WET WINGS & DROP TANKS • Birch Matthews

Wet Wings &

Recollections of American Transcontinental Air Racing 1928-1970

Six Lockheeds were entered in the 1931 Bendix. James G. Hall flew this Altair to sixth place. He is seen here taxiing late in the afternoon at Cleveland after an eleven hour, 55 minute flight from Los Angeles. Credit: Sid Bradd collection

Drop Tanks
Birch Matthews

To Craig:
I'm not to sure how I feel being in a "History" book — until the author told me that I was one of only a few pilots in this book who was still alive!

The best of Luck on the record —

Cheers!
Jack
"1994"

Schiffer Aviation History
Atglen, PA

Acknowledgements

One may reasonably and accurately assert that virtually no book is written in solitary isolation. This is all the more true when treating the subject of air racing where the author must, of great necessity, rely on the generosity of many for their remembrances, photographic illustrations, technical wisdom, overall guidance and encouragement. The integral of these contributions most surely provided the basis for this historical account.

So many contributed to this effort that there is no adequate way of truly acknowledging the extent of their aid. Admitting my limitation, I must nonetheless attempt proper credit where it is due. In this regard, I express great appreciation to John Pappas, Charles Sprinkel, Gordon Cartwright and the late C.L. Chandler for guiding me through the intricacies of aviation weather data gathering and forecasting. Similarly, Dan Whitney graciously allowed me access to his files on Allison and Merlin aircraft engines, a subject he has pursued for years. His knowledge of this subject kept me from straying more than once.

Pratt & Whitney archivist Harvey Lippincott patiently responded to each of my requests for detail on that company's famous family of radial powerplants. Dr. David Lednicer enthusiastically agreed to fire up his computer and model the Gee Bee and Marcoux-Bromberg racers. This was followed by a cogent analysis of the results. His "look back" at these old birds using state-of-the-art methods has never before been done.

My thanks to sport biplane race pilot Don Fairbanks for putting me in touch with Ed Lunken. Through correspondence and telephone conversations, Ed recounted his adventures in the post-war Bendix races and how he "accidently" became the third member of the Paul Mantz racing team in 1948. With great good fortune, I was introduced to Ed Horkey by the late Oliver Aldrich during the 1991 Reno Air Races. Ed maintains contact with many of his former co-workers from the old days at North American Aviation. Thus it was that I learned about such esoteric topics as wet wings, errant drop tanks and cruise control charts from George Gehrkens, Jack Daniels and John Nollan. The effervescent Bill Kerchenfaut, crew chief for Bill Destefani's champion Mustang racer, Strega, kindly provided many technical details about Mike Carroll's Sea Fury. More information on Mike's Fury together with many photographs from the early Reno years were supplied courtesy of Tim Weinschenker, another avid racing historian.

Engineer and superb photographer Jim Larsen, once again came to my aid with pictures, and more important, a kind introduction to Chuck Lyford. Always a fierce competitor, Chuck patiently led me through the story of his Bardahl Special and the frustrating 1964 transcon race. Don Berliner and Dick Phillips dug through their extensive files and provided me a treasure trove of race results and aircraft identities, respectively. Bruce Fraites helped keep me on track regarding a number of the post-war racers. Lockheed P-38 specialist A. Kevin Grantham opened his files and filled in details about the ill-fated McCarthy racer in the 1947 Bendix.

Special thanks go to Phil Krause. Answering a desperate last minute request from me, Phil unlimbered his darkroom and quickly turned out needed photographic prints for illustrations in this book. Phil also introduced me to Chuck Tucker who generously related the story of his 1946 run in the Bendix Trophy Race. Charley Tucker's willing support cannot be overstated. In addition to capturing the essence of this book in his superb foreword, Walt Boyne kindly reviewed drafts on the early years of transcontinental racing, simultaneously urging me to go beyond my typical engineer's short declarative style of writing. Alas, he only partially succeeded. The period from 1928 through 1939 was especially difficult to research. This era could not have been described without the extensive support provided by Sid Bradd and Bob Hirsch. A hearty thanks to both. Howie Keefe's travails in the last Harold's Club race came from Maurice O'Brien, a former co-worker at TRW and ex-crew member for Miss America over several racing season.

Line drawings for the chapter on racing engines were constructed on the MacIntosh computer of pilot and commercial artist, Dave Hargreaves. Ardent collector John Garrett unearthed the pristine color program covers from the "1930 something" era of racing which appear within the book. The striking reproduction of Benny Howard's Mister Mulligan was created by the talented hands of Walt Jefferies, Jr. As in past attempts at writing, I continued to rely on the technical expertise of my friends – Bruce Boland, Pete Law, Gerry Balzer and "Diz" Dean – each time this old mechanical engineer ran afoul of things aerodynamic. Chronologically last in this acknowledgement – but every bit as important to the finished product – are bits and pieces of the story in the form of photographs, news clippings, records and recollections from Roger Besecker, the late Dusty Carter, Al Chute, Jeff Compton, Harry Gann, Al Hansen, Howell Miller, Bob Stepanek, Tom Piedimonte, Dr. Herman Schaub, Emil Strasser, Pappy Weaver and Gary Williams.

In conclusion, I am very grateful to one and all who so willingly contributed their time, collections and knowledge to this essay on transcontinental air racing. I hope the material threads you entrusted to my care have been faithfully woven into an accurate portrayal of the men, women and planes that made these races great.

On the dust jacket

Front:
Chuck Lyford placed second in the inaugural Harold's Club race in 1964. Credit: Jim Larsen

Rear:
This is another Hubbell painting used as the basis for the 1932 race program. In later years, the artist became more literal in his depiction of aircraft. Credit: John Garrett

Page 1:
E.D. Weiner sits in the cockpit of his transcon racer holding the Harold's Club Trophy after winning the 1968 race.
Credit: Birch Matthews collection

Book Design by Robert Biondi

First Edition
Copyright © 1993 by Birch J. Matthews.
Library of Congress Catalog Number: 93-84497

All rights reserved. No part of this work may be reproduced or used in any forms or by any means – graphic, electronic or mechanical, including photocopying or information storage and retrieval systems – without written permission from the copyright holder.

Printed in the United States of America.
ISBN: 0-88740-530-4
We are interested in hearing from authors with book ideas on related topics.

Published by Schiffer Publishing Ltd.
77 Lower Valley Road
Atglen, PA 19310
Please write for a free catalog.
This book may be purchased from the publisher.
Please include $2.95 postage.
Try your bookstore first.

Preface

Air racing chronicles inevitably focus on sprint aircraft, those built or customized for comparatively short closed-course pylon races. To a notable degree the broad history of long distance racing in the United States has been neglected. It seems time to rectify this condition. Some of the most daring pilots, unique aircraft and exciting races were flown in the cloistered isolation of high altitude, cross-country competition.

If one accepts the premise that this form of racing has too frequently received only passing attention from historians, it follows that virtually no consideration has been directed toward the technical aspects of these contests. Nor have the ancillary yet vital topics of weather forecasting, radio communications and racing engines received any recognition. Yet these related technologies played a vital role in the outcome of most cross-country races.

Transcontinental air racing was a melding of men, machines and the elements, with the latter not infrequently the dominant component. For this reason, the ensuing narrative opens with a short history of aviation weather forecasting and wireless transmission. Chapter One deals not with a specific race; rather, it describes the evolution of upper air data gathering and dissemination. The influence upon racing of our ability to predict conditions over a transcontinental route is obvious. The impact of concurrent wireless technology development may be less apparent. Air-to-ground communications during a race seldom occurred. Wireless acquisition of upper air data, though, became all important. Interestingly, the technologies of aviation, weather forecasting and wireless or radio transmission evolved over the years more or less in parallel.

Chapter two summarizes a bit of history behind the important aircraft engines used in transcontinental race planes. Prior to World War II, air-cooled radial engines were used almost exclusively in American cross-country air racing. Following the war, liquid-cooled engines became dominant in the form of Allison V-1710s and Packard-built Rolls-Royce Merlins. In each era, reliable and powerful piston engines were absolutely essential to the sport.

Subsequent chapters introduce many of the personalities and racing machines which took part in these long ago races. Many of the stories have a technical overlay because aircraft are, after all, the products of engineering endeavors. Hopefully, this technical seasoning is not overbearing and merely adds flavor to the story.

While preparing this story, aviation author and historian Don Berliner presented me with a copy of his recent book, *Unlimited Air Racers*. His inscription read: "Just another small step . . ." in the chronicling of air racing history. I hope the reader will find this account yet another small step forward.

Birch J. Matthews
Palos Verdes Peninsula, CA
March 1993

Dedication

This book is gratefully dedicated to Carol and Stephanie, forbearing veterans of many air races.

You on the cutting edge of technology have already made yesterday's impossibilities the commonplace realities of today.

– Ronald Reagan, 40th U.S. President

One goes to Nature only for hints and half-truths. Her facts are crude until you have absorbed them or translated them . . .

– John Burroughs, Signs and Seasons (1886)

*He who, from zone to zone,
Guides through the boundless sky thy certain flight,
In the long way that I must tread alone,
Will lead my steps aright.*

– William Cullen Bryant, To a Waterfowl (1818)

The starting flag was dropped at 6:30 a.m. on 3 September 1949 for the last Bendix piston engine race. Joe DeBona is already rolling on his takeoff. Takeoff was due east. Credit: A.U. Schmidt

Contents

Acknowledgements 4
Preface 5
Foreword 9
Introduction 10

Chapter I: WINGS, WEATHER AND WIRELESS 12
Chapter II: RACE POWER 24
Chapter III: A RACE WITH NO END 46
Chapter IV: DERBIES AND DEPRESSION 58
Chapter V: THE BENDIX TROPHY RACE 70
Chapter VI: YEARS OF STRUGGLE 78
Chapter VII: POTPOURRI 116
Chapter VIII: A LOOK BACK 142
Chapter IX: THE NEW BREED 150
Chapter X: RACE PILOTS 188
Chapter XI: RENO ENCORE 212
Chapter XII: THE FINAL YEARS 224
Chapter XIII: END GAME 244

Appendixes
Appendix A: Major Transcontinental Air Races: 1928-1970 252
Appendix B: Gordon D. Cartwright: Meteorologist 259
Appendix C: Packard-Built Merlin Engines 261
Appendix D: Allison V-1710 Engines 262

Bibliography 265
Index 268

Foreword

Over the years there have been a great many books on air racing, including some truly excellent histories. Most of these have been somewhat narrowly focused, concentrating primarily on the aircraft and the pilots. Birch Matthews cooperated with Dustin Carter in creating the superb, and very different, *MUSTANG: The Racing Thoroughbred*. Now Birch has taken an even more expansive new approach in *WET WINGS & DROP TANKS*, which covers many of the pilots and planes involved in major transcontinental races across the United States, basically from 1928 to 1970. It is unusual in another way, for it is a book that you can both read straight through for pleasure, and then return to again and again for reference.

Long distance air racing had appeal from aviation's beginning, and all over the world, nations competed to create fast, long range aircraft. The geography of the United States lent itself to bringing the sport to an acme of perfection, as beautifully built aircraft sped from coast to coast. Records were set and broken by an endless series of famous pilots – Jimmy Doolittle, Frank Hawks, Roscoe Turner, Jimmy Haizlip, Jackie Cochran, Paul Mantz and Joe Debona. And there were others, not competitors but equally important, colorful characters like Cliff Henderson and Vincent Bendix. Matthews depicts these protean figures with both fidelity and affection.

The author combines with a deft hand the intricate engineering details with anecdotes on the flamboyant personalities of the time, creating a book which will please both the number-crunching buff and the racing newcomer equally well. In it, for the first time ever, he explores the external factors which had such tremendous effect upon the outcome of these races, including wireless, weather and the progressive development of engines. The importance of these external factors is obvious, but Birch is the first writer to take time to do the laborious research necessary to compile the data; fortunately, he also has the experience and intelligence to infer their effect upon the outcome of the races.

His approach to the subject of weather is particularly interesting. While today even the most casual Sunday pilot has the benefit of elaborate weather predicting systems, the early racing pilots had limited information to go on, and much of their success derived from their ability to deduce from scanty data the best routes to fly. Birch records how, over time, as both weather forecasting and wireless transmission of data improved, the more astute racing pilots were able to do a better job.

This is not the sort of book compiled by an amateur researcher laboriously filling out three by five cards in the library. It stems instead from the author's life-long involvement with the racing scene, as well as his engineering background. It is the latter which permits him to validate his approach with unique computer simulations analyzing two of the most famous racers of all time, the Marcoux-Bromberg and the Granville Brothers Gee Bee R-2. Matthews avoids technical jargon as he reviews the respective qualities of the two airplanes. (Knowledgeable readers will know that the Marcoux-Bromberg racer still exists, while Delmar Benjamin is now flying his Gee Bee R-2 replica, as no one believed it could ever have been flown.)

Matthews clearly conveys why racing's popularity has persisted over the years. The sport began with and continues to revolve around a special breed of highly competitive pilots, designers and builders. With his unique background, Birch has captured not only the nostalgia of the past, with its marvelous array of scratch-built racers, but also the impact of a post-World War II generation of converted warplanes, those fabulous Mustangs, Bearcats and Sea Furies which still burn-up the course at Reno.

This is a refreshing, highly readable book, jam-packed with statistics unavailable anywhere else, and adding a great deal of previously undisclosed information to the general store of knowledge. It is at the same time as intensely human as the sport of air racing itself.

Walter J. Boyne
Washington, D.C.
February 25, 1993

Chapter I

WINGS, WEATHER AND WIRELESS

The saga of transcontinental air racing, is inextricably tied to the vagaries of weather and to technology evolved to measure, forecast and disseminate this information. More precisely, the outcome of a race – indeed, the risk to life and limb – was at times contingent upon weather conditions and the availability of predictions. In this context, it is instructive to realize that the development of aviation and the science and art of upper air weather forecasting evolved rapidly during the two decades before World War II. A third factor was the invention of near instantaneous communications in the form of wireless transmission or radio. Radio transmission and reception became a fundamental factor in weather data gathering and dissemination. Fortuitously, all three technologies – aviation, weather and radio – evolved roughly in parallel. This story of transcontinental air racing, therefore, begins not with the recital of a specific air race, but rather with the advent and development of these supporting technologies. Although these topics are peripheral to the main subject, only in this context can the progress and frequently the outcome of long distance air racing in America be fully appreciated.

THE WEATHER BUREAU

Establishment of a national weather service in the United States occurred during the 18th century; February 9, 1870, to be precise. It was the product of a joint resolution of Congress signed by President Ulysses S. Grant, and implemented as a meteorological division of the U.S. Army Signal Service whose work began on November 1, 1870.[1] Some twenty years later, the business of weather forecasting was transferred to civilian hands when the United States Weather Bureau was created within the Department of Agriculture. Today, the "weather bureau" is officially known as the National Weather Service, a component of the U.S. Department of Commerce.

The science and art of weather monitoring and forecasting has grown exponentially over more than a century. We now live in a space age of instant communications and satellite-aided detail weather measurement available to the public on the six o'clock television news as well as to business and the aviation industry 24 hours a day. These forecasts are derived from observations made at 1300 locations in the United States, Canada and Mexico. Something like 40,000 weather observations from the earth's surface are made each day together with satellite weather data, 3000 ship reports, 1500 balloon readings and perhaps as many as 7000 weather messages from aircraft.[2] Ground observed data are augmented by pilot reports, radar reports, balloon soundings and space satellite imagery and temperature data.[3] This complex of activities occurs on an international basis. Interestingly, "the United States has the greatest variety of severe weather of any country in the world."[4] This fact was the bane of more than one transcontinental racing pilot!

Opposite: An improved method of upper air data gathering came about with the development of radiosonde instrument packages born aloft by hydrogen-filled balloons. Barometric pressure, temperature and humidity measurements were recorded and analyzed for use in weather forecasts. Credit: NOAA

This sophistication, among other things, resulted in developing a method of routing commercial airliners from point of origin to destination over a "pressure pattern minimum time track" in place of the great circle routes used for so many decades. The minimum time track method was made possible by measuring and understanding upper air weather conditions and winds. In effect, a flight plan consisting of headings and altitudes is plotted to take advantage of tail winds or minimizes head winds. Ground distance may exceed a great circle route but time of flight is reduced. Toward the end of modern transcontinental air racing, pressure pattern flight planning was utilized by a few pilots – Dick Kestle, Mike Carroll and Tom Kuchinsky – during the Reno Harold's Club races. As we shall see, the luxury of detailed weather-based flight planning was not available during the first two decades of transcontinental air racing.

Weather forecasting was recognized early on as vitally important to the marine industry and as an aid to saving lives at sea and on the Great Lakes when serious storms were anticipated. As the aviation industry matured, the usefulness and need of comprehensive weather forecasts became paramount. Initially, weather forecasts were constrained because observations and measurements were made at ground level. No upper air data were available to early technicians entrusted with weather reporting. This would change at the start of the 20th century as the first halting steps were undertaken to measure upper air properties. Initial efforts to obtain this information involved flying kites and later, hydrogen-filled balloons. By 1926, free balloons, called "pilot balloons," were utilized to obtain these data.

WEATHER KITES

Kite stations were just what the name implied. Large box kites carrying instrument packages were tethered using piano wire coiled on a large rotating drum. The kite was launched and carried aloft on the winds. They were first used in the mid-1700s to measure upper air temperatures. This was done by suspending a thermometer from the kite tail. A line holding the

This photograph illustrates a weather kite launching circa early 1900s, believed to have occurred in the Washington, D.C. area. Large box kites were used to gather upper air temperature data by suspending a thermometer from the kite. Credit: NOAA

Chapter I: Wings, Weather and Wireless

Two Army Air Force technicians at Meeks Field, Iceland, inflate a balloon with helium while a third holds the radiosonde instrument package. A radio transmitter in the package sent data to earth. Helium cylinder is just inside the shelter to the right in this World War II photograph. Credit: NOAA

Radiosonde balloon launching required two people. When the balloon burst at altitude, a parachute lowered the instrument package safely to the ground for use another day. Credit: NOAA

instrument was severed and the thermometer fell to the ground unbroken. Thermometers respond somewhat slowly to temperature change and thus the reading from a recovered instrument was representative of the upper air temperature measured. The technique advanced significantly in 1896, when professor Charles F. Marvin of the Weather Bureau perfected an instrument known as the meteorograph which measured and recorded temperature, barometric pressure and humidity.[5]

Kite stations were established at various points in the country and a more systematic approach to upper air monitoring began. Kites were launched and allowed to rise to several thousand feet on the prevailing winds. They were left in place four to five hours. At the end of the observation period, the kite was reeled in and the meteorograph recovered at which time, analysis of the recorded data was performed. As can be imagined, the kite method had limitations. If the wind velocity was less than ten to 15 miles an hour, the kite could not be flown.

The altitude a kite could reach was limited by the length of piano wire available. The weight of the extended wire became appreciable and further constrained the maximum altitude of the kite. In at least one instance there was a story of one observer at the Grosebeck Kite Station at Palestine, Texas, who claimed "the record for the highest kite flight in the United States Weather Bureau: over 20,000 feet!"[6] It seems he used 18 kites on the same wire to get that much altitude. Can you imagine what a struggle it must have been to launch this sequence of kites?

PILOT BALLOONS

Pilot balloons were used to measure wind velocity. These hydrogen-filled balloons were launched and ascended at a nominal rate of 600 feet per minute. The balloon flight path was tracked using a specially adapted theodolite, an instrument for precisely measuring angles – in this case, elevation and azimuth (direction). This technique provided the two components of velocity; namely, distance and time. Using trigonometry, the speed of the balloon would be calculated at intervals as the balloon ascended. Simultaneous azimuth readings revealed the wind direction.[7] Some amount of error was introduced in these measurements due to the assumed balloon ascension rate of 600 feet per minute.

Today, we are accustomed to near instantaneous communications and results. By contrast, pilot balloon operations and measurements required almost two hours to complete. As the pilot balloon ascended, atmospheric pressure decreased. The differential between hydrogen pressure inside the balloon and atmospheric pressure eventually became great enough to burst the balloon fabric. Atmospheric pressure variation as a function of standard altitude conditions can be appreciated from the data in the table on page 16, which was available in 1935.

Like the kite, pilot balloons had their limitations. To make the desired measurements, one had to continuously track the balloon ascension. Prevailing weather conditions could make this difficult. If the observer momentarily lost his concentration or cloud cover intervened, the balloon flight path would

The U.S. Standard Atmosphere

Altitude Ft.	Temperature[1] °F.	Pressure[1] Lb/In² Abs.	Density[2] Lb/In³
Sea Level	59.0	14.70	0.0765
5,000	41.2	12.21	0.0659
10,000	23.4	10.10	0.0565
15,000	5.6	8.29	0.0481
20,000	-12.3	6.76	0.0408
25,000	-30.1	5.45	0.0343
30,000	-47.9	4.36	0.0286
35,000	-65.7	3.46	0.0237
40,000	-67.0	2.72	0.0187
45,000	-67.0	2.14	0.0147
50,000	-67.0	1.69	0.0116

[1] "W.G. Brombacher, "Altitude – Pressure Tables Based on the U.S. Standard Atmosphere," NACA Report 538, 1935
[2] Computed.

often be lost. Limitations with respect to night balloon flights are obvious although experiments were conducted using paper lanterns and a candle. Later, the lanterns were replaced by battery powered electric lamps. Nonetheless, pilot balloons contributed to a growing knowledge of upper air conditions, a matter of interest to pilots everywhere. Unmanned balloons filled with helium are used to this day albeit with more sophisticated instrumentation in the form of radiosondes. The theodolite has long since been replaced by radar coupled with computer-based software to acquire, reduce and evaluate tracking information and the output of the radiosonde instrument package.

Perhaps the most significant catalyst to develop a systematic and comprehensive aviation weather forecasting service occurred in 1926, with enactment of the Air Commerce Act . . . "to promote safety and efficiency of air navigation in the United States and above the high seas, particularly upon the civil airways . . ."[8] The act led to establishing weather reporting stations at airports along the commercial airways. This did not happen instantaneously. In 1926, when the act became law, no airport weather reporting stations existed. At the time, the Bureau was operating only twenty-one pilot balloon stations and an additional six kite stations across the country. Augmenting this were fifteen stations measuring upper air conditions run by the Army and Navy. Two years later – coincident with the first non-stop transcontinental air race – there were 18 airport stations providing weather reports. This number increased to 50 in 1930, and personnel manning these airport stations started to provided 24 hour service.[9]

AIRCRAFT OBSERVATIONS

In the early 1930s, aircraft were also used to acquire upper air data although not without difficulty and hazard.[10] The first routine airplane observations were made at Chicago, Cleveland, Dallas and Omaha in July, 1931. Contracts were signed with local pilots at each of these locations. Pilots were obligated to equip their aircraft with a mounting suitable for carrying a meteorograph provided by Weather Bureau personnel. The time of observation was fixed at 5:00 a.m. The pilot's contract stipulated that he would receive no compensation unless he ascended to a minimum altitude of 13,500 feet. If the pilot reached that altitude he would be receive $25. For each additional 1000 feet of altitude gained during the flight, a 10 percent bonus was paid. "The initial flight at Chicago gained altitudes of 14,000 feet the first day and 16,000 feet the next day."[11] Like other methods used to obtain upper air data, the airplane did have limitations. As might be expected, poor weather conditions prevented some flights. Marginal weather, mechanical problems and lack of oxygen (at higher altitudes) led to accidents.[12] "Between 1931 and 1938, twelve pilots were killed" while performing observations.[13]

Although the fledgling Weather Bureau was growing, the organization still exhibited serious shortcomings during the early 1930s. A presidential science advisory board was convened to review the Bureau's weather warning system.[14] This board found several weaknesses. The weather service operated on average only about 12 to 15 hours each day. In the case of airport stations, this was extended to 24 hours. At city Weather Bureau offices, only two synoptic observations were made each day at 8:00 a.m. and 8:00 p.m. Special observations were required when major changes in the weather occurred suddenly. Still, in a rapidly changing weather situation, this could lead to unforseen problems for the pilot. All forecasts originated from Washington D.C., often far too distant from critical weather regions or areas. In fairness, Weather Bureau management continually operated with very limited funding during the Great Depression. In spite of this, the extent and refinement of the Bureau's data gathering and forecasting operations continued to improve to meet the ever increasing demands by commercial and general aviation.

WIRELESS COMMUNICATIONS

An invention which became key to the growth and effectiveness of Weather Bureau forecasting operations was the radio. Radio technology fortuitously evolved in parallel with the growth of weather science. Wireless signal transmission is possible due to the phenomenon of electromagnetic wave propagation. The concept of wireless signal transmission was first postulated in a scientific paper by James C. Maxwell in 1864, entitled A Dynamical Theory of Electro-Magnetic Fields read to the Royal Society. In his pioneering paper, Maxwell theoretically showed that electromagnetic waves must exist and they could be propagated through space. It remained for Heinrich R. Hertz to experimentally demonstrate electromagnetic theory some 23 years later when he generated and received such wave forms across the length of a room.[15] "Unfortunately, Hertz died very young in 1894, at the age of 36 and never lived to see his tremendous discovery extrapolated to practical devices."[16] The reduction to practice of wireless transmission is generally attributed to Guglielmo Marconi.

Marconi was born in Bologna, Italy, on 25 April 1874.[17] As a young man, Marconi became interested in the experiments of Hertz. Prior to this, he hoped for a military career. Rejected by the Italian Navy as officer material and later by the University of Bologna because he was not considered too bright, the thin, studious looking Marconi would nonetheless go on to fame. His interest in the work of Hertz was fostered in his teenage years by the lectures of Professor Augusto Righi and simultaneously encouraged by his mother who would play a significant role in Marconi's early years. The young man's father, Giuseppe Marconi, at first thought his experimentation in wireless transmission was a waste of time. Eventually, the elder Marconi began to visualize possibilities in his son's work. Together they sought official support from the Italian Minister of Posts and Telegraphs. Once again Guglielmo Marconi endured rejection. Marconi's mother, an Irish Protestant, pointed out that Marconi's inventions had greatest potential in communication with ships at sea. At that time, England was the greatest maritime nation in the world and there, she thought, was the place to go. This settled, the family migrated to England in February, 1896. Marconi, with the help of friends, succeeded in eliciting support from the British Post Office. He was soon granted his first patent.

Marconi received his first opportunity to demonstrate the commercial value of wireless signals while in Ireland. He was commissioned by the Dublin Daily Express newspaper to transmit from ship-to-shore the results of a yachting regatta. As G.E.C. Wedlake reports in his book, SOS – The Story of Radio Communications, the result was "sensational."[18] From this humble beginning just before the end of the century, radio was soon being used – as Marconi's mother predicted – to save lives at sea.[19] Although not foreseen at that point in history, it would ultimately perform a similar function for the aviation community including dissemination of timely weather information prior to and during flight.

The introduction of Marconi's inventions to the United States revolved around another yachting race, the prestigious America's Cup, which was about to take place off the coast of Long Island. The New York Herald newspaper invited Marconi to cross the Atlantic and report results of the forthcoming race. While in New York, Marconi demonstrated his wireless equipment to the U.S. Navy. As a consequence, a number of his radios were fitted to Navy vessels in 1899. A scant five years later, all Navy ships carried radio apparatus.

Marconi's enterprise resulted in the formation of the Wireless Telegraph Company of America, which later became the giant Radio Corporation of America better known by it's initials, RCA. Development of equipment for the propagation and reception of electromagnetic waves mushroomed after the turn of the century. The leading countries were Great Britain (via Marconi), the United States with RCA and Germany through the Telefunken Company. This leadership would continue through World War II including the subsequent invention of radar in all of its varieties.

Weather reporting and radio were integrated around 1912, and by 1913, a service was provided by Great Britain, the United States and other countries. The two sciences would, from that point on, become interrelated and evolve in parallel. A key figure in American radio development was Lee De Forest, born in Council Bluffs, Iowa, on 20 August 1873. He also became fascinated by the theories of Hertz and the work of Marconi. Perhaps his most important contribution to radio was the invention in 1906, of the triode (under the trade name Audion), an early form of the vacuum tube which became a primary element in radio transmitters and receivers until superseded by the invention of solid state electronic components.

Amazingly, the marriage of aeronautics and the wireless occurred only four years after the Wright Brothers flew at Kitty Hawk, North Carolina. It was a tentative step to be sure,

This photograph was taken at Los Alamitos Naval Air Station in Southern California during the mid-1960s. One sailor has just released the balloon while a second is ready to release the instrument package. The parachute is midway between the balloon and second sailor. Credit: Birch Matthews

but foretold the future. To demonstrate feasibility, a receiver was installed in a captive British Army balloon. "Lieutenant C.J. Ashton ascended in it and successfully received signals in the air" from a ground transmitter.[20] This was followed in short order by wireless transmissions to and from airships and airplanes. The first air-to-ground wireless communication from an airplane occurred in 1910, at the Belmont Park flying meet on Long Island. The pilot was J.A.D. McCurdy (the sixth man to fly in America) using a Glenn Curtiss flying machine.[21,22]

The importance of wireless transmission to the growth and refinement of aviation weather forecasting cannot be overstated. In fact, however, wireless transmission was preceded in the Weather Bureau system by the telegraph. The first practical method of signaling by wire was brought into being by Samuel F.B. Morse. A professional artist during his early life, Morse ultimately devoted himself to science. In 1835, he brought the telegraph to a practical state. The world began to shrink dramatically as people were able to communicate over long distances within hours instead of days, weeks or even months prior to Morse's work. Wireless communication, when it evolved, was the key to obtaining upper air data in a timely fashion.

The process of getting forecasts into the hands of industry and the public was still a bit cumbersome. Data were gathered and forwarded to Washington D.C., where the information was analyzed. Weather forecasts were then prepared and sent to various stations throughout the country. In the very early years, this was done once a day. By the 1920s, weather reports were issued twice daily. In 1927, radio was employed to provide the public with weather information. However, teletype remained a primary method of weather communications for many years to come.

As with any emerging technology, wireless communication was accomplished not without some difficulty. Radio reception was influenced by the often limited reliability of transmitting and receiving equipment and indeed, by the weather itself. Regardless, the role of radio in aviation and in weather forecasting was growing rapidly. In 1929, there were 131 radio stations for all types of aviation requirements including navigation and weather related services. In just over a decade, this number increased fourteen fold.[23]

THE RADIOSONDE

A significant advancement in the Bureau's ability to gather weather information as a function of altitude came with development of the radio meteorograph or radiosonde.[24] The terms are synonymous although it was not until 1938, that the name radiosonde was adopted.[25] As the name implies, the radiosonde was based upon wireless transmission. It is an instrument package born aloft by a balloon into the upper atmosphere to measure temperature, barometric pressure and humidity. A transmitting device in the package sends signals to a ground receiving set. The electrical signal transmitted to the ground station is proportional to the value of the parameter being measured. When the balloon reached an altitude where it burst, the instrument package parachuted to earth and was recovered for use another day.

As with many inventions or discoveries, the radiosonde was being developed concurrently by people in a number of countries during the late 1900s. In the United States, Harvard scientists A.E. Bent and K.O. Lange developed a radiosonde package weighing only three pounds.[26] The year was 1935. Experiments by Bent, Lange and others continued for the next two years and radiosonde-equipped balloons started to replace aircraft observations late in 1938.[27] The number of weather stations using radiosonde balloons grew quickly. By 1941, thirty-four stations were taking daily observations at mid-day.[28]

AVIATION WEATHER SERVICE PERSPECTIVE, 1928-1939

Looking back, aviation weather services available to cross-country pilots were initially a bit primitive though it improved

Chapter I: Wings, Weather and Wireless

Radio Stations Utilized for Aviation Services

Year	Number
1929	131
1930	281
1931	463
1932	579
1933	646
1934	671
1935	678
1936	852
1937	1212
1938	1460
1939	1824

Source: U.S. Bureau of the Census, "Historical Statistics of the United States, Colonial Times to 1957," Washington, D.C., 1960, p.492.

rapidly in the years leading up to World War II. One of the people involved in forecasting during this period was Gordon D. Cartwright. As a young man of 21, he went to work for the Weather Bureau in 1929, during the expansion in aviation weather services brought about by the 1926 Air Commerce Act. Gordon recalls that . . . "aviation weather forecasting was carried on by a number of designated Weather Bureau Centers such as Cleveland, Chicago, Newark, Kansas City, Denver, San Francisco, Los Angeles and Seattle. Weather forecasts were made for all the established commercial air routes, that is, those having light beacons along the route. The forecast interval was normally every twelve hours. Information on the height of a cloud base was obtained by a primitive hand-held clinometer and (later) fixed-beam ceilometer. Cloud layer heights could be had from occasional pilot reports, from APOB (airplane observations) ascents and inferred from pilot balloon data."[29]

Early forecasts were often worded in very general terms. A favorable forecast might read: "Good flying weather today; generally clear sky and good visibility, moderate varying winds (on the) surface and aloft."[30] Adverse forecasts were equally general in nature. Coupled with the limited definition of early aviation forecasts was a sometime tendency of pilots to ignore Bureau forecasts. No less a personage than Charles A. Lindbergh noted that he paid little attention (in the 1920s) to information provided by the Weather Bureau reports. Lindbergh stated that "Chicago (airport station) reports are so unreliable that I do not want to condition my mind with them. I would rather judge weather ahead as I fly."[31] Lindbergh later relied heavily on a New York Weather Bureau Office forecast by the highly respected Dr. James Kimball when he decided to begin his memorable flight to Paris in 1927. Dr. Kimball was the only United States meteorologist at the time with any experience in Atlantic Ocean weather conditions and patterns.

In contrast to Lindbergh's rather terse criticism of Weather Bureau reports, author Donald R. Whitnah notes that some Bureau employees were praised for their work in weather forecasting, notably Henry T. Harrison of Cleveland, "whose opinions as to whether landing fields would be open or not were much in demand."[32] Harrison had a remarkable memory and an intense interest in the weather. According to meteorologist Gordon Cartwright, he "was a private person and one of intense concentration when at work. His pale blue eyes seemed to see everything."[33] Aside from forecasting, Henry was an avid baseball fan and his fabulous memory could recall game statistics of most of the players in both major leagues. It was this talent for remembering details that aided his forecasts. He evaluated current data in context with prior weather events and patterns before making a prediction.

Gordon Cartwright was based at Cleveland Airport from 1932 to 1936, and supports the contention that the Bureau was providing reasonably good forecasts within the limitations of their equipment. He noted that "we were fortunate in having C.G. Andrus, a former Signal Corps balloonist as our station chief, as well as Henry T. Harrison and Wilson Reed, Jr., on the forecast staff. Cleveland had a pilot balloon station as well as an APOB flight. So we had elementary upper air data."[34] However, Gordon cautions "there was very little information on the general upper air circulation" at this time. (Appendix B contains a synopsis of Gordon Cartwright's incredible career.)

During the mid-1930s, an improved method of disseminating weather information evolved. This was the teletype weather map which, according to Cartwright, "had been brought into regular use on the teletype circuits at airports. These maps were produced from a synoptic base chart designed to fit into a page printer teletype machine. The forecaster on duty plotted the current weather data for each of the stations printed on the base chart, drew in the isobars (lines of constant atmospheric pressure) and gave the completed chart to the teletype operator. With the plotted chart in the machine, he typed in the weather data for each station and marked the location of the isobars. All stations on the teletype circuit could then receive the latest synoptic chart. These charts were produced at the main aviation forecast centers and could be pieced together to give the synoptic picture over the entire length of the main transcontinental air routes.

"Before making his final briefing, the forecaster would invariably scan the latest hourly reports from over the route in question. These hourly and special reports were particularly useful in spotting thunderstorms, fog or heavy snowfall. The absence of air-ground communications made amendments impossible once the pilot had taken off. The pilot had to interpret the weather he encountered as best he could in the light of the briefing given before takeoff."[35]

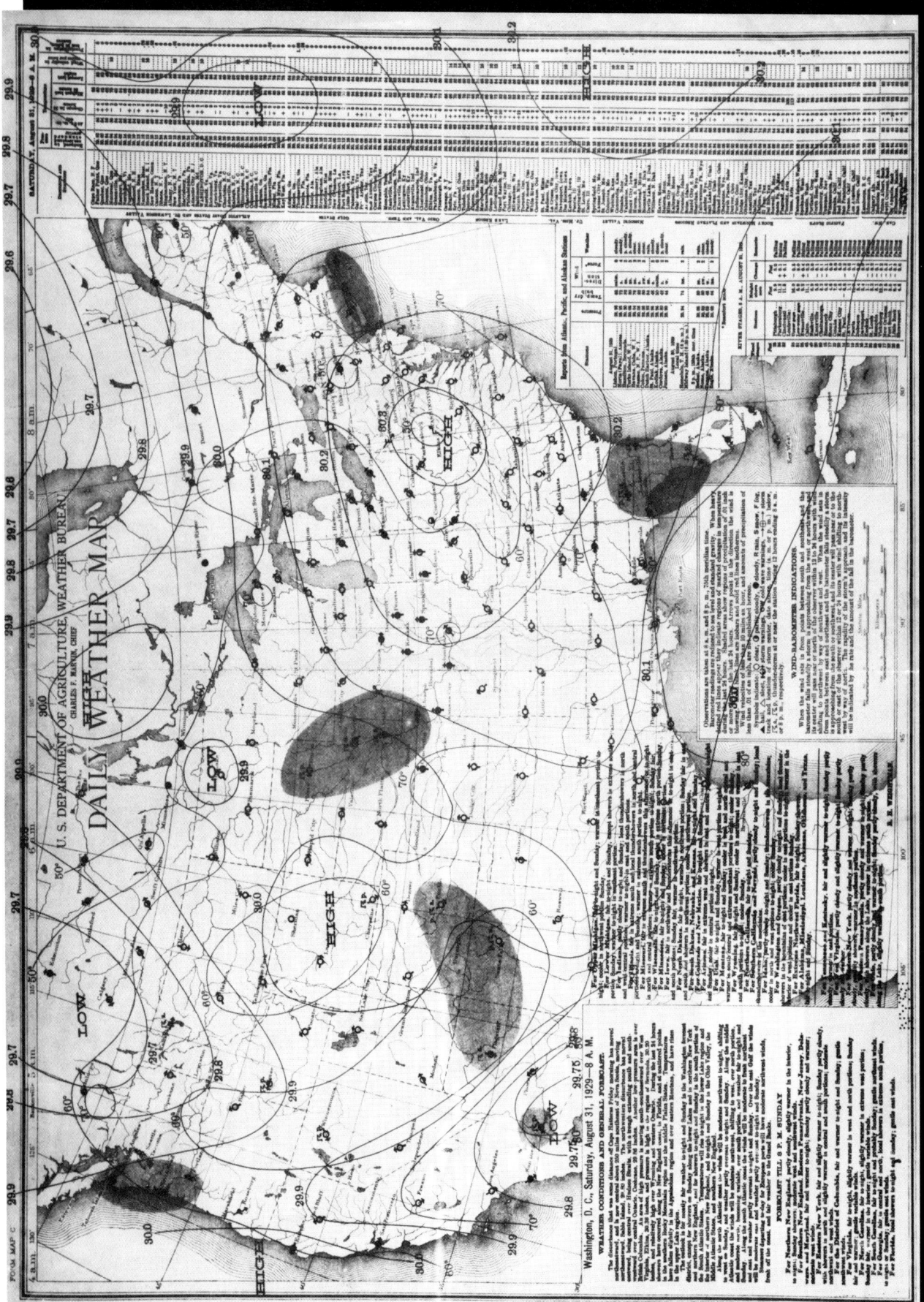

John Wood began the non-stop transcontinental race in the wee small hours of 1 September 1929, and crashed during a violent storm near the California - Arizona border. Shown here is the Weather Bureau map available to Wood before he took off. The low pressure front out of Mexico met the high pressure front from Northern California and created the thunderstorm which caused Wood's death. Credit: NOAA

Chapter I: Wings, Weather and Wireless

Earl Ortman's 1937 Bendix racer encountered weather east of Kansas City. When he tried to climb above it, he got disoriented and off course, a fact which may have cost him first place in the race that year. Credit: D.W. Carter

Jackie Cochran's green P-51B Mustang sitting at Mines Field, Los Angeles before the 1946 Bendix race. She encountered rough turbulence during the first one-third of the race, but otherwise had favorable tail winds and finished second. Credit: Harry Gann

WEATHER AND RACING

One can see that in the early years of transcontinental racing, weather forecasts were available to the competing pilots; however, these reports had limitations and were subject to invalidation if sudden changes occurred. An example of a race in which weather played a decisive and deadly role occurred on 1 September 1929. During the early hours of that day, Major John P. Wood lost his life when the Lockheed Vega he was flying encountered a severe electrical thunderstorm near Needles, California. This storm occurred due to developing weather conditions approximately 24 hours earlier. The previous day, a high pressure cold front rolled across the Northern California Coastline out of the northwest. In meteorology, a

Weather for the 1949 Bendix was generally excellent with favorable tail winds most of the way. Stan Reaver flew this bright red Paul Mantz Mustang to second place at a speed of 450 miles per hour. Credit: Chalmers Johnson via William T. Larkins

front is the interface or transition zone between two air masses of different density. Because temperature distribution is the most important regulator of atmospheric density, a front almost invariably separates air masses of different temperature. In this instance, the cold air mass from Northern California, met a second moisture laden warm air mass from the Gulf of Mexico. The interface zone between these two air masses occurred over California's Mojave Desert. The instability created as the air masses collided resulted in a violent, turbulent thunderstorm.[36] John Wood flew into this chaos during the 1929 race and paid the supreme penalty.

The Weather Bureau West Coast forecast for 31 August – the day John Wood took off for Cleveland – stated: "Southern California and Nevada, partly cloudy tonight and Sunday; local thunderstorms in the mountains."[37] The forecast was accurate. Whether Wood consulted this particular forecast or not, we shall never know.

Ironically, the Bureau's weather map the following day, which would have been based upon 8:00 a.m. observations, made no predictions concerning Southern California weather. The reasons are unknown. Weather observations may not have been made or timely communications proved impossible. The point is moot. Major Wood departed Los Angeles in the wee small hours of 1 September and no more recent weather forecast was available. Fate, as noted by author Ernest K. Gann, is indeed the hunter!

Richard Snyder negotiated the 1964 Harold's Club Trophy race around hurricane Dora to finish fourth. This was the worst storm to hit northern Florida in decades and created havoc with the transcontinental racers that year. Credit: L. Smalley/T. Weinschenker Collection

NOTES:

1 Patrick Hughes, *A Century of Weather Service - 1870 - 1970*, Gordon and Breach, Science Publishers, New York, 1970.
2 Kennedy P. Maize, "Weather Forecasting," Congressional Quarterly, Inc., Washington D.C., 1979, p. 90.
3 Information and data on the current capability of the National Oceanic and Atmospheric Administration's capabilities were provided by Mr. Charles H. Sprinkle, Chief, Aviation Services Branch, Office of Meteorology, via private correspondence with the author dated 3 November 1992.
4 Fact Sheet, National Oceanic and Atmospheric Administration, National Weather Service, Silver Springs, Maryland. Undated.

Chapter I: Wings, Weather and Wireless

5 Hughes, op.cit., p. 51. In 1749, Professor Alexander Wilson of the University of Glasgow developed this technique. Charles F. Marvin would later become Chief of the Weather Bureau.

6 Correspondence to the author from Gordon D. Cartwright, Geneva, Switzerland, dated 28 January 1993.

7 As an example of how the technique worked, consider the following illustration. A pilot balloon is launched at sea level. Theodolite measurements of azimuth (direction) and elevation are recorded after one minute. At that time, the balloon reaches an altitude of approximately 600 feet based upon its predicted nominal rate of ascension. The theodolite elevation angle reading is 50 degrees. Knowing the tangent of 50 degrees and the vertical height (600 feet), we have two components of a right triangle and thus may calculate the horizontal distance the balloon has traveled; in this instance, 715 feet in one minute or just over eight miles per hour. At the same time, the theodolite azimuth reading is recorded as 90 degrees (relative to true north). Therefore, in this hypothetical example, the wind at 600 feet above sea level was moving due east. In actual practice, azimuth and elevation readings were recorded on one minute intervals during the observed balloon flight.

8 Hughes, op.cit., p. 34.

9 D.B. Whitnah, *A History of the United States Weather Bureau*, University of Illinois Press, Urbana, 1965, p. 135.

10 In the jargon of the Weather Bureau, these flights were called "APOBs," an acronym for airplane observations. The propensity for government-inspired acronyms continues to this day!

11 *New York Times*, 3 July 1931, p. 21, and 6 July 1931, p. 16.

12 Prolonged flight at or above 10,000 feet altitude can have an adverse physiological effect on the pilot. This is caused by an oxygen deficiency in the blood and is called hypoxia. The physiological effects are a feeling of exhaustion; an impairment of vision and judgement; and finally, unconsciousness.

13 Hughes, op.cit., p. 58.

14 "Report of the Science Advisory Board, July 1933 - September 1934," Washington D.C., pp. 47-48.

15 This extremely important and seminal experiment occurred in 1887. Hertz's place in scientific history is recognized to this day in that wave frequency oscillations are measured in units of Hertz! One Hertz (Hz) equals one cycle per second.

16 G.E.C. Wedlake, *SOS, The Story of radio-Communications*, Crane, Russak & Company, Inc., New York, 1973, p. 11.

17 W.J. Baker, *A History of the Marconi Company*, St. Martin's Press, New York, 1971, p. 25.

18 Wedlake, op.cit., p. 23.

19 Initial use of Marconi's wireless telegraphy invention did indeed, center on maritime applications. It was soon used by ships to request help in circumstances of danger and distress. By June 1912, an international convention established the letters "SOS" in Morse code as the standard distress signal. The equivalent radio distress signal in aviation is "Mayday," a corruption of the French "M'aider," meaning help me.

20 Wedlake, Op.cit., p. 95.

21 George Hardie, "The Birth of Naval Aviation," American Aviation Historical Society JOURNAL, Vol. 6, No. 1, 1961, p. 5.

22 Anon., *A Chronicle of the Aviation Industry in America*, Eaton Manufacturing Company, Cleveland, 1948, p. 11.

23 U.S. Bureau of the Census, "Historical Statistics of the United States, Colonial Times to 1957," Washington D.C., 1960, p. 492.

24 Radiosonde is a combination of the word radio and the French noun sonde (the e is silent) which is equivalent to the word sound. To sound is to probe or measure.

25 U.S. Weather Bureau, Topics and Personnel, November 1938.

26 *New York Times*, 17 November 1935, Section 10, p. 4.

27 *New York Times*, 18 July 1937, Section 2, p. 4.

28 Whitnah, op.cit., p. 192.

29 Correspondence from Gordon D. Cartwright to author dated 15 December 1992. In his letter, Mr. Cartwright refers to a "clinometer" and a "fixed-beam ceilometer." The clinometer is an instrument designed to measure angles of inclination or slope. For example, if a search light is beamed vertically to a cloud base, an observer standing a known distance from the light can view through a clinometer the point on the cloud base where the light impinges. The instrument measures the angle of inclination. Knowing this angle and the distance from the observer to the search light, trigonometry is used to calculate the vertical distance from the ground to the cloud base. A ceilometer is a more elegant device for measuring cloud height. In its simplest form, a collimated beam of ultraviolet light is projected onto a cloud. The light beam is modulated to a predetermined frequency. Reflected light from the cloud is detected by a photoelectric cell. The geometric relationship of the light source and detector are known and the altitude is calculated once again by triangulation.

30 House Agriculture Appropriations, 1921, 66th Congress, 2nd Session.

31 Charles A. Lindbergh, "The Spirit of St. Louis," Charles Scribner's Sons, New York, 1953, p. 4.

32 Whitnah, op.cit., p. 180.

33 Correspondence to the author from Gordon D. Cartwright dated 28 January 1993.

34 Cartwright correspondence, op.cit.

35 Ibid.

36 Communication with the author and John J. Pappas, Delta Airlines, 14 December 1992. A cold front is the leading edge or transition zone of the more dense air mass behind it and the warmer, less dense air mass ahead. The colder more dense air pushes the less dense warm air out of the way. It is in this dynamic zone that "weather action" such as rain and thunderstorms occur.

37 R.H. Weightman, U.S. "Daily Weather Map, Department of Agriculture," Weather Bureau, Saturday, August 31, 1929.

E.D. Weiner won the 1965 Harold's Club race in this black & white checkered P-51D. Weiner was forced out of the 1964 race after encountering severe weather from hurricane Dora. Picture taken at Long Beach, CA, airport on 29 August 1967. Credit: Birch Matthews

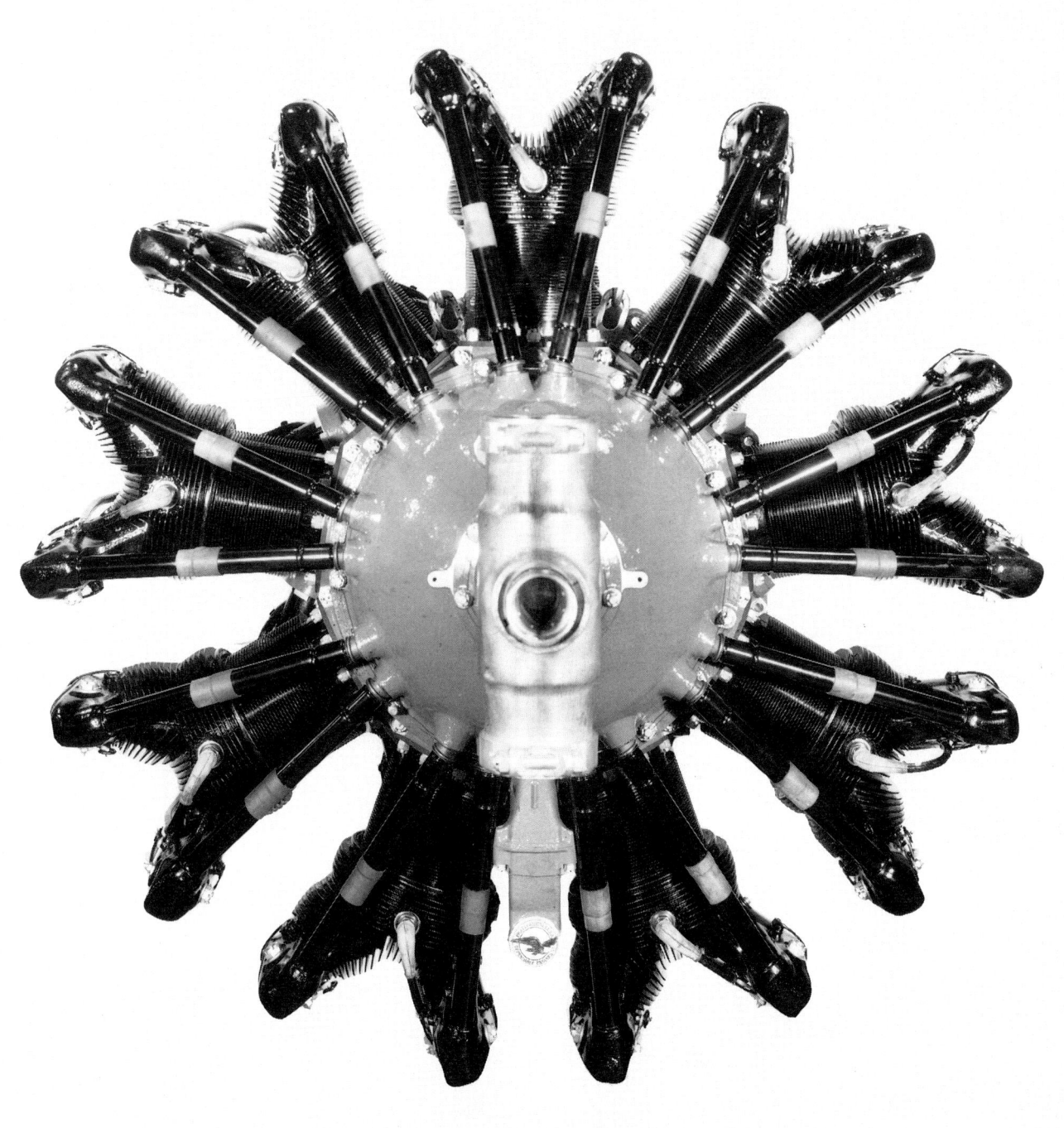

This photograph shows the Wasp Jr. "A" model 985 cubic inch engine, first of a long line of air-cooled radial engines by Pratt & Whitney. Versions of the "A" model were used in a number of early racers. Credit: Pratt & Whitney via the Connecticut Aviation Historical Society

Chapter II

RACE POWER

Air-cooled radial engines reigned supreme in unlimited class transcontinental racing before World War II. There were two major manufacturers of large radial engines, Pratt & Whitney and Wright Aeronautical. The former dominated the racing scene. Pratt & Whitney supported various projects by leasing their products at nominal cost to race plane owners of limited means, which in the Depression, was most of the racing fraternity. The company also provided technical field support during the races, a not insignificant contribution during those years. After the war, most of the entrants selected stripped-down Mustang, Lightning and Kingcobra surplus fighters to compete in the Bendix races and these planes were powered by liquid-cooled Packard-built Rolls-Royce Merlin and Allison V-1710 engines. There were exceptions, of course, but they were few in number. Mike Carroll's 1967 Hawker Sea Fury, powered by a Bristol Centaurus, was the only air-cooled radial engine racer to ever win an unlimited transcontinental contest after 1939.

A variety of piston engines were used for cross-country racing over the years as shown in the accompanying table.[1] A measure of comparison between engines is the rated horsepower developed for each cubic inch of displacement. By this gauge, the Pratt & Whitney Wasp Jr. in Jimmy Doolittle's 1931 Laird Super Solution provided 0.38 horsepower per cubic inch. Eight years later, Frank Fuller's Seversky, powered by a Pratt & Whitney Twin Wasp, produced 0.57 horsepower per cubic inch, a 50 percent increase when compared to Doolittle's 1931 engine. The reasons why Fuller's engine was more efficient by this standard were twofold. All of the early engines were direct drive. In other words, the propeller turned at the same speed as the engine crankshaft. Direct drive engines were more or less limited to around 2000-2200 revolutions per minute. Although the engines were no doubt structurally capable of higher speeds, propellers were the limiting factor. With a direct drive setup, higher engine revolutions quickly led to propeller inefficiency wherein the tips approached sonic velocity. Higher speeds also created structural problems. As propeller speeds increased, centrifugal forces could build up to a stress level where mechanical failure occurred. This was not a pleasant thought for the pilot.

Another limitation for early racing engines involved the quality of available fuel. Before about 1935, premium aviation gasoline was rated at around 80 octane. Octane rating of a fuel is a measure of its detonation resistance. When 87 octane and then 100 octane fuel became available, rated engine power could be raised in many cases with no redesign of the engine. Higher manifold pressures were practical without the fear of destructive detonation. Improved fuels together with reduction gearing for propeller drives resulted in more power at very little cost to the race plane designer. It was a fortuitous combination.

In 1946, racing teams took advantage of the tremendous strides made in engine and fuel technology during the war. Allisons and Merlins could run power settings at altitude far and away above that possible for pre-war Bendix contestants. The major problem for the young ex-military pilots flying the post-war Bendix was how to load enough fuel onboard their racers to fly the route

Representative Engines for Transcontinental Air Racing Aircraft

Engine Model	Aircraft	Race No.	M P In-Hg	Takeoff Rated HP[7]	Rated RPM	Rated Alt.	Prop Drive	Octane Rating	Dry Wt. Lb	Bore Inches	Stroke Inches	Displ. Cu In.	Blower Ratio[5]
WASP JR S2A[1]	Laird Super Solution	400		375	2300	S.L.	Direct	87	575	5.1875	5.1875	985	10:1
WASP JR S2A[1]	Wedell Williams	121		375	2300	7500	Direct	87	575	5.1875	5.1875	985	10:1
WASP JR SB[1]	Rider R-3 (1934)	9		450	2300	5000	Direct	80	585	5.1875	5.1875	985	10:1
WASP S1D1[1]	Rider R-3 (1935)	9		550	2200	5000	Direct	80	763	5.7500	5.7500	1344	10:1
WASP SE[1]	Mr. Mulligan	40	33	500	2200	11000	Direct	87	750	5.7500	5.7500	1344	14:1
WASP S1E[1]	Wedell-Williams	2		500	2200	9000	Direct	87	750	5.7500	5.7500	1344	12:1
HORNET T1C[2]	Wedell-Williams	57		600	2000	S.L.	Direct	80	861	6.1250	6.3750	1690	8:1
TWIN WASP JR S2A5-G[1]	Rider R-3 (1937)	4	33	825	2580	2500	Geared 4:3	87	1130	5.1875	5.1875	1535	11:1
TWIN WASP S1B3-G[1]	Laird-Turner LTR	29	41	1000	2600	6500	Geared 3:2	87	1250	5.5000	5.5000	1830	10:1
TWIN WASP S1A2-G[2]	Seversky SEV-S2	77		1050	2700	11000	Geared 16:9	87	1423	5.5000	5.5000	1830	7.1:1
CONQUEROR SGV-1570-F4[2]	Northrop Gamma 2G			705	2450	7000	Geared 2:1	87	1110	5.1250	6.2500	1587	9.94:1
BRISTOL CENTAURUS 18[6]	Sea Fury FB Mk.11	87	49	2550	2700	4000	Geared	100/130	2695	5.8000	7.0000	3270	6.757:1 9.014:1
PACKARD V-1650-9[3]	NAA Mustang P-51D-25	8	67	1380 1230	3000 3000	S.L. 28,700	Geared 2.09:1	100/130	1745	5.4000	6.0000	1650	6.391:1 8.095:1
ALLISON V-1710-117[4]	Bell P-63C-5	30	55	1325 1100	3000 3000	S.L. 25,000	Geared 2.23:1	100/130	1660	5.5000	6.0000	1710	8.100:1 7.230:1

Notes:
[1] Data from Pratt & Whitney Specifications for each representative engine.
[2] Data from "Aviation Aircraft Handbook," *Aviation Magazine*, New York, 1935, pp. 165-166.
[3] Data from "Model Designations of USAF Aircraft Engines," MCRE Report No.6, Air Material Command, Revised 1 January 1950.
[4] Data from "Service Instructions for V-1710-35, -63, -83, -93, -109, and -117 Aircraft Engines," Army Air Force Document AN 02-5AD-2, dated 5 May 1945, p.30.
[5] Where two numbers are given, they represent the first and second stage of the Merlin supercharger and the engine stage and auxiliary stage supercharger on the Allison, respectively.
[6] Data from Bristol power curves for the Centaurus 18 engine.
[7] Rated takeoff power except where noted.

non-stop. Some pilots, like Paul Mantz and Joe Debona poured fuel into every possible nook and cranny of their custom-sealed wings. Others carried mammoth external drop tanks. They all filled their tanks with 100/130 or 115/145 performance number fuel. These were luxuries heretofore unavailable in air racing.

RACING RADIALS FROM PRATT & WHITNEY

The impetus for powerful radial air-cooled engines traces to the needs of the United States military and in particular, the Navy.[2] In the years following World War I, the U.S. Navy Bureau of Aeronautics – under the able leadership of Admiral William A. Moffett – became enthusiastic over the potential of air-cooled engines to power their new light weight, high performance aircraft. In due course, Navy interest focused on the Lawrance J-1 engine, the design product of Charles L. Lawrance and his small aircraft engine company located in New York City. Eventually, though, the Navy became concerned that Lawrance Aero-Engines did not have the physical and financial resources to assure a reliable supply of J-1 engines. Moffett and his procurement people wanted a larger, financially secure firm to buy Lawrance's company. After several maneuvers on the part of the Navy, Lawrance's company was purchased by the Wright Aeronautical Corporation.[3]

Wright Aeronautical was formed in 1919 from the post-World War residue of the defunct Wright-Martin Company under the guidance of industrialist George Harrison Houston, who specialized in such reorganizations.[4] In forming the new company, Houston acquired among other assets, the old Wright-Martin license to manufacture water-cooled, direct-drive Hispano-Suiza aircraft engines.[5] When the reorganization was complete, Houston turned over the reigns of Wright Aeronautical to a new leader. He was a brilliant, driving young executive named Frederick Brant Rentschler who quickly built Wright Aeronautical into a major aircraft engine manufacturer during the early 1920s.

During this period in time, the American aircraft high-performance engine field was dominated by liquid-cooled designs from Curtiss and Packard. Wright Aeronautical added their product line of water-cooled Hispano engines to the

Chapter II: Race Power

market. These engines were first produced during World War I and production continued into the 1920s. The Navy, however, wanted the air-cooled J engine program and pushed Rentschler to acquire the fledgling Lawrance Aero-Engine Company. Ultimately, Wright did buy the firm and in so doing, unwittingly initiated a series of events that would lead to the dominance of radial engines in the United States until the advent of turbine power.

The marriage of Lawrance and Wright Aeronautical was not without turmoil. Rentschler visited New York prior to the merger and reviewed the J engine production process. What he found was "a completely confused manufacturing operation."[6] Pratt & Whitney historian Harvey Lippincott wrote that after Lawrance Aero-Engines was purchased, "Rentschler swiftly took steps to make a satisfactory engine of it. Shunting C.L. Lawrance aside, he handed the program over to

The Pratt & Whitney Wasp Jr. T1A engine seen here is the same on the exterior as the S2A models raced in Laird Super Solution and Wedell Williams racers of the early 1930s. Credit: Pratt & Whitney via CAHA

The 1935 version of Keith Rider's R-3 Bendix racer used a Pratt & Whitney Wasp S1D1, 1344 cubic inch engine illustrated here. Rider's engine used a 10:1 supercharger gear ratio and was acquired second hand from Boeing where it flew in the prototype transport airplane, c/n 1682, NC13301, used to develop their 247-D air liner. Credit: Pratt & Whitney via CAHA

his Chief Engineer, George J. Mead in whom he had confidence, with orders to straighten the engine out – quick!"[7] Mead was a bright young Massachusetts Institute of Technology graduate with a great deal of experience in engine design and production. He immediately set about redesigning the J-1 engine to strengthen it and make it more suitable for mass production. What resulted was the J-3 model and later still, the famous Wright J-5 Whirlwind engine which came to prominence and popularity in the public's mind when it powered Lindbergh's historic Spirit of St. Louis to Paris in May, 1927.

Long before Lindbergh's epic flight, Rentschler increasingly found himself at odds with his board of directors over the need to invest in research and development for new and improved engines. The directors wanted maximum near-term profit and had little vision toward future engineering products. In the end, Rentschler found no alternative but to leave Wright Aeronautical. He resigned on 1 September 1924. Rentschler's frustrations with Wright directors soon led him to form Pratt & Whitney Aircraft, a pivotal event in the history of American aviation.

The first Pratt & Whitney product was the now famous Wasp engine of 1344 cubic inch displacement. This direct drive nine-cylinder radial was designed to Navy requirements for use in observation and pursuit aircraft. In retrospect, the design origin of this engine was somewhat humble. Designer Andrew Van Dean Willgoos and engineer Earle A. Ryder worked one week in the Willgoos family garage preparing layout drawings for the new engine while Rentschler made arrangements for office space and shop facilities in Hartford, Connecticut. The facilities belonged to the Pratt & Whitney Company, an old line machine tool firm known for quality products. Rentschler incorporated his new company on 23 July 1925, adopting the Pratt & Whitney name in the process. Design work continued for three months at the Hartford factory. The first prototype engine parts were in manufacturing in September, and the engine was completed just before Christmas. It was run for the first time on 28 December 1925, and flown a scant four months later.[8] It was rated at 410 horsepower at 1900 revolutions per minute and weighed just 650 pounds. This engine was the forerunner of an unparalleled piston engine product line.

With respect to transcontinental air racing, five different Pratt & Whitney engine models were used in the twelve years before World War II: the Wasp, Hornet, Wasp Jr., Twin Wasp Jr. and Twin Wasp. In 1928 and 1929, when Lockheed Vega and Air Express airplanes ruled supreme in long distance events, they were typically powered by a Wasp or the larger (1690 cubic inch) Hornet engine. Another popular engine in the very early 1930s was the Wasp Jr., a 985 cubic inch engine designed to compete in the 300 to 400 horsepower market. There were at least five "A" series Wasp Jr. engines used in prominent racing planes from this era. With superchargers having 8:1 or 10:1 gear ratios, the Wasp Jr. was capable of delivering up to 500 horsepower.

One of the many racers to use the Pratt & Whitney Wasp Jr. was this Wedell Williams racer. Jimmy Haizlip flew this airplane to victory in the 1932 Bendix. Credit: Emil Strasser

Chapter II: Race Power

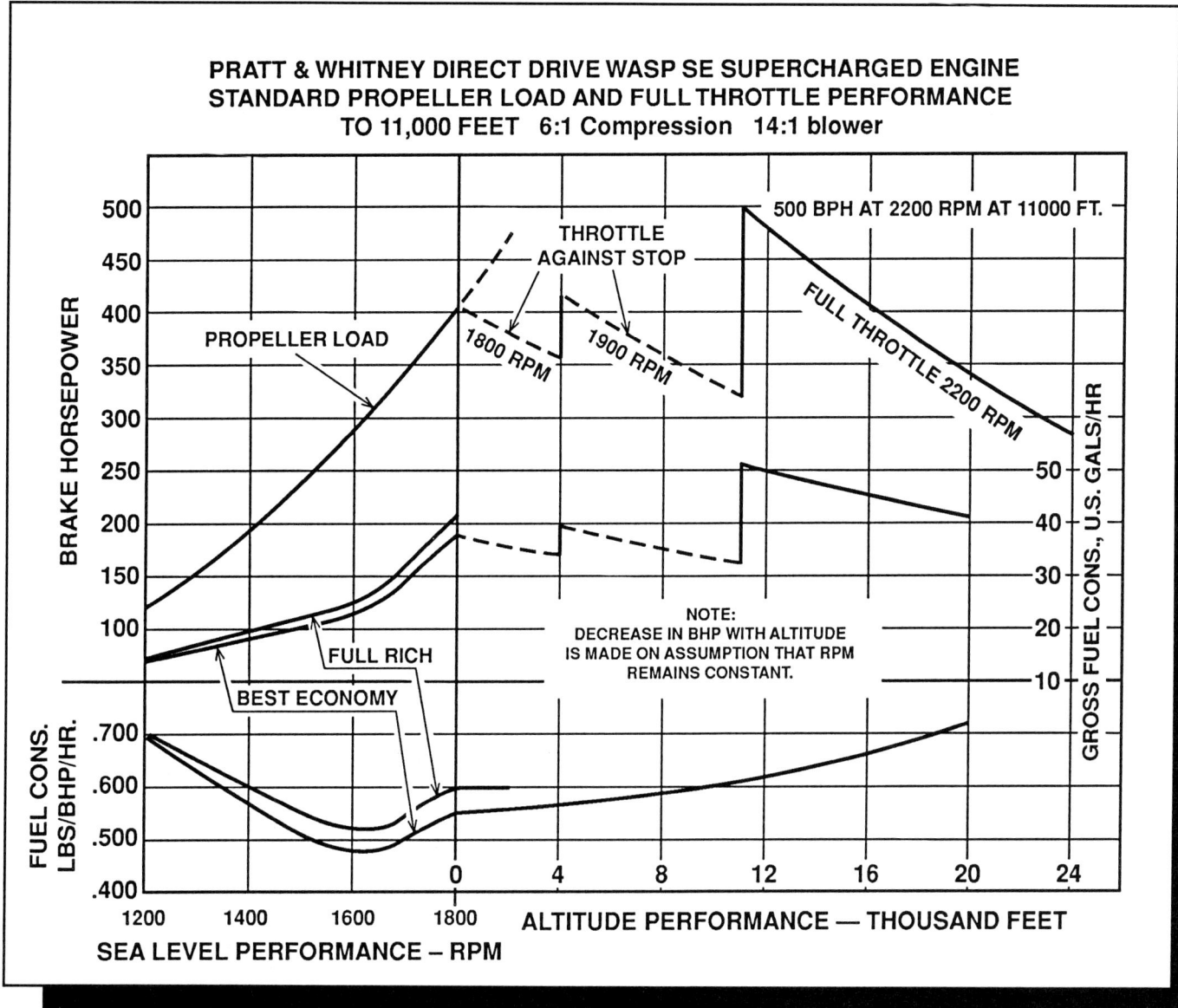

Benny Howard's 1935 Bendix race winner, Mr. Mulligan, was powered by a Pratt & Whitney Wasp SE using a 14:1 supercharger drive gear ratio. This engine is very similar to the Wasp S1D1, a principle difference being the increase in supercharger gear ratio. These performance curves are for the actual engine used in Howard's airplane. Credit Pratt & Whitney, illustration by Dave Hargreaves

The indefatigable Jimmy Doolittle captured the inaugural Bendix Trophy Race in 1931, flying his brilliant green and yellow Laird Super Solution powered with a direct drive A series Wasp Jr.[9] Other famous Bendix contestants using Wasp Jr. engines were Lee Gehlbach in the Granville Brothers Gee Bee R-2; Jimmy Wedell's trio of Wedell Williams racers from the early 1930s; and Keith Rider's sleek new R-3 racer of 1934. Seeking even more power in 1934, Roscoe Turner replaced the Wasp in his Wedell Williams racer with the larger 1690 cubic inch, 650 horsepower Hornet T1C engine in an attempt to wring a bit more speed out of the airplane. In this instance, more available horsepower didn't equate to greater speed. The engine change added a minimum of 130 pounds to the airframe empty weight and greater frontal area drag. It must have been a frustrating outcome for the irrepressible Turner!

One of the more interesting Pratt & Whitney engines raced prior to World War II was hung on the nose of Benny Howard's graceful, white cabin monoplane, Mister Mulligan. The engine was leased to the enterprising Howard who wanted an efficient four-place design with commercial potential. To harvest publicity and a bit of financial remuneration for his work and expense in designing and building the new plane, Howard planned to compete in the Bendix race. "We had to lean toward the last possible 10 miles per hour, so we stuck some extra power into it and stepped up the wing loading."[10] His "extra power" was a built-to-order Pratt & Whitney Wasp SE engine leased to Howard in 1934.[11] This was a D series

The Wasp SE warms up as Benny Howard awaits the signal to take off in the 1935 Bendix. Factory takeoff rating was 500 horsepower. Credit: Roy Russell

Turner is shown here with the newly installed Pratt & Whitney Hornet engine in his Wedell Williams racer. The engine was rated by the factory at 600 horsepower at sea level. Pratt & Whitney, Birch Matthews collection

Chapter II: Race Power

engine equipped with a 14:1 supercharger gear ratio. With this degree of supercharging, the engine delivered 500 horsepower at 11,000 feet while turning 2200 revolutions at full throttle (see the power curve nearby). Howard's strategy for the 1935 Bendix centered on a high altitude flight profile to avoid as much weather as possible. As a consequence, he equipped Mister Mulligan with an oxygen system allowing him to fly the race at "between 19,000 and 23,000 feet."[12] Knowing this and the fact his rate of climb was about 2000 feet per minute at Bendix takeoff gross weight, it is possible to estimate Howard's fuel consumption for the race at approximately 330 gallons.[13,14] Mister Mulligan had a fuel capacity of 300 gallons for the event. Without strong tail winds along the route, the possibility of completing the flight non-stop was quite marginal. For Howard to fly from Los Angeles to Cleveland non-stop would have required a "best economy" cruise power setting. Had he opted to fly the 1935 race non-stop at reduced power, Benny would have almost certainly

The Pratt & Whitney engine shown here is an R-1690 Hornet C model similar to the one used by Roscoe Turner in the 1934 version of his Wedell Williams racer. The dashing pilot captured second place in the 1935 Bendix. Credit: Pratt & Whitney via CAHA

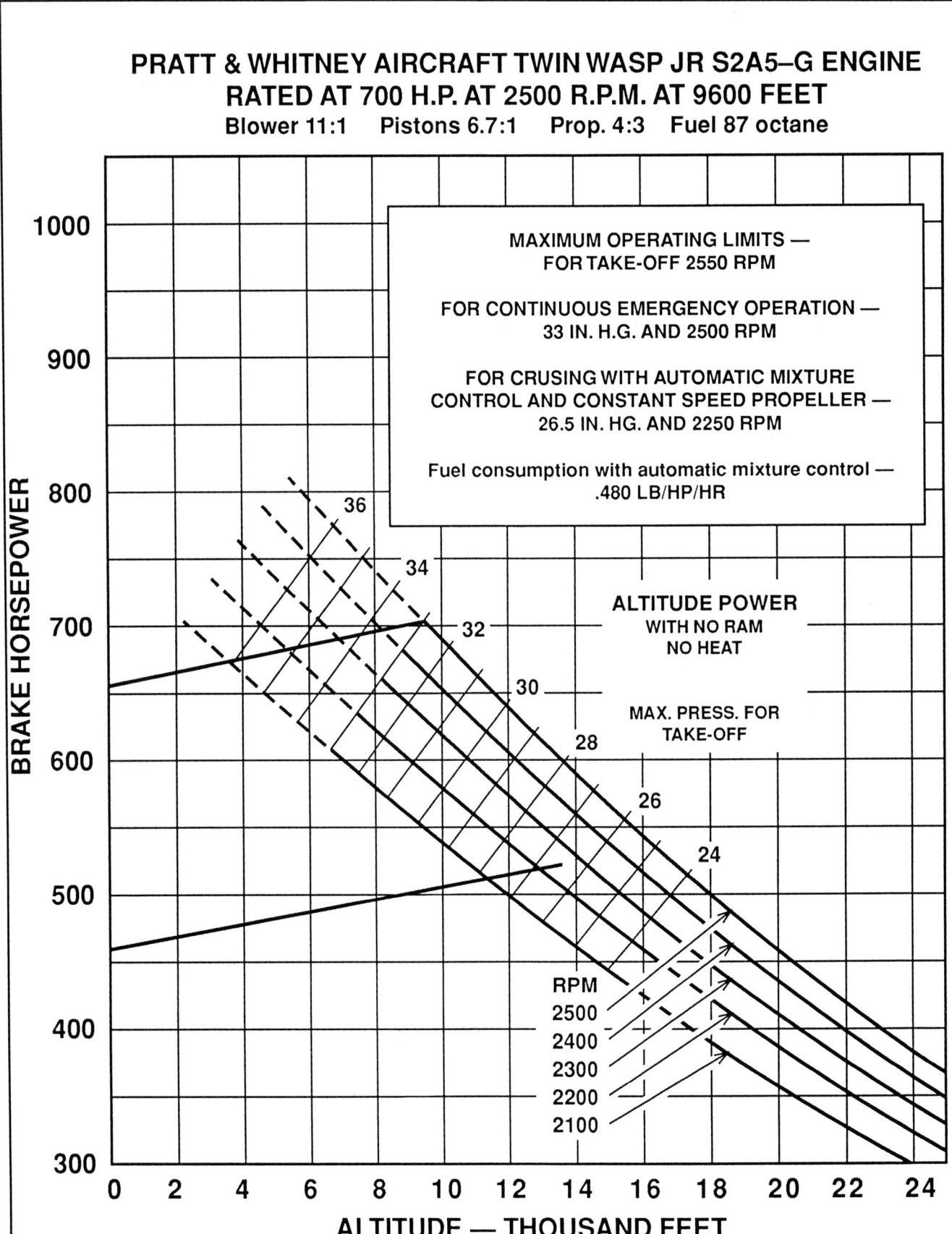

Chapter II: Race Power

The 1937 version of Keith Rider's race plane design, now known as the Marcoux-Bromberg racer, was equipped with a Pratt & Whitney Twin Wasp Jr. S2A5-G engine displacing 1535 cubic inches. The large exhaust collector ring was from a Northrop A-17A. Note the air intake scoop just below the engine for an updraft carburetor. Credit: Robert H. Stepanek

lost the race to Roscoe Turner who finished a scant 24 seconds behind. Instead, Mister Mulligan landed at Kansas City for a brief refueling and won the transcontinental air race by the narrowest margin in history.

HISTORICAL FOOTNOTES FROM THE 1930s

Some may not realize that there were liquid-cooled engines available for racing during the pre-war Bendix years. There was, for instance, the venerable Curtiss 1150 cubic inch D-12 engine with rated outputs varying between 375 to 435 horsepower. Steve Wittman employed the D-12 in his remarkable Bonzo racer which was reportedly entered in the 1936 Bendix Race. Wittman converted the D-12 cooling system from water to Prestone (ethylene glycol), used high compression ratio (8:1) pistons and could run the engine at 2500 to 2600 revolutions per minute to achieve an estimated 485 to 500 horsepower![15] In any event, Steve never flew the Bendix, choosing to concentrate on the closed-course pylon races instead.

Another liquid-cooled powerplant slated for a Bendix racer was the Curtiss Conqueror engine. In 1934, Jacqueline Cochran commissioned John Northrop to build a one-off Gamma 2G airplane powered by a supercharged SGV-1570F4 Conqueror engine. Jackie planned to enter the forthcoming international MacRobertson Race from England to Australia. The engine specified was an experimental Conqueror equipped

Opposite: Engine horsepower as a function of altitude for various manifold pressures and engine speeds is shown for the Marcoux-Bromberg racer using the Twin Wasp Jr. S2A5-G engine. Manifold pressures range from 24 to 36 inches of Mercury (Hg). Engine could deliver 700 horsepower at 9000 feet with 33 inches and 2500 rpm. Credit: Pratt & Whitney, illustration by Dave Hargreaves

In the late 1930s, a number of Pratt & Whitney Twin Wasp R-1830 engines appeared in Bendix cross-country racers. One of the most successful was Frank Fuller's big Seversky, a civilian version of the Army Air Corp P-35. Pictured here is the Twin Wasp SB-G model, similar to that used by both Fuller and Jacqueline Cochran. Credit: Pratt & Whitney via CAHA

with a General Electric supercharger, a fact which caused frustrating and unending problems.

Arthur Nutt designed the Conqueror engine as a next generation to the venerable Curtiss D-12. It was first produced ten years prior to Miss Cochran's order to Northrop. From 1926 to 1932, the 12-cylinder water-cooled Conqueror was built in several versions with ratings of 575 to 650 horsepower. Cochran's engine, using a supercharger, developed 705 horsepower at 2450 revolutions per minute at 7000 feet altitude.[16] Jackie planned to gain experience with the Gamma by flying in the 1934 Bendix Race. It was not to be. "Two days before the Bendix was to start, the General Electric charger

Chapter II: Race Power

This is another view of the Twin Wasp. Roscoe Turner also used a Twin Wasp in his Brown built, Laird modified "Meteor" racer. Slated for the 1937 Bendix, a fuel tank welding accident eliminated the new airplane from starting the race. Credit: Pratt & Whitney via CAHA

blew up on the test stand at the Northrop factory."[17] The supercharger continued to plague Jackie's plans and in the end, the Gamma was withdrawn from the MacRobertson Race as well.

THE FORD-MERLIN ENGINE

The story of Merlin engine manufacturing in the United States begins not with the Packard Motor Car Company; rather, its history started with automobile tycoon Henry Ford. On 16 May 1940, President Franklin D. Roosevelt issued a startling call for American industry to produce 50,000 airplanes to radically bolster the nation's defense. The magnitude of this number is appreciated when compared to an Army Air Corps proposal to increase first-line combat aircraft to 2700 planes only two months earlier.[18] To implement the buildup of aircraft and other weapons of war, Roosevelt created the National Defense Advisory Commission. Danish immigrant William S. Knudsen, formerly president of General Motors, was placed in charge of production planning and to him fell the monumental task of turning FDR's grandiose plan into reality.

One of the industrialists called upon to support the nation was Henry Ford. Only 12 days after Roosevelt made his clarion call for so many airplanes, Henry Ford – in a moment of unabashed enthusiasm – told the Associated Press, "if it becomes necessary the Ford Motor Company could swing into the production of a thousand airplanes a day of standard design."[19] Ford's statement received wide though somewhat skeptical attention both in the United States and abroad. A few

Frank Fuller's beautiful Seversky SEV-S2 racer mounted a Pratt & Whitney Twin Wasp. Takeoff was factory rated at 1050 horsepower. This airframe-engine combination twice won the Bendix Trophy Race. Credit: Dusty Carter

days later, Henry's son, Edsel Ford, met with government officials in Washington, D.C., to discuss possible aircraft production by the Ford Motor Company. Meanwhile, Henry continued his optimistic claims for future aircraft production as long as they were "for defense only; that's the bargain all the way through."[20] Ford was an ardent isolationist and truly did not want the United States entangled in another European conflict.

Edsel Ford returned to Washington in early June and conferred with William Knudsen who proposed that instead of building planes, Ford manufacture 9000 Rolls-Royce Merlins, of which 6000 would go to the British, the remainder to be delivered to the Army Air Corps. The project was subsequently discussed with the elder Ford who, not withstanding earlier pronouncements on making war goods for the belligerents, apparently agreed. Edsel was enthusiastic and set his engineers to work. British drawings were sent to Ford Motor for technical evaluation. Shortly thereafter, all hell broke loose when the irascible Henry angrily announced that he would not do business with the British. With trouble brewing and having already told President Roosevelt that Ford would build the engines, Knudsen flew to Detroit to meet with Henry. He "made a vigorous effort to persuade the Ford Motor Company to produce it," but old Henry was adamant.[21] The meeting degenerated into a confrontation between Ford and Knudsen and the latter departed in a rage. Henry disliked Franklin Roosevelt and his isolationist fervor surfaced once more. The elder Ford was a pacifist, a member of the isolationist America First Committee and certainly no anglophile.[22] That was it. There would never be a Ford-Merlin engine built in the United States! Ironically, the Ford company in Great Britain built thousands of Merlin's.

THE PACKARD-MERLIN ENGINE

On 24 June 1940, representatives of Packard Motor Car Company "called on Mr. Knudsen at his home in Grosse Isle (Michigan). Knudsen came straight to the point: Would Packard build the Merlin?"[23] The reaction to Knudsen's question was positive. The Packard men were receptive and immediately began developing a proposal. After a month or so of negotiations, agreement was reached. In September 1940, 2500 drawings were received from Ford Motor Company and the difficult job of converting these documents to American standards began.[24] Packard engineers and production people performed admirably. By the end of November, 1940, drawings were released to manufacture an improved Merlin incorporating two-piece cylinder block construction. Deliveries began in July of the following year. By the end of the war, Packard manufactured 55,523 Merlin engines.[25] Of this quan-

Chapter II: Race Power

The custom-built Merlin engine shown here was used in Chuck Lyford's beautiful Bardahl Special racing Mustang which placed second in the 1964 Harold's Club Trophy Dash. The engine is mounted on the aft end of truck chassis, dubbed the "Swamp Buggy," and used for engine modification evaluation testing. Credit: Jim Larsen

tity, Packard engineered 26 different models of the engine and produced 22 in quantity (see Appendix C).

Post-war Bendix and Reno Harold's Club Trophy racers were dominated by Packard-built, Rolls-Royce Merlin engines in North American P-51 Mustangs. The engine shown here is a composite of various Packard dash numbers and Merlin Marks built up for Reno era pylon racing. Credit: Birch Matthews

TRANSCONTINENTAL MERLINS

The Merlin is best remembered for delivering exceptional power at high altitude. The basis of this achievement was an outstanding two-stage, two-speed, gear-driven supercharger of Rolls-Royce design. The Rolls engine was a military success and would also shine in the post-war air races. Packard-built dash 3 and dash 9 high altitude engines were best for post-war transcontinental racing and powered the Mustangs of three-time Bendix winner, Paul Mantz and others. The dash 7 Merlin had lower supercharger gear ratios with corresponding less altitude performance and were therefore not as competitive. This was the standard production engine for P-51D Mustangs and was used, at some disadvantage, by two or three Bendix contestants. At least one Merlin-powered Bendix racer flew the dash 225 engine which was a low altitude powerplant. It had a single-stage, two-speed supercharger and was less than ideal for long distance racing.

These same engines became the standard for Reno cross-country racers almost two decades later although by this time, the custom of mixing and matching components of various Merlin models was becoming the norm. One of the hottest racing Merlins to fly in a Reno transcontinental race belonged to Chuck Lyford. He developed his knowledge of modified Merlin engines during his boat racing career. With the help of engine specialist Dwight Thorn, Chuck mounted a modified dash 9 Merlin in his Bardahl Mustang for the 1964 transcontinental trophy race.

Packard-Merlin Engine Superchargers

Engine Model	Impeller Diameter First Stage	Impeller Diameter Second Stage	Gear Ratio Low Blower	Gear Ratio High Blower
V-1650-3	12.0"	10.1"	6.391:1	8.095:1
V-1650-7	12.0"	10.1"	5.802:1	7.349:1
V-1650-9	12.0"	10.1"	6.391:1	8.095:1
V-1650-225	10.25"	–	8.150:1	9.490:1

THE ALLISON V-1710

The contemporary liquid-cooled American engine design was the V-1710, manufactured by the Allison Division of General Motors Corporation. Allison was not always part of General Motors. The company's origin dates to 1915, when wealthy James A. Allison founded an organization to build and repair race cars and engines. The firm was called the Indianapolis Speedway Team Company. It quickly became known for precision custom machining, particularly power transmission gears and shafts. Fourteen years later this small venture would become, through a series of events and maneuvers, the Allison Division of General Motors.

World War was raging across Europe when Allison founded his company. On 6 April 1917, Congress passed a war resolution and the United States officially entered the European conflict. A little over a month earlier, Jim Allison incorporated his company and changed the name to Allison

One of the best known Merlin-powered racers was Paul Mantz's crimson red P-51C. This Bendix winner was powered by a dash 3 Merlin in this 1946 photograph. Credit: Emil Strasser

Chapter II: Race Power

A post-war Bendix competitor of the Merlin was the Allison V-1710 in-line engine. Slightly larger than the Merlin, the Allison gear-driven supercharger performance never matched that of the Merlin. Turbosupercharged models used in Lockheed's P-38 Lightning gave better altitude performance. Credit: Phil Krause

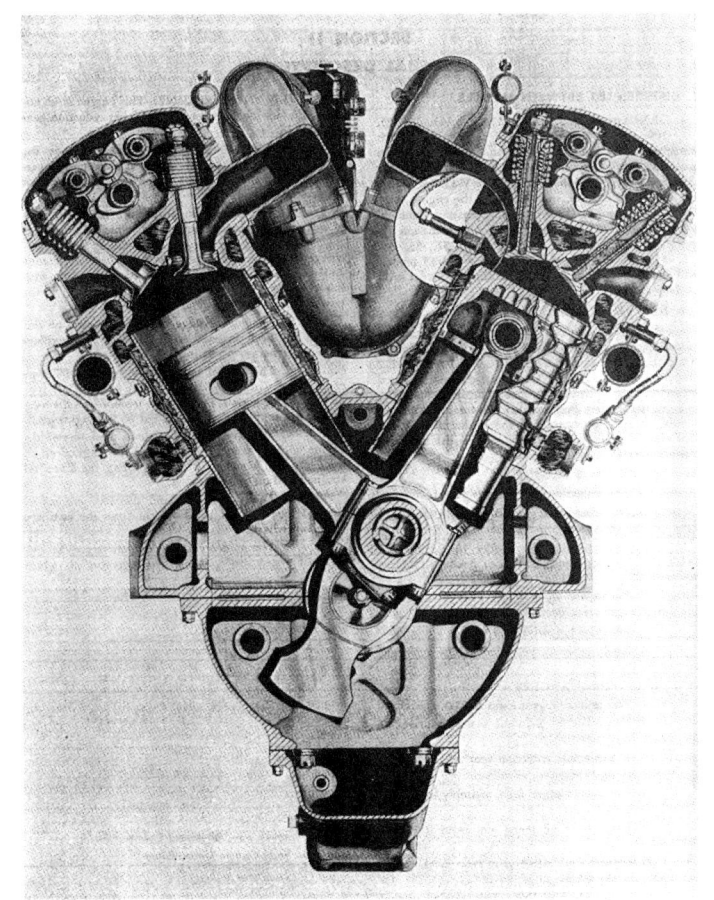

This artist's conception illustrates the internal components of the basic Allison V-1710 power section. The engine cross-section drawing is through the number six cylinder. Credit: Allison Division

Experimental Company.[26] One suspects he saw opportunities for new business as war approached and a less definitive company name might be advantageous. In any event, Allison Experimental obtained several government contracts during the war for specialty gear manufacturing including reduction gear sets for experimental Liberty 12C engines. The company also became a major overhaul facility for Liberty engines.

After the war, the affluent Allison bought a 72 foot yacht which he soon found lacked a suitable marine engine. He directed his chief engineer, Norman H. "Buzz" Gilman – a rotund hands-on automobile racing engine specialist – to develop a V-12 marine engine specifically for his yacht. The engines were smooth and powerful, developing 425 horsepower at 1500 revolutions per minute. Twelve were built with Allison keeping four of the engines. The others found their way into the yachts of his friends and associates.

In 1920, the company name was again changed to Allison Engineering. Around the same time, the small firm received government contracts to rebuild and to redesign the now familiar Liberty engine. A major reason for reworking the Liberty 12 engine was to increase durability by incorporating Allison's unique and well respected lead-bronze, steel-backed engine bearings. The company also designed and produced the self-contained spur-type reduction gear assemblies used on various liquid-cooled Packard aircraft engines. In 1924, Allison designed and built an air-cooled, 24 cylinder "X" configuration, 1200 horsepower aircraft engine for the Army Air Corp.[27] Three years later, another contract was received to design and build a six cylinder, 765 horsepower two-cycle diesel engine for use in U.S. Navy dirigibles. The engine performed well; however, the Navy abandoned this project due to difficulty in recovering ballast water from the exhaust of a diesel, a necessary requirement in their airship program.

At about this time the Army Air Corps Materiel Division at Wright Field became interested in the potential of ethylene glycol as a coolant for liquid-cooled aircraft engines.[28] The perceived advantage of glycol as a coolant was its high boiling

The first Allison V-1710 engine installation in an airframe occurred during 1936, when Bell Aircraft Corp. mounted a V-1710-3 (Allison model C4) into a Consolidated A-11A two-place Army Air Corp attack airplane. The dash 3 engine was used for installation mockup purposes. The first Allison to fly was a V-1710-7 in this same A-11A airframe. Credit: Bell Aircraft via Birch Matthews

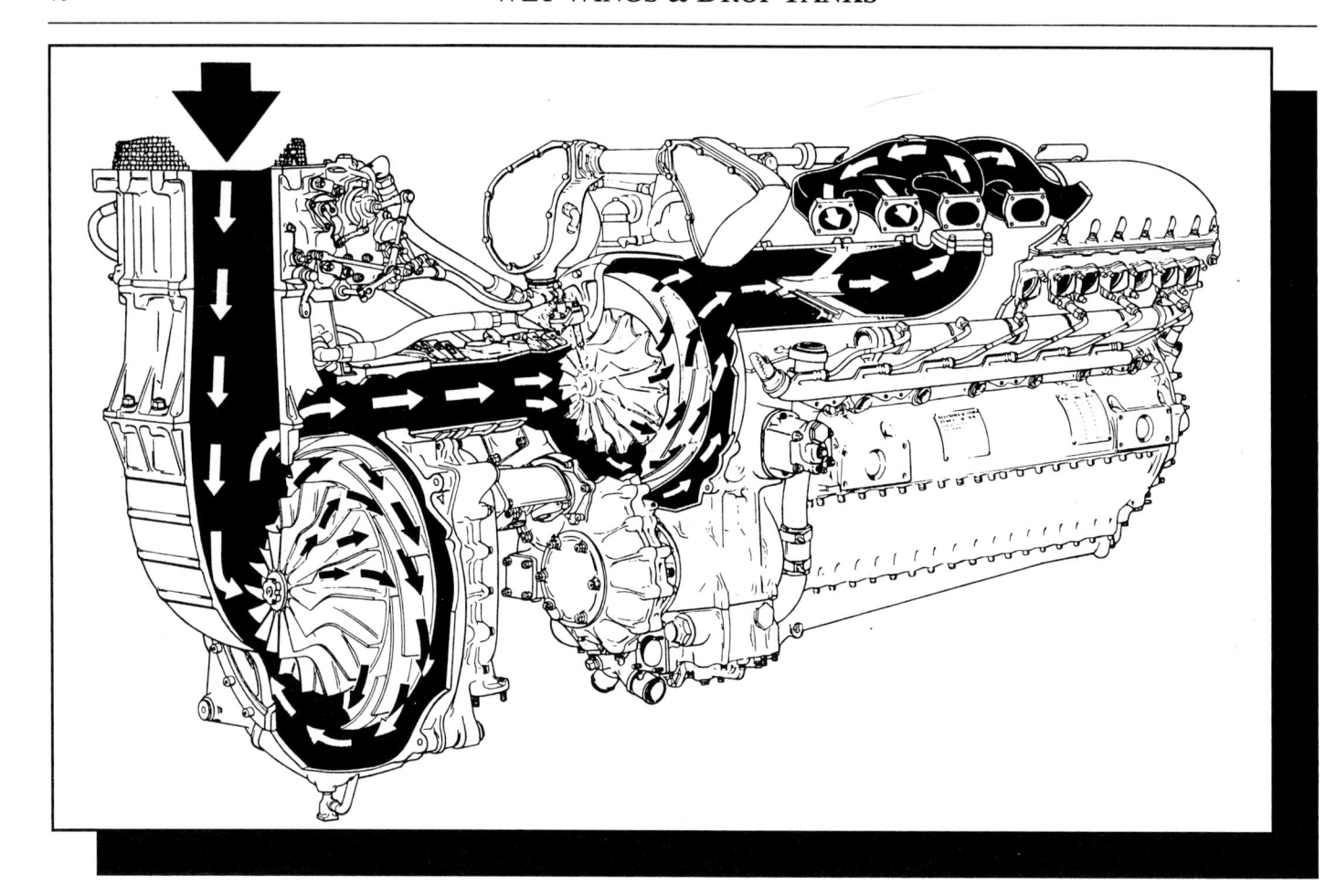

Early Allisons used a single-stage, gear-driven supercharger yielding mediocre altitude performance. Newer versions employed an auxiliary stage supercharger physically separated from the engine stage. This diagram illustrates the air-fuel mixture flow through both supercharger stages, induction passageway and delivery to the cylinder intake valves for the V-1710-117 engine. Credit: Allison Division

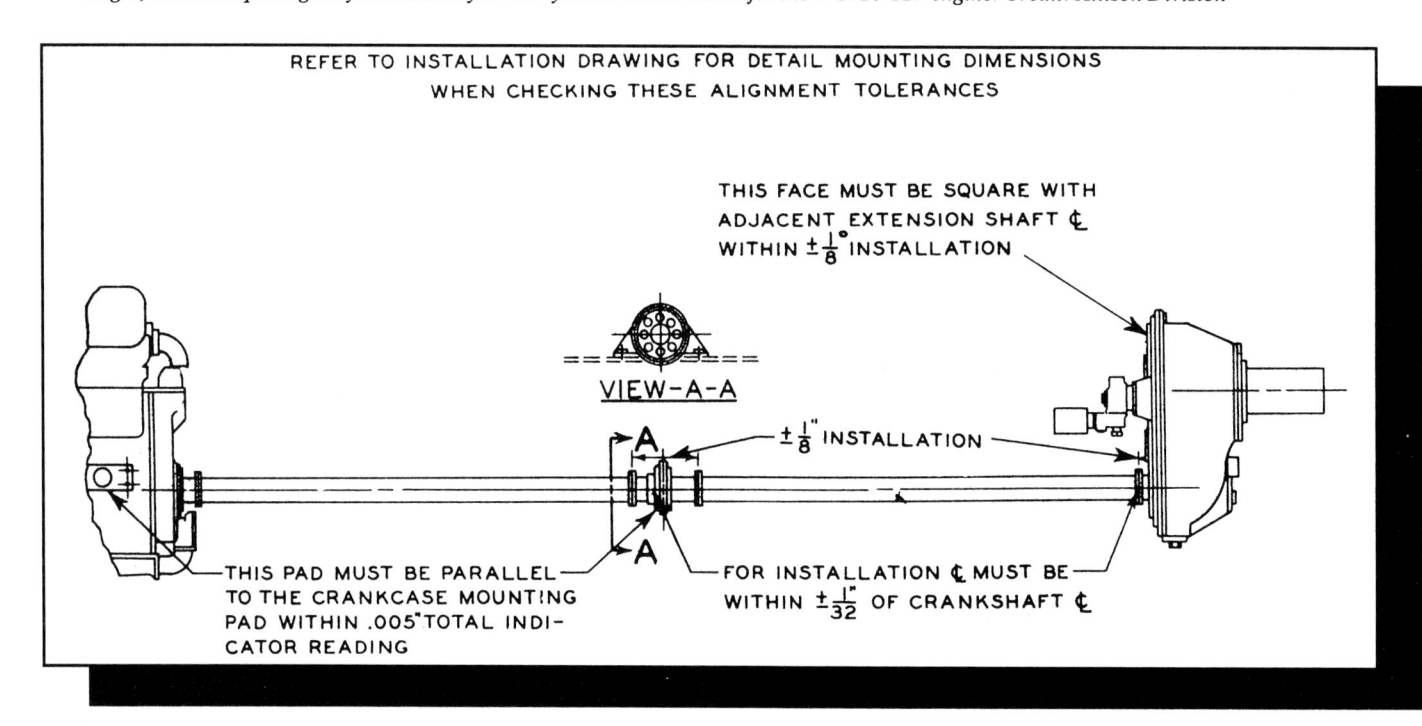

In Bell P-63 and P-39 aircraft, the Allison was mounted amidship. Power was transmitted to the reduction gear box using an extension shaft. This diagram illustrates the rather tight shaft mounting tolerances required. It was for this reason that both fighters were built around a truss-like structure that was extremely rigid. Credit: Allison Division

Chapter II: Race Power

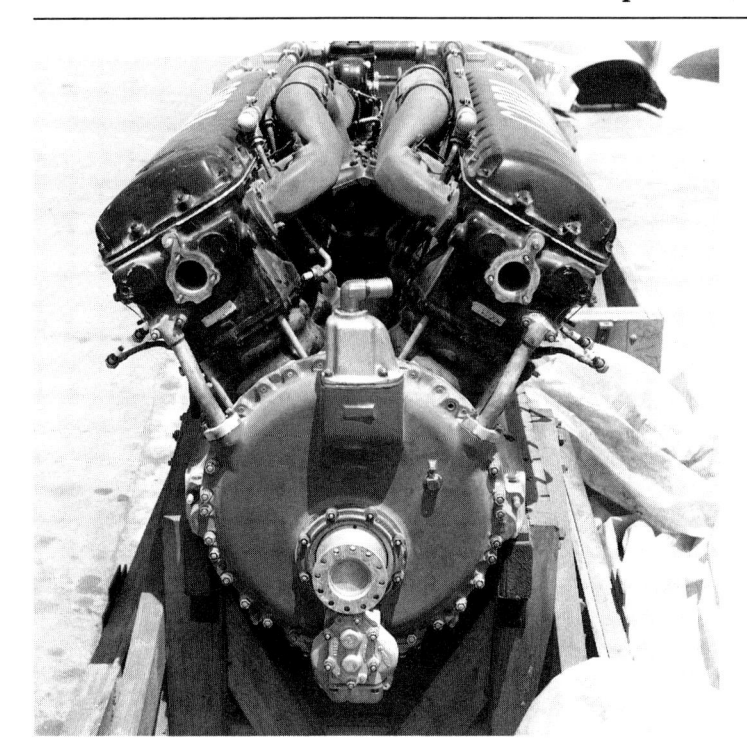

This is a frontal view of an Allison V-1710-85 originally used in Mike Carroll's Cobra racer in 1968. The engine was built by Dave Zeuschel. The photograph shows the extension shaft connection on the forward end of the crankcase. Credit: Birch Matthews

The engine stage supercharger housing on Mike Carroll's V-1710-85 engine is seen in this photograph. It was replaced by a Zeuschel-built V-1710-117 engine for the first flight. The reason the dash 117 engine would fit the small P-39 airframe was that the auxiliary stage supercharger was removed. Credit: Birch Matthews

point of 392°F compared to 212°F for water at sea level. Using unpressurized water in liquid-cooled engines meant that coolant outlet temperatures were restricted to about 180°F. With ethylene glycol, the coolant could rise to 300°F or more, an appreciable increase. The advantage would be smaller cooling radiators with corresponding reductions in aircraft aerodynamic drag and weight.[29] Wright Field engineers tested a Curtiss Conqueror engine to demonstrate feasibility. Glycol as a coolant, however, was not without drawbacks. It tended to attack seals and packing gland materials with some vigor. To take advantage of the higher glycol boiling point meant the Conqueror engine operated at a correspondingly greater temperature. This led to differential thermal expansion between adjoining parts of differing metals, a problem Curtiss – to the frustration of the Army – never resolved.[30]

The innovative Gilman was aware of this Wright Field work and in 1928, began preliminary design and fabrication of a liquid-cooled test engine cylinder suitable for use with ethylene glycol.[31] He approached the Materiel Division seeking a development contract for a new engine designed from the start to use glycol. Gilman was rebuffed. The Army preferred at that time to stay with Curtiss, a well established and familiar engine manufacturer. It was an Army decision that would lead nowhere. Coolant leakage into the Conqueror cylinders from differential thermal expansion persisted. The Army and Curtiss fell into technical disagreement, bickering over the validity of a 300°F (government) coolant temperature requirement versus the engine design. The glycol cooling development problems were never fully resolved. Eventually, the Army stopped development. Within a few years, Conqueror production ceased.

While Jim Allison was not a hands-on manager (that task fell to "Buzz" Gilman), he did control the financial resources available for product development. Gilman needed Allison's concurrence to proceed with the new cylinder concept and extrapolate it into a full fledged engine design. Fifty-five year old James A. Allison was an independently wealthy entrepreneur involved with a number of outside interests, including real estate development projects in Miami Beach and Port Washington, Long Island. Allison's outside pursuits it seems, were not constrained to real estate development. In the early 1920s, his attentions devolved to young Lucille Mussett, the daughter of Miami real estate developer, George W. Mussett. After several years of continued assignations with this very young and attractive women, Jim's wife, Sara Cornelius Allison, brought the scandal to light and sued for divorce charging that Lucille "brought to bear on Allison the fine art of love-making, at which she was a skillful expert."[32] Sara was granted a divorce in June, 1928!

James promptly married Lucille on 1 August at the home of his business associate of many years, Carl Fischer. Three days later, Jim Allison suddenly and unexpectedly died while

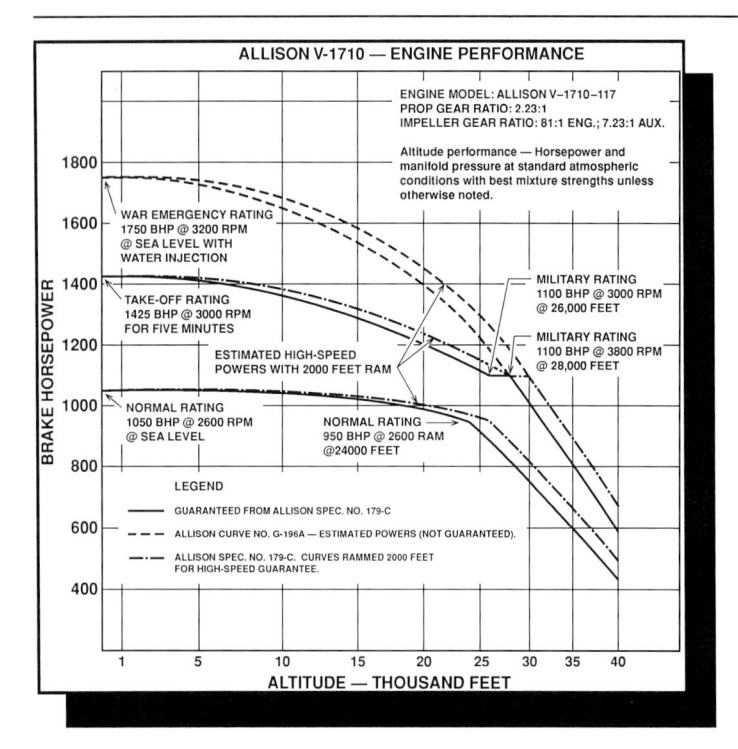

The engine in Charley Tucker's Bell P-63C Bendix racer was an Allison V-1710-117 model. It was not modified for the Bendix race. Performance versus altitude for this engine is illustrated in this figure. At 25 to 30,000 feet where Chuck flew the race, his engine would develop about 1100 horsepower. Credit: Allison Division, illustration by Dave Hargreaves

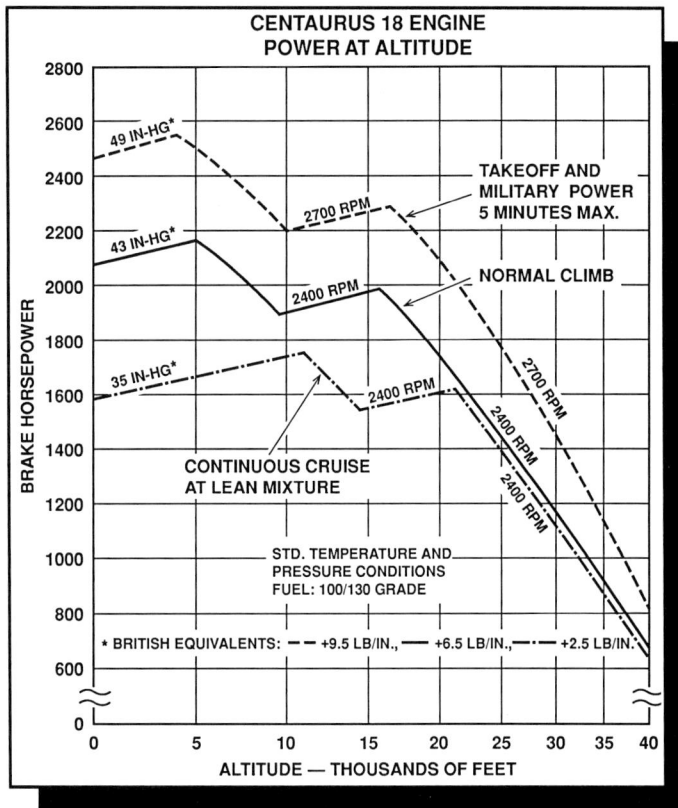

Mike Carroll won the 1967 Harold's Club race with his big yellow Hawker Sea Fury powered by a Bristol Centaurus 18. This sleeve valve, air-cooled radial engine would produce around 2300 horsepower at 17,000 feet using military power. Altitude performance for engine is shown in this figure. Credit: Bristol Aircraft, illustration by Dave Hargreaves

on his honeymoon.[33] The cause of death was variously attributed to bronchial pneumonia and a heart attack. Under the circumstances, his passing was no doubt subject to wide and varied speculation in less sophisticated circles. Ironically, it was a turn of events which led directly to America's only indigenous mass-produced liquid-cooled aircraft engine of World War II.

Allison left an estate valued in the millions. This fact produced a legal suit by his first wife, Sara, who sought a portion of the estate. It was the beginning of a year of legal battles and financial maneuvers by some of the more agile personalities vying for the estate and the company. One of Allison's friends was the famous World War I flying ace, Captain Eddy Rickenbacker. About a year before the industrialist passed away, Rickenbacker approached him with the thought of buying Allison Engineering. Jim really didn't want to part with the company even though he was spending most of his time in Florida, "but when I do come home for the summer," he said, "I like to have a desk I can put my feet on."[34] Although he would not sell the company, he convinced Captain Eddy to buy the Indianapolis Speedway. Absolutely broke at the time, Rickenbacker boldly contrived to have the Union Guardian Bank of Detroit float a Speedway bond issue to finance the purchase. Eddy took control of the Speedway on 1 November 1927.[35]

The funeral services for James A. Allison on 6 August 1928, brought many industrialists and personalities to Indianapolis including Rickenbacker.[36] Eddy apparently lost little time in seeking out the executors of Allison's estate to learn "what was to become of the Allison Engineering Company."[37] It would go to the highest bidder was the answer and Rickenbacker knew this was his real opportunity to acquire the firm. A number of individuals and organizations were very interested in the company; however, Rickenbacker had inside information about their offers and was always able to stay one step ahead of the competition. In the end, Eddy acquired Allison Engineering for a reported $90,000. As with his Indianapolis Speedway acquisition, it is doubtful that Rickenbacker had the resources to buy Allison Engineering. Once again, he was able to secure financing for the full amount, surrounding company acreage being deemed sufficient collateral.

In retrospect, it is not clear whether Captain Eddy really wanted the company or was an interloper for a more well-heeled buyer. Almost immediately, Rickenbacker left Indianapolis heading for Detroit where he contacted the wealthy

Chapter II: Race Power

Fisher Brothers, well known for there automobile body works. The brothers had established the Fisher Investment Trust and it was this organization that next secured ownership of Allison Engineering. The deal was formalized on 22 March 1929, although the name of the new owner was not then publicly disclosed.[38] A month later, Fisher Investment sold Allison Engineering to General Motors. Rickenbacker was rewarded with a "finders fee" of $9000 and everyone, it seems, managed to profit.[39]

Announcing the acquisition of Allison, General Motors president, Alfred P. Sloan, Jr., said ". . . it will be the purpose of General Motors to intensify and expand this company's operations, especially along the lines indicated."[40] Sloan was referring to Allison's earlier work on diesel engine design for the Navy's airships. This work would be redirected toward airplane applications in direct competition with Packard Motor's ongoing diesel development. Allison's future, however, did not reside with diesel aircraft engines – nor did Packard's, for that matter –and Gilman eventually convinced General Motors management to invest resources in the liquid-cooled cylinder design. Early in 1930, a preliminary layout for a 12 cylinder engine of 750 horsepower was completed. The design provided for turbosupercharging and was the genesis of the famous V-1710 Allison aircraft engine of World War II.

NAVY ALLISONS

The V-1710 design was initiated late in 1930, and Allison's first customer was the U.S. Navy. They ordered one experimental engine. This engine was assembled in August of the following year demonstrating a sea level rating of 650 horsepower at 2400 revolutions per minute on 80 octane fuel. Unlike the earliest preliminary design which had provisions for a turbosupercharger, the prototype engine utilized a 7.3:1 ratio gear-driven supercharger.[41] Development continued through 1932, when a 50 hour test was successfully concluded using an increased blower gear ratio of 8.0:1 resulting in an output of 750 horsepower, at 2400 revolutions.

The Navy saw an application for the V-1710 in their airship program. As a consequence, Allison redesigned the basic engine in 1933, eliminating the supercharger and providing a unique reversing mechanism to run the engine in opposite rotation upon demand. As Allison Chief Engineer R.M. Hazen later described this feature, the "engine would reverse from full power in one direction to the same condition in the opposite direction in a matter of eight seconds," a rather imposing accomplishment.[42] The Navy airship program came to an abrupt termination with the untimely loss of the dirigibles Akron and Macon. Navy interest in liquid-cooled aircraft engines vanished.

THE ARMY TAKES A SECOND LOOK

The Army Air Corps began to take notice of Allison's work in 1933. This might never have happened if Curtiss engineering and management been more flexible and forward looking about developing their Conqueror engine for use with ethylene glycol. Curtiss and the Army parted company and the latter felt the need of a liquid-cooled engine for pursuit aircraft. In the event, the Army obtained a modified engine which developed 750 horsepower designated by the manufacturer as the V-1710-C. By 1934, the engine was upgraded to 800 horsepower. The following spring, 1000 horsepower was achieved and the V-1710 was well along in development. By 1937, Allison's V-1710-C8 engine successfully passed a 150 hour qualification, the first engine in the world to produce 1000 horsepower on a military approval type test.[43]

The first Allison engine to fly was the V-1710-7 model.[44] In late 1935 or early 1936, Bell Aircraft Corporation was awarded a contract by Wright Field (W535 ac-7949) to install a V-1710 in a Consolidated A-11 two-place attack airplane. For $24,995, just under the $25,000 major contract limit, Bell designed and fabricated the engine mount and cowling and made the installation. The engine installed at Bell was actually a V-1710-3, later replaced by a V-1710-7 at Wright Field before the airplane was flown in the fall of 1936. It was a milestone in the development of Allison's liquid-cooled engine. This experiment was soon followed by using V-1710s in the Curtiss XP-37 and Bell XFM-1 twin-engined Airacuda. The Army was now committed to the V-1710 and it would go on to power such World War II fighters as the Bell P-39 and P-63, the Lockheed P-38 and early versions of the North American P-51 (See Appendix D for a list of V-1710 models).

RACING ALLISONS

Allison engines appeared only in the 1946 and 1947 Bendix Trophy Races, where they powered Lockheed Lightings and Bell Kingcobras. Most if not all of the post-war Allison engines were run in stock condition. The first post-war Bendix Race saw the largest entry list in the history of the event, over thirty aircraft. The most prevalent aircraft was Lockheed's twin engine Lightning which accounted for 18 of the entries. There were four variants as shown in the accompanying table. Most of these were the F-5G-6 photo reconnaissance version. The Lockheeds were popular because their turbosupercharged engines had excellent high altitude performance. Allison's V-1710-111/113 engines would produce a rated power of 1425 horsepower at 29,000 feet. In addition, P-38/F-5 fighters were in abundant supply in the War Asset Administration inventories, more so than North American Aviation's P-51 Mustang. Another influencing factor may have been the cost of the

Lightning which was almost one-third that of the P-51 in the surplus market.[45]

Only two Bell P-63 Kingcobras flew in the 1946 Bendix. The first was Charley Tucker's race 30, which finished a commendable seventh against a formidable field of competition. The second P-63 flew in 1947, and failed to finish. Both aircraft ran V-1710-117 engines equipped with the Allison auxiliary stage supercharger. This setup provided a respectable 1100 horsepower at 25,000 feet.

As a racing engine, the Allison never matched the Rolls-Royce Merlin. The slightly smaller Merlin had superior supercharging and this proved a deciding factor. Lest the Allison be denigrated, many racing engine rebuilders consider the V-1710 to be the stronger powerplant and indeed, Allison connecting rods have been adapted to the Merlin for that very reason.[46]

LAST OF THE ROUND ENGINES

The only radial air-cooled engine to win a post-World War II transcontinental air race was the big 3270 cubic inch displacement Bristol Centaurus 18 which powered Mike Carroll's equally big Hawker Sea Fury. Mike won the 1967 Harold's Club Transcontinental Trophy Dash in this airplane with its unique British engine.

The engine in Mike Carroll's Sea Fury would produce over 2500 horsepower at high manifold pressures (49 inches of mercury or +9.5 lb/in^2 boost) at 2700 revolutions per minute around five thousand feet. At 21,000 feet, an altitude range where cross-country races were often flown, the mighty Centaurus still delivered a very respectable 2100 horsepower at the same power setting.

The Centaurus was uncommon among air-cooled radials because it used sleeve valves in place of conventional poppet valves. Bristol employed the Burt-McCollum sleeve valve concept. This valve is basically a sleeve surrounding the piston inside the engine cylinder. Like the piston, the sleeve valve moves up and down but also rotates. The rotating motion allows the single sleeve port to alternately uncover intake and exhaust ports during the appropriate piston strokes. Another unique feature of the Centaurus is the method of starting the engine. In place of a battery operated mechanical starter, it uses a Coffman starter which employs a shotgun-type cartridge. When the solid propellant in the cartridge is ignited, it burns rapidly generating a large volume of high pressure gas which propels a mechanism connected to the engine starter gear drive train.

The 18 cylinder Bristol Centaurus series of engines came into being during the early 1940s. These engines were used to power several airplanes including the Tempest II and Sea Fury. Development of the Centaurus began long before World War II. Bristol first built a two cylinder Vee arrangement test engine using the sleeve valve concept in 1927.[47] The first full-scale Bristol sleeve valve powerplant, the nine-cylinder Perseus, was constructed and type-tested in 1932. This was followed by an even larger 14 cylinder Hercules engine which was developed to over 1700 horsepower. The final extension of the sleeve valve design was the Centaurus.

Allison Engines in the Bendix

Aircraft	Air Force Designation	Allison Model No.	Remarks
Lockheed F-5G-6-LO	V-1710-111	V-1710-F30R	Right-Hand Rotation
	V-1710-113	V-1710-F30L	Left-Hand Rotation
Lockheed P-38F-15-LO	V-1710-49	V-1710-F5R	Right-Hand Rotation
	V-1710-53	V-1710-F5L	Left-Hand Rotation
Lockheed P-38L-5-LO	V-1710-111	V-1710-F30R	Right-Hand Rotation
	V-1710-113	V-1710-F30L	Left-Hand Rotation
Lockheed P-38M-6-LO	V-1710-111	V-1710-F30R	Right-Hand Rotation
	V-1710-113	V-1710-F30L	Left-Hand Rotation
Bell P-63C-5-BE	V-1710-117	V-1710-E21	

Chapter II: Race Power

NOTES:

1 Engine parameters compiled in this table were derived from manufacturer specifications. In some instances, power output may be at variance with that claimed by personalities involved in racing. Because these claims are not traceable to test data, they were not used. No doubt some engines were run at marginally higher power settings than the rated values of the manufacturer. In addition, increased power was delivered as aviation fuel quality improved.
2 Robert Schlaifer, "Development of Aircraft Engines," Graduate school of Business Administration, Harvard University, 1950, p. 196.
3 Harvey Lippincott, "The Navy Gets an Engine," American Aviation Historical Society JOURNAL, Vol. 6, No. 4, 1961, p.255.
4 Cary Hoge Mead, "Wings Over the World," the Swannet Press, Wauwatosa, Wisconsin, 1971, p.24.
5 As author Bill Gunston notes, assigning a nationality to the Hispano-Suiza (literally, Spanish-Swiss) company of France is difficult. Engine designer Marc Birkigt was Swiss. In 1904, he established a factory in Barcelona, Spain. Seven years later, Birkigt formed the Société Hispano-Suiza in France, where in 1915, he began production of his first aircraft engine. See Gunston's "World Encyclopaedia of Aero Engines," Patrick Stehpens Limited, England, 1989, p. 77.
6 Anon., "The Pratt & Whitney Aircraft Story," Pratt & Whitney Aircraft Division, United Aircraft Corporation, 1950, p. 28.
7 Lippincott, op. cit., p. 255.
8 The first flight was on 5 May 1926.
9 Engine serial number X-27.
10 Benjamin O. Howard, "Mister Mulligan," Aviation, October 1935, p. 15.
11 Howard built the aircraft with the intention of entering the 1934 Bendix, however, an in-route accident spoiled this plan. The engine was returned to Hartford after the accident where it was overhauled by Pratt & Whitney for the 1935 race.
12 Harvey Lippincott speech before the Society of Air Racing Historians, 4-6 May 1990. Lippincott's comments were based upon a letter from Howard to H. Mansfield Horner following the 1935 Bendix Race.
13 Howard, op.cit., p. 16.
14 An average altitude of 22,000 feet was assumed from Howard's comments in the letter to Horner. He made a fuel stop at Kansas City and thus there were two takeoffs during the race each requiring a time-to-climb of about 11 minutes. Using the Pratt & Whitney power curves for the SE engine, average fuel consumption during climb out was estimated at 0.6 lb/hp-hr assuming 500 horsepower. At altitude, the engine was producing around 300 horsepower and consuming something like 0.76 lb/hp-hr.
15 Hugo T. Byttebier, *The Curtiss D-12 Aero Engine*, Smithsonian Institution Press, Washington, D.C., 1972, p. 83.
16 Northrop drawing No. 576700 notation, courtesy of Gerry Balzer.
17 Richard Sanders Allen, *The Northrop Story, 1929-1939*, Orion Books, New York, 1990, p. 41.
18 Wesley Frank Craven and James Lea Cate, *The Army Air Forces in World War II*, Vol. 6, The University of Chicago Press, Chicago, 1955, p. 264.
19 David L. Lewis, *The Public Image of Henry Ford*, Wayne State University Press, Detroit, 1976, p. 270.
20 Ibid., p. 271.
21 Craven and Cate, op.cit., pp. 309-310.
22 Ted Morgan, *FDR, A Biography*, Simon and Schuster, New York, 1985, p. 581.
23 Beverly Rae Kimes, *Packard, A History of the Motor Car and the Company*, Princeton Publishing, Inc., Princeton, N.J., 1978, p. 505.
24 Paul H. Becker, "Mass Producing the Merlin," *Flying*, March 1946, p. 52.
25 Kimes, op.cit., p. 507.
26 Historical dates compiled by Don O'Brien, Allison Public Relations. This information is on file at the National Air and Space Museum as NASM B1001025. A significant amount of the historical information regarding Allison Engineering was obtained through the courtesy of Dan Whitney, Orangevale, California.
27 This engine is now owned by the New England Air Museum, Bradley International Airport, Windsor Locks, Connecticut.
28 *New York Times*, 12 April 1929, p. 29.
29 The real answer to improved cooling systems was found by using water-glycol solutions in pressurized closed-loop designs. The solution boils at a higher temperature as system pressure is increased. The presence of ethylene glycol was to prevent coolant freezing at high altitudes and cold weather sea level operation. The amount of glycol added to the cooling water varied from 30 to 70 percent depending upon operational needs.
30 Schlaifer, op.cit., p. 261. Army glycol cooling tests were done using a Curtiss Conqueror engine. This engine used aluminum in close contact with steel in the cylinder construction. At higher operating temperatures (the Army insisted on 300°F) differential thermal expansion between the steel and aluminum produced coolant leaks into the engine cylinders. At a given temperature, aluminum expands more than steel.
31 Ibid., p. 274.
32 *New York Times*, 8 August 1928, p. 21.
33 *New York Times*, 4 August 1928, p. 21.
34 Edward V. Rickenbacker, *Rickenbacker*, Prentice-Hall, Englewood, N.J., p. 150.
35 Finis Farr, *Rickenbacker's Luck, An American Life*, Houghton Mifflin Company, Boston, 1979, p. 154.
36 *New York Times*, 7 August 1928, p. 22.
37 Farr, op.cit., p. 159.
38 *New York Times*, 25 May 1929, p. 30.
39 Farr, op.cit., p. 160.
40 *New York Times*, 25 May 1929, p. 30.
41 R.M. Hazen, "The Allison Aircraft-Engine Development," SAE Journal (Transactions), Vol. 49, No. 5, November 1941, p. 489.
42 Ibid., p. 490.
43 Ibid., p. 493.
44 Correspondence to the author from Dan Whitney dated 17 January 1993.
45 William T. Larkins, "War Assets," *Air Classics*, February 1992, p. 28. See table 2.
46 Both engines have identical 6.0 inch strokes.
47 "The Bristol Centaurus," *The Aeroplane*, 6 July 1945, p. 11.

Most of the Allison V-1710s flown in the post-war Bendix powered Lockheed P-38 and F-5 aircraft. Bill Lear, Jr., flew this F-5G-6 to eighth place in the 1947 Bendix. Credit: Birch Matthews collection

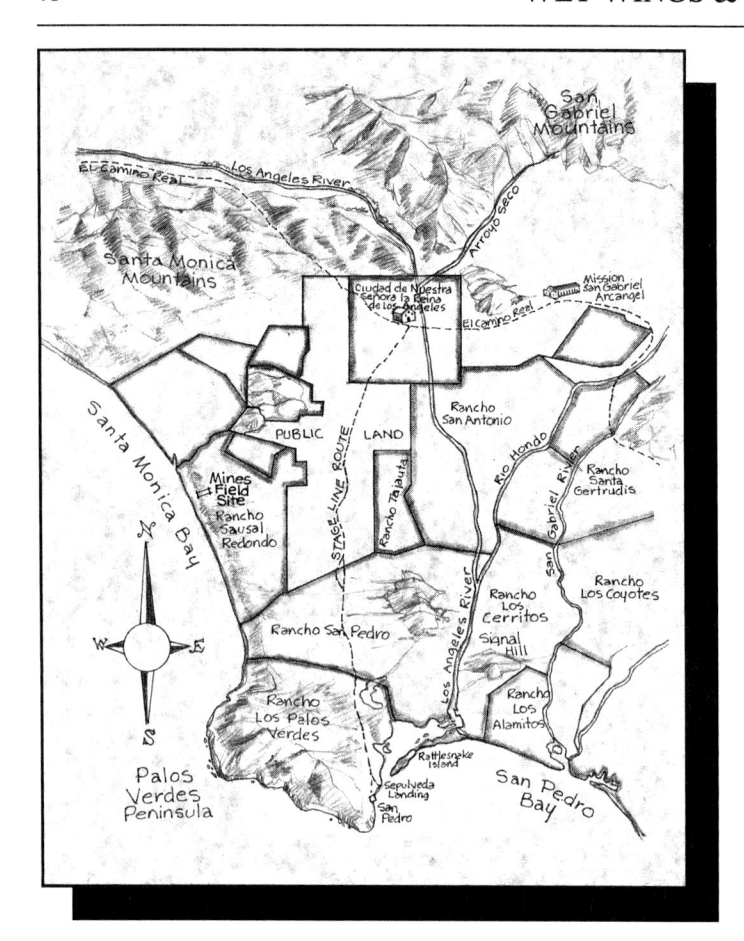

Los Angeles International Airport is situated on what was once a Spanish land grant named Rancho Sausal Redondo. The City of Los Angeles was selected to host the 1928 National Air Races and the present airport site, known then as Mines Field, was chosen for the racing program and exposition. Credit: Birch Matthews collection

After Lindbergh's flight, an aggressive real estate promoter named William W. Mines quickly became a catalyst in the drive to convince the Los Angeles City Council to select the Inglewood site. Mines orchestrated a 640 acre lease on the former rancho and persuasively presented it to the Council. They concurred. Because of his heavy involvement, the new airport was commonly referred to as Mines Field, a name which persisted for years.[2] Legally, the real name was Los Angeles Municipal Airport. The "airport" was no more than a short, level unfinished dirt strip surrounded by fields of wheat and barley. There were no accoutrements like hangars, pavement, or lights, let alone buildings of any kind. What decades later became a busy international port was simply a landing field leased by the city during October, 1928.[3]

AIR RACING COMES TO LOS ANGELES

Southern California was a sprawling amalgamation of cities and towns interspersed with farms, ranches and citrus groves. The people of Southern California were more informal than their eastern counterparts, perhaps due to the generally mild, warm climate of the region. A certain audacious spirit prevailed, attracting the more adventurous to what was – relatively speaking – still the Western Frontier. The area was dynamic, growing and home to an emerging aviation industry. In this context, obtaining the 1928 National Air Races was a highly desirable economic and political objective. It would create revenue and potentially, new business.

Blessed with favorable weather and open land to support this aerial festival, the city fathers aggressively pursued the races.

To make a credible bid, a sponsoring body was formed and christened the California Air Race Association. This organization was managed by an executive committee of seven prominent Southern Californians including Harry H. Wetzel, vice-president of Douglas Aircraft Company, Robert J. Pritchard, editor of Western Flying, Dudley M. Steele, manager of the Richfield Oil Company aviation department and a young, energetic impresario named Clifford W. Henderson, who would simultaneously become managing director of the air races, the aeronautical exposition and director of the new airport.[4] An immediate problem faced Henderson and the rest of the association: Exactly where would the races be held? A study concluded that three possible airfields were suitable, Long Beach, El Monte and Mines Field. The latter was finally selected. A proposal was submitted and the National Aeronautics Association announced that Los Angeles would host the prestigious National Air Races and Aeronautical Exposition of 1928.

THE FOKKER THAT PLOWED THE WEST

California Air Race Association members devised an extravaganza stretching over nine days which offered a myriad of pylon races, cross-country contests and exhibits. To accommodate show aircraft and related aviation displays, a large 200,000 square foot exhibition hall was constructed of wood and covered with canvas. It was located on the southern reaches of Mines Field. North of the exhibition hall, grandstands were built to seat anticipated record crowds of onlookers. It was an ambitious project. The original dirt landing strip was still surrounded by green fields of barley. Only two months before the festivities began, ground was ceremoniously broken for construction of the exhibition hall and the grading of three runways. This traditional ritual was accomplished with fanfare by dragging a plow hitched to the tail of a Fokker F10 passenger plane. Applying a bit of power, the Fokker pilot eased the airplane ahead while the plow was guided by Dr. T.C. Young of Glendale, director of the California Development Association who was also a member of the air race executive committee.[5] It was great press. No doubt more conventional means of locomotion were employed following this publicity event.

Chapter III: A Race With No End

Before the 1928 National Air Races, Art Goebel (l) and Harry Tucker (r) flew this Lockheed Vega 5 to Hartford where Pratt & Whitney technicians overhauled the Wasp engine. The aircraft had just set a west-east transcontinental speed record and was favored in the forthcoming non-stop race to Mines Field. Credit: Pratt & Whitney via CAHA

Possibly the fastest airplane in the non-stop race, "Yankee Doodle" was owned by Tucker and flown by Goebel. The two fought the elements all the way across the country to Prescott, AZ, before having to land. This stop cost them the race, but saved their lives. Credit: Gerry Balzer collection

Transcontinental and inter-city air races were very popular with the public in 1928. Race management devised six of these contests with major emphasis given to a non-stop race across the United States. Contest committee chairman Dudley Steele described these competitions as collectively representing "ten thousand miles of racing."[6] Enthusiasm for transcontinental racing on the part of business as well as the public stemmed from a realization of the potential for aviation which had been glamorized by Lindbergh's remarkable transoceanic flight. Aviation had captured the public's imagination.

The 1928 program included three class races from New York to Los Angeles each with intermediate stops. Two other races were international in nature. One originated from the city of Windsor in Ontario, Canada. The second would start in Mexico City. Two shorter California inter-city races were planned from Oakland and San Francisco to Los Angeles, respectively. The preeminent attraction was a rugged 2700 mile non-stop competition from Roosevelt Field, Long Island, to Mines Field, Los Angeles. It was, however, fated to become "a race with no end."

Preparation for the cross-country races was extensive. Dudley Steele traveled east to New York City to make logistical arrangements. He contacted World War I flyer Captain Charles B.D. Collyer, president of Aviation Service Corporation, to enlist his help.[7] As a consequence of their meeting, another World War veteran, Captain Stephen D. Day, was appointed eastern contest committee chairman. He pursued his assignment with enthusiasm and efficiency. Day did not work alone. In the month remaining before the races began, he organized a committee of 16 people to handle the myriad details of inspecting, servicing and starting the mass of racers.[8]

Following Steele's meeting with Collyer, the New York Times published a press release announcing that entry blanks and race rules were available from the corporate headquarters of Aviation Service at 12 West Fortieth Street, New York.[9] Captain Day, in turn, opened an air race eastern headquarters at the McAlpin Hotel to handle administrative matters and direct preparations. Interest in the derby contests was high. Prize money allocated for the estimated 24-hour grueling non-stop transcontinental race amounted to $22,500, a non-trivial sum in 1928. The winner would also receive the Air Age (magazine) trophy.[10] By Wednesday, August 18, more than 200 inquiries for the various derbies had been received of which 15 expressed interest in the non-stop race.[11] Entrants had until 1 September to file their applications.

Contestants would fly modern aircraft from manufacturers such as Bellanca, Lockheed and Stinson. Pilots were free to select any route they chose and there were no restrictions as to aircraft type, size or engine horsepower. It was truly what today we would call an "unlimited class" race. The only constraints were the race must be flown non-stop and pilots

1928 National Air Races

Transcontinental and Inter-City Derbies

Non-Stop Transcontinental Race	New York to Los Angeles	No aircraft or engine restrictions
Transcontinental Class A Race	New York to Los Angeles	Open to aircraft of 510 cu. in. or less displacement engines
Transcontinental Class B Race	New York to Los Angeles	Open to aircraft of more than 510 but not more than 800 cu. in. displacement engines
Transcontinental Class C Race	New York to Los Angeles	Open to aircraft of more than 800 cu. in. displacement engines and any number of engines
California Class A Race	San Fransisco to Los Angeles	Stock Commercial aircraft of 510 or less cu. in. displacement engines
California Class B Race	Oakland to Los Angeles	Stock Commercial aircraft of 800 or less cu. in. displacement engines
International Air Race	Windsor, Canada to Los Angeles	Open to all types of aircraft to be piloted by citizens of Canada
Pan Amercian Air Race	Mexico City to Los Angeles	Open to all types of aircraft to be piloted by citizens of Latin America

Chapter III: A Race With No End

Lockheed's Vega, Air Express and Orion models, dominated transcontinental air racing during the late 1920s and early 1930s. The monocoque fuselage was made from fine spruce veneer plies molded under pressure to the fuselage contour. The result was an aerodynamically clean airframe. This is a Lockheed factory picture of ten aircraft under construction. Credit: Gerry Balzer collection

had to depart Roosevelt Field between dawn and dusk on 12 September, and arrive at Mines Field between 8 am and 6 pm the following day.

As part of the planning for this race and the other class events from New York to Los Angeles, Dudley Steele embarked on a return flight from New York touring the most likely route across the United States. His homeward mission to the West Coast included investigating enroute terrain and facilities available to the competing aviators. In his own words, Steele stated: "The route of this race is considered by many pilots to be the safest route across the country. At no time was it necessary to fly at an altitude greater than 6000 feet above sea level." Interestingly, his final passage into the Los Angeles basin was through the San Gorgonio Pass, a flight path used by Los Angeles-bound flights from the east to this day. In spite of all the planning by the race association and Steele, this ambitious transcontinental race would in the end prove disheartening.

Meanwhile, Stephen Day was busy preparing for the start of each derby from Roosevelt Field. On Wednesday the 22nd, Day, Lieutenant H.B. Clarke and Carl Schory conducted a lengthy meeting.[12] Clarke was the Roosevelt Field manager and Carl Schory was secretary of National Aeronautics Association contest committee. The three men toured Roosevelt Field as well as nearby Curtiss Field assessing hangar accommodations and service facilities for the expected large amalgamation of racing aircraft. Over 200 entries had been received.[13] It would be a busy time for all concerned.

The non-stop race attracted a number of celebrated pilots. One of the first eager to compete was Harvard graduate and Greenwich Village resident, Oliver Charles "Boots" Le Boutillier. An early acquaintance of Amelia Earhart, Le

This Vega won the Class C (with intermediate stops) transcontinental derby in 1928, piloted by Robert Cantwell. The clean lines in this profile view are evident. Vegas were later equipped with wheel pants and NACA cowlings to further reduce drag. Credit: Gerry Balzer collection

Boutillier contacted socialite Mrs. James A. Stillman with regard to racing her Bellanca airplane, "Northstar."[14] In a telegram from her summer home in Quebec, Mrs. Stillman responded to Le Boutillier saying that she would be . . . "delighted to have you fly North Star."

Others soon joined the game. Arthur C. Goebel and his financial backer Harry J. Tucker, who owned a speedy Lockheed Vega, were quickly established as favorites. Goebel was a well known speed flyer. He and Tucker, a Santa Monica, California, businessman, had recently arrived at Curtiss Field from Los Angeles on Monday (August 20) after setting a non-stop continental speed record of 18 hours, 58 minutes in Tucker's Lockheed, christened "Yankee Doodle." To prepare for the forthcoming race, Goebel flew to Hartford, Connecticut, to let Pratt & Whitney overhaul the Wasp engine. During a flight test after P & W technicians performed their ministrations, Goebel reportedly flew the Vega to a speed of 175 miles an hour.[15]

George Haldeman was another noted aviator of that era. At the time, Haldeman was chief test pilot and a member of the sales staff for Giuseppe Mario Bellanca's aircraft company. Quite naturally, he would race a company product. World War flyer Colonel William K. Thaw II – from the wealthy Pittsburgh family – bought a Lockheed Vega specifically to race in the non-stop transcontinental. He chose fellow Pittsburgher Jack P. Morris to pilot the fast airplane. In his definitive book on single engine Lockheeds, *Revolution in the Sky*, Richard Sanders Allen relates how publisher Bernarr Macfadden purchased Thaw's Vega just before the race. the incentive was a neat $5000 profit on the deal.[16] Thaw and Morris would still fly the race but the purple Vega would carry the name "True Story Magazine" emblazoned on its fuselage giving Macfadden's enterprise due recognition. Winning the first non-stop transcontinental air race would make good copy for the magazine!

Competition promised to be fierce. In the end, there were ten aircraft entries for the non-stop transcontinental air race. Five aircraft manufacturers were represented. The race was dominated by four Bellancas but also included two Stinsons, two Lockheed Vegas, a Buhl Airsedan and one Cessna. The field was reduced to nine when the Cessna was subsequently scratched from the race.

Race day began with the blessing of warm weather and fair skies.[17] The New York temperature soared to a high of 83 degrees and spectators quickly gathered at Roosevelt Field in this balmy Indian Summer weather. Among the crowd were Mrs. Stillman, owner of "North Star," the Bellanca flown by "Boots" Le Boutillier and Charles A. Levine, who owned the Bellanca, Columbia. Another interested bystander was the well known polar explorer Sir Hugh Wilkins.

The crowd of bystanders for the non-stop derby start was enthusiastic. In contrast to current casual trends, the crowd in attendance were more formal in dress and decorum. Most women were clothed in typical 1920s fashion with soft flowing below-the-knee dresses and bell-shaped cloche hats. They were accompanied by men in double-breasted suits or more casual blazers and slacks. Like the women of that day, the men almost universally wore hats.[18] Even many competing race

Chapter III: A Race With No End

pilots adhered to a semi-formal dress standard of white shirt, tie, trousers and, of course, the customary leather flying helmet.

In a retrospective summary of the start of all the transcontinental races, Stephen Day recalled that . . . "In all, seventy planes of varying types were sent off (over four days) without mishap or delay of any kind, with the single exception of the Columbia, which folded up her left landing wheel and ground looped off the runway. No damage was done and after a new wheel had been fitted on, she got away to a beautiful takeoff."[19] Reporter Russell Owen of the New York Times also covered the start of the race. In somewhat more dramatic terms, Owen summarized by saying . . . "No better demonstration of the increased efficiency of commercial airplanes has ever been given than the starts at Roosevelt Field yesterday. With everything against them – a cross wind, a hot day and bumpy thin air – the planes took off successfully one after the other during the day."

It was mid-morning before any of the non-stop racing aircraft departed. First to be fueled and ready to race was Clifford McMillan's Stinson Detroiter. Before buttoning up, his navigator C.A. Herrick got a fond farewell kiss from his wife, faithfully recorded by a press photographer. This familial detail attended to, the Wright Whirlwind engine was cranked to life and the racer eased to the starting line. McMillan led the pack out of Roosevelt Field in his overloaded airplane. His takeoff roll was long using virtually the entire length of the field. Finally breaking ground, McMillan held the racer on a long, low straight out departure. The heavy aircraft labored to reach altitude as it headed west toward Pennsylvania. Ironically, McMillan was not only the first to start the race, he was probably first to leave. Shortly before one in the afternoon after three hours in the air, the Stinson's engine began running rough over northeastern Pennsylvania. With skill, McMillan guided the racer down onto a farm field near Chase, Pennsylvania. His race was over. Although the aircraft would have to

Randolph Page entered a Stinson Junior in the 1928 race, similar to the airplane shown here. Page's airplane was powered by a Warner "Scarab" engine and really was no match for the Lockheeds. Credit: Gerry Balzer collection

An unusual looking plane in the 1928 non-stop contest was the Buhl Air Sedan model CA-3C like the one shown here. It was a biplane configuration called a "sesquiplane," where the lower wing had no more than one-half the surface area of the upper wing. Credit: Gerry Balzer collection

Two Bellanca J airplanes, similar to this airplane, were in the transcontinental race. Bellanca built large rugged airframes characterized by wing struts having an airfoil cross-section. The J model had a wing span of 50 feet. Credit: Gerry Balzer collection

be dismantled and trucked out of the field, it sustained little damage. Both pilot and navigator were uninjured. Their troubles, however, were an omen of things to come!

Following McMillan to the line, Nick Mamer took the red starting flag from George Townsend, opened the throttle on his Wright-powered Buhl Airsedan and trundled slowly down the turf runway. The Buhl bounced once into the air only to settle again, stubbornly landlocked. Realizing he was not going to lift off, Mamer chopped the throttle and returned to the starting line where he braked the lumbering Airsedan through a 180 degree turn for another try. With the engine developing maximum power, Mamer once again released the brakes. When the tail came off the ground, Mamer continued to hold the plane on the runway allowing it to accelerate over a longer distance on this takeoff attempt. Still the racer bounced and porpoised four or five times straining to break free. Finally, to the relief of the crowd and certainly Nick Mamer, the Buhl wings developed enough lift to fly. The crowd applauded in relief. Mamer's luck would not last. He was forced down at 9:38 a.m. the following morning at Rawhide, Wyoming. He too was out of the race.

The starting process continued. Next to takeoff was the red Bellanca named "Veedol" flown by Emile "Hard Luck" Burgin. In spite of his nickname, Burgin coaxed the heavy rugged Bellanca into the air with little apparent effort, swung slightly to the south and then west on his way to the coast. Hard luck indeed caught up with Emile Burgin before the race was out. His Bellanca landed in a corn field near Willard, New Mexico, with mechanical problems although he eventually made his way to Albuquerque.

He was followed by Oliver Le Boutillier in Mrs. Stillman's Bellanca, North Star. After a long somewhat bouncing takeoff roll, Oliver coaxed the lumbering Bellanca into the air. Trouble stalked the Bellanca from the very start. Le Boutillier turned back and landed at Mitchell Field. The compass was vibrating so badly he simply could not read the instrument. Frustrated, he returned to Roosevelt and appealed to the contest committee to be allowed to restart the race later in the day. His request was refused and North Star remained earth bound.

Randolph Page brought the diminutive Warner Scarab-powered Stinson Junior monoplane to the starting line next. After a staggering takeoff and low level departure, he returned to the field and landed. He found it impossible to gain altitude with the fuel load his plane was carrying. Undaunted, Page increased the pitch on his ground-adjustable propeller, reduced fuel load slightly and was off once again. The airplane still struggled to gain altitude. Guiding the racer in a slow gradual turn, Page headed south over the ocean while burning off fuel to lighten the load. Gradually, the Stinson rose higher and Randolph Page headed west. In spite of his plucky performance, Page too encountered engine trouble approaching Allentown, Pennsylvania. He quickly dumped 150 gallons of fuel and set up for a landing in a field unfortunately inhabited by a small herd of unsuspecting dairy cows. Avoid-

Chapter III: A Race With No End

ing the cattle, Page's Stinson rearranged a fence in its landing path. He was unhurt and the aircraft only somewhat damaged. George Haldeman was next to venture forth. His takeoff in yet another Bellanca was, thankfully, uneventful. But Haldeman would not prevail. The Bellanca went out of the race at Albuquerque, New Mexico. Haldeman was a victim of excessive fuel consumption caused by major storms and head winds much of the way. He would eventually fly into Mines Field a day later. The field was narrowing rapidly as the race continued.

Lt. Commander Jack Iseman, commandant of the Rockaway Naval Reserve Flying Station, nudged a heavily ladened Columbia – Charles Levine's Bellanca – to the starting line. Receiving a sharp wave of the starting flag, the short stocky Iseman applied throttle. As Columbia gathered speed, it veered violently. Correcting, Iseman had next to contend with an errant photographer. Side loads caused by his maneuvers were too severe and the left wheel failed. The airplane ground looped, slightly damaging a wing tip. A new wheel was located, installed and the plane hauled back to the starting line. Iseman was furious. The accident cost him a half hour of elapsed time. Resolute, the naval flier once again pushed the racer down the runway fighting all the way against cross winds and an asymmetric lateral load distribution. At last the Bellanca was airborne and climbing out. One can well imagine that owner Levine and pilot Iseman breathed collective sighs of great relief after that adventure. By 4:30 the next afternoon, Iseman too was out of the race having landed at Amarillo, Texas.

Two racers remained at the starting line. These were the Lockheed Vegas of Art Goebel and John Morris. Goebel was somewhat of a fashion plate even when flying. The mere fact he was about to embark on a 24 hour non-stop transcontinental race did not deter him from boarding the Vega dressed in a neatly pressed brown suit adorned with a green handkerchief sprouting from the breast pocket. This affectation could not obscure the fact that he was an excellent pilot. The previous year, Goebel had won the tragedy-marred Dole Race across the Pacific – a distance almost as great as the non-stop transcontinental run he now faced.

Goebel together with his passenger, Vega owner Harry Tucker, climbed aboard the white Yankee Doodle. They were eager to race. Standing up in the cockpit, a smiling Art Goeble strapped on a parachute, sat down in the pilot's seat and closed the cockpit hatch. The big Pratt & Whitney Wasp engine was cranked to life as Goebel monitored temperatures and pressures registered by gages on his instrument panel. He was ready. He expected to win the non-stop race in this fast Lockheed. At the starter's signal, Goebel demanded maximum horsepower from the Wasp engine. The Vega responded, accelerating slowly at first but quickly gaining forward momentum. The takeoff was smooth and rapid. The sleek racer diminished in size until it disappeared to the west. Unknowingly, Goebel and Tucker were on their way to a wild, tumultuous ride.

The Lockheed Vega flown by John Morris with passenger Colonel Russel Thaw, II, was the last racer to depart Roosevelt Field. This aircraft differed from Goebel's Yankee Doodle in that it was powered by a Pratt & Whitney Hornet engine. With a reported 650 gallons of fuel onboard, the graceful Vega lifted off with no difficulty into an early evening sky and sped westward chasing Art Goebel. The first non-stop transcontinental air race was underway. In summing up events of the day in what could never be classified as an understatement, reporter Russell Owen wrote that . . . "Everything happened but a tragedy."[20] This was quite a tag line for the inaugural non-stop transcontinental race!

John Morris and Russel Thaw were destined for serious trouble as they plunged westward over Pennsylvania and Ohio. Nighttime quickly enveloped Columbia. As Morris crossed into Indiana air space, an oil line suddenly ruptured. The failure, probably vibration induced, caused engine oil pressure to fall rapidly threatening catastrophic consequences. Morris and Thaw quickly loosed a parachute flair and located what appeared to be a suitable field for emergency descent. As Morris set up for landing, the flair extinguished and he was

Jack Iseman flew this Bellanca WB-2 named "Columbia." He was forced out of the race at Amarillo, TX. This same airplane with Clarence D. Chamberlain and Charles A. Levine aboard, flew non-stop from New York to Eisleben, Germany, a distance of 3,905 miles in 42 hours, 15 minutes. Credit: International Newsreel Photo, Gerry Balzer collection

Owen Haugland entered the 1928 non-stop race with a Wright J5 powered Cessna BW-5, like the one shown here. The airplane was scratched from the race before it began. Credit: Cessna, Gerry Balzer collection

Cesare Sabelli applied to race in the 1928 non-stop transcontinental derby very late in the game. His entry was refused. The aircraft is a Bellanca K model with a stub lower wing blending into a strut supporting the main wing. Credit: Gerry Balzer collection

essentially flying blind. A crash ensued. The aircraft tore through a fence and was severely damaged. Both men were trapped in the wreckage on a farm some 15 miles south of Decatur, Indiana. It was past midnight and they lay in the wrecked Bellanca until 6:00 in the morning when they were found by a farmer and rescued. Their injuries, although not life threatening, were serious. Thaw dislocated his hip. Morris fractured both his collar bone and pelvis. One more bird was down. The non-stop race was taking a heavy toll.

Unlike many of his competitors, Art Goebel and Harry Tucker sped westward free of mechanical problems. The big Wasp engine droned steadily and reliably, pulling the Vega on a great circle route to Los Angeles and Mines Field. What Goebel did face, however, was increasingly poor weather and stiffening head winds. The first stormy weather he encountered was over the Allegheny Mountains. Past this barrier, Goebel struck out for Pittsburgh, Terre Haute and Wichita eventually veering south over the badlands to Albuquerque. The storms were past, but the head winds persisted. The two men fought through vicious turbulence accompanied by stomach wrenching down drafts for much of the way. Tucker would later say that it was his "most awful experience in the air and I firmly believe that no other flier in the world could do what Art did" in bringing the Vega safely through the weather.

With the arrival of daylight, Harry Tucker went about throwing empty gas cans – the earliest known form of drop tanks – out the cabin door. A sudden gust wrenched the door from his hand and it tore away from the fuselage. This didn't help the aerodynamics of the clean Vega and forward speed was reduced some five miles per hour in addition to the penalty already imposed by strong head winds. Goebel was also experiencing carburetor difficultly. Fuel consumption was abnormally high due to the persistent head winds. With fate rapidly enveloping him, Art Goebel wisely chose to land at Prescott, Arizona, to regroup, repair and refuel. Goeble and Tucker were on the ground for an hour. As brief as this was, it cost them the race, but may well have saved their lives.

Refuelled, Goebel and Tucker lifted the Vega away from Prescott and forged ahead toward Los Angeles. Flying past San Gorgonio Mountain, the Vega at last was within sight of her destination. The exhausted men closed the distance to Mines Field, dipped low and streaked passed the finish line. Within minutes, the proud Lockheed Vega named Yankee Doodle touched down on the oiled dirt landing strip afforded by Mines Field. Goebel braked the racer to a stop. The two men were immediately greeted by contest committee chairman Dudley Steele and Aero Digest publisher Frank Tichenor. In the ensuing fragmented conversation, no one thought to ask Goebel if he had made a stop enroute. Reporters fled to telephones to relate the story of Goebel's victory in this first non-stop transcontinental race.

In a special wire report to the New York Times, correspondent Lauren Lyman later described the scene. "No one apparently thought to ask Goebel at first if by chance he had made a landing anywhere on the way and the flier himself did not have a chance to say a word for many minutes. Finally, he recognized a friend in the cheering crowds pressing around him and in answer to the question which no one else had thought to ask, he said that he had landed at Prescott, Arizona, this morning because his gas was very low and a carburetor was acting wrong. This of course disqualified him for the non-stop race but he is likely to get sweepstakes prize (sic) for the fastest time in crossing the country."[21] Reporter Lyman described Goebel's appearance as pale and drawn after his ordeal of flying 23 hours and 50 minutes without sleep and through precarious weather. It was indeed a test of human

Chapter III: A Race With No End

endurance and if anyone deserved to win the prize money and trophy, it was Arthur Goebel and Harry Tucker. But it was not to be. Not one aircraft finished the first non-stop transcontinental air race.

As often happens, disappointment in the race result soon turned to acrimony. Apparently some felt Stephen Day, starting committee chairman, should not have begun the derby because fliers ran into adverse weather and strong head winds along the way. Day reacted immediately declaring that everything possible was done to safeguard the contestants. "We (Day and his chief assistants) were in almost constant telephone communication with the weather office at Hadley Field and with points throughout Pennsylvania, and everywhere flying conditions were reported excellent. No committee can be held responsible for the storms which are apt to pop up on any hot summer day."[22] In retrospect, Stephen Day had to depend upon an evolving weather service system possessing only limited upper air data and forecasts made at least twelve hours before the start of the race. In the end, only four non-stop derby aircraft limped into Mines Field. Jack Iseman and "Hard Luck" Burgin eventually arrived joining Goebel and Haldeman. It was indeed a race with no end.

NOTES:

1 Paul D. Friedman, "Birth of an Airport," American Aviation Historical Society JOURNAL, Vol. 23, No. 4, 1978, p. 287.
2 The name Los Angeles International Airport was not adopted until 11 November, 1946. During the following month, the major airlines moved from Lockheed Air Terminal to the newly dedicated Los Angeles airport.
3 The origins of Los Angeles International Airport were compiled in March 1978, by Paul D. Friedman, a graduate student, University of California at Santa Barbara. The information was released in pamphlet form by the Los Angeles Department of Airports, #1 World Way, Los Angeles, CA, 90009. Airport land was first leased for 50 years by the city during October 1928, at a cost of $124,800 per year. Construction was started on two 100 square foot hangars. The only runway consisted of a 2000 foot oiled dirt strip. Nine years later in October, 1937, the City of Los Angeles purchased the airport property outright.
4 Composition of the executive committee consisted of: Theodore T. Hull, President (president of the American Aircraft Corp.); Harry Wetzel, vice president; D.E. McDaneld, secretary-treasurer (president of the Southern California Chapter of the National Aeronautics Association); Dr. T.C. Young (director of California Development Association); Robert J. Pritchard; Dudley M. Steele; and Cliff Henderson.
5 Anon., "The National Air Races," *Aviation*, 4 August 1928, p. 401.
6 Dudley M. Steele, "Ten Thousand Miles of Racing!," *Western Flying*, August 1928, page 26.
7 *New York Times*, Section IV, page 17, 1 July 1928.
8 Stephen Day was the committee chairman. He was assisted by aides Henry Boynton and B.L. Orde. George M. Townsend was the chief starter and utilized William A. Rogers and George B. Post in the capacity of assistant starters. Talbot O. Freeman, Sidney Bowen and John J. White were respectively, chief timer and assistant timers. James B. Taylor, Jr., served as referee while Frank L. Tallman, Jr., was clerk of the course. A technical subcommittee was formed consisting of Harry Booth, George McLaughlin and Hubert Huntington. Hugh C. O'Reilly supervised ballast and weighing of the class racers. H.B. Clarke and Lt. Max Balfour were responsible for operations. Details of the working committee are found in "Start of the Transcontinental Air Races," by Stephen D. Day, *Aero Digest*, October 1928, p. 728.
9 Ibid.
10 The winner of the race would receive $12,500. Second place was worth $6,000 while third and fourth place finishes were valued at $3,000 and $1,000, respectively.
11 *New York Times*, 18 August 1928, p. 4.
12 *New York Times*, 8 August 1928, p. 4.
13 Ibid.
14 Mrs. Stillman originally purchased the Bellanca monoplane and sponsored Thea Rasche's transatlantic flight attempt which was ultimately canceled.
15 New York Times, 5 September 1928, p. 28.
16 Richard Sanders Allen, *Revolution in the Sky*, The Stephen Greene Press, Brattleboro, Vermont, 1967, p. 44.
17 The start of the non-stop race was described in great detail by Russel Owen in the *New York Times*, 13 September, 1928. See pp. 1 and 10.
18 Dress styles of yesteryear seldom find contemporary reference. See for example, "Summer in the Twenties" by Jean Cook Barkhorn and Robin Whitney, Town & Country, Vol. 145, No. 5134, July 1991.
19 Stephen D. Day, Op cit.
20 Ibid.
21 Reporter Lyman's description of the arrival of Goebel at Mines Field was published in the September 14 edition of the New York Times, page 1.
22 *New York Times*, 15 September 1928, p. 8.

1929 NATIONAL
AIR RACES
AND AERONAUTICAL EXPOSITION
50
WELCOME

Chapter IV

DERBIES & DEPRESSION 1929-1930

Nineteen twenty-nine was the beginning of a period now fondly referred to by some as the "golden age" of air racing, a characterization dedicated retrospectively some time after World War II.[1] It was a brief but colorful period and 1929 was the genesis of this era. This year marked the onset of a proliferation of specially-built racing planes for competition in closed-course pylon races as well as cross-country events. It was concurrently a time of design individualism. Racing aircraft designers like Jimmy Wedell, Larry Brown, Benny Howard, the Granville Brothers, Clayton Folkerts and Keith Rider dominated the scene with their unique creations. These creative men wrapped Pratt & Whitney and Menasco engines into tightly packaged aerodynamic shapes that caught the public's imagination. In major transcontinental racing during 1929 and 1930, however, one production aircraft reigned supreme. Lockheed's Vega and Air Express models, aerodynamically clean and aesthetically pleasing, were simply unrivaled.

ON TO CLEVELAND

The 1929 National Air Races and Aeronautical Exposition had moved across the continent from Los Angeles to Cleveland, a city destined to become the center of air racing in this country for many years. Once again, Cliff Henderson would be managing director for the entire affair. Western Flying Magazine reported that the city of Los Angeles granted Henderson a leave of absence from his position as director of municipal airports.[2] The accuracy of this reporting appears in some dispute. At the time, Cliff Henderson was Director of Airports reporting to the Los Angeles City Council. Paul Friedman states that Henderson resigned this post under pressure in April, 1929. He was criticized for allocating too much of his time to National Air Race affairs at the expense of the Department of Airports.[3]

Henderson was an extraordinary showman in the tradition of Barnum & Bailey. His approach to racing spectacles was unparalleled. Later air race promoters have tried to emulate Henderson's style without complete success. Cliff demonstrated his métier in a period when aviation was extremely popular with the American public. Fortuitously, his timing was perfect.

Opposite: The 1929 National Air Race program was one of the most ambitious shows ever staged by Cliff Henderson. It is doubtful there has ever been one like it in all the years since. Shown here is the announcer's stand at the center of the grandstands. Credit: Birch Matthews collection

PROHIBITION AND FINANCIAL TURMOIL

Nineteen Twenty-Nine was an unforgettable year for many reasons. It would be the last dance in a decade-long wild interval known as the "roaring twenties." These often uninhibited years were not restricted to matters on Wall Street. For instance, a great liquor prohibition became law of the land and represented a daring if not universally appreciated attempt at social engineering.[4] Suffice it to say the temperance movement, as vociferous as it was, did not appreciably alter the social habits of many if not most Americans with respect to adult beverages. What prohibition did, though, was spawn a new generation of criminal entrepreneurs or bootleggers supplying product of varying quality to underground networks of liquor distributors and thence to clubs known as "speakeasies."[5] America's thirst wasn't really quenched by the social engineers.[6]

With little doubt, the most infamous bootlegger during this period was Chicago's own Alphonse "Scarface" Capone. Reputedly, it was Capone who masterminded the notorious Saint Valentine's Day massacre although at the time, he was happily engaged in an elaborate social gathering given at his Florida home in Miami.

The twenties were passionately extreme in other ways. Florida real estate speculation suddenly blossomed and then just as quickly imploded. Investment in corporate stocks including burgeoning aviation enterprises flourished nationally. For some it became an obsession. Small investors and large were drawn into a financial vortex with the promise of ever greater gain. Stocks were purchased using margin accounts – wherein up to 90 percent of the price was borrowed – profitably sold and margin loans repaid. As long as the market was ascending the process worked. By early 1929, signs of increasing financial instability were manifested in a turbulent marketplace. On March 25, Wall Street suffered a sharp reversal, but soon rebounded and climbed again. This continued rise could not be sustained. Seven months later on October 23, the market crashed with a resounding thump. It turned into a desperate economic collapse which few foresaw or indeed perceived at the time. This was the beginning of "The Great Depression." For many, the roar of the twenties quickly faded to the quiet despair of the thirties. It was against this tumultuous backdrop that the 1929 National Air Races were staged in Cleveland.

THE SHOW BEGINS

The raucous times provided a fitting backdrop for what may have been the greatest air show and racing forum of all time. The 1929 National Air Races offered a full course menu with innumerable events of great variety and imagination. Races and flying demonstrations were held at the Municipal Airport

Clifford W. Henderson poses for a publicity shot in this Great Lakes 2-T-1 biplane. Great Lakes Aircraft was located in Cleveland, Ohio, and apparently provided one of their products to Henderson during the races. Paint scheme is believed to be red, white and blue. Credit: Sid Bradd collection

Chapter IV: Derbies & Depression: 1929-1930

A smiling Henry Brown takes congratulations from one of the race officials after winning the 1929 non-stop derby. The race was actually part of a delivery flight from Lockheed in Los Angeles to the General Tire and Rubber Company in Akron, Ohio. Credit: Sid Bradd collection

Second place winner in the 1929 Los Angeles to Cleveland non-stop derby, Lee Schoenhair, is seen here on the right in a 1930 photograph with Charles "Speed" Holman (center) and aircraft designer Matty Laird. The airplane is the Laird LC-DW 300, winner of the 1930 Thompson Trophy race. Credit: Sid Bradd collection

southwest of downtown Cleveland. There were flying demonstrations, aerobatic routines and closed-course pylon races. There were competitions for Navy pilots, Army airman, the National Guard and civilian men and women flyers. Interspersed was a special event to break the world's solo endurance record as well as parachute jumping and a dead stick landing contest. It was truly a festival of colorful sights and discordant sounds lasting from August 24 through September 3. All in all, it was enough to satiate even the most ardent enthusiast.

By no means was all activity confined to Cleveland's large Municipal Airport. An aviation exposition was simultaneously held in the municipal auditorium in downtown Cleveland. Exhibits ranged from static displays of the latest aircraft and engines to aviation related accessories. A number of technical meetings took place and aeronautical societies and personalities gathered. Hotels in Cleveland were packed. The Carter Hotel served as the locus for many of the racing fraternity and aviation personalities. Even the streets were congested. Distinguished visitors flocked into town. Cleveland City Manager W.R. Hopkins greeted aviation personalities from across the country and Europe: Transatlantic flyer Charles A. Lindbergh and his wife Ann Morrow Lindbergh; Assistant Secretary of Commerce for Aeronautics, William P. MacCracken, Jr., to mention but two.[7] For ten days during August and September, Cleveland was quite literally a center of the aviation universe.

While thousands attended the downtown exposition and concurrent meetings, tens of thousands trekked into Cleveland Municipal Airport for the flying venue. Surrounding fields were crowded with Ford Model T's and other contemporary automobiles. Traffic jams were frequent and only the presence of horse-mounted police alleviated the time consuming task of entering and leaving the airfield. Cleveland's airport was one of the largest and busiest in the country. A measure of the airfield's size is the fact that a gigantic air show was conducted without disrupting commercial traffic. Grandstands on the field stretched the length of three or four city blocks. In describing the spectacle in the October, 1929, issue of Aero Digest, Russell C. Johns told of how "thousands of members of the aviation industry who attended agreed that nothing like it has ever been seen in America before, and no such variety of attractions has ever been offered to the visitor at any aeronautical event anywhere."[8] The magnitude and

Air mail pilot Henry J. Brown won the 1929 non-stop transcontinental derby flying a Hornet-powered Lockheed Air Express 3. When he landed he was just about out of fuel and taxied across the finish line simultaneously kicking up a cloud of dust behind the airplane. Credit: Sid Bradd collection

breadth of the affair was absolutely without parallel, then or now.

The 1929 races saw top notch civilian pylon competition in what heretofore had been a field dominated by the military. Doug Davis, flying the "mysterious" Travel Air company entry in event twenty-nine – a free-for-all speed contest – was victorious whipping the military's best pursuits. This particular closed-course contest would become the classic Thompson Trophy Race the following year. The contemporary press and future historians made much of the fact that Davis' racer

Second place in the 1929 non-stop derby was captured by Lee Schoenhair flying this Lockheed Vega 5A model owned by B.F. Goodrich. Aircraft was named "Miss Silvertown," for the company's premium automobile tire product line. Credit: Pratt & Whitney via CAHA

Chapter IV: Derbies & Depression: 1929-1930

Roscoe Turner flew this Vega 5 to third place in the 1929 non-stop derby. The aircraft was originally owned by F.C. Hall and was the first "Winnie Mae." Sold back to Lockheed by Hall, the Vega was acquired by Nevada Airlines and flown by Turner. Credit: Sid Bradd collection

was faster than first line Army pursuit aircraft, forgetting in the process that this racer was a single purpose design. The military needed airplanes capable of fulfilling a variety of requirements, not just all out speed.

OUT OF GAS

The 1929 program was also significant with regard to American cross-country racing. There were no less than nine cross-country races listed as "derbies." Now a derby is a race typically open to anyone seeking the offered prize. The word today is commonly associated with horse racing, probably the best known example being the Kentucky Derby. But in those bygone days of aviation, it was an appellation frequently appended to cross-country air races as well. Cliff Henderson managed to put together such events as the Women's Derby, the All-Ohio Derby, the Rim-of-Ohio Derby and the Philadelphia-to-Cleveland Derby. Others competed over longer distances. One "on to Cleveland" race originated in Miami, Florida. Even more strenuous events were staged for racers starting from Portland, Oregon, and Oakland, California. But once again, the toughest and indeed principal cross-country race was the "Non-stop Derby: Los Angeles to Cleveland." Floyd Logan, contest committee chairman, stated the non-stop race rules which were simple and few: Contestants could depart the West Coast any time from August 25 through September 2; they were required to land at the Cleveland airport any time between two and five in the afternoon; and,

if not satisfied with their elapsed time, could return to Los Angeles and start again.[9] One entrant, Major John P. Wood, took advantage of the restart option. It would be a fatal decision!

One day before the National Air Races were to start, a rainstorm swept over Cleveland drenching the airport. By afternoon the storm cleared. Airport manager Major John Berry declared the field would be in shape the next day provided no further storms occurred. As it turned out, a hot sun the next morning coupled with steady winds dried the airport completely. Festivities began at two in the afternoon that first day with a grand mile-long parade including "84 floral floats, scores of bands and hundreds of marchers."[10] The parade theme centered on transportation modes beginning with covered wagons followed in turn, by horseback riders, stage coaches, high-wheeled cycles and vintage automobiles. Downtown Cleveland was also treated to a noisy fly over of planes completing a good will tour of Ohio. It was a glorious beginning.

In the transcontinental non-stop derby, eight pilots submitted entry applications. Only four actually started.[11] Among the entrants were several noted aviators of that period including Frank Hawks and Lee Shoenhair, both transcontinental record setting pilots. A third entrant was Art Goebel, 1927 Dole Race victor who struggled through the 1928 non-stop race almost winning this event. Rounding out the list were Henry J. Brown, Cleveland air mail pilot; Robert Cantwell of Tulsa, Oklahoma; Major John Wood, winner of the 1927 National Air Tour; Oliver C. Le Boutillier of New York and

The domination of Lockheed airplanes in transcontinental air racing continued in 1930. Wiley Post flew F.C. Hall's Vega 5B named "Winnie Mae" to victory in 1930. The all-white Vega was trimmed in blue and named for Hall's daughter. Credit: Sid Bradd collection

Roscoe Turner who would become one of the best known race pilots in history. With the single exception of "Boots" Le Boutillier, all entries used Lockheed's sensational Vega and Air Express airplanes. In the end, Le Boutillier did not start the race thus leaving the entire field to Lockheed products. Of the seven remaining entries, Hawks, Goebel and Cantwell would not start for unknown reasons.

The premier derby was captured by Cleveland resident and airmail pilot Henry J. Brown. He flew for National Air Transport, but was on leave at this time to compete in the race under the colors of the General Tire & Rubber Company. Brown raced a Pratt & Whitney Hornet-powered Lockheed Air Express. This all-black, parasol-wing racer was purchased from Lockheed just days prior to the National Air Races. When Brown flew the race, he was simultaneously making the delivery flight to General Tire.[12]

Brown flew into Cleveland on Sunday, September 1. Ironically, he almost forfeited his victory. Very low on fuel, Brown made a straight in approach and immediately landed. He was almost out of fuel, virtually running on fumes. Author Richard Sanders Allen wrote that, "Five miles from Cleveland Airport the engine began to sputter, and then cut out entirely."[13] According to the New York Times, Brown "almost lost the race in the last hundred yards, for he landed just before he crossed the finish line."[14] An alert timer, according to this newspaper account, ran onto the field and advised the pilot of his oversight. Some five minutes elapsed during this confusion but Brown finally taxied across the line. He flew the distance in 13.25 hours for an average speed of 156 miles per hour. Although Henry Brown was the winner of the 2072 mile derby, this was not immediately confirmed. Pilots were allowed to depart the West Coast any time during race week. The winner would be judged on the lowest elapsed flying time. All flights had to be completed and timed before results could be compared. Eventually, Brown would claim the $5000 first prize.

Actually, Henry was the second pilot in the derby to land at Cleveland that Sunday. First to fly in was young Lee Shoenhair flying the B.F. Goodrich Vega, race number 36, named "Miss Silvertown." Although Shoenhair arrived ahead of Brown, he also departed Los Angeles earlier and his elapsed time was some thirty-six minutes greater. His speed of just under 150 miles per hour earned him second place and a $2500 prize. One other pilot had completed the transcontinental run the previous evening. This was Roscoe Turner in a Nevada Airlines five-passenger Vega. Turner was disqualified because he arrived in Cleveland after the 6 p.m. deadline decreed in the race rules. His average speed was a modest 134 miles per hour. Only Major John Wood remained on the West Coast at this point.

LIGHTNING STRIKE

Born in 1896, Major Wood was a native of Buffalo, New York. He attended Carnegie Institute of Technology in Pittsburgh before World War I. In 1917, he enlisted in the U.S. Army Air Service and was commissioned a lieutenant. After the war, Wood entered commercial aviation. He flew in the 1927 National Air Derby and won the 1928 National Air Tour. Wood subsequently earned third place in one of the class races from Roosevelt Field to Mines Field during the 1928 National Air Races. Major Wood was an accomplished pilot. He was also an entrepreneur. He established the Northern Airways Company in Wausau, Wisconsin, while managing the Wausau and Oshkosh airports as well. John was an active man.

Thirty-three year old John Wood followed Roscoe Turner out of Los Angeles on Saturday, 31 August. Race officials on the West Coast dutifully notified their counterparts in Cleveland that Wood and Turner were airborne. Crossing into New Mexico, Wood encountered engine trouble. He and his mechanic, twenty-five year old Ward Miller, landed for repairs at the tiny town of Willard, New Mexico, some 60 miles southeast of Albuquerque.[15] By Saturday afternoon, Wood and Miller were back in Los Angeles for an engine change and another try at the non-stop race.

Just after midnight in the early Sunday darkness with Miller again aboard, Wood lifted the Wasp-powered Vega away from the airport runway in Los Angeles. Once again, Cleveland was notified of Wood's second departure. With a fuel load of 2910 pounds (485 gallons), the airplane climbed slowly upward to bridge the San Gabriel Mountains separating the California coast from the desert beyond. Leaving the mountain range behind, the Vega sped in darkness across the Mojave Desert, a hot desolate unforgiving landscape. According to an estimate by Miller, the Vega forged eastward at an altitude of about 2000 feet over the desert. Cloud formations loomed ahead. Unknown to the two man crew, the racer was charging headlong into a fierce desert electrical rainstorm.

Air turbulence became violent tossing the Lockheed about as if it were a leaf in the wind. Rain pelted the airplane in waves as the downpour continued. In the midst of this turmoil, Ward Miller was attempting to transfer fuel from the auxiliary tank to the main tank while John Wood fought to control the plane. The racer was approaching Needles, California, situated near the Colorado River. As Miller was pumping fuel, he later recalled that ". . . they were almost blinded by a lightning flash. The plane sideslipped and fell into a whirling tailspin."[16] Miller sensed disaster. He unfastened his seat belt. The stricken airplane continued to lurch and spin as Wood fought for control. Setting himself by the fuselage door, Miller opened the latch to bail out only to have the aircraft reel sharply pitching the mechanic into the tempestuous night. He automatically pulled the "D" ring on his parachute and felt the shock as his canopy blossom overhead. It was still pitch black except for momentary flashes of lightning. Miller never saw the ground as it neared. He hit the ground apparently striking his head and became unconscious.[17]

Miller regained consciousness and was able to judge the direction of Needles as the sun came up. Bruised but not otherwise injured, the lucky mechanic first sought to find Major Wood and the stricken Vega. He climbed several sand mounds for a better view of the terrain, but to no avail. Frustrated, Miller made his way into Needles and sought help. Local authorities immediately sent out men on horseback to scan the area around the desert town. Miller also called Lockheed officials who dispatched Harry Bromley in another Vega to Needles to conduct an air search. As word spread, local pilots joined the rescue effort. The search continued on land and in the air for the remainder of the day. Preparations were made to air drop water and food should the missing pilot be located. The rescuers continued their hunt after dark in a somewhat forlorn hope that Major Wood, if able, might light a fire.

Wreckage of the Lockheed was located late Tuesday afternoon, sixty hours after the search had begun.[18] Impact occurred approximately 38 miles northwest of Needles at an obscure, isolated place called Piute Springs. The crash site was on the Fort Mohave Indian Reservation. The fate of Major John Wood was discovered Wednesday morning when flyers E.B. Smith and Bobby Loutt flew to the site. Risking an accident, Smith and Loutt nonetheless landed their biplane on the desert floor and approached the wreckage. Sadly, they found John Wood dead in the cockpit of his demolished Vega. Strangely, with all the fuel onboard the racer, there was no fire. One wing was missing from the crash site, apparently disjoined from the fuselage during the lightning strike. The main tank in a Vega was located overhead in the wing center section. Smith and Loutt inspected the crash site and concluded the Wasp engine was running at the time of impact. This could have been determined based upon engine instrument readings frozen at impact.

Exactly what happened to Major Wood that terrifying night can only be suggested. The fact that one wing was missing from the immediate crash site indicates structural failure at the time of the lightning strike or shortly thereafter. Lightning may have penetrated through to the main gasoline tank causing an explosion as Ward Miller later reconstructed. More likely, the lightning strike weakened the wing and it failed momentarily afterward as the plane went out of control. John Wood was wearing a parachute. Extricating himself, however, from the relatively small overhead cockpit canopy hatch while experiencing high centrifugal forces as the Lockheed lurched wildly and spun out of control would have been extremely difficult.[19] Whatever the cause of the accident, it was a sad footnote to the 1929 non-stop derby.

Estimated Takeoff Weight of "Winnie Mae" in 1930 Derby		
Component	Weight/Lb.	Remarks
Fuel	3000	
Oil	188	
Trapped Fuel	12	Est. 2 Gal.
Trapped Oil	4	Est. 0.5 Gal.
Pilot	180	With Parachute
Added Fuel Tanks	120	Estimated
Fuel System Plumbing	10	Estimated
Aircraft Seats Removed	2490	Estimated
Airframe Empty Weight	-50	Model 5B Spec.
Estimate At Takeoff	5954	Pounds

by relying on Gatty's carefully prepared charts. He arrived in Chicago believing that a transcontinental record was out of reach. Wiley Post won the non-stop transcontinental derby of 1930, beating Art Goebel by 30 minutes. Ironically, Goebel was flying Vega NR7954 which was the first Winnie Mae. The coincidence was further compounded when Post learned that Goebel had also relied upon a flight plan prepared by Harold Gatty!

The 1930 transcontinental race was devoid of any high drama. By the same token, it marked the debut of Wiley Post as a long distance flyer. The characteristics of meticulous attention to detail with regard to his airplane and reliance upon expert navigation planning by Gatty would define his future global flights. Post would become the consummate aviator in his time.

Art Goebel flew this Vega 5 to second place in the 1930 non-stop race. Aircraft was the same one used by Roscoe Turner the previous year and once owned by F.C. Hall. Credit: Sid Bradd collection

General Tire owned this Lockheed Air Express when Henry J. Brown won the 1929 non-stop derby. The plane was sold to Gilmore Oil Company in 1930 and painted cream color with red trim. Roscoe Turner placed fourth in the 1930 race. Credit: Birch Matthews collection

Turner's 1930 racer is seen here in full Gilmore Oil colors. Marking on the vertical tail and wheel pants is the Gilmore lion, a corporate emblem. Credit: Pratt & Whitney via CAHA

Chapter IV: Derbies & Depression: 1929-1930

NOTES:

1 Precise attribution for the term "golden age of air racing" is unknown. One of the first to publish this phrase was Truman C. "Pappy" Weaver in his book, *The Golden Age of Air Racing*, Experimental Aircraft Association Aviation Foundation, Inc., 1983.
2 *Western Flying*, April 1929, p. 165.
3 Op cit., p. 290.
4 Depending upon one's point of view, the enactment of prohibition was a salutary state of affairs or a totally frustrating intervention of government upon the populace.
5 The word "bootlegger" literally derives from a practice of hiding a liquor bottle in one's boot.
6 One might reasonably ask what bootlegging has to do with aviation? Be assured that more than one case of Canadian whiskey and Mexican tequila traversed the U.S. border via air transport. More than one air racing pilot was at some time or another engaged in "rum running."
7 Cleveland's municipal airport would one day be named for Hopkins.
8 Russell C. Johns, "Observations at the National Air Races and Exposition," *Aero Digest*, October 1929.
9 *New York Times*, 23 August 1929, p. 3.
10 *New York Times*, 24 August 1929, p. 2.
11 *New York Times*, 17 August 1929. Page 3.
12 Richard Sanders Allen, "Barrel-Nosed Cigars," American Aviation Historical Society JOURNAL, Vol. 9, No. 1, 1964, p. 33. According to Allen, this Lockheed was purchased F.O.B. Akron, Ohio, the location of General Tire & Rubber Company. Date of purchase was 27 August 1929.
13 Richard Sanders Allen, *Revolution in the Sky*, The Stephen Greene Press, Brattleboro, Vermont, 1967, 47.
14 *New York Times*, 2 September 1929, p. 4.
15 Ibid.
16 *New York Times*, 4 September 1928, p. 3.
17 The author made many parachute jumps while in the U.S. Army. A parachutist is alerted to ground proximity during a night jump if there are trees present. Even on a dark night, you can sense when you reach the tree line. This alerts the jumper to prepare for landing. In Ward Miller's case, he was in the middle of the Mohave Desert. There was no tree line to look for and the terror of the storm was all about him. In retrospect, he was fortunate not to have been severely injured under the circumstances.
18 *New York Times*, 5 September 1929, p. 8.
19 What probably saved Ward Miller's life was that he was virtually thrown out of the airplane and somehow had the presence of mind to activate his parachute.
20 Stanley R. Mohler and Bobby H. Johnson, *Wiley Post, His Winnie Mae, and the World's First Pressure Suit*, Smithsonian Annals of flight, No. 8, Smithsonian Institution Press, Washington, D.C., 1971, p. 1. The Mohler and Johnson publication presents a rather detailed description of Post's early life and introduction to aviation.
21 Op cit., p. 4.
22 The engine in Post's second Vega was Pratt & Whitney serial number 3088.
23 This resulted in a supercharger speed seven times faster than the engine crankshaft was turning.
24 Wiley Post and Harold Gatty, *Around the World in Eight Days*, Orion Books, New York, 1989, p. 19.
25 These changes to a stock Lockheed Vega required that the registration be changed to a restricted license, a process F.C. Hall readily agreed to.
26 Post and Gatty, op.cit., p. 191.

Roscoe Turner's penchant for publicity was seldom equalled. The lion cub he is holding in this publicity photograph was named "Gilmore," and flew with him during the 1930 transcontinental race. Credit: Pratt & Whitney via CAHA

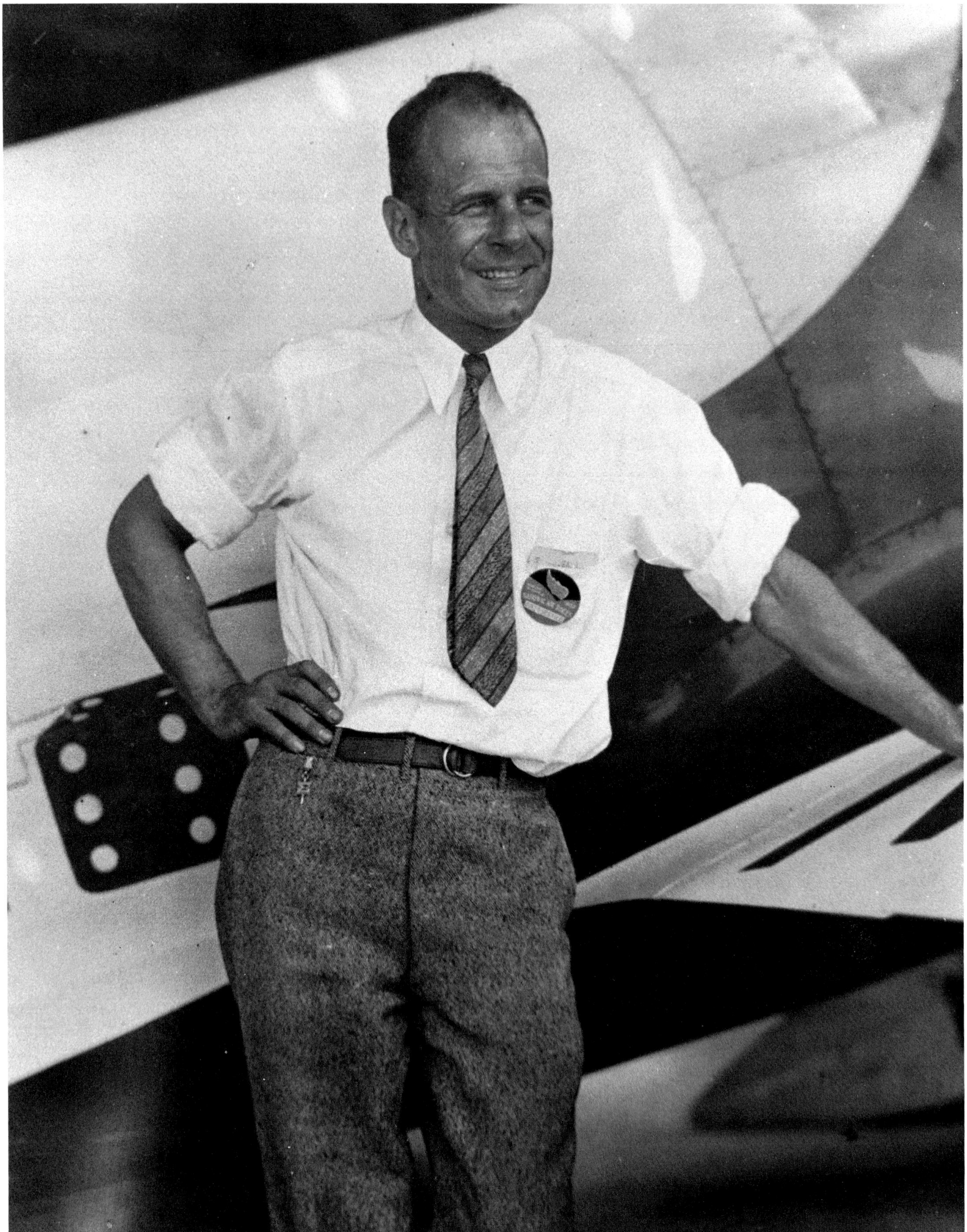

Chapter V

THE BENDIX TROPHY RACE

Nineteen thirty-one marked a turning point for the National Air Races. Senator Hiram Bingham, President of the National Aeronautics Association (NAA) announced that agreement was reached with the Cleveland Chamber of Commerce, the National Air Races of Cleveland, Incorporated, and the Cleveland Chapter of the NAA, to make the city a permanent home for this national event.[1] In the past, the National Air Races had been held in a different city each year. Of the various locations, only the Cleveland, Spokane and Chicago affairs yielded a profit. Cleveland hosted the 1929 races and realized a profit of $100,000 which exceed by far the amounts realized in Spokane and Chicago.

A prominent business leader in Cleveland, industrialist Louis W. Greve, spearheaded the drive to make the city the permanent host for the races. Greve was president of National Air Races, Inc., as well as the Cleveland NAA chapter. He was also chairman of the aviation committee of the Cleveland Chamber of Commerce and thus well placed to coordinate and sell the city as a center of aviation and racing. Greve was successful in his quest. Senator Bingham noted that Cleveland was a central location with a large population, facilities and an airport to stage the races and perhaps most important, a strong civic organization dedicated to the idea of the National Air Races.

Cliff Henderson knew this was an important turning point. He went about preparing for the 1931 Nationals by visiting manufacturers in various parts of the country seeking ideas as well as reactions to previous race programs. He arrived in New York City around mid-March for day long discussions with a number of well known aviation personalities including C.S. "Casey" Jones, Amelia Earhart, Al Williams, Edward P. Warner, and George Haldeman. Their meeting lasted well into the night.[2] From this ad hoc group came a recommendation that several cross-country derbies should again be part of the 1931 program. In addition, a new race was planned with a purse of $10,000 or more. It would be a "free-for-all" long distance speed event meaning there would be little or no restriction on airframes, engines and supercharging.[3] The race could be flown non-stop or with in-route refueling. A final caveat was that some western city be selected as the starting point.

Returning to Cleveland, Henderson called a press conference to announce some of the findings from his survey around the country. He told of his, "... plans for innovations at the races to create new speed dash records and to imprint the meaning of rapid flight more strongly on the consciousness of the spectator."[4] These noble objectives also meant that Cliff Henderson was driving for more race fans, contestants and especially prize money. One of the things on his mind was obtaining a sponsor for the planned new transcontinental feature race.

Jimmy Doolittle was a superb pilot. His skills were complimented by a keen analytical mind. This photograph was taken during the 1932 National Air Races. Jimmy won the Thompson Trophy that year flying a Granville Brothers Gee Bee racer. Credit: Sid Bradd collection

Cliff Henderson poses long enough for the photographer to take this picture before a local flight in this 1930 Great Lakes Special 2T-2 powered by a 95 horsepower Cirrus Ensign. The company provided this aircraft for the 1931 National Air Races. Credit: Sid Bradd collection

THE SPONSOR

Henderson wanted the rotund, cigar smoking industrialist, Vincent Bendix to become the patron of this new transcontinental speed event. Bendix was born in Moline, Illinois, during 1881. Young Vincent ran away from home when he was 16 to work on the railroads. After initially studying law, he became interested in engineering and the automobile. The industrious Vincent ultimately became a self-made millionaire and holder of numerous patents. His best known innovation was the automobile starter mechanism.

The Bendix Corporation was prominent in both the automotive and aviation fields. Their involvement in aviation dated to World War I when starters for aircraft engines were developed by a predecessor company, the Bijur Starting and Lighting Company. Back in 1914, Bijur worked with Packard, Curtiss and Wright Field to develop aircraft engine starters. Bijur was subsequently purchased by the Eclipse Machine Company which in turn, was bought by the Bendix Aviation Company in 1929. Bendix also owned Stromberg Carburetors and the Eclipse-Pioneer Division, makers of flight instruments.

The Great Depression was in full swing by 1931, and sponsors were not easy to find. For several months, Cliff Henderson attempted to meet Bendix without success. In his chronicle, "They Flew the Bendix Race," author Don Dwiggins notes that the persistent Henderson finally caught up with Bendix in the club car of New York Central's Commodore train on the Chicago to New York run.[5] Henderson approached Bendix somewhat cautiously. After preliminary formalities, Henderson launched into a pitch for sponsorship of the planned new transcontinental race. He was seeking fifteen thousand dollars, a sum to be matched by the National Air Race Committee. He didn't receive an immediate answer that night on the train. But he did get an invitation to contact Bendix again with a suitable trophy concept. Henderson's salesmanship proved irresistible and the sponsorship was soon in place. What had heretofore been termed a free-for-all derby was now officially the Bendix Trophy Race. Vincent Bendix elected to sponsor the race no doubt for corporate promotional reasons, but also in the belief that development and research might be fostered in the field of aeronautics. The Bendix became a civilian race classic which ran from 1931 to 1949 with the exception of six years during World War II.[6]

THE SUPERB SOLUTION

The inaugural 1931 Bendix Race was captured by Army reserve airman, Major James H. Doolittle. Early in 1930, Doolittle left active Army Air Corps duty to take a job with Shell Oil Company. Shell had been interested in aviation as early as 1909, when Louis Bleriot used their gasoline to make

Chapter V: The Bendix Trophy Race

the first English channel crossing by airplane. In the United States, Shell operated in a number of regions including San Francisco where an aviation department was formed late in 1929. Shell hired Lieutenant John A. Macready to manage this aviation department and promote Shell products. Macready proposed hiring Jimmy Doolittle together with James Haizlip, another well known flyer. His idea was to have both pilots establish inter-city flight records and compete in air races promoting Shell products. An offer was made and Doolittle accepted joining Shell in mid-February. A little over a year later, Jimmy Doolittle was an entrant in the first Bendix Race true to the plan envisioned by Macready.

Cliff Henderson wanted to insure the inaugural Bendix Trophy Race would be an extraordinary event, hopefully accompanied by new speed records to Cleveland and to the East Coast as well. The entry list once again included a fleet of Lockheed airplanes – a Vega, two Orions and three Altairs. These craft were fast, indeed capable of flying the route non-stop. It was doubtful, however, that these machines would break the existing transcontinental record of twelve hours and twenty-five minutes set in 1930 by Frank Hawks.

A seventh entry in the 1931 Bendix was an airplane known as the Travel Air Mystery ship to be flown by Walter Hunter. This was an impressive three year old record-setting design with a number of inter-city and transcontinental records to its credit. Henderson and some associated with promoting the National Air Races in Cleveland believed a new racer was needed to spur interest in the Bendix. In late June or early July of 1931, a group of local business leaders put together an organization named the "Cleveland Speed Foundation." In reality, the Foundation was a financial vehicle. It is thought to have been hurriedly pieced together at the urging of Cliff Henderson to sponsor a purpose-built racer for the 1931 Bendix. In the first week of July, the Foundation contracted with Chicagoan E.M. "Matty" Laird – builder of a fast line of biplanes – to construct a super fast racer. Laird began work on July 8 and finished 45 days later.[7] The Speed Foundation paid Laird $12,500 to build the airplane ". . . with engines, propellers, instruments, wheels and brakes to be provided" separately.[8] Actually, two engines were planned for the new racer. Both were Pratt & Whitney Wasp Jr powerplants, the first a direct drive and the other built with a 3.2:1 ratio propeller reduction gear. The geared engine was planned for the Thompson Trophy contest while the direct drive version would be used in the Bendix race.

Matty Laird possessed special credentials. His small company, E.M. Laird, Inc., located at Ashburn Field – 83rd and Cicero Avenue in Chicago – built the 1930 model LC-DW 300 racer which pilot Charles "Speed" Holman flew to victory in the Thompson Trophy Race. The aircraft was completed in a dreadfully short time, finished literally just before the Thompson Trophy Race began. It was called the Laird "Solution." The designer's response to the 1931 race plane con-

Industrialist Vincent Bendix, with one of his ever present cigars, chats with young Douglas "Wrong Way" Corrigan (right) who flew his nine year old Curtiss Robin non-stop from Floyd Bennett Field, N.Y., to Dublin, Ireland, in July 1938. His excuse for the unauthorized flight was that he just headed in the wrong direction. Credit: Sid Bradd collection

struction contract was to improve on the 1930 design using more streamlining and greater horsepower while still retaining the biplane configuration. The result was the "Super Solution." The racer was aptly named. In the hands of a superb pilot, it was the solution to victory in that first Bendix Trophy Race. The superb pilot, of course, was Jimmy Doolittle whose own racer – a modified Travel Air – disintegrated during a test flight over St. Louis about the middle of August. By this time, work on the Super Solution was underway and the Cleveland Speed Foundation signed Doolittle as pilot for the Laird racer.

The 1930 Solution and 1931 Super Solution race planes were similar in design, Laird tending to refine and build on previous successes. Both designs descended from a long line of "Speedwing" aircraft. Heritage of the model LC-DW 500 ("LC" for Laird Commercial, "D" was the series, "W" indicated a Wasp powerplant and "500" approximated engine horsepower) Super Solution was indisputable. The plane was a small close-coupled design very similar in form to the LC-DW 300 Solution. Aerodynamic and physical differences were limited as shown in the accompanying table. The Super

A Comparison of the Laird Solution Racers

Parameter	1930 LC-DW 300	1931 LC-DW 500
Length	17 ft. - 8 In.	19 ft. - 6 In.
Span (Upper Wing)	21 ft. - 0 In.	21 ft. - 0 In.
Span (Lower Wing)	18 ft. - 0 In.	18 ft. - 0 In.
Wing Area	108 Ft.^{2}	108 Ft.^{2}
Empty Weight	1380 Lb.	1580 Lb.
Gross Weight	1845 Lb.	2500 Lb.
Fuel Capacity	50 Gal.	112.5 Gal.
Oil Capacity	Unknown	8 Gal.
P & W Engine	Direct Drive	Direct Drive
Supercharger Ratio	None	6:1
Horsepower	300	530
Rev./Min.	2200 (Est.)	2600
Prop. Dia.		8 Ft.
Airfoil	NACA M-12	NACA M-12
Wing Loading	17.08 Lb./Ft.^{2}	25 Lb./Ft.^{2}
Power Loading	6.15 Lb./HP	4.7 Lb./HP

Solution displayed an obvious attention to drag reduction employing wheel pants, faired landing gear structure and elimination of the strut located between the wheels. The latter was replaced by a streamline tension wire of considerably less surface and frontal area. Initial flight testing revealed a condition of directional instability which increased in magnitude at higher velocities. As Jimmy Doolittle stated ". . . the airplane was barely manageable at a speed of 200 miles per hour."[9] He concluded the directional stability problem in the Super Solution was "due to the increased fin area (vertical surface) forward, resulting from the longer NACA cowl employed with the geared engine, the large (wheel) pants and the fairing which filled in the space between the front and rear landing gear struts."[10] The deficiency was corrected by adding nine inches in height to the vertical stabilizer and rudder. By comparison, lateral and longitudinal stability characteristics of the racer proved quite satisfactory.

THE FIRST BENDIX

That first Bendix Race was run September 4, 1931. Roll-out of the Laird Super Solution occurred a scant fourteen days earlier at Ashburn Field. Three hours of test flying time were accumulated by both Jimmy Doolittle and Matty Laird to resolve the typical problems encountered with a new airplane design. On August 28, Doolittle flew west to Kansas City and Wichita on his trip out to the West Coast for the start of the Bendix race. After an overnight stay in Wichita, he flew on to Los Angeles. The new racer had logged just nine hours flying time. The next few days were spent readying the Super Solution for the grueling 2046 mile Bendix Race and planned continuation to the East Coast. In Los Angeles, the plugs, magnetos, carburetor set up and airframe rigging were checked and checked again. Another thirty minutes of local flying time was accumulated to verify readiness.

It was dead of night on the Pacific Coast when at close intervals, each Bendix racer took off for Cleveland. Following Beeler Blevins in his Lockheed, Doolittle was flagged off at 2:35 a.m. Pacific Daylight Time. Leaving Burbank's United Airport, Jimmy Doolittle – dressed in knickers, shirt and tie, leather flying jacket, helmet and goggles – banked the Super Solution and headed east. Departing the Los Angeles area, Doolittle climbed rapidly to 5000 feet then lessened his ascent until reaching 11,000 feet as he cleared the San Bernardino Mountains. A crosswind forced Jimmy to hold a degree or two of left rudder as he flew. At this time in the race, the rising sun was directly ahead, a bright yellow ball low in the sky. Beeler Blevins in his Lockheed Orion had taken off before Doolittle. Winging along over the desert, he watched incredulous as the small viridian green and Kodak yellow Super Solution streak past him, disappearing into the distance. Reporters interviewing Blevins after the race noted his reaction when he said Doolittle passed him " . . . just like I was standing still. I thought I was flying backward." Doolittle needed this speed as the Laird did not have fuel capacity for a non-stop flight.

Chapter V: The Bendix Trophy Race

The Lockheeds in contrast, could negotiate the entire distance without refueling, albeit at a lesser speed.

After reaching altitude, Jimmy began a gradual 100 feet per minute decent over the Arizona landscape. Crossing over Flagstaff, the Laird had dropped down to 6000 feet. Doolittle piloted the plane to Albuquerque wasting no time in his approach and touchdown. His planned refueling stops on the way to Cleveland were at Albuquerque and Kansas City. Like everything else Jimmy did, his refueling plans were laid with care. Shell aviation research assistant Eugene F. Zimmerman, stationed crews at both intermediate stops while he went on to Cleveland to attend this chore personally.

Zimmerman's preparation paid off handsomely. Doolittle's elapsed time on the ground at Albuquerque was exactly seven minutes with a similarly brief refueling at Kansas City. At each stop his crews rapidly loaded Shell 87 octane aviation gasoline into the fuel tank and added a few quarts of oil. Doolittle's time for the first leg of his race was three hours and two minutes. At 5:44 a.m. West Coast time, Doolittle was again airborne, headed for Kansas City. His physical stamina was an integral part of the flight. The cockpit of the tiny Laird racer was confining. Forward visibility was essentially limited to a narrow field of view on each side of the airplane unless he peered over the top wing. Flight instrumentation was minimal. The staccato roar of the Wasp Jr. engine was constant, only slightly attenuated by the leather helmet Doolittle was wearing. In that era, there was no climate-controlled, hermetically-sealed cockpit environment with digital instrument displays. Navigation was sometimes by dead reckoning and weather forecasts were tenuous at best. Weather radar was an invention still years into the future. The Laird's cockpit was not a place for the hesitant nor anyone with claustrophobic tendencies.

Doolittle flew a course he hoped would maximize tailwinds, a methodology practiced today in more sophisticated form and known as pressure pattern minimum time track flight planning. In other words, the fastest flight route is not necessarily the shortest physical distance between two points. Rather, it may be a series of headings and altitudes designed to minimize headwinds and maximize tailwinds such that a destination is reached in the least time although over a longer distance.

The Laird "Super Solution" was built for both the 1931 Bendix and the Thompson Trophy races by E.M. "Matty" Laird. This photograph was taken before the first flight of the new airplane. Jimmy Doolittle is in the cockpit. The man in shirtsleeves on the left is Laird. Parallel wing struts and small vertical fin and rudder were later replaced. Credit: Birch Matthews collection

This photograph illustrates the higher vertical tail surfaces as well as the single inter-wing strut added to the airframe after it was built. Doolittle flew the Super Solution in this configuration during the 1931 Bendix race and transcontinental record flight. Credit: Birch Matthews collection

Under Doolittle's steady hand, the Laird arrived in Kansas City by 11:50 a.m. eastern time, just three hours and six minutes out of Albuquerque. His average speed at this point was 230 miles per hour. Once again, Zimmerman's pre-positioned refueling crew had Doolittle underway in a matter of minutes. He veered a bit to the south and headed for Cleveland. By now, Jimmy realized he had a good chance of beating Frank Hawks' transcontinental record. Weather, thus far, was excellent and the winds favorable. Unfortunately, this condition wouldn't last. Doolittle encountered heavy weather over Western Ohio in his approach to Cleveland. The Weather Bureau forecast accurately predicted local thunderstorms over the lower Great Lakes region. The route from Cleveland to New York promised little better with cloudy skies, showers

Doolittle also flew the Super Solution in the Thompson Trophy race using the same direct drive Wasp Jr. engine raced in the Bendix. Unfortunately, a damaged piston forced him out of this race during the seventh lap. Credit: United States Air Force

and south winds shifting to the west up to 1000 feet. This meant either crosswinds or moderate headwinds as Doolittle attempted to set a new transcontinental record.

THE TRANSCONTINENTAL RECORD

Before worrying about a coast-to-coast record, Doolittle first had to reach Cleveland. He was getting close as he raced above the northern Ohio countryside. Below him, rain pelted the rifle and pistol matches held annually at Camp Perry, Ohio, by the National Rifle Association. The rainstorm troubled Doolittle too. By the time he arrived at the Cleveland airport, the rains became intense. Most of the scheduled events were canceled due to the inclement weather. Landing, Jimmy taxied to a refueling truck where he was greeted by a throng of well wishers. His only intent at this point was to refuel as quickly as possible and resume his record-breaking journey to the east. Gene Zimmerman was on hand to assist in the refueling process which took about ten minutes amid the excitement and chaos of the moment. Doolittle's wife rushed over to the airplane to hand him a sandwich. He refused not wanting to take time to eat lest he loose additional precious minutes. He was too busy refueling the Laird.

With a clean windscreen and enough fuel to reach the East Coast, Doolittle wasted no time leaving Cleveland. Flying low beneath a leaden overcast sky, he forged on, his speed varying dramatically depending upon the turmoil of the weather front.

The Allegheny Mountains passed underneath as the tiny Laird headed eastward. An hour and forty-nine minutes later, the thunderstorms were behind. Doolittle was just west of Newark, New Jersey. The airfield in sight, he entered his approach and touched down at eleven hours, fifty-one minutes and ten seconds after leaving California. The record was his. The event was witnessed by less than three hundred spectators, but that really didn't matter. His goal was achieved and he wanted to return to Cleveland and his family as soon as possible. After a brief interlude with the press, he departed Newark and flew back to Cleveland, winner of the first Bendix race and holder of a new transcontinental speed record. It was quite a day's work.

NOTES:
1 *The National Aeronautic Magazine*, January 1931. p. 50.
2 Lauren D. Lyman, "Derbies to Feature Air Races," *New York Times*, 22 March 1929, Section IX. Page 1.
3 *New York Times*, Section X, 22 March 1931, p. 8.
4 *New York Times*, 22 March 1931, p. 19.
5 Don Dwiggins, *They Flew the Bendix Race*, J.B. Lippincott Company, New York, 1965, p. 14.
6 Beginning in 1946, the Bendix had two divisions, one for piston engine airplanes and the other for jets. After 1949, the Bendix trophy was awarded to the military flights of outstanding achievement.
7 E.M. (Matty) Laird, "The Laird Super Solution Speedwing," *Aero Digest*, November 1931, p. 76.
8 George Hardie, Jr., *E.M. Matty Laird's Super Solution*, EAA Aviation Foundation, Inc., 1981. p. 7.
9 James H. Doolittle, "Racer Ramblings," reprinted in the American Air Racing Society Newsletter, Vol. 5, No. 6, November 1976.
10 Ibid.

Harold Johnson finished in second place with this Lockheed Orion 9. He had just stepped out of the airplane when this picture was taken. His elapsed time was one hour and four minutes longer than Doolittle in the Laird Super Solution. Credit: Sid Bradd collection

*The Rider R-3 was assigned race number 9 for the MacRobertson race and retained this number for the 1934 Bendix race. Mechanical problems kept it out of the Bendix. This illustration shows the airplane being pushed out of Jim Granger's hangar at Clover Field, Santa Monica, California.
Credit: Roy Russell*

Chapter VI

YEARS OF STRUGGLE

The Great Depression was in full swing during the early 1930s. Sponsors for racing aircraft and air races were few and far in between. In spite of the times, there was still keen public interest in aviation and a scattering of people able and willing to finance new aeronautical projects. Thus in late 1933, plans were under way for a long distance international air race the following year from London, England, to Melbourne, Australia. The race was to help commemorate the City of Melbourne's centennial celebration. A wealthy Australian, Sir MacPherson Robertson stepped forward to sponsor this race. He established a $75,000 purse – a quite large sum of money in those days – provided the race would be named "MacRobertson" after his candy manufacturing business.[1] It would be a grueling test of endurance and speed for the proposed route stretching over 11,300 miles, nineteen countries and seven seas. The race would begin 20 October 1934.

RIDER'S RACER

Announcement of the forthcoming race spurred several people into action including such notable American pilots as Roscoe Turner, Wiley Post, Clyde Pangborn, Louise Thaden, Jimmy Wedell and Jacqueline Cochran. Another person anxious to participate was Keith Rider, a young aircraft designer just beginning to gain recognition. Rider was bitten by the air racing bug. He was fascinated with the idea of fast airplanes. His early endeavors resulted in the design and construction of three Menasco-powered racers identified as the B-1, the R-1 and R-2. These were small airplanes designed for limited (engine) displacement pylon races.

Rider was enthusiastic about the long distance MacRobertson race. His creative mind built upon his first racing machines, expanding the basic design concept to a larger airframe capable of greater range and speed. Regardless of his ambitions, Keith Rider faced the classic problem of obtaining financial backing.[2] He found his "financial angel" in the person of Edith Boydston Clark, a lady of some means, from Santa Monica, California. Mrs. Clark was an aviation enthusiast and owner of a Travel Air biplane. Edith, in her early thirties, was also secretary-treasurer of the Pacific School of Aviation. If Keith Rider wanted Edith's financial backing, he apparently also had to accept her choice of who would fly the new racer. Her choice was 41 year old Jim Granger, president of James E. Granger, Inc., a fixed-base operation located at Clover Field Airport in Santa Monica. In addition to performing aircraft maintenance and renting hangar space, Jim was the local dealer for Swallow biplanes.[3] He was also president of the Pacific School of Aviation for flight training which occupied a portion of the Granger hangar building.

Granger was a prominent local pilot who two years earlier flew a Wright-powered Swallow to seventeenth place in the Cord Cup transcontinental handicap race. Earlier in 1934, Granger captured the 200 horsepower class race as well as the free-for-all race at a local meet held at the

Keith Rider's R-3 racer was designed to compete in the 1934 MacRobertson race from England to Australia. The airplane is shown here in its original as-built configuration. It was powered by a 400 horsepower Pratt & Whitney Wasp Jr. engine. Credit: Birch Matthews collection

The R-3 offered little in the way of creature comfort during long distance races with its cramped, open cockpit. When the landing gear was retracted, one-half of the wheel was exposed and could be used in that position for an emergency landing. Credit: Roy Russell

Chapter VI: Years Of Struggle

Compton Airport in Compton, California. The aircraft he flew to victory in these races was Edith Clark's Travel Air biplane.[4] Jim's wife, Glema Granger, was also a pilot of some accomplishment. She flew a plane belonging to Waldo Waterman winning a women's event at the Compton races.

Keith Rider accepted Edith's money and her pilot. As Rider completed drawings for the aircraft, construction was begun in West Los Angeles.[5] The construction site was an abandoned sash, door and window frame factory, no doubt a victim of the economic times. Although Rider designed the basic airframe, he received assistance from Douglas Aircraft powerplant engineer Ivar Shogran who, it turns out, was Keith's brother inlaw. Ivar designed the engine mount for the Wasp Jr. engine which Keith arranged to lease from Pratt & Whitney. It was the beginning of a loose and informal association between Rider and several personnel from Douglas.

The racing machine which took shape that summer of 1934, employed an all-metal fuselage of very clean design. The airplane had a small cramped open cockpit with a simple one-piece plexiglass windscreen. Emphasis on streamlining and minimum frontal area drag left precious little room for creature comforts during a long race. The confining cockpit would not change with time, however, a subsequent modification did enclose the pilot's head with a plexiglass canopy. The cantilevered wing was constructed of wood and covered in wood veneer. The empennage was of conventional metal construction with fabric covered control surfaces. The vertical stabilizer incorporated Rider's personal signature in the form of an extreme sweep to the leading edge, a trademark he used on all of his designs.[6]

A significant difference in Rider's new design was use of an air-cooled radial engine in place of the Menasco in-line powerplants installed in his previous racing machines. Rider made arrangements with Pratt & Whitney to lease an engine and the company rebuilt a Wasp Jr., serial number X-27, in April 1934.[7] Before this 375 horsepower engine was shipped from the factory, Rider changed his mind. He needed more horsepower. Pratt & Whitney obliged and rebuilt a Wasp Jr. "A" model converting it into a supercharged SB configuration. This engine, rated at 400 horsepower, was shipped to Keith Rider in Santa Monica on 30 July 1934.[8] It would be the first of three different Pratt & Whitney engines to power this Rider racer.

Entries for the MacRobertson Race were accepted through Thursday noon, 31 May 1934, a date later extended to 1 June.[9,10] Keith Rider's application was submitted and accepted and he was assigned racing number "9" which was duly painted on the sides of the new airplane.[11] In addition to American contestants, there were flyers entered from Great Britain, France, Italy, Holland, Ireland, Sweden, Denmark and Australia. It was truly going to be an international affair. In the end, 64 aircraft were officially entered although for various reasons, only 21 racers actually arrived at Mildenhall

Actress Mary Pickford was an honorary official at the 1934 National Air Races. She was photographed here with Cliff Henderson on the left and Jimmy Doolittle on the right. Credit: Sid Bradd collection

Aerodrome, some 60 miles north of London.

With airframe construction underway, Jim Granger departed California for Europe in June, some four months before the race would start. He planned to fly with the Dutch airline K.L.M. to Batavia, look at the proposed route, check airfields and gather all the route maps and charts he could locate.[12]

Keith Rider was nothing if not optimistic about the performance potential of his new racer. He estimated that Granger and the R-3 would complete "the race in forty-four hours total time, including a five-hour lay over in Singapore to give Jim a nap."[13] The extent of Rider's optimism is illustrated by the fact that British pilots C.W.A. Scott and T. Campbell Black would win the speed division of the race with an elapsed time of nearly 71 hours.

Work on the new racer was completed in late summer, 1934. After the aircraft was finished it was trucked to Jim Granger's hangar at Clover Field in Santa Monica, for final assembly and flight test. The MacRobertson Race starting date was closing in rapidly leaving precious little time for testing, perfecting and shipping the airplane to England. Coupled with this agenda, Rider entered the racer in the Bendix Trophy Race which preceded the much longer and grueling MacRobertson contest anticipating that this would be a useful shakedown for his newest creation.

Roscoe Turner sits in his Hornet-powered Wedell Williams racer sponsored by the H.J. Heinz food company. Mechanical problems grounded him on the day of the 1934 Bendix. The next day, he established a coast-to-coast speed record in the same airplane. Credit: Birch Matthews collection

HOLLYWOOD DIGRESSION

The fourth annual Bendix Trophy Race was scheduled for Friday, 31 August, and would be held with all the fanfare Clifford Henderson could muster. Never one to overlook ways of promoting the National Air Races, Cliff arranged for Hollywood motion picture star Mary Pickford – "America's Sweetheart" – to be honorary starter for the race.[14] Mary Pickford came to prominence in the silent screen era and was one of the few stars to successfully make the transition to talking motion pictures. Her first "talkie" was Coquette, produced in 1929. Although not critically acclaimed, it was a

Lee Gehlbach flew Jackie Cochran's Gee Bee "Q.E.D." in the 1934 Bendix. Cowling attachment fittings failed during the race forcing Lee to remove the cowl at Des Moines and fly the rest of the way to Cleveland without it. He arrived after the 6 p.m. deadline and out of the money. Credit: Marvin Border

John Worthen flew this Wedell Williams Model 45 racer in the 1934 Bendix. This photograph was taken at Patterson, Louisiana, not long after the airplane was built. At this point, it mounted a Pratt & Whitney R-985 Wasp Jr. engine. It was the first Wedell model to feature retractable landing gear. Credit: Birch Matthews collection

hit with her public. Her final movie was Secrets released in 1933, amid a turbulent estrangement from her husband, Douglas Fairbanks.

Fairbanks entered into an affair with British-born actress Sylvia Ashley which quietly persisted for several years. Finally in the summer of 1933, his assignations became public. On July 3, Hollywood gossip columnist Louella Parsons revealed Mary's troubled marriage. As Pickford biographer Booton Herndon wrote, "Louella broke the story under headlines of the size usually reserved for war, and papers around the world followed the example."[15] The public and the media avidly followed Mary's life on a daily basis. Probably no other Hollywood movie star at that time could guarantee air race promoter Cliff Henderson as much focus by the media as Mary Pickford!

Henderson originally planned to have Mary act as honorary starter for the Bendix. A day or two before the race was to start, this plan was hurriedly changed and Mary and her agent, N.A. McKay, made arrangements to leave Grand Central Air Terminal at 4:00 p.m. on their way to Chicago via TWA transport. She would be met in Chicago by Vincent Bendix and Major James Doolittle who would fly the actress to Cleveland for the races. Her new role would be to participate in the opening ceremonies on Friday and present the Bendix Trophy to the winning pilot. Mary's stay in Cleveland would be brief.

A favorite in the upcoming Bendix was Roscoe Turner flying his golden Wedell Williams racer sponsored by the H.J. Heinz food company. He had won the Bendix Trophy the previous year and hoped to repeat in 1934. The irrepressible Turner arrived at Grand Central Thursday afternoon and met with the blond movie star before her departure. He towered a full head and shoulders over her as news photographers captured the meeting. Turner, current holder of the coast-to-coast speed record seldom missed an opportunity for publicity. Resplendent in a loose fitting quasi-military attire and elegant waxed mustache, Roscoe smilingly posed with the actress to the delight of the assembled newsmen. The Los Angeles Times headlined their meeting writing, "Speed Ace Bids Star Adieu." Actually, the meeting was brief. As she was leaving, Mary turned to Roscoe declaring simply, "I hope I can return the trophy to you."[16] With that, the actress with the famous long blond curls boarded her plane for the flight east.

SIX TO GET READY, TWO TO GO

The day before Mary Pickford's send off from Grand Central, all of the Bendix race pilots gathered in the office of Union Air Terminal manager Fred Denslow to resolve apparent confusion over the number of race entries and their assigned starting times. They met with Joe Nikrent, W.H. Hitchman and Larry

Roy Minor was hired by the Granvilles to fly this composite R-1/R-2 Gee Bee racer in the 1934 Bendix race. The aircraft was damaged in a pre-race accident and never made the starting line. Credit: Phil Krause collection

1934 Bendix Race Schedule Departure Times

Pilot	Aircraft	Race No.	Scheduled Time
Roscoe Turner	Wedell Williams	57	3:00 a.m.
Douglas Davis	Wedell Williams	44	3:05 a.m.
Lee Gehlbach	Gee Bee Q.E.D.	77	3:10 a.m.
Murray Dilley	Vance		3:15 a.m.
John Worthen	Wedell Williams	45	3:20 a.m.
James Granger	Keith Rider	9	3:25 a.m.

Therkelson, all officials of the National Aeronautics Association responsible for the Bendix start.[17] At one point, nine pilots planned to fly in the race. On the day of the race, the field was reduced to six. The number had rapidly narrowed when two aircraft were damaged in pre-race accidents. The unfortunates were Harold Neumann and Roy Minor. Neumann and co-pilot George Cassidy were flying Benny Howard's brand new cabin monoplane – "Mister Mulligan" – out to the West Coast for the race. Historian Mike Kusenda relates that Neumann tried to fly above a western storm when he and Cassidy "were overcome by anoxia."[18] Veteran air race chronicler Truman Weaver suggests that both oxygen and fuel system problems forced Neumann down during the flight at an "unfinished airport" near Hawthorne, Nevada.[19] The ensuing landing wrecked the landing gear, damaged the wing and bent the propeller. Mulligan was definitely out the race.

Roy Minor was hired in 1934, to resuscitate the flagging fortunes of the Granville Brothers by flying their most recent creation, the newly fashioned Gee Bee composite R-1/R-2 racer, in the Bendix Race. The racer had been assembled using components from both the Gee Bee R-1 and R-2 and further modified by adding 18 inches to the fuselage aft of the cockpit together with more rudder surface. Minor flew the aircraft two times at the Springfield, Massachusetts, airport for familiarization. At the end of the second flight, he landed long, ran into a drainage ditch beyond the field and damaged the hybrid racer.[20,21,22] The airplane was finished for the 1934 season. A third racer, the Wedell Williams 92, was also flown to the West Coast for the Bendix but didn't start presumably due to mechanical problems.

Six planes lined up at Burbank for the race. Three of the racers were Wedell Williams airplanes piloted by Doug Davis, John Worthen and Roscoe Turner. Lee Gehlbach was there with the big Gee Bee Q.E.D., a name adopted from the Latin phrase meaning "which was to be shown or demonstrated."[23] The racer was built for Jacqueline Cochran to fly in the MacRobertson Race. Murray Dilley was to fly the Vance "flying wing," conceived as a long range air freight carrier by the late Claire Vance. This airplane could fly the distance nonstop and although slower than the pure racing ships, would not loose time with refueling stops along the way. Last but not least, Jim Granger would drive the newly built Keith Rider R-3. For him, the Bendix was a precursor to the MacRobertson race.

The 1934 Bendix proved a disappointment to race fans and the sponsor, alike. At 3:00 a.m. on the morning of the race, Roscoe Turner – the pre-race favorite and first scheduled to depart –was unable to takeoff due to mechanical problems. Minutes later, Doug Davis in the red and black Wedell Williams racer roared down the runway and headed toward Cleveland. Two more racers launched that morning, Lee Gehlbach in the corpulent Gee Bee "Q.E.D." and Johnny "Red" Worthen in a brand new Wedell Williams racer featuring retractable landing gear. Like Roscoe Turner, Dilley and Granger were grounded with frustrating mechanical problems.

Doug Davis won the 1934 Bendix race, but not without experiencing a physically punishing flight. Davis climbed away from Union Air Terminal to 14,000 feet to clear the coastal mountain range. He quickly dropped down to 10,000

When Worthen flew the Bendix, the model 45 used a Wasp R-1344 engine. Worthen overflew Cleveland, landing at Erie, Pennsylvania. After a quick refueling, he back tracked to Cleveland. This navigation error cost him the race. Doug Davis beat him by 34 minutes. Credit: A.B. Bradley

This front view of the Wedell model 45, taken in 1933 when the aircraft was built, shows detail of the inward retracting landing gear. Wedell proposed a pursuit aircraft design similar to the model 45, designated by the Air Corp as the P-34. Wedell was killed in an airplane accident and the project was never completed. Credit: Birch Matthews collection

Chapter VI: Years Of Struggle

An interesting racing plane intended for the 1932 Bendix was Bob Hall's "Bulldog." This is the original short vertical stabilizer version. Unfortunately, the airplane never made it to the starting line. Credit: Pratt & Whitney Aircraft

feet and headed for Goodman, Kansas, and his first refueling stop. Within ten minutes, Davis was again airborne. He fought poor weather and head winds most of the trip. At times, the turbulence was so rough that his head hit the cockpit canopy. A second brief fuel stop was completed at Ford Airport in Illinois. Fighting fatigue, Davis began the final leg of his transcontinental run. Finally approaching Cleveland, he located the airport and wasted little time in getting the swift Wedell Williams racer onto the ground. He was one tired pilot after that exhausting flight. Davis was greeted with a congratulatory handshake from a smiling Vincent Bendix who told him that he was the first pilot to arrive. His elapsed time was a relatively slow nine hours and 26 minutes due to the adverse weather conditions. This was over an hour more than the record time set by Jimmy Haizlip in 1932. Nonetheless, it was good enough to win the race.

About 30 minutes later, Johnny Worthen lowered the gear on his Wedell Williams racer and landed at Cleveland. Expectations for Worthen's new racer were not realized. He became lost during the latter part of the race winding up over Lake Erie and had to retrace his route back to the airport.[24] The third aircraft to depart Union Air Terminal was the new Gee Bee racer named Q.E.D. Financier Floyd B. Odlum bought the Q.E.D. for Jackie Cochran who desperately needed a racer for the MacRobertson international air race. She had planned to race her brand new Northrop Gamma 2G. Royal Leonard was ferrying the Gamma east when the specially built supercharger for the Curtiss Conqueror engine failed. A crash landing which followed eliminated the unique Gamma from the MacRobertson.[25]

Lee Gehlbach lifted the Q.E.D., painted Lucky Strike green, away from Union Terminal early in the morning hours of 31 August. The Bendix Race was to be a shakedown run for the forthcoming MacRobertson Race. The idea of flying the racer in the Bendix was sold to Floyd Odlum by Gehlbach and he wanted to make a good showing; however, fate would not be kind to Lee. Somewhere during the first part of the race, "the big NACA cowl loosened up and Lee landed in Des Moines with the prop grinding hard into the leading edge."[26] The cowl attachment fittings proved too weak.[27] The cowling was removed at Des Moines and Gehlbach flew on to Cleveland at a low cruise speed arriving after the deadline.

Airshow events and pylon racing continued on into the afternoon at Cleveland. It soon became apparent that Lee Gehlbach, the third and last racer to leave California, was not going to beat the elapsed time of Doug Davis and he was declared the Bendix winner. Cliff Henderson and Vincent Bendix were anxious to recognize the Bendix Trophy Race

Jackie Cochran bought a Northrop Gamma 2G for the MacRobertson race. The airplane was powered by a liquid-cooled, supercharged Conqueror engine. Jackie entered the 1934 Bendix race as a tuneup for the longer England-to-Australia race. Credit: Northrop Corp. via Gerry Balzer collection

Cochran's two-place Gamma was a relatively large airplane with a wingspan of 47 feet, 10 inches and a fuel capacity of 438 gallons. Credit: Northrop Corp via Gerry Balzer collection

Supercharger problems plagued the Gamma 2G. Cochran was forced to withdraw from the Bendix when the supercharger failed two days before the race was to start. Credit: Northrop Corp via Gerry Balzer collection

Chapter VI: Years Of Struggle

victor before the day's program drew to a close. It was disappointing enough that only two planes finished the race and some ceremony was deemed necessary before the crowds left the field. Actress Mary Pickford was brought to the microphone at the announcers stand to offer congratulations and officially present the trophy to Doug Davis. The triumphant Davis was photographed in front of his racer receiving congratulations from Bendix, Cleveland Mayor Harry L. Davis and Louis E. Greve of the National Air Races governing body. It was a Phyrric victory. Davis died three days later when his Wedell crashed in the eighth lap of the Thompson Trophy Race!

Late on the evening of 31 August, Vincent Bendix – disappointed at how the race had turned out – hurriedly offered a consolation prize of $2500 to the remaining three pilots on the West Coast for the fastest flight to New York via Cleveland. If a new transcontinental speed record was established, the lucky pilot would receive an extra $1000.[28] All three of the stranded pilots – Turner, Dilley and Granger – quickly announced they would seek this special offer.[29] Only the stylish Roscoe Turner was able to take advantage of this unexpected windfall. He took off the next morning for Cleveland and then the East Coast. A record setting ten hours, two minutes and 51 seconds later, Turner set the golden Wedell Williams racer down at Floyd Bennett Field, the proud recipient of Bendix's largesse. In stark contrast, Murray Dilley and Jim Granger were still unable to get their mounts into the air.

DISASTER STRIKES THE RIDER RACER

A tragic post script to the trouble plagued Bendix Race involved Keith Rider's new racer. In spite of the problems which prohibited Jim Granger from starting the Bendix, preparations went ahead for the MacRobertson Race in October. Flight testing continued during September with Granger going aloft perhaps a dozen times in all.[30] As fate would have it, he would make only one more flight attempt. Late on Tuesday afternoon, October 2, mechanics lifted the aft fuselage of the racer and placed the tail skid on a two-wheel dolly.[31] The airplane was pulled out of Granger's hangar onto the ramp. His leather flying helmet and goggles in place, Jim slid into the cockpit. The Pratt & Whitney Wasp barked to life. The engine idled as Granger watched his instruments for any telltale sign of problems. Satisfied, he taxied out to the east end of Clover Field, ran the engine up checking the magnetos and then moved onto the runway.

Local interest in the racing project drew scores of spectators. Among them was designer Keith Rider and test pilot Vance Breese. They watched as Granger opened the throttle on the Wasp engine and the racer began to accelerate. Over-

Doug Davis receives a congratulatory handshake from Vincent Bendix after winning the 1934 Bendix race. On the near side of the airplane are Jimmy Doolittle and Jimmy Haizlip to the left of Bendix. Credit: Birch Matthews collection

head a Douglas DC-2 circled patiently waiting for the racer to clear the runway. As Granger began his takeoff roll, the tail came up rapidly and too far. The propeller struck the runway. Momentum carried the craft over flipping it inverted where it came to rest. Watching the accident, Vance Breese recalled that it seemed to be happening "in slow motion." Jim Granger struck his head on the runway surface as the vertical stabilizer failed structurally upon impact. When the accident occurred, two police officers sped out near the runway to wave off the Douglas transport turning final for landing. At the same time, Rider and Breese together with some mechanics and spectators ran to the crash site and pulled the pilot free of the cockpit.

Jim Granger was rushed to Santa Monica Hospital where Dr. Elmer Mortenson examined him and initially concluded that he would survive, suffering from a severe concussion and lacerations of the scalp. Early Wednesday morning, however, the pilot lost consciousness. He died later that afternoon apparently of a skull fracture.[32] All thought of competing in the MacRobertson Race evaporated with Granger's death.

What caused the accident? There was some disagreement among witnesses. Some years later, Keith Rider related that Granger compensated for engine torque by using the brakes. The brakes subsequently locked and the aircraft went over.[33] Engineering test pilot Vance Breese saw the accident from yet another perspective. In late 1961, he wrote that the airplane had "insufficient elevator (control) to lower the tail during takeoff." Stated another way, "pitch control was inadequate at low speed relative to the landing gear position (location) in relation to the center of gravity. The tail had to be held low for a takeoff run."[34] In his view, Granger brought the tail up a little too far and the propeller hit the runway causing the aircraft to

Jim Granger sits in the cockpit of the R-3 in preparation for a test flight. The airplane had poor low speed elevator control. During a takeoff from Clover Field, the tail rose too high and the propeller struck the ground flipping the airplane on its back. Granger died from injuries sustained in the accident. Credit: Roy Russel

Following the Clover Field accident with the Rider R-3, the racer was rebuilt, this time with a sliding cockpit canopy. Vance Breese performed limited testing on the airplane after the rebuilding process was finished. This photograph was taken prior to March, 1935. Credit: Emil Strasser collection

somersault onto its back. According to a Los Angeles Times report the engine sputtered suddenly causing Granger to abort his takeoff. One might infer from this that Granger reacted by hitting the brakes which caused the nose to pitch down and the propeller to strike the runway.

Of the three analyses, the newspaper account of an engine malfunction can probably be discounted. Neither Keith Rider nor Vance Breese indicated an engine problem. Both, however, acknowledged ineffective aerodynamic control at low speed. From Rider's account, torque produced by the engine was not completely overcome as Granger applied opposite rudder and thus he used braking to augment yaw control. Breese on the other hand, was concerned by the lack of adequate elevator (pitch) control at low speed once the pilot allowed the tail to come off the ground. If Granger let the tail get a bit too high, the elevator was inadequate to regain control. Vance Breese's technique for takeoff was essentially to lift the airplane off the runway in a three-point attitude to avoid low speed control deficiencies. In retrospect, the two explanations are not totally inconsistent.

Damage to Rider's new airplane was not really extensive. The cowling was deformed, the propeller twisted and the windscreen crushed. When the aircraft inverted, the vertical stabilizer took the brunt of the impact and sustained damage. The airframe was repaired and subsequently flown by Vance Breese during one or two familiarization flights. Gilmore Oil Company posted a modest amount of prize money for a record setting flight between San Francisco and Los Angeles. Vance took the R-3 to San Francisco and proceeded to make a speed dash (under one hour) between the two cities. The record gained some favorable publicity for Rider and also put a little money in the coffers.

ANOTHER YEAR, ANOTHER TRY

Cliff Henderson was getting ready for another year of racing. Interviewed by Julian Griffin of the Cleveland Press, Henderson acknowledged that . . . "it's going to take more than just a bunch of flyers racing and stunting to hold the interest of people here. But I feel sure our four-day program, beginning August 30, packs enough thrills and spectacular aerobatics to keep any group of spectators on the edge of their seats."[35] The Bendix lineup would prove Henderson's contention. The disappointing conclusion of the 1934 Bendix Trophy Race did not dampen enthusiasm for this year's contest when early on, it looked like as many as fourteen aircraft might be on hand for the start. There was a real chance the race would include foreign competition for the first time. "Officials in France are considering sending three planes, led by Maurice Rossi, co-holder of the world's distance record," according to newspaper accounts.[36,37] Rossi was planning to fly a French Renault racer. The French never appeared. Most likely the cost of sending a team to the United States proved too expensive. The depression, after all, was virtually world wide.

As so often happens, the field of racers began to dwindle rapidly as the starting date approached. The Wedell Williams Corporation had signed Waco Aircraft test pilot Bill Ong to fly their race 92. Ong ferried the racer from Patterson, Louisiana,

Earl Ortman was the third pilot to fly the Rider R-3. In July, 1935, Gilmore Oil Company sponsored a three-country record flight between Canada and Mexico. Earl made the flight and Rider finally made a little bit of money.

Chapter VI: Years Of Struggle

on his way to Burbank. He landed in Texas to refuel, took off again only to have the oil filler cap fly off. Oil splattered across the windshield and Ong quickly brought the airplane down, only to run into a ditch at the end of his landing roll.[38] The aging racer was out of the 1935 race.

CHEROKEE PILOT

The next pilot to fly the sleek Keith Rider racing plane was 23 year old Earl H. Ortman. Earl was born in the small town of Fort Gibson, Oklahoma. Of medium height and slender build, his dark hair and facial features betrayed a Cherokee Indian heritage. Ortman's family migrated from Fort Gibson to Ohio, while Earl was still a child. At some point later in life, Earl ventured out to the West Coast. He had a fascination with airplanes and flying and the West Coast offered opportunities.

Young Earl Ortman attended the Hancock Foundation College of Aeronautics in Santa Maria, California, located some 135 miles northwest of Los Angeles between the Coastal Range and the Pacific Ocean. The aviation college was established on the Santa Maria Airport in October 1928, by Captain G. Allen Hancock.[39] While learning to fly at the school, Earl became acquainted with classmate, Jack L. Bromberg.[40] It was through Bromberg that Earl got to fly the Rider R-3 racer. After college, Jack went to work as an engineer with Douglas Aircraft Company in Santa Monica, in what would become a long successful career. He ultimately retired as a vice president with the Douglas Missiles & Space Division. Jack met Hal Marcoux, Douglas chief of plant protection who, in turn, knew Keith Rider. He later recalled that Hal Marcoux had invested some money in Rider's (R-3) race project. As Bromberg explained it, "Earl's flying ability and urging by Hal and myself led to Keith's choice of Earl (as pilot) after Jim Granger's death."[41]

Ortman first flew the R-3 racer in June, 1935.[42] To gain publicity for the airplane, a record three-country flight attempt was planned from Canada to Mexico. The promotional flight was sponsored by Gilmore Oil, the Los Angeles company founded by Earl Gilmore and originally known as the Gilmore Petroleum Company. Gilmore's father, Arthur Fremont Gilmore, backed into the oil business quite by accident while drilling for water in 1903.[43] One oil strike quickly grew to 24 wells by 1918. Arthur's son Earl then established the Red Lion chain of gasoline stations along the West Coast and made his own fortune. Earl was a sportsman and aviation enthusiast with an interest in air racing. In 1932, he sponsored Roscoe Turner's Wedell Williams racer. Keith Rider turned to Gilmore and also succeeded in gaining his patronage. The wealthy Angelino would sponsor the airplane. This provided the money for the record flight attempt and "on the morning of July 3rd, Ortman lifted the R-3 away from Vancouver airport and pointed her nose southward. He sped into Mexico touch-

This view shows the Rider R-3 after the three-country record flight. The racer was finally beginning to demonstrate its potential, much to the relief of Keith Rider. Credit: Roy Russell

The travails of Keith Rider were not over. He entered the R-3 in the 1935 Bendix with Ortman as pilot. A Wasp S1D1 replaced the Wasp Jr. for added power. The main fuel tank developed a leak forcing Earl out of the Bendix at Kansas City. Credit: Roy Russell

ing down at Agua Caliente just 5 hours, 27 minutes and 48 seconds after takeoff bettering the old record by 1 hour and 12 minutes. The approximately 1400 mile distance had been negotiated at an average speed of about 250 miles per hour."[44]

After the record flight, Rider decided to install a more powerful engine in the racer. He acquired a used Wasp engine (serial number 5492) from United Airlines.[45] This was originally one of two S4D1-G models built and shipped to Boeing during October 1933, for use on the prototype 247-D transport.[46] The engine was converted at Boeing to a S1D1-G configuration by reducing the supercharger gear ratio from 12:1 to 10:1. When Rider acquired this engine, it was a direct drive configuration with a rating of 525 horsepower at 2200 revolutions per minute.[47] In addition to the engine change, the racer now sported a full cockpit enclosure adding a touch of streamlining to its overall appearance.

DOWN AND OUT AT KANSAS CITY

The re-engined racer was ready just 24 hours before the start of the 1935 Bendix. The modifications were made in a hurry, Ortman recalled, "with very limited funds, Mrs. Clark being away on a world cruise."[48] On August 29, Earl flew the R-3 in a final test flight only to have the cowling loosen (shades of the Q.E.D.) and pull forward into the propeller arc. He landed safely and it was discovered that damage to the cowl and propeller would not keep the racer out of the Bendix. Hurried repairs were made that would allow the airplane to fly the race.

At 4:25 a.m. the next morning, floodlights illuminated the gleaming polished silver finish of the Rider racer. The big radial engine ticked over at idle speed. Earl sat in the confined cockpit of the R-3 waiting for the starter's signal, his adrena-

This in-flight photograph over Southern California, shows the R-3 as it appeared during late 1935. The protruding landing gear wheel is clearly seen. Ortman is flying with the cockpit canopy open.

Chapter VI: Years Of Struggle

Earl Ortman sits on the wing of the rebuilt racer one week before the 1936 National Air Races held this year in Los Angeles. Credit: Emil Strasser

line pumping at peak capacity. At precisely 4:30 in the pre-dawn early morning darkness the starter's flag dropped. Ortman released the brakes, added throttle and the racer began to move.[49] Holding the tail down and applying rudder, Earl eased the racer into the air from a near three-point attitude. He immediately swung east toward a refueling stop at Kansas City on his way to Cleveland. Somewhere along the route, a crack developed in the fuselage fuel tank resulting in a gasoline leak. Earl landed at Kansas City for emergency repairs. He was out of the Bendix. With temporary repairs in place, Ortman proceeded to Cleveland in hopes of flying the Thompson Trophy Race. The race committee thought otherwise in view of the temporary cowl repair, gas tank leak and a scuffed propeller (from the previous incident with the loose cowling) and prudently declared the racer unsafe to fly let alone enter the Thompson. Years later, Earl would agree with their decision although at the time, he was no doubt very disappointed.

After the 1935 races, the R-3 was repaired by Jim Borton, owner of General Airmotive Corporation at Cleveland's Municipal Airport. Repairing the fuel leak meant that Borton had to pull the engine, mount and firewall before removing the main tank. "It seemed," Borton said, "as if the airplane had been built around the gas tank."[50] Indeed it was! The main gas tank extended from aft of the firewall to just in front of the cockpit. A second tank was located in the wing center section.

TOUGH TIMES

In addition to mechanical problems with the racer, Ortman was broke. Jim Borton loaned the pilot enough money to return to California while the plane was being repaired. In the end, Borton turned to Gilmore Oil Company to collect on his repair bills.[51] Gilmore had sponsored the racer in the Bendix and became a court of last resort for the Cleveland fixed-base operator. Times were tough. The Depression weighed heavily throughout the country. Ortman was finally able to fly the racer back to California, only to have it grounded by a mechanics lien against the Rider-Clark Aeroplane Corporation which held title.[52]

A NEW LEASE ON LIFE

Nineteen thirty-six marked a turn around of sorts for Ortman and the R-3. Earl was working as a mechanic for Douglas Aircraft and his association with Jack Bromberg and Hal Marcoux solved the immediate financial problems. In the end, Marcoux bought the airplane taking title on 18 July. His financial support at this juncture was crucial. Keith Rider was now out of the picture. He would go on to create other pylon racers, returning once again to the popular Menasco racing engines as the basis for his designs.

There would be no Bendix Trophy Race for Earl Ortman in 1936. The National Air Races moved to Los Angeles this year and apparently the team of Marcoux, Bromberg and Ortman collectively decided not to dilute their efforts with a costly, time consuming flight to the East Coast where the Bendix would begin. Their focus was on the closed-course Thompson Trophy pylon race. The airframe was extensively reworked in 1936. Bromberg designed another cowling to shroud the direct drive Wasp. The engine was overhauled by Ralph Bushey while the airframe was being rejuvenated by replacing large sections of fuselage skin. A new fuel tank was fabricated and installed. The wing was modified by blunting the leading edge of the NACA 2218 airfoil to improve stall

Gilmore Oil sponsored Ortman's racer in 1936. The aircraft was cream colored with red trim, the Gilmore colors, and carried race number 54. Ortman did not compete in the Bendix this year. Credit: Birch Matthews collection

Plans were made for extensive modifications to Ortman's racer after the 1936 races as depicted in this artist's sketch. A Pratt & Whitney Twin Wasp Jr. engine would be installed, the cockpit moved aft, the vertical fin modified and fairings added aft of the landing gear wheels in the retracted position. Credit: Jack Bromberg via Birch Matthews collection

characteristics. A one-eighth inch veneer was added to the wing surface for added strength. The oil tank was relocated behind the cockpit to improve balance and compensate for the S1D1 engine, some 150 pounds heavier than the earlier Wasp SB model. A final alteration was the return to an open cockpit. This was done for two reasons. The new large cowling took a toll on forward visibility. Cockpit ventilation was also poor and with the canopy in place it became very warm. There wasn't time to devise and install improved ventilation before races. The open cockpit was an expediency.

The reconditioned racer performed well. Flight tests produced an indicated speed at sea level of 312 miles per hour with a power setting of 2425 revolutions and 49 inches of manifold pressure. With sponsorship again provided by Gilmore Oil, Ortman was able to capture second place in the Thompson Trophy Race behind Frenchman Michael Detroyat. The latter's victory caused quite a stir among American air racing circles. Many felt the French Government subsidized Detroyat's machine and that this represented unfair competition to the private enterprise race plane builders in this country. In any event, the Marcoux-Bromberg racer – as it was now called – finally earned some prize money and this helped support modifications made the following year.

ONE MORE BENDIX RACE

The Marcoux-Bromberg-Ortman team envisioned an improved racing machine for 1937. The basis would be a still more powerful engine. Once again, they turned to Pratt & Whitney for assistance. As a consequence, arrangements were made to lease a Twin Wasp Jr., R-1535-11 production engine which would be modified for Ortman's racer. The engine Ortman would receive was a Model S1AG (serial number 422) originally used as a test unit to evaluate lubrication design improvements. This work took place in the Pratt & Whitney Experimental Department toward the end of March, 1936. A month later, the engine suffered a major failure during the test program. This failure was roughly coincident with the Marcoux-Bromberg team's request for a Twin Wasp Jr.[53] As a consequence, serial number 422 was rebuilt into an S2A5-G differentiating it from production engines then being supplied for Northrop's A-17A attack aircraft.[54] The principal change was installation of new blower gears providing a ratio of 11:1. The increased gear ratio allowed rated power up to 9600 feet.

The airframe was extensively rebuilt in 1937, under the critical eye of F.J. Roberts, another Douglas Aircraft employee. Work took place in an abandoned casket factory suggesting that the Marcoux-Bromberg team was not particularly superstitious. The rebuild was necessitated by the heavier more powerful Twin Wasp Jr. engine which imposed higher stress levels on the airframe. Heavier longitudinal stringers were added and the fuselage skin was replaced with heavier gage aluminum stock from the cockpit forward.[55]

Jack Bromberg calculated the thrust and static loads to the engine mount which would occur when the Twin Wasp Jr., and three-blade Hamilton Standard controllable pitch propeller were installed. A new welded tubular steel engine mount was built and attached to the firewall. The exhaust collector ring and cowling from an experimental Northrop A-17A completed the engine installation. This cowling was several inches greater in diameter than the fuselage resulting in a less than desirable aerodynamic condition.[56] Unfortunately, there

Chapter VI: Years Of Struggle

Racing Engines Used in the Marcoux-Bromberg Racer

Engine Model	Wasp, Jr. SB S/N 199[1]	Wasp S1D1 S/N 5492[2]	Twin Wasp Jr. S2A5G, S/N 422[3]
Horsepower Rating	400	525	700
Rated RPM	2200	2200	2500
Rated Altitude, Ft.	5000	5000	9600
Cruise Fuel Consumption, Lb/HP/Hr	0.60	0.48	0.48
Oil Consumption, Lb/HP/Hr.	0.035	0.035	0.035
Cylinder Bore, In.	5-3/16	5-3/4	5-3/16
Cylinder Stroke, In.	5-3/16	5-3/4	5-3/16
No. of Cylinders	9	9	14
Displacement, In.3	985	1344	1535
Overall Diameter, In.	45-3/4	51-7/16	44-1/8
Overall Length, In.	41-3/32	42-5/8	53-1/4
Compression Ratio	6:1	6:1	6.7:1
Blower Ratio	10:1	10:1	11:1
Prop. Gear Ratio	Direct Drive	Direct Drive	4:3
Dry Weight, Lb.	585	736	1070

Notes:
[1] Wasp, Jr., A series engine used in experimental P & W work converted to SB configuration and then shipped to Keith Rider.
[2] Acquired as a used engine from United Airlines.
[3] P & W serial number 422 was originally built as an R-1535-11 (S1A5-G), later modified to S2A5G.

was no time to deal with this deficiency before the races.

The fuel system was again reworked and the capacity increased. Total fuel capacity after modification was 240 gallons. The main tank alone held 125 gallons. All three fuel tanks utilized Douglas Aircraft filler necks permitting the use of two and three refuelling hoses at the same time, an advantage during the Bendix Race.

Externally, the lines of the racer changed somewhat due to the new engine and cowling. More subtle, however, was relocation of the cockpit approximately one foot aft of the former location and the return to an enclosed cockpit. Moving the cockpit aft also made room for the third fuel tank. The oil cooler was relocated to the lower aft portion of the fuselage in a small tunnel air scoop. The amount of air flowing through the scoop and oil radiator was regulated using a shutter thus giving a measure of oil temperature control. These extensive changes were necessary in large part because the new power package including engine, mount, cowling and propeller weighed considerably more than the old design. The Twin Wasp Jr., alone, was 175 pounds heavier than the previous Wasp S1D1. As a consequence, the airframe center of gravity shifted forward. With the relocation of the oil cooler, the center of gravity returned to a an acceptable location.

The rebuilt racer gave promise of better performance. The big Twin Wasp Jr. engine was factory rated at 700 horsepower. Ortman could pull perhaps 800 to 825 horsepower out of the engine at 2500 revolutions and manifold pressures in excess of 45 inches. What would the R-3 do in its new form? No documentation exists to specifically answer this question. In a pre-race press release, Jack Bromberg ". . . made some high speed calculations on Ortman's plane ranging from 366 to 389 mph."[57] In retrospect, this top speed appears somewhat optimistic. Years later, Earl Ortman recollected that the racer . . . "indicated great improvements in speed, smoothness of air flow and general handling characteristics . . .", although he acknowledged that: "No really accurate speed checks were made at this time, but I believe about 340 mph was available at sea level."[58]

The Marcoux-Bromberg team had great hopes for their entry. They believed it capable of winning the Bendix and had hopes of establishing a new transcontinental speed record by continuing on to the East Coast. Tempering this optimism was a formidable array of competition.

THE COMPETITION

There were twelve and by some newspaper accounts, as many as fifteen aircraft, entered in the 1937 Bendix. The newest and possibly the fastest racer – Roscoe Turner's "Meteor" – was

Statistical Details
Marcoux-Bromberg Racer

	1936	1937
Engine Model	S1D1	S2A5-G
Overall Length	21 Ft., 7 In.	23 Ft., 2 In.
Major Fuselage Dia.	40 Inches	40 Inches (46 Inches at cowl)
Wing Span	25 Ft., 5-1/2 In.	25 Ft., 5-1/2 In.
Wing Area	106 Ft.²	106 Ft.²
Maximum Chord	5 Ft., 7-1/4 In.	5 Ft., 7-1/4 In.
NACA Airfoil	2218 @ Center Section 2210 @ Wing Tip	2218 @ Center Section 2210 @ Wing Tip
Gross Wing Loading	39.4 Lb./Ft.²	48.5 Lb./Ft.²
Gross Weight	4175 Lb.	5142 Lb.
Empty Weight	2875 Lb.	3474 Lb.
C.G. Station	173.6 In.[1]	174.0 In.[1]
Fuel, Main Tank	117 Gallons	110 Gallons
Fuel, Tank No. 2	N/A	65 Gallons
Fuel, Wing Tank	50 Gallons	50 Gallons
Oil Capacity	15 Gallons	15 Gallons

Notes:
[1] Staion reference is the tail post which is station zero.
[2] Gross weight includes pilot, chute, fuel and oil

Left: Bromberg designed a new engine mount for the big Twin Wasp Jr. engine. The fuselage was beefed up to take the static and dynamic loads generated by the larger engine. Credit: Roy Russell

The racer was modified and rebuilt in an abandoned casket factory. Heavier skin was added to the fuselage. The men posing in back of the fuselage are from left to right, ?, ?, Frank Yamaguchi, Bud Pearson, Jack Bromberg and Hal Marcoux. Credit: Roy Russell

Chapter VI: Years Of Struggle

This photograph shows the Pratt & Whitney Twin Wasp Jr. S2A5G engine at the time of installation in the rebuilt racer. Credit: Birch Matthews collection

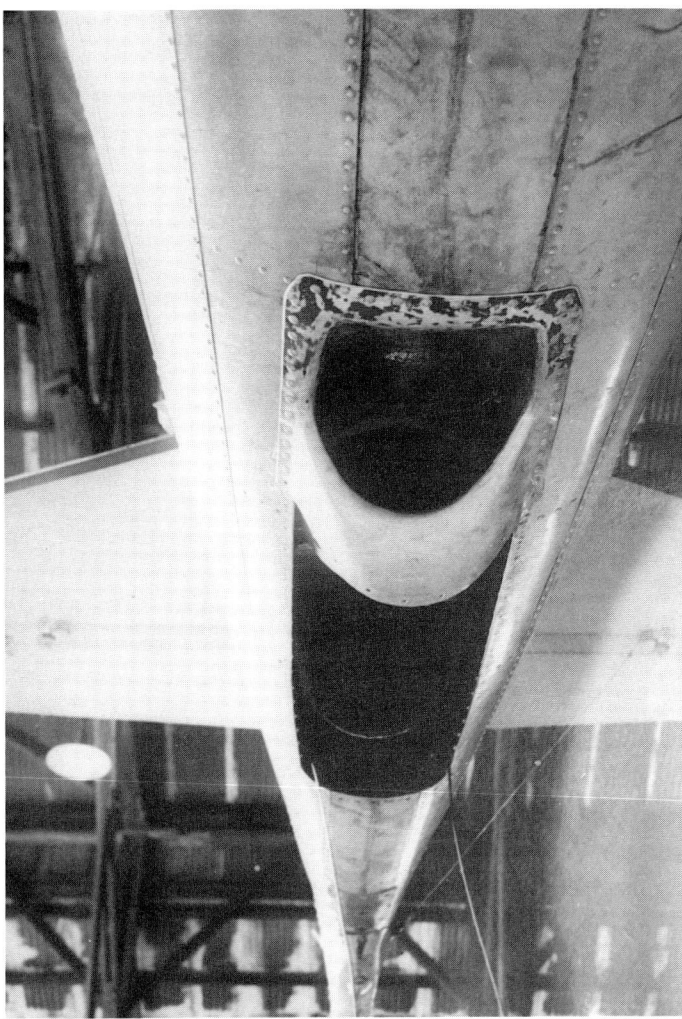

The oil cooler was moved to the aft fuselage and installed in a small duct. The move was necessary to correct the center of gravity location due to the heavier Twin Wasp Jr. engine. Credit: Birch Matthews collection

rolled out of Matty Laird's hangar in Chicago and flown for the first time on Saturday, 28 August 1937. After a 20 minute test flight, Turner announced that "the ship performed nicely in the air. It was the first time it has been off the ground," he told the press, "and I've still got to make some adjustments before racing."[59] Only six days remained before the start of the Bendix Race. Turner flew the silver Meteor again on Sunday and Monday. He took off for the West Coast on Tuesday only to become stranded in Albuquerque with a rough engine. The problem was corrected and Turner hurried into Burbank. He was still dogged by trouble. One of the fuel tanks was leaking. An attempt to make a welding repair resulted in a gasoline vapor explosion ruining the tank and damaging the airframe. Roscoe was out of the 1937 Bendix.

Three fast Seversky racers were entered in the Bendix. These were civilian versions of the relatively new Army Air Corp P-35 pursuit built by the exuberant Russian emigree Major Alexander P. de Seversky and his Seversky Aircraft Company in Farmingdale, Long Island. The Army selected the P-35 design in a contract tendered to Seversky for 77 aircraft on 16 June 1936, after a somewhat convoluted design competition beginning in 1935.[60] The military configuration of this airplane design had a top speed of 281 miles per hour at 10,000 feet. At cruise power, the P-35 had a range of up to 1000 miles. In racing form, these craft were undoubtedly lighter weight than their military counterparts.

Two of the Seversky racers were factory entries to be flown by Seversky and his chief test pilot, Frank Sinclair. The third plane belonged to wealthy San Francisco sportsman flyer Frank Fuller. Alexander Seversky planned an assault on the east-west transcontinental record on his flight to Burbank where the Bendix race would begin. Prior to leaving New York, Seversky flew to Hartford, Connecticut, to have Pratt & Whitney and Hamilton Standard technicians go over the engine and propeller. Returning from Hartford, Seversky entered his approach to Floyd Bennett Field and eased the

The finished 1937 Marcoux-Bromberg racer is shown in this illustration. The aircraft was all black except the cowl which was natural aluminum metal finish. Ortman is running an engine check in this late afternoon picture. Credit: Dusty Carter collection

This perspective of the Marcoux-Bromberg racer shows the small inlet beneath the cowl for the updraft carburetor. By today's fluid dynamic standards, this was a relatively inefficient scoop design. Credit: Dusty Carter collection

racer onto the runway. Suddenly, the left wheel started to squeal as the brake locked. The aircraft veered left, the landing gear collapsed and the racer ground looped to a standstill. Fire erupted as Seversky staggered away from wreck, shocked but basically unhurt. The fire was put out in short order. The racer was disassembled and ignominiously trucked back to Seversky's Farmingdale factory.[61] Seversky planes would still be represented in the Bendix because both Fuller and Sinclair flew to Burbank without incident.

Earlier that same day, Jackie Cochran departed North Beach Airport in her D-17W Staggerwing Beechcraft bound for the West Coast with an intermediate overnight stop in Kansas City. She arrived at Union Air Terminal on Sunday afternoon, 29 August together with Milo Burcham in a twin-engined Lockheed 12 owned by oil millionaire F.C. Hall. This was the same Hall that owned the Lockheed Vega, "Winnie Mae," and sponsored Wiley Post. Hall and his wife would be passengers in the Lockheed 12 during this year's transcontinental dash.

Eastern weather and an assortment of problems kept other entrants from reaching Burbank the next day and Bendix officials waived the requirement that all contestants arrive 48 hours in advance of the race. By Tuesday, Turner's second Bendix entry – the now aging Wedell Williams racer – arrived on the West Coast. It would be raced by Joe Mackey from Findley, Ohio. Another arrival was Earl Ortman in the black Marcoux-Bromberg after a short hop from Mines Field. At this point in his career, Ortman was the personal pilot of movie actor Wallace Beery. Yet another to arrive was Clevelander E.C. "Sonny" Sundorph and co-pilot John Yost in the high wing all-metal Sundorph Special. Bendix race officials had been concerned for their safety until Sundorph finally landed at 8:00 p.m. almost an hour later than his scheduled arrival.

TAKEOFF

Floodlit Union Air Terminal was busy in the wee hours of Friday morning, 3 September, as officials prepared to launch contestants for the 1937 Bendix Trophy Race. First off was Jackie Cochran in her green Beech Staggerwing at just after 3 a.m. Starter Larry Therkelson waved seven more contestants away that morning. One near tragedy occurred when Bob Perlick's takeoff was aborted by a collapsed landing gear on his fast Beechcraft A-17F Staggerwing.

The fastest aircraft in the 1937 Bendix race were the two remaining Seversky racers and Earl Ortman's revamped Marcoux-Bromberg. The Serversky's had greater range and were equipped with oxygen systems. In fact, Fuller ran his race at altitudes up to 16,000 feet.[62] He refueled once in route at Kansas City, flashed across the finish line at Cleveland without landing, took the checkered flag and climbed away headed for Bendix, New Jersey. His one refueling stop was enough for the transcontinental hop. Fuller's elapsed time to Cleveland was just under eight hours, enough to garner first place.

Earl Ortman was the last to leave Burbank with an 8 a.m. departure. Unlike the two Seversky racers, Earl didn't have oxygen onboard his plane forcing him to fly at lower altitudes. Leaving California behind, Ortman flew almost due east to Amarillo, Texas, for his first fuel stop.[63] Out of Amarillo, Earl pointed the racer northeast and a second stop at Kansas City for more fuel. Beyond Kansas City, Earl ran into some unpleasant weather. He tried to climb over the weather and this was a mistake. He went too high and became dazed and disoriented due a lack of oxygen. Earl let the racer drift north off course and wound over Lake Michigan before he finally realized his problem.[64] It was a mistake that might have cost

Cliff Henderson staged the first National Air Race program to occur in Los Angeles. The stylized art on this 1928 race program cover was fashionable during that era. Credit: John Garrett collection

The Experimental Aircraft Association restored the Laird Super Solution which Jimmy Doolittle flew to victory in the inaugural Bendix Trophy Race of 1931. Credit: EAA

Matty Laird gave a lot of thought and attention to drag reduction for this airplane. It paid off. The racer was far and away the fastest entrant in the 1931 Bendix. Credit: EAA

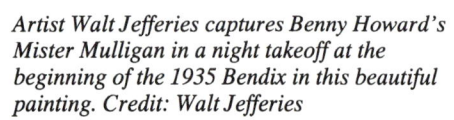

Artist Walt Jefferies captures Benny Howard's Mister Mulligan in a night takeoff at the beginning of the 1935 Bendix in this beautiful painting. Credit: Walt Jefferies

Artist Charles Hubbell created this 1931 air race program cover. Hubbell was retained by Thompson Products, Inc., to produce a series of aircraft paintings for the company's calendars which soon became collectors items. Credit: John Garrett collection

Originally designed by Keith Rider, the Marcoux-Bromberg racer was always a contender in the National Air Races. The old veteran was restored by the New England Air Museum and is on display to the public. Credit: Bob Stepanek

The Marcoux-Bromberg racer was restored to the colors and markings of its 1939 configuration. The restoration is exceptionally clean. The airplane looks ready to fly! Credit: Bob Stepanek

Color Gallery

This 1938 cover is from a Bendix race program issued for the start of the classic transcontinental contest at Burbank, CA. Credit: John Garrett collection

Above: This illustration is a computer generated representation of the Gee Bee R-2 racer. Analysis of the R-2 was done using a computer code to calculate the subsonic flow field about the airframe. The analytical model is known as VSAERO and was developed by Analytical Methods, Inc. Credit: David Lednicer

Above right: This is another view of the R-2 computer generated image. The pressure coefficient distribution about the airframe is shown by color index. On the color scale to the right, dark blue represents stagnation pressure where air velocity is zero. The middle of the color scale, yellow to green, shows a pressure and velocity close to the free air stream conditions. Colors between the middle of the scale and red are areas of suction or very low pressure. Credit: David Lednicer

Right: Another way of visualizing pressure distribution is presented in this computer image of the R-2 racer. The lines are called isobars and represent constant pressure coefficient values. The leading contour of the wheel pants and wing leading edge are dark indicating stagnation pressure conditions. The wings show dark red lines indicating low pressure on the upper surface. Credit: David Lednicer

Below: The Marcoux-Bromberg racer was also modeled using VSAERO. This illustration represents the 1937 version when the Twin Wasp Jr. engine was installed. A six inch differential existed between the cowl and major fuselage diameter, a not very satisfactory aerodynamic condition. Credit: David Lednicer

Below right: The Marcoux-Bromberg racer model was adjusted to reflect the 1939 configuration when a 42 inch long fairing was added just aft of the cowl to eliminate the previous discontinuity. The fairing blended the contour from the cowl to the fuselage thereby reducing a bit of drag. Credit: David Lednicer

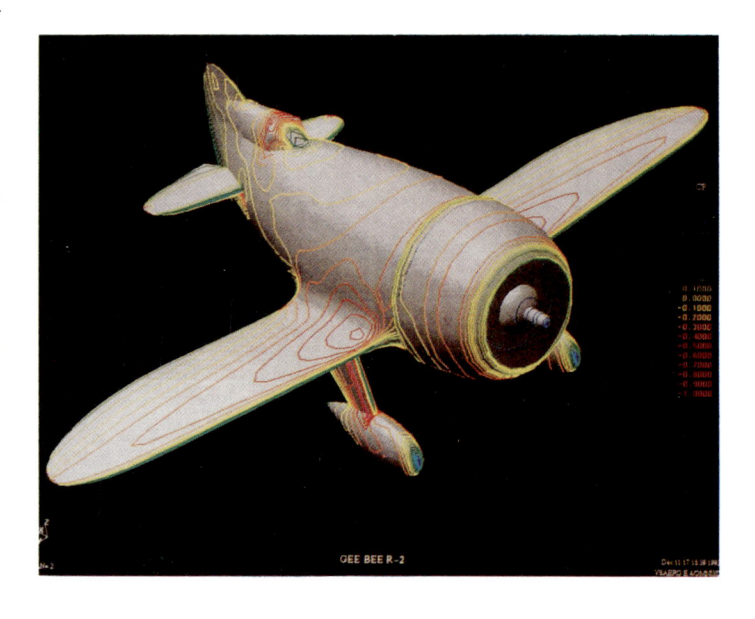

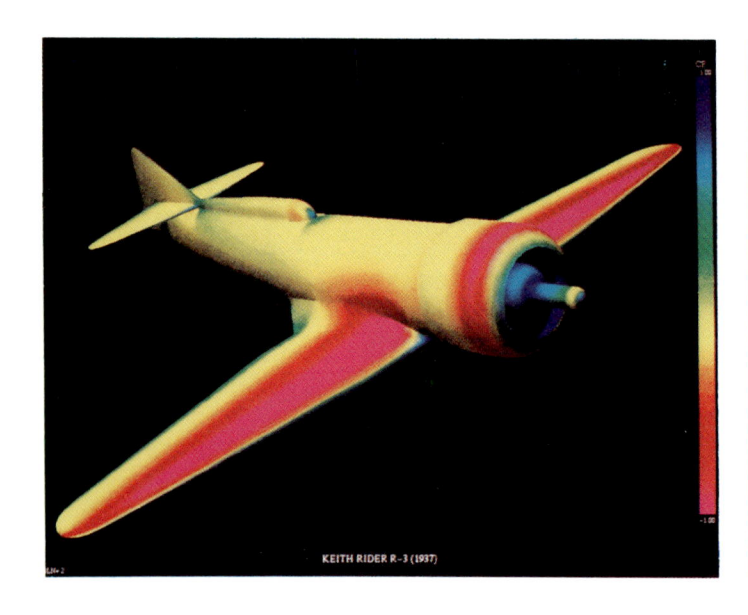

The last National Air Races before World War II were held at Cleveland in 1939. Hitler's invasion of Poland coincident with the races brought an end to air racing. Credit: John Garrett collection

The National Air Races resumed after the war in 1946. Note that the price of a program only increased by ten cents from the 1928 program cost. A 1992 Reno air race cost $4, over eleven times the 1946 program price! Credit: John Garrett

Color Gallery

Paul Mantz flew N1204 to victory in the 1948 Bendix Trophy Race. The airplane was part of the Tall-Mantz Museum collection at the Orange County airport for many years. This photograph was taken in June 1968. Credit: Dusty Carter

Jane Page placed ninth in the 1947 Bendix with this F-5G-6 Lockheed Lightning. The aircraft was all natural finish with red racing and license numbers. Credit: William Greeley

Chuck Tucker is seen in this photograph standing on the wing of his white P-63C-5 Thompson Trophy racer. This was the fastest Kingcobra that ever raced on a pylon course. Credit: Phil Krause collection

Color Gallery

109

Although the colors on this 1946 photograph have deteriorated with age, it is still possible to see that Tommy Mason's Bendix racer had red wings and a red spinner. The remainder of the plane was unpainted. Credit: Birch Matthews collection

Herman "Fish" Salmon raced Mantz's N1202 Mustang to third place in the 1949 Bendix. The airplane was taxiing in front of the Cleveland grandstands when this picture was taken. Credit: Fred Buehl

World flyer Bill Odom flew from Honolulu to New Jersey in this vee-tailed Beech Bonanza. The aircraft was named Waikiki Beech. Odom is seen here at the 1949 air races. Credit: Birch Matthews collection

Stan Reaver placed second in the 1949 Bendix race. Both Paul Mantz Mustangs had identical paint schemes differing only by race and license numbers and the name of the pilot. Credit: Fred Buehl

Color Gallery

Jackie Cochran decided to enter the 1946 Bendix race in the eleventh hour. She didn't have a wet wing to compete with Paul Mantz. Nonetheless, she finished second in her "green machine." Credit: Paul Penrose via Steve Sheflin

Benny Howard smiles for the camera in one of the official cars at the 1946 National Air Races. Howard was a race consultant to Jackie who is sitting next to him. Credit: Paul Penrose via Steve Sheflin

Jackie left nothing to chance in her determination to excel in the Bendix. Before the 1946 race, she had a priest bless her Mustang racer. Credit: Paul Penrose via Steve Sheflin

Before Jackie decided to fly in the 1946 Bendix, she was considering Paul Penrose as the pilot. Paul is seen here on the wing of Jackie's airplane. Jackie is in the cockpit. Credit: Paul Penrose via Steve Sheflin

Chapter VI: Years Of Struggle

When the Twin Wasp Jr. engine was installed in 1937, there was a six inch discontinuity between the engine cowl and major fuselage diameter. This poor aerodynamic condition was carried over into 1938 when the racer flew in the Oakland, California races. Credit: Birch Matthews collection

The cowl-fuselage discontinuity was eliminated for the 1938 National Air Races as shown in this photograph. A 42 inch long fairing extended from the aft end of the cowl to the fuselage. The scoop on top of the fuselage fed fresh into the cockpit. Credit: William Yeager

1937 Bendix Race Start

Race No.	Pilot	Aircraft	E.S.T.[1]
13	J. Cochran	Beechcraft D-17W	3:04:00
17	E. Sundorph	Sundorph SPL	3:20:00
12	M. Burcham	Lockheed 12	4:44:00
63	F. Sinclair	Seversky SEV-1XP	6:39:00
23	F. Fuller	Seversky SEV-S2	6:55:00
4	E. Ortman	Marcoux-Bromberg	8:00:00
25	J. Mackey	Wedell-Williams	Did Not Finish
64	R. Perlick	Beechcraft A-17F	Crashed on Takeoff

Notes:
[1] Eastern Standard Time
[2] Source: Official 1937 National Air Race Results

him the race although this is doubtful. Ortman's racer and the Seversky airplanes had roughly comparable top speeds, but Fuller's mount could span the continent with only one fuel stop, a decided advantage. Back on course, he raced for Cleveland arriving only eleven minutes before the six o'clock deadline. His elapsed time, however, was still good enough for second place. In three tries at the Bendix, the racer had finally finished in the money. An odd footnote to Earl's Bendix finish is the fact that his average speed was posted at just under 225 miles per hour. This was a timer's calculation error perpetuated now for well over five decades! His real average speed was a little less than 208 miles an hour (see Appendix A).

NOTES:
1 Venlo Wolfsohn, "World's Greatest Air Race," *American Modeler*, December 1959, p. 14.
2 Financing air racing projects remains an obstacle in this day and age. Fortunately, there are still wealthy individuals interested in the sport who are willing to finance new and innovative projects.
3 Manufactured by the Swallow Airplane Manufacturing Company founded by financier Jacob Melvin Moellendick.
4 *Western Flying*, July 1934, p. 24.
5 On 16 May 1934, the Department of Commerce granted a certificate of title to Keith Rider for his new design. The certificate listed the model number as A-1 and a registration (license number) of X-14215 signifying an experimental airplane. The racer was never commonly referred to as the "A-1."
6 This was a relatively common practice among most aircraft designers during the 1930s and 1940s. Note, for instance the series of twin-tailed Lockheeds, the similarity in general empennage configuration on Douglas DC series aircraft as well as others.
7 The serial number signified this engine was the 27th one built in Pratt & Whitney's experimental department. This particular engine was originally installed in James H. Doolittle's 1931 Bendix Trophy winning Laird Super Solution, based upon correspondence to the author from Harvey H. Lippincott, Pratt & Whitney Aircraft, 26 July 1961.
8 Ibid.
9 *New York Times*, 31 May 1934, p. 17.
10 *New York Times*, 2 June 1934, p. 9.
11 *Western Flying*, September, 1934, p. 11. This same number would be retained for the abortive attempt to race in the 1934 Bendix Race.
12 Lippincott, op.cit. This letter quotes a report filed by a Pratt & Whitney representative who visited Keith Rider in June, 1934.
13 Ibid.
14 *Los Angeles Times*, 30 August 1934, Part II, p. 1-2.
15 Booton Herndon, *Mary Pickford and Douglas Fairbanks*, W.W. Norton & Company, Inc., New York, 1977, p. 290. Mary Pickford filed for divorce on 8 December 1933, and the dissolution of the marriage became final a year later.
16 *Los Angeles Times*, 31 August 1934, Part II, p. 1.
17 Ibid.

Earl Ortman poses beside the Marcoux-Bromberg racer. It took a skilled pilot to handle this marginally stable airplane. Earl was the only pilot to race the airplane. Credit: Birch Matthews collection

Chapter VI: Years Of Struggle

18 Mike Kusenda, "Mr. Mulligan", American Aviation Historical Society, Cleveland Chapter Newsletter, March 1975, p. 3. Anoxia is an abnormally low content of oxygen in the body tissues in this instance caused by flying at very high altitudes without a supplemental oxygen source.
19 S.H. Schmid and Truman C. Weaver, "The Golden Age of Air Racing," Vol. 2 EAA Aviation Foundation, Inc., (undated) p. 340.
20 Charles G. Mandrake "The Gee Bee Story," The Robert R. Longo Company Inc., Wichita, Kansas, 1957. p. 73.
21 Phillip C. Brown, "The Fabulous Gee Bees," American Aviation Historical Society JOURNAL, Vol. 24, No. 3, Fall, 1979, p. 198.
22 Henry A. Haffke, "Gee Bee," VIP Publishers, Inc., Colorado Springs, 1989, p. 138.
23 Q.E.D. is short for the Latin phrase "quad erat demonstrandum" and is a term frequently used in mathematical proofs.
24 *Los Angeles Times*, 1 September 1934, p. 2.
25 Jacqueline Cochran, *The Stars At Noon*, Little, Brown & Company, p. 52.
26 Robert H. Granville, *The Q.E.D. Racer, The Golden Age of Air Racing*, second revised edition, S.H. Schmid and Truman C. Weaver, EAA Aviation Foundation, Oshkosh, Wisconsin, p. 329.
27 Cowl attachment fittings on the Q.E.D. probably failed due to one of two reasons. A detail stress analysis on the fitting design may not have been done or the load assumed in the analysis was too small. The other likely failure mode was defective material due to design or manufacture resulting in a stress concentration ultimately leading to a part failure. The state-of-the-art for structural analysis and for non-destructive testing was embryonic in the early 1930s compared to today.
28 *New York Times*, 1 September 1934, p. 15.
29 Ibid.
30 Correspondence from Keith Rider to the author dated 23 September 1961.
31 *Los Angeles Times*, 3 October 1934, Section II, p. 1.
32 *Los Angeles Times*, 4 October 1934, Section II, p. 2.
33 Rider, op.cit.
34 Correspondence from Vance Breese to the author, circa late 1961.
35 Julian Griffin, "Pylon Polishers," *The Cleveland Press*, 14 August 1935, Section II, p. 1.
36 Ibid.
37 *Los Angeles Times*, 28 August 1935, Part II, p. 8.
38 Bob Hirsch, "Wedell-Williams Air Service Corporation and Air Racing," American Aviation Historical Society JOURNAL, Vol. 34, No. 2, 1989, p. 132.
39 Robert F. Schirmer, "AAC & AAF Civil Primary Flying Schools, 1939-1945, Part VIII, Santa Maria Primary," American Aviation Historical Society JOURNAL, Vol. 37, No. 4, 1992, p. 300. According to Schirmer, the name of the school was subsequently shortened to Hancock College of Aeronautics.
40 Correspondence from Jack L. Bromberg to the author, 19 May 1961.
41 Ibid. Ortman knew Keith Rider in 1934, and flew the Rider R-2, known as the Bumblebee, during the 1934 National Air Races.
42 Correspondence to Mrs. Ruth M. Fox from Earl Ortman, dated 27 April 1947.
43 *Los Angeles Times*, 11 January 1993, p. B3.
44 Birch J. Matthews, "Often a Bridesmaid," American Aviation Historical Society JOURNAL, Vol. 7, No. 2, 1962, p. 11.
45 Apparently Rider and Ortman got a real bargain price from United. In a letter to the author from Harvey H. Lippincott, dated 29 June 1961, it was noted that "Mr. (Ray) Peck recalls that Ortman purchased the engine for a ridiculously low sum from United Airlines."
46 The "G" designation indicated that propeller reduction gearing was incorporated.
47 In a direct drive engine, the propeller turns at the same speed as the engine crankshaft. In a geared engine, propeller speed is lower than the crankshaft speed by an amount equal to the reduction gear ratio.
48 Ortman correspondence, op.cit.
49 Matthews, op cit., p. 11.
50 Interview by the author with James Borton, President, General Airmotive Corporation, 11 March 1961.
51 Ibid.
52 The Rider-Clark Aeroplane Corporation was formed in early 1935, with an address listed as 1800 Pontins Avenue, West Los Angeles, California. Keith Rider was listed as president. The name implies that Mrs. Clark was still supplying financial backing. On 30 April of that year, the racer was sold by Rider to the corporation. It might be assumed that Edith Clark supplied the purchase price and this became the capital for the new company. Among other things, this probably allowed Rider to obtain and install the used Wasp S1D1 direct drive engine.
53 Subsequently, another S1A5-G was built up for the Army to replace the test engine that failed. H. H. Lippincott correspondence, 23 June 1961, op cit.
54 Because the engine was not delivered as part of the Air Corps contract, it never received an Air Corp serial number and thus retained the manufacturer's serial number.
55 Fox correspondence op.cit. Consideration was being given to installing a new engine of even more horsepower to the R-3 airframe and entering it in the post-war National Air Races. Ortman advised against doing this as he believed the airframe was not stressed to accommodate an engine of greater weight and power. He did believe that installation of a water injection system, use of improved fuels and spark plugs might make the old racer somewhat competitive. In the end, the project was abandoned.
56 This deficiency was corrected in the 1938 version of the racer.
57 National Air Race press release dated 2 September 1937.
58 Ortman correspondence, op. cit.
59 *New York Times*, 29 August 1937, p.22.
60 Edward T. Maloney, *Sever The Sky - Seversky Aircraft Evolution*, World War II Publications, Corona Del Mar, California, 1979, pp. 17-18.
61 *New York Times*, 2 September 1937, p. 14.
62 *New York Times*, 4 September 1937, p. 7.
63 National Air Race Press Release dated 2 September 1937.
64 "The Races," *Western Flying*, October 1937, pp. 11-12.

Gee Bee
SUPER
SPORTSTER
7
NR 2101
Granville Bros. Aircraft
Springfield Airport
2410

Chapter VII

POTPOURRI

During the early years, the Bendix was won by airplanes specifically designed to meet the singular criterion of maximum speed. These were single point designs unencumbered with a variety of complex often competing requirements related to military or commercial operations. With respect to pure speed, however, the Bendix race demonstrated aeronautical development through refinements in aerodynamic streamlining and the application of copious amounts of horsepower. These races also illustrated that the continental coasts were less than 12 hours apart, a time increment that would continue to shrink as the years advanced.

TERRIFIC TRIO

The Bendix Trophy Race ran uninterrupted for nine years before World War II. After Jimmy Doolittle captured the inaugural race in 1931, the "Model 44" design of race plane builder Jimmy Wedell from Patterson, Louisiana, overshadowed all competitors for the next three years compiling a fantastic record of three victories, three second and two third place finishes. Perhaps the most impressive feat was Jimmy Haizlip's 1932 Bendix win at 245 miles per hour, a record that would stand for five years. Haizlip eclipsed Doolittle's elapsed time by almost an hour. This string of victories nearly extended into 1935, when Turner in his aging Wedell racer ran second behind Benny Howard's Mr. Mulligan racer losing by a fraction of a minute in the closest transcontinental race in history.

James Robert "Jimmy" Wedell was born in the small Gulf Coast town of Texas City, Texas, on 3 March 1900, at the turn of the century.[1] Handsome, slightly built with an unruly shock of hair over his forehead, Jimmy was a self-taught technician, an amazing feat considering his limited ninth grade education. He had an insatiable appetite for reading especially about things mechanical. This led to an interest in flying and eventually to a life of barnstorming along the Gulf Coast and running contraband across the Mexican border in a Curtiss JN4. Jimmy finally concluded this might well be an unhealthy business with an uncertain life expectancy. About 1927, Jimmy and his brother Walter migrated to New Orleans and began a fixed base operation consisting of aircraft maintenance, flight instruction and charter service.

Quite by accident, Wedell ran into a rich Southern gentleman by the name of Harry Williams and this meeting would lead to air racing history. Life long air race historian Bob Hirsch best describes how this occurred. Jimmy Wedell was flying "in the Louisiana State Aerial Tour about September, 1927, and was in the lead when on the last leg (of the tour) back to New Orleans, he was about 75 miles west when his engine quit. He spiraled down looking for a field and found one near the lake shore at Patterson, Louisiana. Jimmy got a lift to town where he met and talked with a wealthy sportsman and business entrepreneur as well as town mayor, Harry Palmerson

Opposite: Wealthy sportsman pilot Russell Boardman ordered two new Gee Bee racers in 1932. He poses in this 1933 picture with the transcontinental version, the Gee Bee R-2. Credit: United Technologies Corp., John Garrett collection

Williams."[2] While repairing his airplane, Wedell decided that the Patterson area was an excellent location for his flying operations. With the help of his new friend, Harry Williams, Jimmy acquired land, built a hangar and started his business. Williams continued his interest in Jimmy's flying enterprise eventually financing what became the Wedell-Williams Air Service Corporation.

Jimmy Wedell built his first air racer in 1928. It was not until 1932, though, that Wedell designs became famous. Wedell built three airplanes for racing that year and they were informally identified as the model 44 design based upon Jimmy's long time interest in firearms. Two were owned by the Wedell-Williams Corporation. The third airplane was built under the sponsorship of Gilmore Oil Company for the flamboyant Roscoe Turner. Interestingly, each of the three airframes would win the Bendix Trophy Race in succeeding years, a remarkable achievement and superb testimony to the talent of Jimmy Wedell. Ironically, Jimmy Wedell would never be in the Bendix winner's circle, placing second in 1932, and again in 1933.

JIMMY HAIZLIP

The most notable Bendix winner flying one of Wedell's creations was Jimmy Haizlip in the black and white racer 92 in 1932. Haizlip stood only four-feet, eleven-inches. If he was short in stature, he was long on ability and drive. Sitting on the starting line in Burbank, California, Haizlip pushed the throttle forward on his Wasp Jr.-powered Wedell-Williams at exactly

Cliff Henderson poses beside a Stinson Model R which was the official plane for the Cord Corporation, sponsor of several cross-country events during the 1932 National Air Races. Credit: Sid Bradd collection

3:45 a.m.[3] Heading east in the empty blackness of pre-dawn, Jimmy guided the racer across the northern reaches of Arizona and into Colorado. Crossing the Rocky Mountains, Jimmy was fast approaching a familiar landmark under his left wing tip, Pike's Peak. East of the mountain, he flew over Colorado Springs and began his long downhill run toward the flatlands of Kansas. His first refueling would take place at Goodland, Kansas, in the northeastern corner of the state.

A quick landing at Goodland for 80 octane aviation gasoline took no more than ten minutes and Jimmy Haizlip was once more in the air headed for the Chicago area. South

Wedell-Williams Model 44 Racers

Year	Bendix Position	Race No.	License Number	Pilot
1932	1st	92	NR536V	James H. Haizlip
	2nd	44	NR278V	James R. Wedell
	3rd	121	NR61Y	Roscoe Turner
1933	1st	2	NR61Y	Roscoe Turner
	2nd	44	NR278V	James R. Wedell
1934	1st	44	NR278V	Douglas Davis
	2nd	45	NR62Y*	John Worthen
1935	2nd	57	NR61Y	Roscoe Turner

* Wedell-Williams Racer NR62Y was designated a Model 45. It was a derivative of the Model 44 incorporating retractable landing gear among other variations.

Chapter VII: Potpourri

The three Wedell Williams racers are lined up in front of the Thompson Aeronautical Corporation (TAC) hangar at Cleveland airport. TAC was a subsidiary of Thompson Products, sponsors of the Thompson Trophy Race. Haizlip's 92 is on left, Wedell's 44 in center and Turner's 121 on the right. Credit: Birch Matthews collection

Jimmy Wedell (arms folded) and his crew pose for a photograph in front of the speedy number 44 Wedell Williams racer. The airplane was painted a glossy red and black. Credit: Birch Matthews collection

Number 44 sits uncowled in the Thompson hangar, ready for maintenance. The racer was light, weighing in at under 2000 pounds empty. Credit: Birch Matthews collection

Jimmy Haizlip flew this black and white Wedell Williams racer to victory in the 1932 Bendix race at an average speed of 245 miles per hour. Credit: Birch Matthews collection

of the heart of the city, Jimmy landed the Wedell at Lansing, Illinois, close to the Indiana state line. This refueling stop was even shorter than Goodland. Haizlip was on his way within five minutes, headed out across the southern tip of Lake Michigan bound for Cleveland. Weather had not been much of a factor in the flight thus far, but this changed as he approached Ohio. Jimmy ran into rain showers so common to the northern Ohio region in early September. Sliding and bouncing in the turbulence beneath the dark rain clouds, Haizlip found the Cleveland airport and briefly circled, loosing altitude. He roared across the Bendix finish line in front of the grandstands at low altitude to alert the timers, climbed eastward and disappeared in the sky.

Haizlip did not touch down at Cleveland. He continued eastward in his quest for a new coast-to-coast flying record. Over the center of Pennsylvania, he broke out of the rain and clouds catching a welcome late afternoon sun. Passing north of Allentown, Jimmy soon picked up the distinctive skyline of New York City as he lost altitude. Haizlip settled the small black and white racer onto Floyd Bennett Field two hours after flashing past the Cleveland airport. As his wheels touched the ground, Charles Gale of the National Aeronautics Association marked the time at four minutes past six in the afternoon.

The Wedell racer rolled to a stop before an excited crowd. Tired and hungry from his ordeal, a happy Jimmy Haizlip nonetheless smiled and waved at photographers and well

Jimmy Haizlip's wife, Mary Haizlip, was an accomplished pilot in her own right. She placed second in the Cleveland Pneumatic Tool Company Race for women pilots flying the number 92 Wedell during the 1932 races. Credit: Birch Matthews collection

In this photograph, five of the Bendix pilots are pictured before the race. They were, from left to right, Lee Gehlbach, Jimmy Haizlip, Roscoe Turner, Jimmy Wedell and Claire Vance. Credit: Acme photo from Sid Bradd collection

Chapter VII: Potpourri

AT CHATEAU BENDIX, SOUTH BEND, INDIANA, SEPTEMBER 7TH, 1932
Guests of Mr. Vincent Bendix, President Bendix Aviation Corporation at conclusion of National Air Races

Major James H. Doolittle, winner of 1931 Bendix Trophy Race and Transcontinental Record, 11 hours, 16 minutes; Capt. James C. Haizlip, winner of 1932 Bendix Trophy Race and Transcontinental Record, 10 hours, 20 minutes; James Wedell, winner of second place Bendix Trophy Race; Col. Roscoe Turner, winner of third place Bendix Trophy Race and also breaking previous Transcontental Record. Lieut. Placido Abreau of Portugal, Lieut. Jean Assolant of France, Flight Commander R. L. R. Atcherly of England, Col. George Kossowski of Poland, Herr Emil Kropf of Germany, and Lieut Andrea Zotti of Italy, comprising 1932 team of International flyers; Major Alexander P. de Seversky, Russian Ace, and Mrs. de Seversky; Mr. James Mattern, Trans-Atlantic flyer; Major E. E. Aldrin, Chairman Stanavo Specifications Board and Manager International Team of Flyers; Mr. Cliff Henderson, Managing Director of National Air Races; Bendix Executives and South Bend guests.

Wealthy industrialist, Vincent Bendix, hosted a gathering at his Chateau Bendix in South Bend, Indiana, after the 1932 races. Among the luminaries were Wedell, Haizlip, Doolittle, Turner and de Seversky. Credit: Bendix Corporation, Sid Bradd collection

Jimmy Wedell's beautiful black and red number 44 racer was named "Miss Patterson." This 1933 picture was taken at Pratt & Whitney, Hartford, CT. The Wasp Jr. engine had been replaced with the more powerful Wasp engine covered by a new cowling. Credit: Pratt & Whitney, Phil Krause collection

Wedell took second place in the 1933 Bendix, losing to Roscoe Turner in another Wedell Williams racer. This photograph of race 44 was made at the Chicago air races in 1933. Credit: A.B. Bradley

There was no doubt that the Gee Bee design possessed a rather wide girth as shown in this full rear view. In spite of this, it was a well thought out design based upon wind tunnel experimentation. Credit: United Technologies, John Garrett collection

was level or appeared to be so indicating that wing failure was not due to high "g" load."[5]

In other words, the wing structurally failed prior to the nose pulling up and the start of the snap roll. The Model Z ailerons were neither statically nor dynamically balanced. The airplane was traveling at maximum velocity and vibrations induced by aileron flutter could easily have resulted in a structural failure. Modern accident investigation methods including metallurgical examination of components might have conclusively revealed the cause of the accident. Absent this type of information, one can only speculate with the information available.

Opposite: A smiling Russell Thaw poses in front of the Gee Bee R-2, now powered with a Wasp engine. Thaw, after witnessing Russ Boardman's sickening crash during takeoff from Indianapolis, promptly withdrew from the Bendix. Note what appears to be a rectangular air scoop beneath the cowl for an updraft carburetor. Credit: United Technologies, John Garrett collection

Cecil Allen purchased the gee Bee R-2 remains, lengthened the fuselage, installed a Pratt & Whitney Hornet engine and entered the 1935 Bendix. He crashed fatally during takeoff. Credit: Dusty Carter collection

Chapter VII: Potpourri

Benny Howard's snow white cabin monoplane, Mr. Mulligan, won the 1935 Bendix race. It was clean and fast. Howard was the first Bendix pilot able to fly at high altitude to avoid as much weather as possible en route. Credit: Roy Russell

Ben Howard entered the 1936 Bendix with his wife, Maxine "Mike" Howard as co-pilot. Mulligan shed a propeller blade over New Mexico and crashed. Fortunately, both Howard and his wife survived. Credit: Birch Matthews collection

ENTER RUSS BOARDMAN

The tragic accident very nearly brought to an end the racing activities of Granville Brothers Aircraft. In 1932, however, another personality entered the scene. This was 35 year old Russell N. Boardman, a wealthy sportsman, businessman, rancher and pilot with homes on Cape Cod, in Boston and Brookline, Massachusetts. Boardman had an appetite for speed and adventure. He won local fame as a daring motorcyclist. He raced motorboats narrowly escaping serious injury when a boat he was driving blew up. He learned to fly in 1921, and spent time barnstorming the West where he formed a partnership with another man to operate the Rimrock Ranch near Cottonwood, Arizona. His first airplane accident occurred at the Cottonwood Airport during a night takeoff. It would not be his last. Returning to Boston, he bought the Hyannis airport on Cape Cod and formed Boardman Aviation Corporation, running a seaplane service between Boston and Cape Cod.

Ever looking for a new challenge, Russell Boardman began planning a good will tour of European capitals in connection with the 1930 American Legion convention to be held in Boston. He enlisted the aid of Captain Harry W. Lyon, navigator of the Southern Cross on Major Kingsford-Smith's dramatic flight across the Pacific. Lyon became disenchanted with Boardman's approach to the proposed European flight and withdrew from the venture. Harry Lyon damned him with faint praise! "Boardman has a great plan," he declared, "but he is greatly enhancing his chances of an unsuccessful flight by lack of thorough preparation."[6] Preparations for the flight, or the lack of them, stalled the project. It was the beginning of September and weather over the North Atlantic became problematic at best. Boardman rescheduled his adventure to the following year. His objective changed too. The new goal was a record non-stop distance flight from New York to Istanbul, Turkey. He needed a co-pilot for this ambitious flight and found him in the person of fellow New Englander, John L. Polando. The stocky Polando was an accomplished aircraft mechanic, however, his flying experience was limited, having obtained his pilot's license but two years earlier.

Russ Boardman gained international fame and recognition when he and John Polando completed their record 1931 non-stop flight of 5011 miles from New York to Istanbul. The deed earned both flyers the Distinguished Flying Cross.[7] Ever restless, Boardman flew a Granville Model Y to victory in a free-for-all race at Omaha, Nebraska, in May, 1932. Later that same month, he announced publicly his involvement with the Granville Brothers ordering the construction of two new racing planes which became known as the Gee Bee Model R-1 and R-2.[8] The two new racers were nearly identical differing only in the choice of engines and fuel tank capacity. The R-1 mounted a 1344 cubic inch Pratt & Whitney Wasp engine while the sister ship employed the 985 cubic inch Wasp Jr. The R-2 carried 604 gallons of gasoline, almost twice that of the R-1. Boardman and the Granvilles planned an assault on both the Thompson and Bendix races using the R-1 for the former and the R-2 for the latter.

Russell Boardman climbed aboard the R-1 on 13 August 1932, and took the airplane up for the first time.[9] He was generally pleased requesting only that more vertical fin and rudder area be added for directional control. Three days later, before he could make a second flight in the new racer, Boardman took off in a Warner-powered Gee Bee Model E Sportster. "Some say it was his first flight in the aircraft. Boardman was a hot shot aerobatic pilot and frequently did things to thrill onlookers at the field. Eye witnesses tell of

Chapter VII: Potpourri

Boardman leaving the ground in the Warner-powered Sportster and going into a loop during the takeoff."[10] However, William Heaton, a Federal aviation inspector who witnessed the crash said that "the machine went into a low roll" and then spun into the ground.[11] Boardman had performed stunts on takeoff before in the more powerful Senior Sportster which used the Wasp Jr. engine. This time though, he misjudged the capability of the 110 horsepower Warner-powered airplane and crashed. Boardman was badly injured with a very severe concussion and internal injuries. Doctors at Springfield hospital initially gave him a fifty-fifty chance of living but later were encourage by his response to their care.[12] Any chance of Boardman flying the new Gee Bee R-2 in the National Air Races evaporated with this mishap. Jimmy Doolittle was hired to replace Boardman and the rest is history. The amazing Mr. Doolittle went on to win the 1932 Thompson Trophy Race in the Gee Bee R-1 and also set a land plane speed record of 296 miles per hour in the Shell Petroleum Speed Dash.

GEE BEE R-2, RACE 7

The Bendix Trophy Race that year was another matter. Boardman was not planning to fly in that contest. Lee Gehlbach, a former Army Air Corps flyer and experienced test and racing pilot, was selected to race the Gee Bee R-2.[13] He made an uneventful trip to the West Coast on 24 August. The R-2 was a fast airplane for its day and offered first class competition to the Wedell-Williams racers running in the Bendix. During the race, Lee made excellent time across the continent until he reached Illinois when an oil line cracked. Oil sprayed all over the windscreen and canopy forcing Gehlbach to land at Chanute Field. Apparently the problem could not quickly be repaired for Lee removed the cockpit canopy on the ground at Chanute, added more oil and flew on to Cleveland. He arrived with an oil-drenched fuselage and fourth place in the Bendix at a comparatively slow average speed of 210 miles an hour. In the absence of mechanical difficulties, could the R-2 Gee

An unusual entry for the 1935 race classic was this Breese-Dallas transport. Vance Breese never arrived to start the race. Jackie Cochran reportedly planned to fly it in the 1936 Bendix with a new Twin Wasp engine installed. Once again, it was a "no-show." Credit: H. Gardiner via Marvin Border

Amelia Earhart with Allan Loughead, Carl Squirer and Cliff Henderson in front of Vega c/n 22 which Amelia used for the first women's transatlantic solo flight. She flew a similar Vega to fifth place in the 1935 Bendix. Credit; Gerry Balzer collection

Bee have beaten any of the Wedell racers across the continent? It doesn't seem likely. In the Shell Speed Dashes which followed the Bendix, the R-2 was 20 to 30 miles an hour slower than the three Wedell-Williams racers.

The R-2 Gee Bee was modified in early 1933, with wing panels of increased area (32 ft^2 added), landing flaps, a larger rudder and the Pratt & Whitney Wasp TD used the previous year in the R-1. A Pratt & Whitney Hornet was installed in the R-1. Russ Boardman, still feeling the effects of his accident, flew the revised airplane out of the mud and snow of Springfield Airport on 25 March for the first time and was apparently satisfied.[14] This year he planned to enter each racer in both the Bendix and the Thompson. Selection of a pilot for race number 7 was up in the air. The Granvilles wanted Lee Gehlbach again but he was already committed to one of the Wedell-Williams racers. Boardman, on the other hand, preferred his 1930 partner on the run to Istanbul, John Polando.[15] In the end, 24-year old Russell Thaw was named publicly in late June as the other pilot possibly as a compromise between the Granvilles and Boardman.[16]

FATAL TAKEOFF

Russell K. Thaw was the son of Evelyn Nesbit Thaw, an artist's model and chorus girl, and Harry K. Thaw, scion of an extremely – one might say absurdly – wealthy Pennsylvania family. The Thaw's came into scandalous prominence in 1906, when Harry murdered architect Stanford White. After ten years of antics, court trials, law suits and copious amounts of family money, the elder Thaw was finally released into society. Russell was born into this turbulence in the city of

Berlin on 25 October 1910, while Evelyn – estranged from her erratic husband – was traveling abroad.[17] Somehow, the son managed to grow up productively in spite of his heritage becoming a very respected pilot.

The Bendix that year was run from Floyd Bennett Field in New York to Mines Field in Los Angeles, a great circle distance of almost 2500 miles. Weather reports predicted clouds and showers between New York and the Mississippi River. Indeed, a violent electrical storm swept over New York at dusk that evening before the race began, providing a measure of relief from sweltering 90 degree temperature.

Thaw and Boardman got away on July 1 without difficulty after the other three contestants – Jimmy Wedell, Roscoe Turner and Amelia Earhart – had departed in the early morning darkness. Thaw planned to refuel at Kansas City and Amarillo, Texas. Boardman's racer carried 280 less gallons of fuel than Thaw's and his larger engine had a greater fuel consumption rate. As a consequence, his plans included refueling at Indianapolis as well as Wichita and Amarillo. Following the plan, Boardman flew directly to Indianapolis and landed. As he taxied in to fill the tanks, he was surprised to see Thaw and the R-2 already on the ground in an unscheduled stop. Bob Granville recalls that after Thaw landed, "a (landing gear) shock strut went down as he was turning around and he did damage a wing tip slightly. It had to be fixed in order to continue."[18]

After refueling, Russ Boardman climbed into the R-1 cockpit, fired up the big Hornet engine and taxied out for takeoff. The chubby racer roared down the runway, lifted off and promptly stalled about 40 feet in the air. Flipping over on its back the Gee Bee smashed into the ground fatally injuring its pilot. Boardman was disentangled from the cockpit by rescuers and rushed to City Hospital in Indianapolis. He was

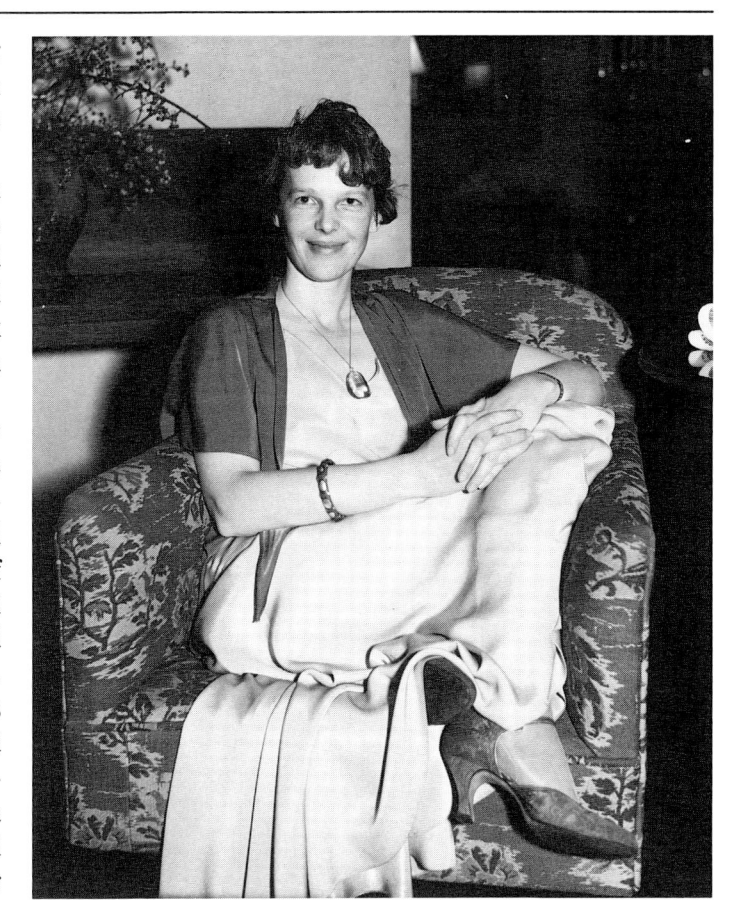

Amelia Earhart never won the Bendix, but she was a vocal advocate of women's participation in air racing and aviation in a time when men frowned upon such things. Credit: Sid Bradd collection

in critical condition with a fractured skull, broken shoulder and punctured lung. This time, his injuries were beyond the skills of his doctors and he died early on the morning of 3 July.

Neither Gee Bee completed the 1933 Bendix. Witnessing the terrible crash, Russell Thaw withdrew from the race on the spot. In fact, he chose not even to fly the R-2 back to Springfield. For all intents and purposes, the Gee Bee epoch was over.

COMMERCIAL RACERS

After 1934, the complexion of the transcontinental race changed. More and more, the contesting aircraft were existing commercial designs occasionally modified to carry extra fuel tankage in place of passenger seats. In this respect, the race began to lose a bit of luster and drifted from the purpose Vincent Bendix originally envisioned. It became more of a sporting event for the wealthy. The reasons for this are not difficult to discern. Designing and building increasingly competitive racing machines was a very expensive proposition. The country was in the midst of a highly depressed economy

Amelia Earhart, Laura Ingalls and Roscoe Turner gather at Laura's Lockheed Orion 9D in this 1935 photograph. Ingalls placed second in this aircraft in the 1936 Bendix. Credit: Sid Bradd collection

Roscoe Turner flew his gold Wedell Williams racer to second in the 1935 Bendix, losing to Benny Howard literally by seconds. This year, the Hornet engine had a new cowl smaller in diameter, but with bumps to cover the engine rocker arms. Credit: Dusty Carter

Blanche Noyes and Louise Thaden won the 1936 Bendix flying this Beech C-17R Staggerwing. It was the year of the woman as three of the first five places were taken by Louise Thaden, Laura Ingalls and Amelia Earhart. Credit: Beech Aircraft Corp, Al Hansen collection

making it virtually impossible for individual designers to get financial backing for new and better creations. Unlike the international Schneider Trophy Race, there was no government involvement and funding to cover the costly process of developing special racing engine airframes for Bendix competition.

Aircraft manufacturers were disinterested in the race. Army and Navy contracts offered the only substantial market for their products although the commercial airline business was beginning to mature with the advent of the Boeing 247 and Douglas DC-2 and DC-3 passenger liners. Racing was often perceived by the public as a carnival of daredevil pilots all to often involved in tragic accidents. This was hardly the image major aircraft manufacturers wished to portray.

The trend toward commercial airplanes dominating the field of transcontinental racing began in 1935. Benny Howard's high wing cabin monoplane won the race that year. Although it was a sleek well thought out design, it was in reality a prototype for a line of future Howard aircraft fashioned for the private sector. In other words, it possessed utility for more than just racing. A year later, every aircraft finishing the race was an existing commercial product. The last three post-war

This is the Lockheed 10E Electra flown by Amelia Earhart to fifth place in the 1936 Bendix. Credit: Sid Bradd collection

Chapter VII: Potpourri

Above and below: George Pomeroy flew this 14 passenger Douglas DC-2 into fourth place in the 1936 Bendix. This picture was taken 4 October 1934. Pomeroy's DC-2 was owned by Swiftlite and was one of the first large corporate airplanes. Credit: Both photos, McDonnell Douglas courtesy of Harry Gann

races were won by civilian derivatives of the Seversky P-35 pursuit aircraft and the supporting cast of contestants were strictly commercial aircraft with the single exception of Earl Ortman's rebuilt, but aging Marcoux-Bromberg racer. The only unique design built solely for race competition was Roscoe Turner's new ship which appeared in 1937. He intended to fly the Bendix that year and the airplane would have been a formidable competitor fully capable of winning the race. Unfortunately, he was forced out due to a pre-race welding accident which damaged the aircraft.

Nineteen thirty-six was the year for women pilots in the Bendix. Victory would go to Louise Thaden and copilot Blanche Noyes at the controls of a stagger wing Beechcraft C-17R. Laura Ingalls in a Lockheed Orion took second place and Amelia Earhart finished fifth in another Orion. Wealthy San Francisco sportsman pilot Frank Fuller, Jr., acquired a commercial version of Alexander de Seversky's military P-35 fighter aircraft in 1937. This airplane and two more "civil" P-35s were entered in the Bendix that year. Seversky planned to fly one and his company test pilot, Frank Sinclair, would pilot the other. Seversky never made it to the race having damaged his aircraft in a landing accident at Floyd Bennett Field on his way to California. The other two Seversky aircraft did arrive on the West Coast and were obviously the ones to beat. Their entry marked the first time a military fighter would compete in the race. It was, however, truly an omen of events to follow.

Frank Fuller won the 1937 race establishing a speed record of 258 miles an hour. Fuller's flight finally broke Jimmy Haizlip's 1932 mark of 245 miles per hour in the Wedell Williams racer. Jimmy Wedell's design and Haizlip's feat are all the more remarkable when one considers that in five years, what was essentially a stripped down military design exceeded the old record by just five percent! What Fuller's flight demonstrated though, was the markedly increased range of the Seversky compared to the small Wedell design. With a single refueling stop at Kansas City, Fuller spanned the continent from Burbank to Bendix, New Jersey. His average speed to the east coast was 255 miles an hour, just slightly under his average to Cleveland. By contrast, the old Wedell Williams racers required three to four refueling stops to span the nation.

The 1938 race was captured by Jacqueline Cochran who had by this time switched from her Beechcraft to one of Seversky's fighters. In reality, the big Seversky pursuits had no serious competition in the cross-country race. Times were changing rapidly as the thirties drew to a close. The National Air Races diminished in relevance as a sporting event and certainly as a contributor or proving ground for aviation. The financial and technical resources needed to create new unlimited class racing planes overwhelmed the means of individual designers. This was the province of major aircraft companies. The world was changing also. Of serious concern nationally were the gathering war clouds in Europe. It was a sobering time for all even though the economic depression was starting to ease. It was in this growing environment of uncertainty that the 1939 races were held.

The Bendix race that year seemed to hold exciting promise. In the September, 1939, edition of Aviation Magazine, Charles F. McReynolds surveyed the entries and gave readers his forecast. Lamenting the absence of industry innovations in racing, he simultaneously acknowledged possible drama in the Bendix. At the time, rumor spread that millionaire eccentric Howard Hughes would enter his transcontinental record setting racer. In 1937 Hughes had flown this plane across the continent from California to New York in seven hours and twenty-eight minutes. This beautiful airplane with a gleaming metal fuselage and deep blue wings was certainly a leading contender and reportedly, Vance Breese was to be the pilot. However, McReynolds went on to say that... "as this is being written the entry of the Hughes plane is still in doubt. The ship is now the property of the Timm Aircraft Corporation and design work is being pushed on the development of a military pursuit modification with higher power. Timm is understood to have purchased full design rights from Hughes and also to have the continuing cooperation of Hughes and his engineers in development of the new pursuit."

Competition for the Hughes Racer would come, McReynolds soundly reasoned, from the two Seversky fighters entered by Jackie Cochran and Frank Fuller. In the end, he predicted Cochran would be victorious with a winning time of seven hours, certainly an optimistic assessment of the Seversky's speed potential. The basis of this foresight was the fact that Cochran would be flying the latest variant of the

Roscoe Turner wanted to enter his new racer in the 1936 Bendix, but wasn't satisfied with Larry Brown's construction. The airframe was shipped to Matty Laird for completion. This is the original narrow chord wing version built by Brown. Credit: Birch Matthews collection

Turner's rebuilt "Ring-Free Meteor" appeared like this just before embarking for the West Coast and the 1937 Bendix. Credit: Birch Matthews collection

Right: Jackie Cochran garnered third place in this classically beautiful Beechcraft C-17R Staggerwing. Her average 1937 Bendix speed was 195 miles an hour. Credit: Sid Bradd collection

Chapter VII: Potpourri

Frank Fuller had just arrived at Grand Central Air Terminal when this picture was taken. He bought the airplane from Seversky and planned to enter the 1937 Bendix Trophy Race. Credit: Sid Bradd collection

Seversky which appeared cleaner in design relative to Frank Fuller's mount. If it actually flew the race, the Hughes Racer was predicted to finish second in seven hours and ten minutes while Fuller was relegated to third with an elapsed time of seven hours and 30 minutes. In addition to Breese, Cochran and Fuller, there were five other entries. They consisted of Frank Cordova in a Bellanca trimotor, Paul Mantz in his now familiar red Lockheed Orion, two stagger wing Beechcrafts flown by Bob Perlick and Max Constant, Inez Gibson, Burbank air charter service operator behind the stick of a Northrop Gamma and automobile race driver Wilbur Shaw in a Vultee.

How did Charles McReynolds fair in his prognostications? Certainly he was prudent in qualifying his speculation that the Hughes Racer would place high if it indeed actually started. Conforming to Hughes' growing reputation for eccentric behavior, the airplane did not participate for whatever reason. It was unfortunate. The Hughes Racer was a grand design execution coupled with superb workmanship. Viewed in the National Air and Space Museum today, one can still appreciate the talent required to create this machine. Also unfortunate was the fact that Jacqueline Cochran decided not to start the race. Her decision was forced by heavy fog that very early September morning. This is not an unusual weather phenomenon in Southern California. Two times Jackie had the Seversky rolled out for takeoff and each time concluded the risks were unacceptable. Her last decision to withdraw from the race was made after eight in the morning. To meet the six o'clock Cleveland deadline, she would have had to maintained a 285 mile per hour average, a feat perhaps marginally beyond the Seversky's potential. In the end, Jackie flew via commercial transport into Cleveland to see the races.

Frank Fuller, head of a large paint manufacturing concern in Northern California, won the Bendix Trophy Race in 1939. It was his second victory. He broke his own speed record with a posted seven hours, 14 minutes and 19 seconds elapsed time computing to an average speed of 282 miles per hour. His flight, for the most part at fourteen thousand feet, was relatively uneventful. Occasional air turbulence was his only companion. Fuller executed a refueling stop at Goodland, Kansas. Here, with the help of a United Air Lines refueling crew, he was off again inside of 12 minutes. Fuller later praised the support of this United crew as one reason for his victory. Frank continued on from Cleveland to flash across the Bendix, New Jersey, airport. William C. Zink, a representative of the National Aeronautical Association, timed Fuller's arrival at Bendix. Not positive that the timer had seen his airplane, Fuller circled the field and twice crossed over the finish. With that, he proceeded to Floyd Bennett where he landed. His speed across the continent was just under 236 miles per hour.

Left: Seversky pilot Frank Sinclair wound up fourth in the 1937 Bendix in this SEV-1XP model at a rather slow speed of 185 miles per hour. Seversky Aircraft, Tim Weinschenker collection

Frank Fuller was back for the 1937 races with his civilian version of the Seversky P-35 pursuit. He flew the entire race at 17,000 feet and wound up second behind Jackie Cochran who reportedly flew as high as 22,000 feet, apparently with more favorable winds. Credit: Dusty Carter

WAR INTERRUPTS

On Friday, September 1, one day before Frank Fuller launched his Seversky toward Cleveland in the 1939 Bendix race, German armies raced into Poland. Newspapers across the continent rushed extra editions onto the streets of America with fateful headlines declaring "GERMAN ARMY ATTACKS POLAND." Armor, infantry and tactical air units advanced across the Polish corridor separating Germany from East Prussia. A major target was Danzig, artificially created as a "free city" following World War I. The conquest of Poland would be rapid and foretold of virtually unimaginable strife to come.

Momentous world events were very much on the minds of spectators attending the 1939 National Air Races. The public address system periodically interspersed news announcements with air show commentary. Race fans could be seen with portable radios following the pace of events. News of world affairs rapidly overshadowed the races. As if foreboding news wasn't enough, Cleveland's weather turned sour and storms forced postponement of the Labor Day Thompson Trophy classic until Tuesday, September 5th. The day before, Louis W. Greve, president of the National Air Races, announced the retirement of both Cliff and Phil Henderson as managers of the races. Cliff Henderson had investment and business interests in Southern California to take care of and his brother Phil was suffering from ill health. For many reasons, the National Air Races would never be the same.

Chapter VII: Potpourri

Jackie Cochran was victorious in the 1938 Bendix with this Seversky AP-7. Landing gear retracted to the rear. Wheels were covered by the fairing extending down near the wing trailing edge. Credit: Seversky, Gerry Balzer collection

The airplane Sinclair flew in the 1937 Bendix race was a Seversky Sev-1XP two-place pursuit. It is pictured here as it appeared sometime in 1935. Credit: Gerry Balzer collection

MORE RACES FOR 1940?

In spite of war in Europe, hopes for a continued National Air Race program still resided in some minds. A March 1, 1940, New York Times article declared: "Newark's Airport To Get Air Races."[19] In a press forum Friday evening, February 29, Newark Mayor Meyer Ellenstein told reporters the races would be held in his city over a five or six day period surrounding Labor Day weekend. A marketing survey conducted during February by a certain Robert Kenworthy representing National Air Races, Incorporated, indicated the event would draw one million people from the surrounding area. Kenworthy believed that Newark was "ideally suited" for the races. There was, however, political opposition based mainly on securing financial resources necessary to back the planned races. Unlike Cleveland, there was no established core of civic leaders and local industrialists interested in promoting air racing. In spite of the optimism expressed by Kenworthy when he told reporters: "I am going to Cleveland tomorrow with an attorney for the city of Newark and a representative of the Mayor to settle the last few details," the probability for races that year was tenuous.[20]

That there was serious intention on the part of some persons to hold the races in 1940, seems little in doubt. During the first week in February, veteran race pilot Earl Ortman surveyed a potential layout for closed-course pylon racing in the vicinity of the Newark airport. The course was to have been ten miles in length with either five or six pylon turns. Ortman took particular notice of emergency landing opportunities from anywhere on the course and concluded it was relatively safe. There was only one stretch where the race pilots would have to cross over railroad tracks and high tension wires. "On almost every leg of the proposed course it would be possible," Ortman said, "for a plane to put down if necessary."[21]

Practical matters concerned with staging the National Air Races centered on repaving some of the Newark runways and erecting suitable grandstands. It was estimated the cost of this work would amount to $300,000, not an inconsiderable amount in 1940. Earl Ortman returned to Canada where he was employed as a DC-3 copilot for Canadian Pacific Airways. In the near future, Earl would resign from the air line and

Fuller won the 1937 Bendix and continued on to Bendix Airport, Hasbrouck Heights, N.J. He spanned the continent in nine hours, 35 minutes. Credit: Sid Bradd collection

Lee Gehlbach was back for the 1938 Bendix in the now outclassed and aging Wedell racer, number 92. Credit: Birch Matthews collection

Paul Mantz flew his Orion 9C in both the 1938 and 1939 Bendix races taking third place each year. The old red and white Lockheed was still a pretty airplane but no match for the Seversky fighters. Credit: C. Karvinen

volunteer for service with the Atlantic Ferrying Organization. Ortman went to war before most pilots in the United States.

The National Air Races were not held in 1940. At the end of April, Mayor Ellenstein announced that . . . "he had abandoned efforts to obtain the 1940 National Air Races for Newark airport because of failure to find a sponsor to underwrite expenses."[22] By this time, the estimate for expenses had risen to $400,000. This was a large sum for an economy just emerging from the greatest economic depression the world had ever known. World events were overpowering as well. By March 10th, the German Army was on the move flooding into the Lowlands and then south into France. In a matter of weeks, the fighting was over and the Battle of Britain would soon begin.

The last flicker of hope for another air race occurred a year later when Mayor Fiorello La Guardia of New York, appointed a committee to study the possibility.[23] The committee consisted of Major Elmer Haslett, manager of La Guardia Airport, O.N. Mosher, vice president of American Airlines and I.S. Randall, assistant chairman of the board of Trans World Airways. Labor Day weekend was selected for the anticipated program. The small committee gave the matter serious consideration. Their overall conclusion was that the location was "potentially excellent." A lot of work would be required to actually implement the races, however. Additional runways would be required to minimize interference with commercial traffic during the races. Grandstands would have to be erected. Perhaps the idea holding the races in the Fall of 1941, wasn't a pipe dream, but it lacked a certain degree of reality. Europe was in flames and America was rearming. There would be no air racing in the foreseeable future.

CONTRASTS AND COMPARISONS

Comparing various disparate racing aircraft is an imprecise adventure at best and more likely a futile assignment. Nonetheless, some gross assessment seems possible. Two nearby tables present physical characteristics and power comparisons for six different racers designed for transcontinental events during the decade of the thirties. Three of these aircraft

Sixth place in the 1938 Bendix went to John Hinchey in a Spartan Executive. Hinchey was along for the ride. His average speed was a slow 177 miles an hour. Credit: Dusty Carter

Ross Hadley piloted this sleek Beechcraft D-17S to fifth in 1938. Like the Spartan Executive, the sleek Staggerwing couldn't keep up with the faster Seversky racers. Credit: Birch Matthews collection

Weight and Power Comparisons
Representative Transcontinental Air Racers: 1930-1937

Component	Vega 5B (1930) NR105W	Wedell Williams (1932) NR536V	Gee Bee R-2 (1932) NR2101	Northrop Gamma 2G (1934) NX13761	Howard DGA-6 (1935) NR273Y	Marcoux Bromberg (1937) R14215
Empty Weight, Lb.	2490	1950	1796	4687	2600	3474
Pilot/Chute, Lb.	185	185	185	185	370	185
Fuel Weight, Lb.	3012	1218	1812	2628	1800	1350
Oil Weight, Lb.	192	75	150	217	225	113
Misc. Weight, Lb.	50	118		160	360	20
Takeoff Gross Wt., Lb.	5929	3428	3943	7877	5355	5142
Engine Model	Wasp C	Wasp Jr. S2A[1]	Wasp Jr. A[2]	Conqueror SVG-1570-F4	Wasp SE	Twin Wasp Jr. S2A5-G[3]
Serial Number	3088	133	2	Unknown	5640	422
Rated T/O Power[4], HP	500	515	515	705	500	825
Power Loading Ratio[5]	11.86	6.66	7.66	11.17	10.71	6.23

Notes:
[1] With over boost/over speed power setting.
[2] Engine modified to S2A equivalent before installation in R-2. With over boost/over speed.
[3] Engine modified with 11:1 supercharger gear ratio.
[4] Sea Level power using 87 octane fuel.
[5] Ratio of gross weight to takeoff horsepower.

Physical Characteristics
Representative Transcontinental Air Racers: 1930-1937

Parameter	Vega 5B (1930) NR105W	Wedell Williams (1932) NR536V	Gee Bee R-2 (1932) NR2101	Northrop Gamma 2G (1934) NX13761	Howard DGA-6 (1935) NR273Y	Marcoux-Bromberg (1937) R14215
Wing Span, Ft.-In.	41-0	26-0	25-0	47-10	31-8	25-5.5
Wing Area, Ft.²	275	103	101.9	363	137	106
Wing Loading, Lb./Ft.²	21.6	33.3	38.7	21.7	39.1	48.5
Airfoil - Root	Clark Y-18	M-10 Modified*	M-6 Modified*	NACA 2415	NACA 2412	NACA 2218
- Tip	Clark Y-9.5	M-10 Modified*	M-6 Modified*	NACA 2409	NACA 2412	NACA 2210
Overall Length, Ft.-In.	27-8	22-6	17-9	32-11.5	25-1	23-2
Fuel Capacity, Gal.	502	115	302	438	300	225
Oil Capacity, Gal.	25.6	10	20	29	30 (Est.)	15
Estimated Max. Speed	230	272	247	230	287	340
Seating	7	1	1	2	4	1

*NACA airfoil designation.

Frank Fuller was back again in 1939 when he entered his redecorated Seversky one more time. He is shown here just after he won the last pre-war Bendix race. Credit: Sid Bradd collection

– the Lockheed Vega, Northrop Gamma and Howard DGA-6 – are fundamentally commercial designs stripped of unnecessary equipment which was replaced by extra fuel tanks. The remaining three were single-point designs created for maximum speed. The Gee Bee R-2 and Marcoux-Bromberg racers were designed specifically for long distance racing. The Wedell-Williams plane was used to compete in the Bendix as well as contemporary pylon races. It is obvious from the tables that the three commercial aircraft are larger and heavier because they were designed to have a useful load capability for commercial purposes. The Northrop Gamma and Lockheed Vega were relatively large single engine airplanes of their time and dwarfed the pure racers. The Vega had 2.6 times the wing area and 60 percent more span compared to the racers. The Northrop Gamma was even larger. The pure racing machines were remarkably similar in dimension. The Marcoux-Bromberg – designed two years later than the Gee Bee and Wedell-Williams machines – was more advanced as evidenced by a retractable landing gear, cantilevered wing, newer airfoil section and monocoque metal fuselage construction. The 1937 Marcoux-Bromberg was significantly faster than the 1932 Wedell racer due largely, one suspects, to the fact it had over 37 percent more available power. How did the 1934 Marcoux-Bromberg compare to the 1932 Wedell? The latter was perhaps slightly faster because it was lighter. Regardless of statistics and technicalities, these old airplanes were exciting and they fostered the glamour and romance of a fascinating motor sport during a period in our nation when it was needed most.

Chapter VII: Potpourri

Fuller poses with the Bendix Trophy and floral horseshoe after his 1939 victory. Germany invaded Poland the day before Frank won his second Bendix Trophy. It was the end of an era and seven years would elapse before another Bendix race took place. Credit: Sid Bradd collection

NOTES:

1 Bob Hirsch, "Wedell-Williams Air Service Corporation and Air Racing," (Part I, The Corporation), American Aviation Historical Society JOURNAL, Vol. 32, No. 3, 1987, p. 182.
2 Ibid., p. 185.
3 *New York Times*, 30 August 1932, p. 1.
4 Henry A. Haffke, *Gee Bee*, VIP Publishers, Inc., Colorado Springs, 1989, p. 8.
5 Philip C. Brown, "The Fabulous Gee Bees," American Aviation Historical Society JOURNAL, Vol. 24. No. 3, 1979, p. 200.
6 *New York Times*, 2 September 1930, p. 6.
7 *New York Times*, 28 July 1932, p. 7.
8 *New York Times*, 22 May 1932, Section II, p. 3.
9 Haffke, op.cit., p. 102.
10 Ibid., p. 103.
11 Ibid.
12 *New York Times*, 17 August 1932, p. 19.
13 Lee Gehlbach was the only pilot to fly both the Granville Brothers and Wedell-Williams racers in National Air Race competition.
14 Robert H. Granville, "The Gee Bee in '33", published in *The Golden Age of Air Racing*, EAA Aviation Foundation, Inc., Oshkosh, Wisconsin, 1991, p.233.
15 Ibid., p. 234.
16 *New York Times*, 25 June 1933, Section II, p. 1.
17 Michael MacDonald Mooney, *Evelyn Nesbit and Standford White*, William Morrow and Company, Inc., New York, 1976.
18 Granville, op.cit., p. 235.
19 *New York Times*, 1 March 1940, p.7.
20 Ibid.
21 *New York Times*, 7 April 1940.
22 *New York Times*, 30 April 1940, p. 24.
23 *New York Times*, 12 May 1940, p. 6

The Gee Bee model was devised using the VSAERO computer code to calculate the subsonic flow field about the airframe. In this view, the cowling is removed revealing the curved beginning of the fuselage aft of the cowl. Refer to the color illustration gallery which shows the flow field results. Credit: David Lednicer

work helped validate the basic airframe configuration including the wing-to-fuselage intersection.

To analytically assess the Gee Bee, drawings of the R-2 were obtained from Vern Clements and the aircraft was modeled using VSAERO. David's conclusion was that overall the racer was rather well thought out and designed, although there is little longitudinal stability margin. He goes on to say that "the engine installation is quite good. The forward cowl is well shaped and appears to have about the correct amount of inlet area. Behind the engine, the fuselage starts as a curved (as opposed to a conical) fairing over the accessories, to provide a smooth flow path for exhausting the engine cooling air."[3] The Gee Bee did not have cowl flaps, however, David's analysis indicates the exit area was well sized. The absence of comments on engine cooling problems in the historical literature substantiates this conclusion.

The Gee Bee wing was externally braced with flying wires. The airfoil selected was the NACA M-6 section which was thinned to 65 percent of its designed thickness. Considering the state of airfoil development at the time, this was a reasonable design selection. The M-6 section is somewhat reflexed meaning that the trailing edge is bent upward which helps reduce trim drag. In his research on the Gee Bee, David Lednicer was unable to determine if any degree of twist was built into the original wing. The term "twist" literally means building the wing structure so that the tip is at a slightly lower angle of incidence than the wing root. Twist in a tapered wing forces the inboard regions of the wing to reach stall angle before the outboard sections, keeping the ailerons effective as the stall progresses and preventing a severe roll-off that would result at stall without twist. Gee Bee R-2 replica builder Delmar Benjamin put about one and a half degrees of twist

Chapter VIII: A Look Back

Delmar Benjamin's fantastic replica of the Gee Bee R-2 is shown in this photograph as it appeared during the 1992 Reno National Championship Air Races. In developing his analyses, David Lednicer consulted with Benjamin on handling and design characteristics of the replica. Credit: Dan Whitney

into the wing of his airplane. Even then he states, the wing stalls rather abruptly, but without roll-off.

The original airplane may not have had any wing twist based upon Russell Boardman's fatal accident on takeoff at Indianapolis. He pulled the heavily loaded racer off the runway apparently at a steep angle of attack and it promptly stalled about 40 feet above the ground. The aircraft immediately rolled inverted and fell to the ground suggesting the wing tips stalled first and lateral control was lost. Delmar Benjamin notes that the worst problem with his Gee Bee is the aileron reversal that the aircraft experiences at higher angles of attack. This is because the wing with the downward aileron stalls before the upward oriented aileron on the opposite wing. If Boardman was applying lateral control during his Indianapolis takeoff, aileron reversal may well have caused the accident.

The analysis performed by David Lednicer indicates the Gee Bee R-2 has only marginal longitudinal stability. Pilot Delmar Benjamin further states that directional stability on the racer is worse than longitudinal stability. The Gee Bee R-1 and R-2 racers were clearly not for the inexperienced or careless as they could be very unforgiving. At that point in time, the Gee Bee was near the outer limits of pilot experience with respect to speed and handling qualities. Even Jimmy Doolittle treated the airplane with a great deal of respect flying the Thompson high and wide with comparatively gentle low "g" turns.

The original Gee Bee R-1 and R-2 racers no longer exist. In recent years, however, replicas of each have been constructed. A facsimile of the famous R-1 can be found in the New England Air Museum on static display. Most well known is Delmar Benjamin's R-2 replica which he flies at air shows and races across the United States. One can't help but believe Zantford Granville would be amazed to witness Delmar's aerobatic routine in this 1932 vintage racing plane design!

THE 1937/1938 MARCOUX-BROMBERG RACER

The Marcoux-Bromberg design by Keith Rider used the NACA 2200 series airfoil, a popular state-of-the-art section in the early 1930s which was also incorporated in the Supermarine Spitfire. Unlike the Gee Bee, the 1934 vintage Marcoux-Bromberg featured a cantilever wing, split wing flaps and a retractable landing gear.[4] It was a compact design right from the start. In 1937, after the larger Pratt & Whitney Twin Wasp Jr. engine was installed, the wetted area of the airframe was

This perspective of the 1937 Marcoux-Bromberg racer is comparable to the computer generated image in the adjacent figure. The similarity between the computer image and the actual aircraft is excellent. In the photograph, Earl Ortman has the cowl flaps wide open during a ground run up of the engine. This accentuates the excessive gap between the cowl and fuselage. The obvious deficiency was corrected before the 1938 National Air Races. Credit: Dusty Carter

still only 458 square feet, 16 percent less than the rotund Gee Bee.

In analyzing the Marcoux racer, Lednicer noted the airfoil thickness to chord ratios used in the wing were a bit on the high side being 18 and 12 percent at the root and tip, respectively. This is probably explained by structural design requirements for the wooden cantilevered wing as well as the need to partially house the main landing gear wheels in the retracted position. Part of the wheel was exposed after retraction. The axle of each wheel nestled against stops when the gear was up and the wheel was free to turn. In the event the landing gear couldn't be lowered, enough wheel was exposed to prevent damage to the fuselage during a forced landing. This design approach first became popular when it appeared on the early Douglas transports through the DC-3 series. Keith Rider's association with various Douglas people led him to design the racer with this feature.

Like the Gee Bee, there was no evidence of any twist in the wing. Coupled with the tapered wing planform, stall likely began near mid-span. "Luckily, the thick airfoils probably resulted in a gentle stall," David concluded.[5] He went on to say that the wing incidence on the Rider design is rather large and would result in a bit of fuselage drag penalty. The Marcoux-Bromberg racer does have a generous wing-to-fuselage fairing, reminiscent of the British Spitfire. This would help performance to a degree but simultaneously added a bit of wetted area to the airframe.

The 1937 version of the racer which flew in the Bendix race that year used a Pratt & Whitney R-1535 Twin Wasp Jr. engine. When this installation was made, an A-17A cowling was incorporated. The cowling diameter was six inches greater than the major fuselage diameter and this resulted in a poor aerodynamic configuration. The exit area for engine cooling air passing through the cowl was excessive. Cooling air flow was not properly throttled and, therefore, not adequately accelerated as it left the cowling. This represented an increased drag penalty. Jack Bromberg undoubtedly realized the poor cowling-fuselage design relationship and lacked time before the 1937 races to correct the problem. Prior to the 1938 National Air Races, the fuselage was further modified with a

Chapter VIII: A Look Back

KEITH RIDER R-3 (1937)

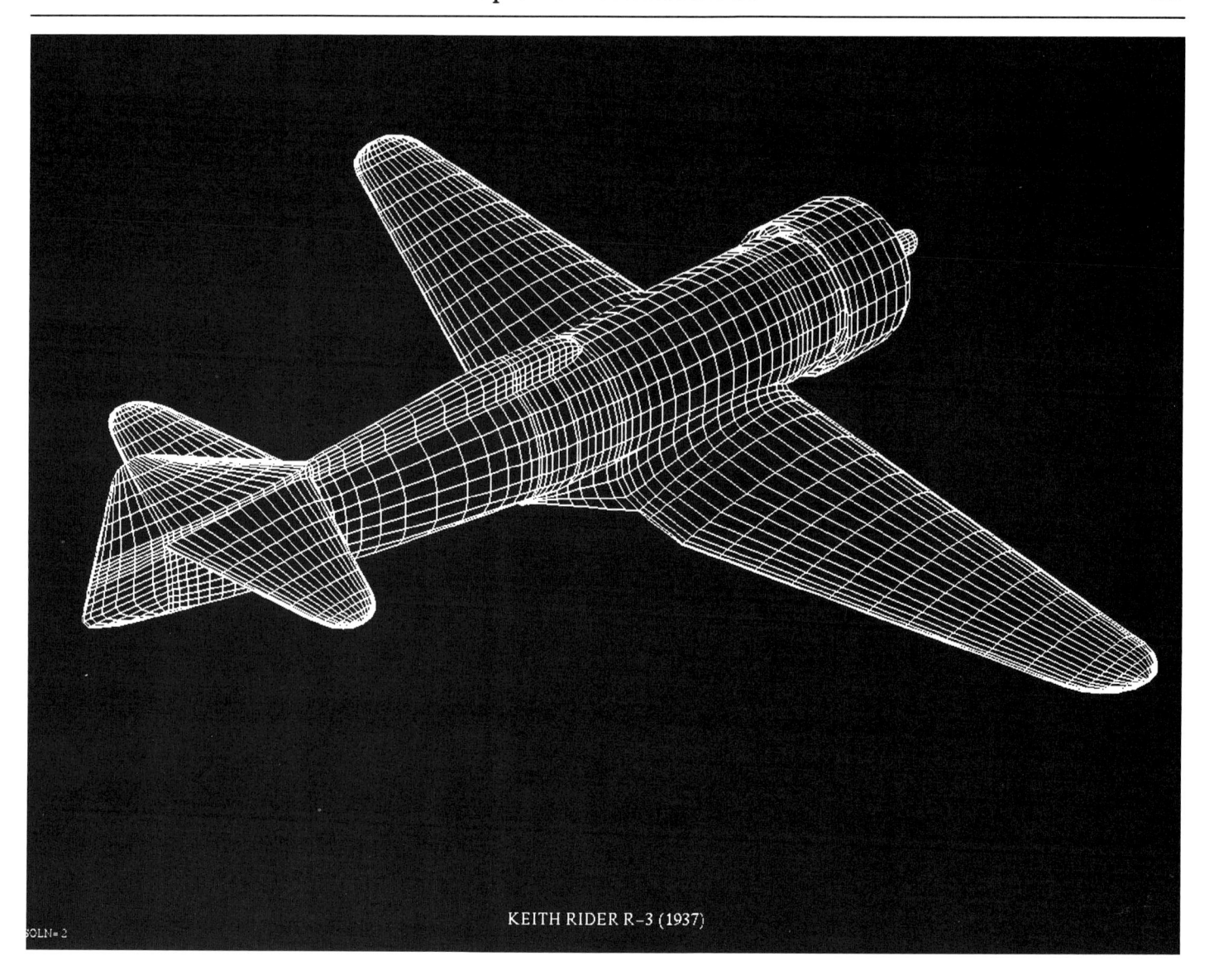

The flow field analysis is derived from incremental evaluation of the airframe surface geometry. This picture illustrates the quadrilateral, three-dimensional modeling elements used to represent the 1937 Marcoux-Bromberg racer. If the elements are sufficiently small, the airframe geometry is accurately represented for modeling purposes. Once the basic geometry is defined, flow field characteristics can be calculated. The color gallery illustrations show lines of constant pressure coefficient and coefficient gradations by color index. Credit: David Lednicer

42-inch long fairing extending aft from the cowling trailing edge until it intersected the fuselage major diameter, greatly improving engine cooling air flow at the cowl exit.

Pilot Earl Ortman assessed the handling qualities of the racer following the 1937 modifications. He noted that the wing loading was increased significantly with the Twin Wasp Jr. engine and the airplane had "a marked tendency to mush at anything less than about 80 percent power."[6] Earl went on to state that "some directional instability was noted" and that longitudinal stability was very poor. He found that at low speeds, elevator control was quite marginal, a condition that Vance Breese found when he flew the airplane after Jim Granger's fatal accident.

Other changes were planned for the Marcoux-Bromberg racer before the 1937 races. As originally envisioned, a custom engine cowling contoured to meet the major fuselage diameter was to have been made which would have eliminated the drag penalty already mentioned. Either time or money constraints precluded this change and the A-17A cowling was fitted to the racer. Landing gear fairings were also designed to smooth the flow aft of the wheels. The proposed configuration was similar to that employed on Seversky's P-35 airplane. The fairings were never used because the structural attachments proved unreliable.[7] A revised vertical stabilizer was also considered but abandoned because it would have reduced the rudder surface area which was already considered minimal.

After World War II, plans were made to install a still more powerful Pratt & Whitney engine in the old Marcoux-Bromberg racer and enter it in the Thompson Trophy Race. Two brothers, Earl and Robert Benjamin of Cleveland, bought the plane

KEITH RIDER R-3 (1937)

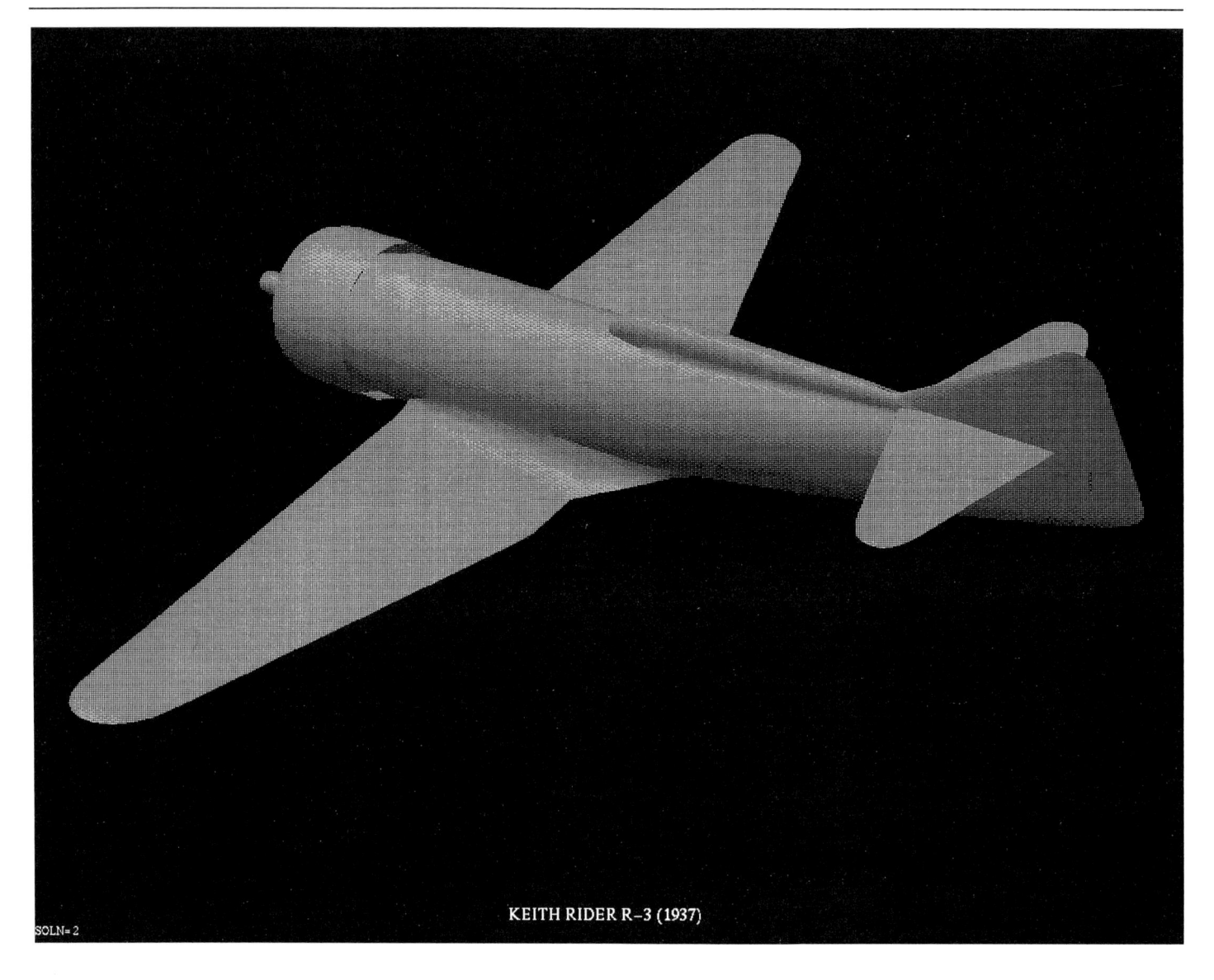

This perspective computer generated view shows the 1937 version of the Marcoux-Bromberg racer, originally designed by Keith Rider in 1934. There is a six inch differential between the large cowling used with the Pratt & Whitney Twin Wasp Jr. and the major fuselage diameter. An objective of the analysis was to compare this with the 1938 version which eliminated this abrupt change in diameter. Credit: David Lednicer

from Hal Marcoux in early 1948.[8] Bob Benjamin flew P-51s in the Air Force and planned on flying the reconstituted airplane. The project never got off the ground. Earl Ortman was contacted and he indicated the present fuselage structure was stressed to the limit with the Twin Wasp Jr., and a larger, heavier engine installation was not advisable. The vintage racer had seen its last race. Today, it is owned by the New England Air Museum where it was refurbished and placed on display.

IN RETROSPECT

The unlimited class racers of the 1930s were single point designs with but one purpose: maximum speed. In many instances, the handling qualities of these aircraft were marginal and totally unforgiving. Most of these speedsters were quite small and confining. The cockpits were devoid of creature comforts with little room to stretch or move. That Earl Ortman could pilot the Marcoux-Bromberg almost ten hours straight across the United States in the 1937 Bendix Race is a credit to his stamina as well as his skill.

NOTES:

1 Analytical Methods, Inc., 2133 - 152nd Avenue, N.E., Redmond, Washington, 98052.
2 David A. Lednicer and Ian J. Gilchrist, "A Retrospective: Computational Aerodynamic Analysis Methods Applied to the P-51 Mustang, American Institute of Aeronautics and Astronautics, 9th Applied Aerodynamics Conference, Baltimore, Maryland, 23-25 September 1991.
3 Correspondence to the author from David A. Lednicer, 14 December 1992.
4 Wing flaps were adapted to the Gee Bee R-3 in 1933, to lower the landing speed and permit landings at the relatively short field available at Springfield.
5 Correspondence to the author from David A. Lednicer, 16 November 1992.
6 Correspondence to Mrs. Ruth M. Fox from Earl H. Ortman, 27 April 1948.
7 Correspondence to the author from Jack L. Bromberg dated 28 June 1961.
8 *The Cleveland Press*, 1 April 1948, p. 24.

ASSETS OF WAR

The 1946 National Air Races brought a brand new look to this spectacle. Contestants would fly surplus military aircraft. Gone were the colorful and unique one-of-a-kind designs that fascinated so many before the war. For those with an ardent nostalgic leaning, these new machines would never supplant those of earlier years. For younger generations, however, it was the birth of a fresh and exciting period with a new and much faster breed of racers.

What forever changed the character of air racing was the Federal Government's decision to sell surplus military equipment – including aircraft – to the general public. The first move toward this end was the Surplus Property Act passed by Congress in early 1944, to establish policy. Surplus aircraft sales were initially the responsibility of the Defense Plant Corporation, a Government entity. Later, aircraft sales came under the authority of the Reconstruction Finance Corporation which was another Federal organization dating to the Great Depression years. In January, 1946, the War Assets Administration was formed and assumed responsibility for military aircraft disposal.[2]

With the end of the war, thousands of Army and Navy airplanes were no longer needed by the military. Many were factory fresh while some were war-weary combat veterans. A large number of planes were flown or shipped from overseas bases to the United States while others were delivered directly from the factory. Aircraft sales took place at well over 100

This is a factory fresh P-51B-10 Mustang nearly identical to the airplane Jackie Cochran flew in the post-war Bendix races. The familiar dorsal fin is absent. The fin was a field modification applied first to D model Mustangs. Credit: North American Aviation via Gerry Balzer collection

Mustang serial number 42-103644 was a P-51C-5, manufactured by North American at their Dallas, TX, facility. Basically the same as the B model from the Inglewood, CA, plant, the P-51C was used by Paul Mantz. The clean lines of the Mustang are evident in this photograph. Credit: North American Aviation via Gerry Balzer collection

airfields across the country. Most fighter planes sold to individuals – many of which were used for air racing – came from just a handful of large storage facilities.

Major Surplus Aircraft Storage Fields
Altus, Oklahoma
Augusta, Georgia
Clinton, Oklahoma
Kingman, Arizona
Ontario, California
Walnut Ridge, Arkansas

One of the largest was located five miles outside of Kingman, Arizona. This was the old Kingman Army Airfield adjacent to U.S. Route 66 in the dry, hot Arizona desert. Surplus bomber and fighter planes began arriving at Kingman in early October, 1945. By December, the flow of planes to this field was so great they were landing at the rate of one every minute.[3] Unlike Kingman, the majority of airfields contained utility and training aircraft or aircraft of little application in civilian life. The destiny awaiting most of this vast war plane armada was the smelting furnace. For those with cash in hand, though, there were bargains to be had. Surplus aircraft were sold for a tiny fraction of what the Government originally paid. As a consequence, a large pool of fast, modern aircraft were readily available for the sport of air racing.

War Assets Administration
1946 AIRCRAFT SALE PRICES

Bendix Racers	Price
Bell P-63	$1000
Goodyear FG-1	$1250
Douglas A-26	$2000
Lockheed P-38/F-5	$1250
Martin B-26	$3000
North American P-51	$3500
Republic P-47	$3500

Source: William T. Larkins, "War Assets," *Air Classics*, February 1992, p. 28.

BASIC AIRCRAFT CHARACTERISTICS

Military fighter planes were far and away the most popular candidates for pylon and transcontinental racing. Of the available surplus Army and Navy models, Lockheed's P-38 and F-5 Lightnings were highly regarded for Bendix competition. The F-5 was a photo reconnaissance version of the P-38 in which five cameras replaced the standard compliment of machine guns. Their competition consisted primarily of North American P-51 Mustangs and Bell Aircraft P-63 Kingcobras.

The D model Mustang is the most numerous variant found in air racing, past and present. Ed Lunken and Bill Eddy both flew the P-51D aircraft in the Bendix. The airplane shown here is a P-51D-20. Credit: North American Aviation via Gerry Balzer collection

This Lockheed Lightning started out as a P-38L-5 and was subsequently converted into the F-5G-6 photo reconnaissance version at a modification center. More F-5G-6 Lightnings were entered in the 1946 Bendix race than any other type of airplane. Credit: Lockheed via Gerry Balzer collection

The Lockheed Lightning was an excellent high altitude fighter. The two Allison V-1710 engines were equipped with turbosuperchargers. The turbos were installed on top of the booms in proximity with the wing trailing edge. The airplane shown here is a P-38L-5, three of which started in the 1946 Bendix. Credit: Lockheed via Gerry Balzer collection

Military Fighter Performance Comparison

Parameter	P-38L	P-51C	P-63C
Engine	V-1710-111/113	V-1650-7	V-1710-117
Takeoff Power	1500 HP[1]	1490 HP	1325 HP
Maximum Speed at 25,000 Ft.	414 MPH	439 MPH	410 MPH
Service Ceiling	44,000 Ft.	41,900 Ft.	39,600 Ft.
Rate of Climb	2857 Ft./Min.	2898 Ft./Min.	2500 Ft./Min.
Internal Fuel Capacity	415 Gal.	269 Gal.	126 Gal.

Notes:
[1] Takeoff power for each engine.

Sources:
1 Ray Wagner, *American Combat Planes*, 3rd Edition, Doubleday & Co., Garden City, New York, 1982.
2 Bell Aircraft Model Specification, P-63C-5-BE, Report No. 33-947-007, dated 15 November, 1944.
3 Robert W. Gruenhagen, *Mustang*, Arco Publishing, Inc., New York, revised edition, 1976.

All three fighters had excellent 400+ mile per hour maximum speeds as shown in the nearby table of performance. The Mustang had a performance edge at 25,000 feet, however, the turbosuperchargers on the P-38 gave it a service ceiling advantage over the other two fighters. The rate of climb for all three airplanes was reasonably good with the P-38 and P-51 basically equivalent while the P-63 was about 400 feet per minute slower. The Mustang was powered by the superb Packard-built Rolls-Royce Merlin engine with its integral geared two-speed, two-stage supercharger. Unlike the Mustang, the P-38 was equipped with turbosupercharged Allison engines.

Bell's P-63 also used an Allison, but with a gear-driven supercharger or blower. The Allison gear driven supercharger staging was quite different from the Merlin. The Allison engine had an integral single stage supercharger and a second or auxiliary stage blower physically separated from the engine stage. This approach yielded a less than optimum packaging configuration when compared to the Merlin. The Allison supercharger design arrangement evolved from mass production considerations influenced heavily by General Motors production engineering people associated with the engine program. Their goal was to absolutely maximize production with a minimum of changes. By separating the auxiliary stage, the basic engine and blower (called the engine stage supercharger) did not have to be redesigned and re-tooled. Auxiliary blower design, tooling and production could be carried out separately without disrupting basic engine production.

Weight statements for the three fighter types are given in a nearby table. The Kingcobra was the lightest of the three at just under 6900 pounds while the Mustang was slightly heavier. At 12,780 pounds empty weight, the P-38 was almost twice as heavy as the two single engine fighters. Internal fuel capacity for the three military airplanes varied considerably. On a per engine basis, the Mustang had the greatest capacity at 269 gallons, a decided advantage as the basis for setting up

Drop Tank Installations

Fuel Cap. Gallons	Tank Empty Wt.-Lb.	Wing Pylon Wt.-Lb.	Fuel Weight Lb.	Number of Tanks	Total Wt. Lb.
75	60	16	450	2	1052
110	90	16	660	2	1532
165	115	16	990	2	2242

Source: E.J. Horkey and J.G. Beerer, "Performance Calculations for Model P-51D Airplane," North American Aviation, Inc., Report No. NA-46-130, dated 6 February 1946.

Chapter IX: The New Breed

Chuck Tucker flew a Bell P-63C-5 in the 1946 Bendix like this Kingcobra ready for delivery to the Free French Air Force. The aircraft shown here is equipped with 75 gallon drop tanks. Credit: Bell Aircraft via Birch Matthews collection

a cross-country racing machine. Lockheed's P-38 carried 208 gallons of gas per engine while the P-63 was a poor third in this evaluation category with only 126 gallons. The amount of fuel carried by each airplane could, of course, be augmented with auxiliary drop tanks (refer to the tabulation of drop tank installations). Without a heavy combat load of ordinance, the external fuel load a fighter could carry was sizable amounting to 2000 pounds and more of extra gasoline when long range ferrying operations were required. All three fighters had significant maximum weight capability. The P-51C Mustang, for instance, could takeoff at 12,000 pounds gross weight while the P-63C could lift off at around 11,000 pounds. When the aircraft were stripped for racing, this useful load capacity translated to large fuel quantities for transcontinental flight.

RACING AIRCRAFT CHARACTERISTICS

There was a perception on the part of many race pilots that a few entrants were strongly backed by the aircraft manufacturers. There was some substance to this suspicion although none of the prominent airframe companies cared to advertise the fact. Sponsorship, if that's what it could be called, was much more subtle. For the lucky few, engineering talent was contributed on a voluntary basis after working hours. Facilities were occasionally made available while management looked the other way and took no active role. If their product won, it might be noted and pleasure expressed. Employees of North American and Bell Aircraft, for instance, worked on their own time preparing racers. Larry Bell insisted that Jack Woolams, Alvin "Tex" Johnston and Charles "Slick" Goodlin divorce their efforts from the corporation by using a separate legal entity for their racing activities.[4]

Comparative Weight Values Military Fighter Configurations

Component	P-38L	P-51C	P-63C
Wing	1,860	1,066	1,152
Tail	417	183	178
Fuselage	1,454	509	676
Landing Gear	886	781	607
Engine Section	471	274	(1)
Engine(s)	2,730	1,670	1,710
Engine Accessories	321	(1)	114
Engine Controls	81	30	41
Propeller(s)	827	483	460
Starting System	82	25	58
Cooling System	1065	663	346
Supercharger(s)	614	(1)	(1)
Lubrication Systems	194	101	135
Fuel System	506	320	343
Instruments	73	48	46
Surface Controls	234	108	141
Hydraulic System	209	57	(3)
Electrical System	321	176	202
Commo Equipment	162	163	146
Armament Provisions	176	246	378
Furnishings	96	85	93
Other	2	(3)	30
Total Empty Weight	12,780	6,988	6,856

Notes:
(1) Included in engine weight
(2) Not broken out for P-63
(3) Not given

Source:
Aircraft specification weight statements.

In truth, most participants acted in their own behalf and enlisted the aid of friends, family and acquaintances as volunteer race crew members. Pilots directly or informally connected with Lockheed, North American, Bell, Goodyear and United Aircraft did have a decided advantage due to their familiarity with the company's product and access to engineering talent. A rare exception was Jacqueline Cochran whose wealth could buy any necessary expertise. Others, such as Earl Ortman and Charley Tucker lacked any serious sponsorship and relied upon past experience, volunteer help and intuition. Their situation was the norm. Only a handful of pilots enjoyed the indirect support of prominent aircraft or engine manufacturers.

JACKIE COCHRAN'S GREEN MACHINE

Louis Wait, head of flight testing for North American Aviation, entered a P-51 in the 1946 Bendix.[5] Wait didn't own the airplane. He entered the stripped down Mustang for the well known Jacqueline Cochran who yearned to be involved in the transcontinental classic one more time. A week before the race she told the press of her intention to enter a racer. Jackie said her industrialist husband, Floyd B. Odlum, "and some of her friends think that, having won the race once and not really needing the prize money, I might better sit this one out."[6] She was exploring the possibility of having Western Air Lines captain Paul Penrose fly her Mustang. Jackie obviously was toying with the idea of flying the plane herself. A day or so later, Jackie put aside her husband's objections and decided to fly the race.

Cochran was undecided about racing in the Bendix. She was considering having Western Air Lines pilot Paul Penrose (left) fly the P-51. Louis Wait (right) was a North American test pilot and originally entered the plane in the Bendix, presumably at Jackie's request. Credit: Birch Matthews collection

Jackie Cochran's green P-51B-15 Mustang was fitted with 165 gallon drop tanks. The aircraft is shown here at North American's Inglewood, CA, facility prior to the race. The date was 28 August 1946. Credit: Birch Matthews collection

Chapter IX: The New Breed

Jackie Cochran's Mustang is ready for a flight from Mines Field in Los Angeles. The massive size of the drop tanks can be seen in this view. Credit: Birch Matthews collection

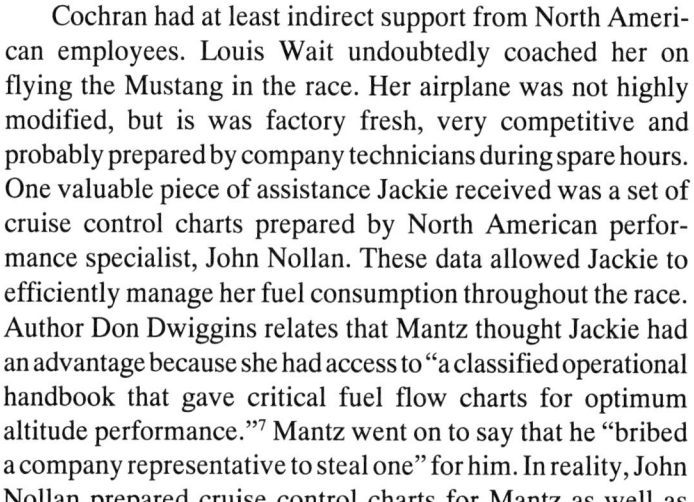

In this photograph, Jackie's Mustang is sitting on the ramp in front of the Aviation Maintenance hangar at Van Nuys airport on the day before the 1946 Bendix. Credit: Dusty Carter via A. Kevin Grantham

Cochran had at least indirect support from North American employees. Louis Wait undoubtedly coached her on flying the Mustang in the race. Her airplane was not highly modified, but is was factory fresh, very competitive and probably prepared by company technicians during spare hours. One valuable piece of assistance Jackie received was a set of cruise control charts prepared by North American performance specialist, John Nollan. These data allowed Jackie to efficiently manage her fuel consumption throughout the race. Author Don Dwiggins relates that Mantz thought Jackie had an advantage because she had access to "a classified operational handbook that gave critical fuel flow charts for optimum altitude performance."[7] Mantz went on to say that he "bribed a company representative to steal one" for him. In reality, John Nollan prepared cruise control charts for Mantz as well as Cochran. He was certainly aware these two strong personalities had little use for each other, a condition that dated to before the war.[8] John exercised great care in keeping his work for each of them well separated![9]

Jackie's Irish green P-51B Mustang was essentially stock although stripped of non-essential military gear for the 1946 race. It retained the self-sealing wing and fuselage tanks. She wanted to wet the wing of her airplane because she apparently knew Mantz had made this modification. "I was late in getting my Mustang," Jackie related in her autobiography, "and there was no time for such work. So I decided to carry exterior drop tanks."[10] There would be a drag penalty with the large external tanks, most of which would be eliminated when she released them during the race.

A smiling Jackie Cochran gets ready to climb out of the cockpit shortly after arriving in Cleveland. She was awarded second place after a timing error was straightened out. Credit: Birch Matthews collection

Cochran has just lifted off the runway at Van Nuys on her way to Cleveland. The big drop tanks damaged the wing trailing edge when she released them giving her trim problems for the remainder of the flight. Credit: A.U. Schmidt via Birch Matthews collection

The empty weight of Cochran's racer after removing unnecessary equipment was about 6500 pounds. To carry enough fuel for a non-stop race, 165 gallon drop tanks were installed on the wing pylons. This gave Jackie a total fuel capacity of 599 gallons. The takeoff gross weight of the racer with pilot, parachute, fuel and oil was close to 10,900 pounds, a third of which was aviation gas. With good fuel management based upon the work of John Nollan, Cochran could negotiate the Bendix without refueling but there was little margin for error. She would climb out of Van Nuys Airport to around 25,000 feet and it would take her some 15 minutes and about 24 gallons of fuel. Her plan was to cruise with an engine power setting of 61 inches of manifold pressure and 2700 revolutions letting the mighty dash 3 Merlin digest ten quarts of oil and 120 gallons each hour of the race. With favorable tail winds along the way, she would arrive in Cleveland with a small reserve of fuel. It was a good plan.

Paul Mantz introduced the wet wing concept to post-war transcontinental air racing. His P-51C-10 Mustang was beautifully prepared for the race. It is shown here on the Cleveland airport a day or so after he won the 1946 Bendix at 435 miles per hour. Credit: Emil Strasser

PAUL MANTZ'S RED BARON

Transcontinental air racing after World War II was truly the era of wet wings and drop tanks. Most of the contestants added the largest available drop tanks to the wings or fuselage of their aircraft intending to make one fast refueling stop on the way to Cleveland. Ideally, one loaded enough fuel onboard to fly the race non-stop above the weather at maximum power. This was a tall order because more than 800 gallons of gasoline would be needed for a stripped-down, single engine fighter plane to complete the race under these conditions.

One individual solved the problem though, and that was Hollywood movie pilot Albert Paul Mantz. He was the first of the post-war pilots to seal the wings on his airplane creating two really big fuel tanks. During the middle of February, 1946, Paul Mantz and two associates bought a large fleet of various war surplus planes speculating that many would be needed in war movies which they felt were sure to come.[11] Indeed, Mantz was right and some of the aircraft appeared in various movies. Most would be sold for scrap. The planes were located at the old Clinton Naval Air Station about half-way between Oklahoma City and the Texas state line. Mantz had one of his mechanics, Bob King, select two of the best looking Mustangs from his newly acquired "air force" with orders to get them ready for return to California.[12] The airplanes King chose were both P-51C-10 models, subsequently licensed NX1202 and NX1204. Both would go into the record books of the Bendix Trophy Race.

Chapter IX: The New Breed

Paul had piloted a plane in the Bendix twice before the war placing third each time in an aging Lockheed Orion. He wanted badly to win the Bendix in 1946, and this time he had the basic ingredients for victory. The P-51C Mustang was a superb airframe with a slightly lower fuselage drag coefficient than the later D model. It also used the Merlin V-1650-3 which was an excellent high altitude engine ideally suited for the Bendix race.

To win the race, Mantz needed to fly non-stop at full power meaning 67 inches of manifold pressure and 3000 engine revolutions using high blower. This power setting would eat up fuel at a prodigious rate, better than 160 gallons an hour. If he could do this without external fuel tanks, the airplane parasitic drag coefficient would be significantly reduced.[13] Drag reduction, of course, meant higher speed at no increase in power.

The Mantz Mustangs were carefully prepared by his trusted mechanics, Cort Johnson and Bob King at the Grand Central Air Terminal located in Glendale, California. The solution to Mantz's need of greater internal fuel capacity revolved around making the wing structure into a gasoline tank. This was done by removing the heavy self-sealing military fuel bladders and stripping the ammunition and gun bays. The outer wing panels and the wing fuel tank cavities (where the bladders had been) were treated with a viscous form of zinc chromate which acted as a sealant. The 85 gallon fuselage tank bladder was removed and a replacement thin wall metal tank installed. This yielded an impressive internal fuel volume of 856 gallons!

Mantz P-51C-10 Mustang Fuel Capacity 1946 Bendix Racer

Location	No. of Tanks	Gallons Per Tank	Total Gallons
Sealed Wing Tanks	2	110	220
Sealed Outer Wing Panels	2	160	320
Sealed Wing Leading Edges	2	75	150
Fuselage Tank	1	175	175
Total Volumetric Capacity			856

In spite of this prodigious fuel capacity, it could still be a marginal amount for a non-stop race at full throttle especially if Paul ran into adverse winds or weather. Mantz's fuel consumption rate for the race was most likely something over 170 gallons per hour. Allowing for some reserve and the possibility of weather along the way suggested that a greater margin would be prudent. Once again, the innovative Mantz

Mantz chilled the aviation gas with dry ice before filling his tanks. He was able to load a massive 875 gallons for his non-stop flight to Cleveland. The aircraft is shown here at Van Nuys before the race. Credit: Dusty Carter

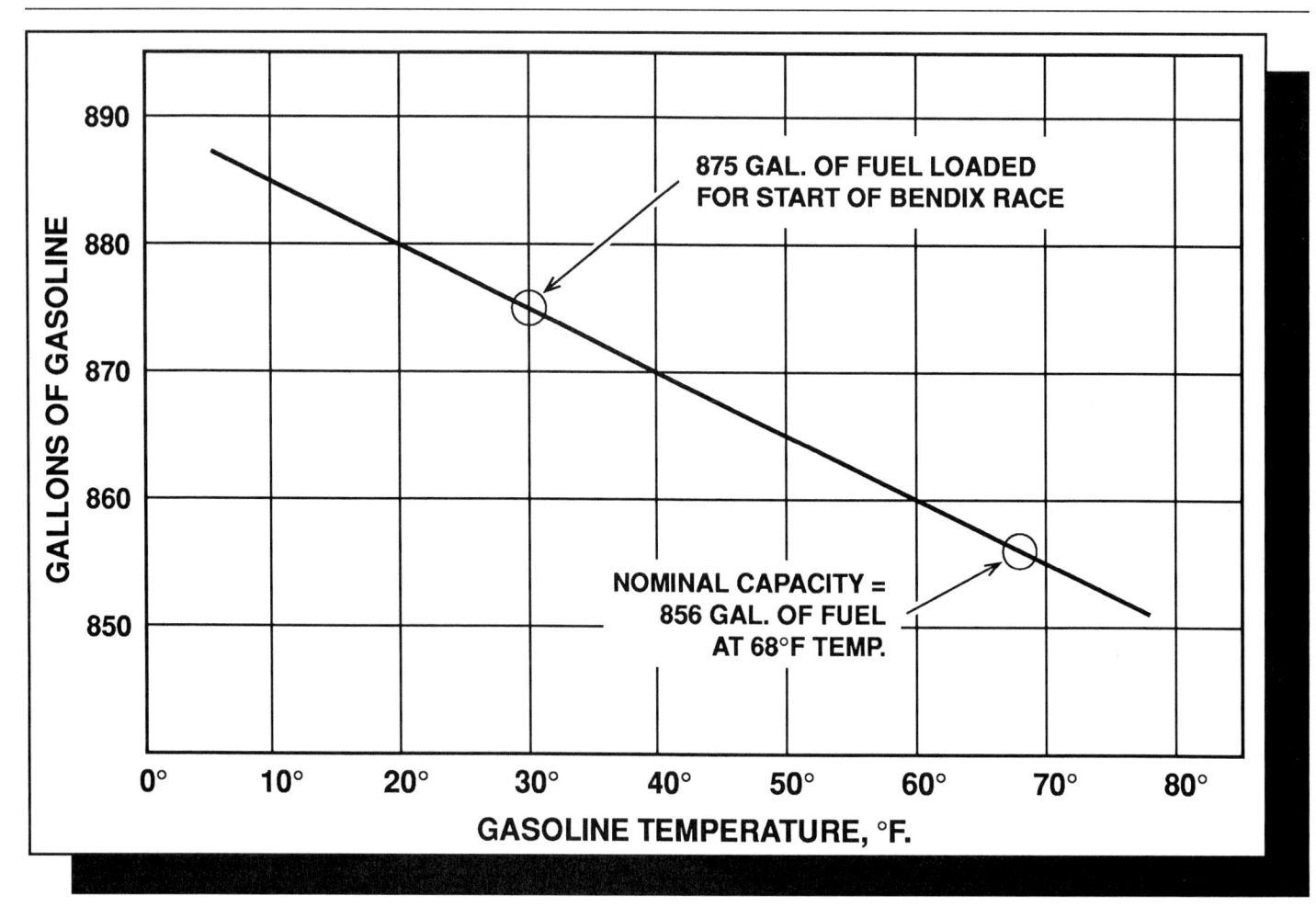

This curve shows the affect of chilling gasoline to make it more dense. At 68 degrees F., Mantz could put 856 gallons in his racer. Lowering the temperature about 38 degrees resulted in an equivalent volumetric capacity of 875 gallons, quite an increase. Once the chilled fuel was loaded, Mantz covered the wings to insulate against heating from the sun. Credit: Birch Matthews, illustration by Dave Hargreaves

came up with a solution. He would chill the gasoline to make it more dense. The day before the race, his crew placed containers full of dry ice into a Standard Oil tank truck and began the process of lowering the gasoline temperature.[14] A parametric thermal analysis of this cooling process suggests it required somewhere between 10 and 16 hours to chill the aviation fuel from ambient temperature to perhaps 30 degrees Fahrenheit. Once the fuel was chilled, Mantz was able to load 875 gallons into the racer.[15] He now had that extra margin. Mantz's airplane was truly a flying gasoline tank and very heavy at lift off, weighing over six tons! Paul's crimson red racer was ready.

Mantz's bright red Mustang is seen here taking off from Van Nuys in the 1946 Bendix race. His flight took four hours, 42 minutes. Credit: A.U. Schmidt via Birch Matthews collection

Color Gallery

Wayne Adams won the inaugural Harold's Club Transcontinental Trophy Dash flying this P-51D-25 Mustang. The airplane is shown as it appeared in 1966 at Reno. Credit: Birch Matthews

E.D. Weiner's checkered Mustang racer won four transcontinental air races and placed second in another event. This is a record unmatched by any other pilot or aircraft. Credit: Dusty Carter

Doug Wood entered this P-51D-25 in the 1965 Harold's Club race and placed seventh. This photograph was taken during the 1965 races at Lancaster, CA. Credit: Birch Matthews

When Mike Carroll bought his Sea Fury from its Canadian owner, the fighter was red with gold trim. Modifications had just started when this photograph was taken in August, 1965, at Long Beach, CA. Credit: Birch Matthews

Color Gallery 163

During a takeoff at Long Beach, Mike nearly lost the Sea Fury by retracting the gear to soon. The wing tip is inches off the ground and all five propeller blades were ground as they struck the runway. Credit: Emil Strasser

Dick Kestle was second in the 1966 transcontinental race. The race ended here at Palm Springs where the temperature was 114 degrees in the shade! Credit: Birch Matthews

There was no Harold's Club race in 1966. Mike brought his Sea Fury to Reno where Lyle Shelton flew it in the pylon events. Mike flew this same airplane to victory in the 1967 cross-country race. Credit: Birch Matthews

Race 14 was second in the 1967 race. E.D. must have been a bit surprised when he made his pass over Stead Field at the finish of the race and saw Mike Carroll's Sea Fury sitting in front of the stands. Credit: Ken MacLean collection

Color Gallery

Jim Ventura crashed fatally in this P-51D-30 during the 1967 cross-country race to Cleveland. The airplane is seen here at Palm Springs, CA, where the race started. Credit: Birch Matthews

H.F. "Mick" Rupp was forced out of the 1967 Trophy Dash shortly after takeoff. The aircraft is seen here at Rockford, IL, where the race started. Credit: Ken MacLean

This stock P-51D-20 was flown by Dr. Mark R. Foutch in the 1968 race. The racer was forced out at Laramie, WY, with engine problems. Credit: Jim Morrow

Fifth place in the 1968 transcon race was earned by Tom Kuchinsky in this P-51D-25. His average speed was 246 miles per hour. Credit: Birch Matthews

Color Gallery

Walt Ohlrich, Jr., entered his Grumman F8F-2 in the 1968 race equipped with external fuel tanks. Walt didn't start the race that year, but did go on to place eighth in the 1969 race. Credit: Harry Gann

For the 1968 race, E.D. Weiner modified his transcon racer and changed the checker paint scheme from black and white to yellow and black. He won the race with this beautiful Mustang. Credit: Birch Matthews

E.D. Weiner's checkered Mustang won the 1967 Harold's Club race. The airframe, although very clean, was essentially stock. Credit: Jim Larsen

Color Gallery

This rare and beautiful Grumman F8F-1 placed seventh in the 1969 race. It was owned and flown by Gunther Balz. Credit: Jim Larsen

The first Bearcat to compete in the Harold's Club race belonged to Bob Kucera. His F8F-2 finished fourth in the 1968 race. Credit: Birch Matthews

Jim Fugate entered this P-51D-25 Mustang in the 1968 race, but didn't start. He did fly in the pylon races that year. Credit: Birch Matthews

Color Gallery

Dick Kestle was a consistent entrant in the Reno transcon races. His airplane appeared as shown here at the 1968 races. Credit: Birch Matthews

John Sliker raced this P-51D-30 and took second place in the 1969 Harold's Club race. He finished just one minute behind Dick Kestle. Credit: Birch Matthews

This P-51D-30 was entered in the 1969 race by Bob Guilford. The aircraft did not start the race, but arrived in Reno later in time for the pylon events. Credit: Birch Matthews

In 1969, Tom Kuchinsky flew this P-51D-25 to third place. Although his plane carried race 18 again, it was a different Mustang than the one he flew the previous year. Credit: Birch Matthews

Color Gallery

E.D. Weiner landed in his pylon racer as shown here after having a heart attack during a 1969 Reno heat race. He was taken to a Reno hospital and died a few days later. Credit: Birch Matthews

The 1969 Harold's Club Race victor was Dick Kestle in his now familiar P-51D-20. The aircraft was essentially unchanged from the previous year. Credit: Birch Matthews

Sherm Cooper bought Mike Carroll's racing Sea Fury and entered the 1969 transcon race. Cooper was unable to start and subsequently flew in the pylon events that year. This photo was taken at Long Beach 1 April 1970. Credit: Birch Matthews

Although E.D. Weiner entered the 1969 race with his transcon Mustang and a new sponsor, he was unable to compete. His sponsor this year was STP and the racer was repainted. Credit: Dusty Carter

Color Gallery

Ron Reynolds entered the last Harold's Club race in 1970 with this Grumman F8F-2 Bearcat. He was forced out of the race at Sioux City with engine trouble. Credit: Birch Matthews

Burns Byram flew in the last three Harold's Club races. He placed fifth in this P-51D-25 in the 1970 race. Credit: Birch Matthews

Dick Kestle captured the 1969 and 1970 transcon races. His Mustang is seen here as it appeared the last race in 1970. Credit: Birch Matthews

Howard Keefe's beautiful P-51D-30 Mustang finished fourth in the 1970 Harold's Club race. Credit: Birch Matthews

Chapter IX: The New Breed

One other D model Mustang was entered by 34 year old Paul J. Franklin, a former North American Aviation test pilot and then operating a flying service and school in Culver City, California. Franklin purchased his P-51 from the War Assets Administration at Walnut Ridge, Arkansas, on 24 June 1946. He wanted to enter the Bendix and it's believed that he also wet the wing of his Mustang. Civil Aeronautics Administration records for this airplane tell of fuel system modifications made by Franklin for the purpose of racing and exhibition flying.[16] At the eleventh hour, he ran into debilitating carburetor problems which kept him from starting the race.

Mantz had trouble retracting the landing gear on his racer after leaving Van Nuys. The landing gear door to the left of the landing light retracted ahead of the wheel when the sequencer valve malfunctioned. He recycled the gear and it tucked away into the wing properly. Credit: North American via Gerry Balzer collection

THE OTHER MUSTANGS

In addition to the P-51s of Paul Mantz and Jacqueline Cochran, three other Mustangs were entered in the 1946 Bendix. Tommy Mayson flew the second Mantz P-51C which also had a wet wing. The fourth Mustang in the race was flown by William Eddy of La Jolla, California. His airplane was a P-51D model, the only one in the 1946 race. Curiously, Eddy flew without drop tanks apparently using only the stock 269 gallon internal tank capacity of the P-51 and refueling enroute.

Estimated Takeoff Weight Mantz P-51C-10 Bendix Racer

Component	Weight Pounds
Military Empty Weight	6,988
Less Armament	-246
Less Furnishings	-85
Less Miscellaneous	-200
Pilot and Chute	200
21.5 Gallons of Coolant	266
21 Gallons of Oil	158
3.75 Gallons of Hydraulic Fluid	28
875 Gallons of Aviation Gas	5,250
Gross Weight at Takeoff	12,359

Paul Mantz gets towed after the Bendix race. The airplane has been washed down and cleaned up following the grueling transcontinental race. Credit: Birch Matthews collection

Mantz had two Mustangs set up for the Bendix race. His second airplane is shown here at Van Nuys before the race. Tommy Mayson, one of Mantz's charter pilots, flew this P-51C-10. Credit: Dusty Carter

Mayson finished third in the Bendix in 1946. Only the wings of this Mustang were painted and smoothed to take advantage of the laminar flow airfoil. Credit: Warren Bodie

CHARLEY TUCKER'S P-63C

Born and raised in Philadelphia, Charley Tucker migrated to California, and attended Pasadena Junior College. While going to school, he received his first ride in a Luscombe airplane and he knew he wanted to learn to fly. He joined the Civilian Pilot Training Program and obtained his private license in a Piper J2 Cub at the old Alhambra airport. Chuck went on to take an advanced course at Vail Field flying a Waco UPF biplane.

With this foundation, Tucker enlisted in the Army Air Corp as a flying cadet. He was sent to Santa Maria, California, to attend the Hancock College of Aeronautics, one of nine original civil contract schools in the Army's primary flight training program.[17] After completing primary, Chuck went on to Luke Field in Arizona, for advanced training. Charley Tucker won his wings and commission in the Air Corp on 9 January 1942, shortly after America entered the war. By April, Chuck was in China where he cajoled his way into General Chenault's 14th Air Force serving under John Allison, commanding officer of the 75th Fighter Squadron.

Returning to the United States in 1944, Tucker was one of the very early jet pilots flying twin-engine Bell P-59s at Muroc Army Air Field. It was after his return to the States that Chuck first flew the Bell P-63 Kingcobra and grew to like it even more than the P-51 Mustang. He was discharged from military service in 1945. "When the National Air Races came along, I was just loafing and playing some golf," Chuck remembers.[18] He decided to go racing. "I had some money saved up and this sounded like a hell of an idea." He needed an airplane. Actually, he needed two airplanes; one for the Bendix and one for the Thompson Trophy race. "I thought gee, the P-63 is $1,000 and the P-51 is $3,500. I'll take the P-63. I can get two for the price of one. So I did. I bought two of them."[19] Both

Paul Franklin entered this P-51D-10 in the 1946 Bendix, but was unable to start because of carburetor problems. This same airplane was flown in the 1947 race by Joe Debona. Credit: Roger Besecker collection

Bill Eddy flew this stock P-51D-20 Mustang to fourth place in the 1946 Bendix race. This photograph was taken at Van Nuys before the race. Credit: Dusty Carter via A. Kevin Grantham

Right: Eddy's Mustang is shown here at Cleveland after the race. Aside from race number 31, there were virtually no markings on the airplane. Credit: Warren Bodie

Chapter IX: The New Breed

Chuck Tucker's P-63C-5 sits on the ramp at Van Nuys in this photograph taken before the race. With the tip mounted tanks, this Kingcobra lifted off from Van Nuys with over 2700 pounds of Mobil aviation gas onboard. Mobil furnished the fuel for the race. Credit: Dusty Carter

were P-63C-5 Kingcobras purchased from the War Assets Administration office at Kingman, Arizona.

Tucker's Bendix racer was licensed NX63231 and carried race number 30. This airplane was built by Bell Aircraft at their plant on the Niagara Falls Airport in Wheatfield, New York, and accepted by the Army on 2 June 1945. The Kingcobra was flown to Sioux City, Iowa, where it had a brief undistinguished military existence for four months. In late October, the airplane was declared surplus and flown to Kingman where it became the property of the Reconstruction Finance Corporation.[20] The Kingcobra languished at Kingman until purchased by Charley Tucker in June, 1946.

The task of preparing two airplanes for the races was a bit more time consuming than Tucker anticipated. His "race team" consisted almost entirely of himself and his younger brother. Seeking advice on how to modify his airplanes for the races, Chuck contacted Bell Aircraft chief engineer, Robert M. "Bob" Stanley. Stanley told him the fighter had too much wing for racing and he should reduce the span. This he did with

The Kingcobra had cockpit doors and roll-down windows like an automobile. Chuck Tucker poses long enough for this candid photograph while in the cockpit of his P-63. Credit: Charles Tucker collection via Phil Krause

Estimated Takeoff Weight
Tucker P-63C-5 Bendix Racer

Component	Weight Pounds
Military Empty Weight	6,856
Less Ventral Fin	-15
Less Armament	-378
Less Armor Plate	-169
Less Furnishings	-64
Less Miscellaneous	-100
Wing Tip Tanks (2)	230
Tank Mounts (2)	20
Lines, Fittings, Etc.	10
Pilot and Chute	175
Internal Fuel (126 Gallons)	756
Tip Tanks (330 Gallons)	1,980
Trapped Fuel (2 Gallons)	12
Oil (19.4 Gallons)	146
Reduction Gear Box (2 Gallons)	15
Coolant (13.1 Gallons)	121
Gross Weight at Takeoff	9,601

The relative size of the external tanks is shown in this photograph as Chuck Tucker stands next to the left wing tip. The airplane is at Van Nuys airport ready for the 1946 Bendix race. Credit: Charles Tucker collection via Phil Krause

Tucker could not fly the Bendix non-stop. He made arrangements to refuel at Garden City. He landed and refueled hot, never shutting down the big Allison. This picture shows the ground crew filling the wing and external tanks simultaneously. Credit: Charles Tucker collection via Phil Krause

Spiro "Sammy" Dilles flew this P-63C-5 in the Bendix. He was forced out with mechanical problems at Winslow, AZ. Credit: Repla-Tech via Tim Weinschenker

a vengeance on the Thompson racer literally sawing off almost ten feet. Alterations to the Bendix plane were much more modest. Chuck and his brother simply removed the wing tips where the wing spars ended. This left a wingspan of 34.6 feet, about four feet less than a stock wing. Wing area after the tips were removed was just over 227 square feet, some eight percent less than the military P-63C wing. This gave a wing loading of 42 pounds per square foot at a gross takeoff weight of 9600 pounds at the start of the Bendix.

Chuck bought two 165 gallon drop tanks and attached them to the spar ends. The tip tanks were plumbed into the existing fuel system. To enclose the tank structural attachments, fairings were fashioned from aluminum sheet stock. The only other airframe modification to race 30 was removal of the ventral fin, saving some 15 pounds of weight. The ventral fin was added to the C-5 model of the Kingcobra to increase directional stability and make the airplane into a better gun platform.[21] It was certainly not needed for a racing machine. In addition to these external changes, all unneeded weight was removed from the airplane including navigation equipment. Chuck would fly the Bendix using only a directional gyro correcting any deviations by observing ground terrain features. He retained only one four channel radio for air-to-ground communications which would allow him to contact the tower at his refueling stop.

Charley Tucker could not fly the Bendix non-stop. The Allison V-1710-117 engine was unmodified except that the water injection system was not used. Without a wet wing, Chuck simply couldn't carry enough gasoline to feed the big Allison at a competitive power setting. Instead, he arranged with the Air Force base commander at Garden City, Kansas,

Chapter IX: The New Breed

The laminar flow wings on Tucker's P-63 were painted white and the remainder of the airframe was in natural finish. He finished seventh in the Bendix with an average speed of 367 miles per hour. Credit: Airphotos

to refuel enroute. His flight profile would range between 25,000 and 30,000 feet with the Allison running at 50-55 inches and 3000 revolutions.

THE UBIQUITOUS LOCKHEED LIGHTNING

The 1946 Bendix list of entrants was the largest in the history of this event. There were a minimum of 27 aircraft entered.[22,23] Five would not start for one reason or another narrowing the field to 22 aircraft. One contemporary newspaper article claimed as many as 50 participants might fly the race.[24] This number may represent the number of inquiries received by the contest committee. Statistically, Lockheed was well represented at the start of the race. Of the 22 aircraft departing Van Nuys on race day, no less than 14 were P-38 and F-5G Lightnings. The F-5G was a photo reconnaissance version of the ubiquitous Lockheed fighter.

That the Lockheed Lightning was so popular was probably due to one of several reasons. The airplane had two turbosupercharged Allison V-1710 engines giving it excellent high altitude performance and twin engine reliability providing a nice comfort factor during a grueling 2000 mile transcontinental race. Compared to a P-51, the cost of a Lightning was quite reasonable. Surplus Mustangs were not as readily available to civilian buyers in 1946.[25,26]

Automobile race driver Rex Mays flew this F-5G-6 Lightning to 13th place in the 1946 Bendix. It was sponsored by MacMillan Oil and like Roscoe Turner's 1937 racer, was called the "Meteor." Credit: Dusty Carter via A. Kevin Grantham

Red-haired Nadine Ramsey was one of the first to fly into Van Nuys airport for the race, arriving on 19 August. Nadine was enthusiastic about her chances saying she would "win if Jackie Cochran doesn't get into it."[27] She figured she was "a cinch to be in the money at Cleveland," because there was a special prize of $1000 for the first woman to cross the finish line.[28] At that point, she was the only women entered. Nadine's dreams would not be realized. Mechanical problems forced

Number 70 was raced by Harvey M. Hughes and his F-5G-6 was named "Paul Bunyan." Hughes finished a respectable 8th right behind Chuck Tucker. Credit: Birch Matthews collection

The "Paul Bunyan" sits outside weathering in the years following the Cleveland races. This was the fate of many ex-warbirds after 1949. Credit: Roger Besecker collection

occurred, Paul climbed over Palmdale and put the heavy Mustang through a loop that shook the gear loose. He recycled the landing gear and this time everything worked as it should. Mantz was on his way to Cleveland.

With the airplane cleaned up, Mantz went to a full throttle power setting of 67 inches and 3000 revolutions per minute. The Merlin responded smoothly. Paul flew by the reading on his manifold pressure gauge, increasing or decreasing altitude to maintain 67 inches which on this day, ranged between 30,000 and 35,000 feet. He reported some cloud cover, but not enough to prohibit locating his first visual check at Pueblo, Colorado. Aided by a modest tail wind, he crossed the Colorado River, racing over the Arizona desert wasteland, past the Continental Divide and on into the flat prairies of the midwest. When he arrived over Fort Bend, Indiana, Mantz put the scarlet red Mustang into a shallow dive and began a long fast decent toward Cleveland. Advising race control that he was nearing the airport, Paul brought the racer down to 1000 feet, flashed over the finish line and with bravado, performed a slow victory roll as he climbed away preparing to land. He had flown the Bendix in four hours and 42 minutes at an average speed of 435 miles per hour, shattering the old record of 282 miles an hour set by Frank Fuller in 1939. With the sweet taste of victory came $10,000 in first place money.

Behind Paul Mantz was a steady stream of aircraft strung out across the country. Each pilot was intent on making Cleveland and picking up part of the prize money awarded to the first seven pilots crossing the finish line. One of those in the hunt was Jackie Cochran in her bright green Mustang racer. She was in for a rough ride. Cochran's Mustang was flagged away from Van Nuys at 8:51 a.m. Thundering down runway 34, the Merlin pulled her P-51 into the air without missing a beat. Jackie wheeled the fighter around and climbed for altitude and the long flight east.

Jackie had a full fuselage tank at the start of the race and this put the aircraft center of gravity so far aft that longitudinal stability of her racer was marginal. She had to fly with caution. If she lost control and the airplane dived, a steep pull out would result in a reversal of control stick forces. This could spell disaster. The racer could shed a wing. The problem was so severe that during the war, North American added "a 20 pound bob weight to the elevator control system of all Mustangs, increasing the stability to a point where the airplane was marginally stable with approximately 35 gallons of fuel remaining in the fuselage tank."[32] Jackie had to consume at least

Pilot John Schields flew this P-38L-5 into Cleveland after the six o'clock Bendix deadline and didn't place. This photograph was taken in 1950 at Mitchell Field, Milwaukee, and is another example of how so many of the racers deteriorated from neglect.

The only FG-1D Corsair entered in the Bendix was flown by Thomas Call. The aircraft was all white and carried a single external drop tank on the fuselage centerline. Credit: Birch Matthews collection

Chapter IX: The New Breed

The ramp area outside the Aviation Maintenance hangar was filled with airplanes for the 1946 Bendix race. Credit: A.U. Schmidt

The "Caribbean Queen," out of Miami FL, was flown by Don Husted. The A-26C-55 carried race number 45 and finished in 6th place. Credit: Harold G. Martin via Tim Weinschenker

This is another view of the 1946 Bendix airplanes before the race. Ten aircraft are visible in this photograph. Credit: A.U. Schmidt

50 gallons from this tank before she could feel more comfortable. With the fuel management charts provided by John Nollan, Jackie began the race using this tank to feed the Merlin.

Thirty or forty minutes into the race, Jackie switched to the drop tanks. The sooner these were depleted, the quicker she could shed the tanks and reduce drag. Timing was important for another reason. The external tanks had to be released over desolate unpopulated country or they could not be dropped and the drag penalty they presented would endure throughout the race. To make matters more complicated, a cloud layer obscured the ground and Jackie's radio failed somewhere over the California-Arizona border. Over the Grand Canyon, she ran into turbulent weather and attempted to climb on top only to encounter a surge in engine power as her speed and manifold pressure bled off. She had no choice. Jackie lowered the nose of the airplane letting it build up speed so that ram air pressure to the supercharger would increase. This put her right back into the weather front which was really turbulent.

When she passed beyond this tempest, Jackie released the big 165 gallon drop tanks over the Rocky Mountains only to receive another rude surprise. As the tanks were released, they rotated in the slipstream. The aft end of the tanks collided with the wing trailing edge. The impact deformed the wing and altered aircraft trim. Jackie adjusted the trim tabs to the extreme without completely overcoming the problem. Describing the difficulty after the race, Jackie told reporters that she . . . "had by force to hold the stick far out of neutral to maintain flying attitude," for the remainder of the race.[33]

The external tanks Jackie carried on the race were quite long, extending well beyond the wing trailing edge which no doubt exacerbated the situation. The phenomenon of drop tanks colliding with the Mustang airframe as they were released was not completely unusual. North American aerodynamicist Jack Daniels recalled that this happened occasionally and that many hours of wind tunnel tests were expended using scale tank models to evaluate and understand tank trajectories.[34] In spite of her compounding problems, Jackie Cochran roared into Cleveland to capture second place.

North American P-51 Mustangs swept the top four places in the race. By coincidence, all of the Mustangs were flown by California pilots. Thomas Mayson, flying the second Mantz airplane, took third place while Bill Eddy ran fourth. Eddy's takeoff caused a moment of concern when after liftoff, the P-51 rolled left unexpectedly. He corrected his flight path and continued to climb.[35] Eddy's Mustang did not have a wet wing and he had to make one fast five minute refueling stop. Over Jolliet, Illinois, Bill's oxygen system failed at 26,000 feet.[36] He descended to 16,000 feet and finished the race, but it cost him valuable time. When he landed, the Mustang was out of gas. Bill had nearly cut things too fine!

Chuck Tucker knew he would have to refuel enroute to Cleveland. Before the race, he contacted the base commander at Garden City, Kansas, and made arrangements. As it turned out, Garden City would also refuel the Lockheed P-80 fighters competing in the jet division of the Bendix, a brand new feature on the race program for 1946. Charley climbed out of Van Nuys and pointed the nose of his P-63 toward Kansas. He loved to fly the P-63 Kingcobra while simultaneously acknowledging it was noisy and rattled a lot with that long drive shaft running between his legs from the hard-mounted Allison behind the seat to the gear reduction box ahead. When asked to contrast a Mustang to the P-63, Chuck admits the P-51 is a Cadillac by comparison. It is quieter and the Merlin engine mount featured shock mounts to minimize vibration. Nonetheless, having many hours in each type of fighter, he preferred the P-63.

Charley Tucker, like so many of the Bendix pilots, had no deep pocket sponsor. The expenses were all out of his own pocket. He did manage to persuade Mobil Oil to furnish aviation gas for the race and in turn, he put their flying red horse emblem on his racer. Leaving Van Nuys, Chuck climbed to 30,000 feet urging the Allison to 55 inches and 3000 revolutions as he headed for Kansas. He made a fast landing at Garden City Air Force Base where he refuel hot – with the engine running. When the P-63 rolled to a stop, his refueling crew swarmed about the racer pouring in hundreds of gallons.

When the gasoline fueling hoses were swept away, Chuck opened the throttle and lifted the Kingcobra away toward Cleveland. He arrived over the finish line five hours and 34 minutes after departing Van Nuys and took seventh place with an average speed of 367 miles per hour. He was 40 seconds behind sixth place finisher Don Husted's Douglas A-26 and only three minutes behind Jim Harp who took fifth place in an F-5G. It was a very credible performance and one he would long remember.

Aside from Jim Harp's fifth place finish, the P-38s and F-5Gs did not fare well. Nine out of ten Lockheeds finishing the Bendix ran out of the money. A P-38L flown by John Schields arrived after the 6 p.m. deadline and three other Lightnings were forced out of the race before reaching Cleveland. Bill Lear's F-5G was one of the Lockheeds finishing well down the list. He had to refuel once during the race and "landed as planned, at Kansas City and set some sort of record for refueling eight tanks. I landed downwind and rolled to a stop right between four gas trucks. Four and a half minutes later I was back on my way but the P-38 – that love of my life – wasn't quite fast enough to keep up with the P-51s."[37]

The first post-war Bendix Trophy Race was history. Mustangs swept the field establishing a trend that, with one exception, would continue until the last unlimited class transcontinental race was run.

NOTES:
1 *New York Times*, 16 September 1945, p. 12.
2 William T. Larkins, "War Assets," *Air Classics*, Vol. 28, No. 2, February 1992, p. 22.
3 *New York Times*, 1 April 1946, p. 13.
4 Birch Matthews, "Cobra," American Aviation Historical Society JOURNAL, Vol. 8, No. 3, 1963, p. 186.
5 Registration of Cochran's plane with the National Air Race contest committee is somewhat confusing. The "Press and Radio Manual" for the 1946 National Air Races shows North American Aviation as the entrant for race 13, NX28388. The "1946 Race Plane Registry," prepared by race management officials shows Louis S. Wait as the entrant for this plane. The registry document was obtained from the archives of the National Air and Space Museum.
6 *Los Angeles Times*, 27 August 1946, p. 8.
7 Don Dwiggins, *They Flew the Bendix*, J.B. Lippincott Company, Philadelphia, 1965, p. 114.
8 Don Dwiggins, *Hollywood Pilot*, Modern Literary Editions Publishing Company, New York, 1967, p. 162.
9 Interview by author with John Nollan on 12 March 1993.
10 Jacqueline Cochran, *The Stars at Noon*, Little, Brown and Company, Boston, 1954, p. 67.
11 Bill of sale issued by the War Assets Administration dated 19 February 1946.
12 Interview of Bob King by Dusty Carter circa July, 1988.
13 E.J. Horkey and J.G. Beerer, "Performance Calculations for Model P-51D Airplane", North American Aviation, Inc., 6 February 1946, pp. 29-30.
14 Dry ice is really carbon dioxide cooled until it freezes. Dry ice has a temperature of -165 degrees Fahrenheit.
15 Dwiggins, op.cit., 1965, p. 114.
16 Data extracted from the Federal Aviation Administration files on aircraft NX33699. Data compiled by Malcolm L. Gougon and provided courtesy of Dick Phillips in correspondence dated 27 June 1992.
17 Robert F. Schirmer, "AAC & AAF Civil Primary Flying Schools, 1939-1945," American Aviation Historical Society JOURNAL, Vol. 37, No. 4, 1992, p. 300.
18 Charles Tucker interview by Oliver Aldrich, 16 September 1986.
19 Ibid.
20 Aircraft Record Card, Air Force serial number 44-4126.
21 Harold I. Johnson, "Resume of NACA Stability and Control Tests of the Bell P-63 Series Airplane," NACA Memorandum Report for the Army Air Forces, NACA CMR Report No. L4J19, 19 October 1944.
22 "Press and Radio Manual," 1946 National Air Races, Cleveland, Ohio. See biographical notes on pilots, p. 10.
23 "1946 Race Plane Registry," National Aeronautic Association historical files located in the National Air and Space Museum, Washington, D.C.
24 *Cleveland (Ohio) Press*, 9 August 1946.
25 Personal correspondence to author from J. Skinner, dated 8 April 1963, concerning Earl Ortman's attempts to acquire a surplus P-51. Details of a Mustang acquisition were related during an interview of P.J. "Sep" Mighton by Jerry Skinner in early April, 1963.
26 Robert Hull, *A Season of Eagles*, Bob Hull Books, Bay Village, Ohio, 1984, p. 224.
27 *New York Times*, 25 August 1946, Section II, p. 11.
28 *Los Angeles Times*, 20 August 1946, Part II, p. 1.
29 *Cleveland Plain Dealer*, 16 August 1946.
30 Bill Lear, Jr., "Bill Lear Jr. and His P-38," *Sport Flying*, Vol. 6, No. 4, August, 1972, p. 52.
31 *Los Angeles Times*, 30 August 1946, p. 2.
32 Louis S. Wait, "Briefing for P-51 Pilot Instructors," North American Aviation, Inc., Report No. 8679, 8 August 1945, p. 4.
33 Cochran, op.cit., p. 70.
34 Telephone interview with Jack Daniels by the author on 11 March 1993.
35 *Los Angeles Times*, 31 August 1946, p. 5.
36 *New York Times*, 31 August 1946, p. 8.
37 Bill Lear, Jr., op.cit., p. 54.

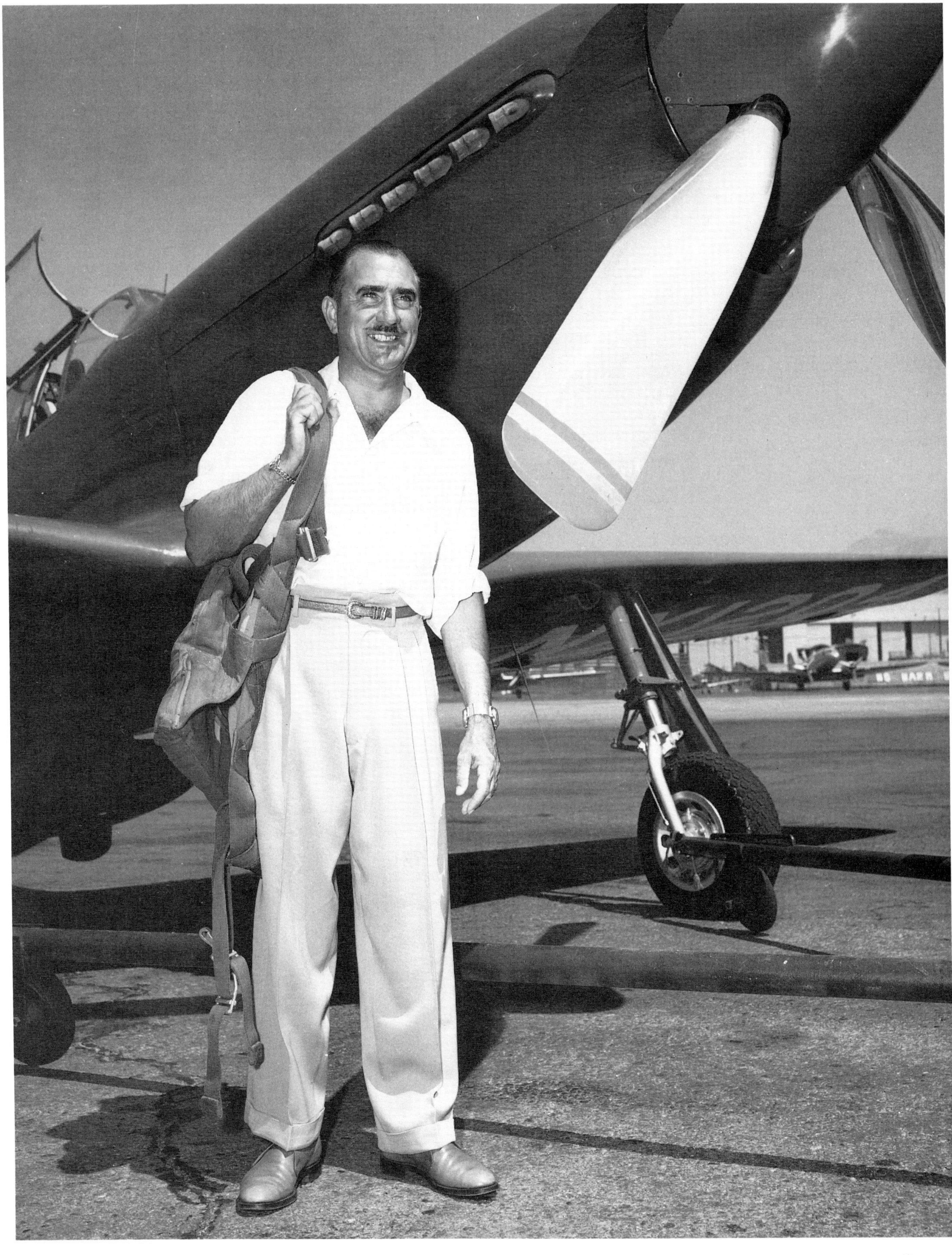

Chapter X

RACE PILOTS

The piston engine division of the Bendix Trophy Race was run for three more years, 1947-1949. These were the glory years for the Mustang transcontinental racing machines. They were simply unbeatable taking the gold, silver and bronze positions every year.

NINETEEN FORTY-SEVEN

The number of contestants entering the 1947 Bendix was drastically reduced compared to the previous year. Only 13 aircraft arrived at the Aviation Maintenance hangar on the Van Nuys airport to run in this year's race. Twelve airplanes took off on the day of the race, but only nine finished. The lone non-starter was Bill Odom who once again was unable to get his big YP-47 Thunderbolt off the ground. This time, he developed fuel leaks which could not be repaired in time to race. In 1946, a needle in the ignition harness kept him on the ground.

Paul Mantz was back again with his wet wing Mustang, but this time, he had some stiff competition from newcomers Joseph C. DeBona and Edmund Lunken. Both had wet the wings of their D model Mustang racers. Tommy Mayson would again fly the other Paul Mantz P-51 and Bruce Gimbel was chosen to fly Jacqueline Cochran's P-51. While her plane still sported external drop tanks, it could be counted on to give the others a run for the money. The sixth Mustang in this race would be flown by William Eddy. His racer was basically unchanged from the previous year and he would need to refuel during the race.

The distaff side of the aviation community was well represented by 25-year old Jane Page Hlavacek from Wilmette, Illinois, flying a Lockheed F-5G. Jane was an experienced pilot having served 19 months as a WASP (Women Air Force Service Pilot) during the war. The other woman pilot was Dianna Cyrus of Santa Paula, California.

The 24-year old Dianna entered a Douglas A-26B powered by two supercharged Pratt & Whitney R-2800-71 Double Wasp engines each generating 2000 horsepower at 1500 revolutions for takeoff. The A-26B Invader, named "Huntress," was a sleek looking design utilizing a National Advisory Committee for Aeronautics six thousand series laminar flow airfoil. Stripped of military equipment and armament, the civil version of this attack aircraft would be considerably lighter and certainly capable of flying the race non-stop. With a gross weight of somewhere between 27,000 and 30,000 pounds at takeoff, Dianna Cyrus' A-26 could do in excess of 350 miles per hour at altitude.[1] Her airplane wouldn't challenge a wet wing Mustang, but she might well place in the money.

A lone Bell P-63C Kingcobra was entered by Joseph M. Kinkella of Kingman, Arizona. Young 22-year old Kinkella was an ex-military fighter pilot with two and one-half years in the Army Air Force. In spite of his youth, he was an experienced pilot having learned to fly when he was only 16 years old. His racer belonged to another Kingmanite, William Bricker, and Joe leased

Opposite: Paul poses before his Mustang at Lockheed Air Terminal in Burbank. He was undecided about flying the race and at the time, was considering Ed Lunken, Stan Reaver and "Fish" Salmon as candidates. Credit: A.U. Schmidt

Ex-WASP pilot Jane Page Hlavacek flew this Lockheed F-5G-6 in the 1947 Bendix. It was the same aircraft raced by Harold Johnson the pervious year. Credit: Roger Besecker collection

Dianna Cyrus was the only other woman in the 1947 race. She flew this A-26B which developed a malfunctioning compass causing her to land in Michigan, out of the race. Credit: Birch Matthews collection

the airplane for the race. While his mechanics stripped excess weight from the P-63 and installed wing pylons and two 75 gallon drop tanks, Kinkella flew a BT-13 east to review the route he would take during the race.[2] He wanted to be thoroughly familiar with his navigation check points, refueling arrangements and the finish line at Cleveland.

Globe girdling record holder Bill Odom was back again with the same Republic YP-47 Thunderbolt that did not start in 1946. His sponsor was industrialist Milton Reynolds who accompanied Odom on the first round-the-world flight in the Douglas A-26, "Reynold's Bombshell." Odom was convinced that his airplane could beat Paul Mantz and win the Bendix. The big fighter had been set up in Houston, Texas, and Odom looked forward to adding this race to his laurels. He arrived at Van Nuys on Friday, 29 August flying in with his friend, R.A. Cole, at the controls of the famous Bombshell.

A Navy FG-1D Corsair flown by Tom Call in the 1946 race was back again for this year's contest. Entered by Dave Weyler, the gull wing Corsair would be raced this time by Marine Air Corp Reserve pilot, Frank P. Whitton. The balance of the field was made up of Bill Lear's F-5G and James C. Ruble's P-38F Lockheed Lightnings.

TEXAS LIGHTING

Ruble's P-38 represented an interesting and provocative challenge to Paul Mantz. This Lightning was one of 4,822 surplus warplanes including 1,165 fighters stored at Walnut Ridge, Arkansas.[3] The entire lot was purchased during June, 1946, by the Texas Railway Equipment Corporation, a company owned by George and Herman Brown of Houston, Texas. These entrepreneurs planned to scrap the aircraft after salvaging salable components and selling the aviation gasoline drained from the fuel cells. Few of the planes escaped the smelter; however, one that did was P-38F-15, Air Force serial number

Bill Odom returned for the 1947 Bendix with the big black and white YP-47M. The aircraft developed a fuel leak which could not be repaired in time to start the race. Credit: M.P. Mayo

Odom completed a record breaking around-the-world flight in this A-26 named the "Reynolds Bombshell." The aircraft was on display at the start of the Bendix. Credit: M.P. Mayo

Chapter X: Race Pilots

The P-38F-15 in the foreground was flown by Jim Ruble, chief pilot for oil and hotel man Glenn McCarthy. The racer was P-80 gray with green trim. It carried four external tanks for a planned non-stop race. Credit: Birch Matthews collection

Young Joe Kinkella entered this Bell P-63C-5 Kingcobra, the only one of its type in the 1947 race. He used two 75 gallon drop tanks and planned to refuel en route. Joe was forced out with mechanical problems at Pueblo, CO. Credit: M.P. Mayo

Ruble lost the starboard tip tank on takeoff from Van Nuys. His troubles weren't over. The port turbo failed over northern Arizona and started a fire. Ruble bailed out safely. Credit: Birch Matthews collection

43-2181. This early model Lightning was acquired from Texas Railway Equipment by Ivis V. Hill in June, 1947, and subsequently sold to the McCarthy Oil & Gas Corporation of Houston, Texas.[4]

Wealthy oil man and hotel magnate Glenn McCarthy was out to win the 1947 Bendix and he had the financial resources to indulge this pursuit. Former Army Air Force captain Jim Ruble would be his pilot. The P-38F was licensed N5101N and ferried to Van Nuys for racing modifications. In addition to stripping weight from the airframe, the cockpit windscreen and canopy profile were lowered and smoothly blended to the existing fuselage contour. Tip tanks were attached to the spar ends. The tank mounting arrangement was faired to the under surface of the wing just inboard of the wing tips. Two additional drop tanks were mounted on wing pylons inboard of the engine nacelles. Ruble intended to fly the race non-stop releasing empty external tanks during the flight.

The aircraft was painted a light shade of gray, the same color Lockheed used to finish their new P-80 Shooting Star jet fighter. In recognition of Glenn McCarthy's heritage, the P-38 was trimmed in green and christened the "Flying Shamrock." The Shamrock was a Houston hotel McCarthy owned. He reportedly spent $100,000 having the ex-fighter prepared for

Paul Mantz pushed his wet wing Mustang hard and again won the Bendix in 1947, at a very fast 460 miles per hour. The aircraft is seen here as it taxis past the grandstands at Cleveland. Credit: Pete Bowers

Tommy Mayson waits for the starter's flag in Paul Mantz's second Mustang racer. The racer had a wet wing and a very large fuselage tank. In 1947, the fuselage was painted yellow and the wings were red. Credit: Birch Matthews collection

the Bendix and was confident his racer would beat all the others including Mantz's crimson Mustang.[5] News of McCarthy's supreme confidence reached Paul Mantz. Always ready for competition, Mantz wired Glenn McCarthy offering to wager $10,000 that his Mustang would beat Jim Ruble in the P-38.

Complaining to a Los Angeles Times reporter, "I never got a reply," Paul said, "but I'm going to call him again and see if we can make a deal."[6] Within hours, Mantz and McCarthy agreed to the side bet of $10,000, a sum equivalent to the Bendix first place award. Paul Mantz was nothing if not absolutely confident in himself. With tongue in cheek, he allowed as how he and Tommy Mayson, pilot of the other Mantz racer, were seriously "considering flying formation to Cleveland for a one-two finish," with Mayson as wingman, of course.[7]

MORE MUSTANGS

Edmund P. Lunken of Cincinnati, would prove to be a worthy contender with his D model Mustang. His P-51 airframe was absolutely stock except for a bit of external cleanup including fairing over the side fuselage air induction grills used for desert operation, six machine gun ports and wing tip running lights.

Southern California real estate broker Joe DeBona was another newcomer to the Bendix race in 1947. Joe's entry was a jet black P-51D equipped with a Merlin 68, an engine similar to the Packard V-1650-7 engine.[8] DeBona's Mustang carried civil registration NX33699. It was the same Mustang Paul Franklin entered the previous year which failed to start because of carburetor problems. Franklin apparently wet the wing on this P-51 and beside competing in the Bendix, wanted

Chapter X: Race Pilots

to establish some inter-city records. He worked with the airplane for a few months after the 1946 race, finally selling the racer to Thomas F. Call in April of the following spring.[9] Call, it may be remembered, flew in the 1946 Bendix race finishing fifteenth in a snow white FG-1D Corsair entered by Dave Wyler. Joe DeBona flew Thomas Call's newly acquired P-51D in the 1947 race.

Bruce Gimbel would fly Jackie Cochran's P-51B this year. The aircraft was unchanged from 1946, and would once again carry large drop tanks. These were the same type of tank that damaged Jackie's racer in the 1946 race. When these tanks were installed, they extended well beyond the leading and trailing edges of the Mustang wing. To prevent a recurrence of last year's problem, detachable struts were placed between the lower wing surface and the aft end of the big tanks. As the tanks fell away, the struts deflected them away from the airplane. It was a technique North American engineers tested during the war when the problem first developed.

Ed Lunken was a newcomer to the 1947 Bendix race. He took off with no pre-planned refueling stop. His high blower wouldn't function due to a faulty solenoid and he ran the entire race in low blower. His speed of 409 miles per hour was still good enough for third place. Credit: Emil Strasser

Joe DeBona's Mustang originally belonged to Paul Franklin. Joe pushed this P-51D-10 across the country to collect second place, only one minute, 18 seconds behind Mantz. Credit: Bob Burke Photographers

THE RACE

An estimated 20,000 people gathered early Saturday morning, 30 August 1947, to watch the Bendix airplanes leave Van Nuys. The sun was still low in the eastern sky and the racers cast exaggerated shadows as each contestant taxied out for takeoff. They were using runway 16 which was over a mile long. Bespectacled Larry Therkelsen, dressed in a double-breasted business suit and tie, sent each pilot on his way with a smart stroke of his checkered flag.

Jane Page was the first to launch having received permission to depart at 4:36 a.m. West Coast time to reach Cleveland for another race. She had a busy day ahead. Three hours later, the other pilots were ready to go. Bill Eddy was first off followed by Bill Lear, Jr. Jim Ruble was next to leave in Glenn McCarthy's very expensive and very modified Flying Shamrock. Seconds after Ruble's plane left the runway, the starboard wing tip tank tore loose and struck the ground. The impact ruptured the tank and 165 gallons of high octane aviation gasoline erupted in a fireball sending a dense black plume of smoke skyward.[10] Ruble managed to maintain control of the P-38 in spite of the sudden unbalanced trim condition and continued to climb away from the airport. If it wasn't for Jim Ruble's bad luck, he wouldn't have had any luck at all that day.

Destiny caught up with Glenn McCarthy's swift Lockheed racer 35,000 feet over northern Arizona, when the port turbo-supercharger failed and started a fire. Jim parachuted out of the stricken airplane and landed safely on an indian reservation. All Mantz had to do now was finish the race to collect the $10,000 side bet.

Tommy Mayson almost didn't get off in the second Mantz P-51 racer when a vehicle, driven by an airport employee, backed into the right wing tip causing an immediate fuel leak in the wet wing. Mechanics made a hasty repair and the red and yellow Mustang was able to tale off. The other contestants departed without incident except Bill Odom. He had a fuel leak in his big Republic YP-47 Thunderbolt and once again the airplane was grounded. By the time the leak was repaired, it was too late for Odom to takeoff and reach Cleveland before the 6:00 p.m. deadline.

Paul Mantz streaked across the country in record breaking time to win his second consecutive Bendix race. Aided by a favorable tail wind, he completed the flight in four hours, 27

Starting Sequence
1947 Bendix Trophy Race
Piston Engine Division

Position	Pilot	Race No.	Aircraft Type
1	Jane Page	63	F-5G-6
2	Bill Eddy	31	P-51D-20
3	Bill Lear, Jr.	25	F-5G-6
4	Jim Ruble	88	P-38F-15
5	Bruce Gimbel	13	P-51B-15
6	Paul Mantz	46	P-51C-10
7	Thomas Mayson	60	P-51C-10
8	Dianna Cyrus	91	A-26B
9	Frank Whitton	99	FG-1D
10	Ed Lunken	33	P-51D-20
11	Joe DeBona	90	P-51D-10
12	Joe Kinkella	92	P-63C-5
–	Bill Odom	42	YP-47M

DeBona's Mustang was fast and he was an excellent former Army pilot. Joe would return to race again in the Bendix in another Mustang. Credit: Warren Bodie

Bruce Gimbel flew Jackie Cochran's green P-51B in the 1947 race. Detachable struts were added between the wing undersurface and the drop tanks to prevent damage to the airframe when the tanks were released. The struts are visible in this photograph taken at Van Nuys before the race. Credit: Dusty Carter

Chapter X: Race Pilots

Gimbel waits for the starting flag at Van Nuys in this photograph. The overhead plexiglass panel in the cockpit canopy was removed and replaced by sheet aluminum in 1947. Otherwise, the aircraft was basically unchanged. Credit: Birch Matthews collection

Larry Therkelsen is about to flag Bill Eddy away from Van Nuys on race day. Eddy was the second to take off that morning behind Jane Page who had permission to leave before the official starting time. She planned to enter a pylon race at Cleveland later that same day. Credit: Birch Matthews collection

minutes at an average speed of just over 460 miles per hour. Stepping from the cockpit, he shouted to Glenn McCarthy: "Is that $10,000 I bet (still) safe?" McCarthy greeted Mantz and told him about Ruble's accident, shook Paul's hand and assured him that he had indeed, won the bet. "Thanks pal," Mantz replied, "it's certainly nice to see you under such circumstances then." McCarthy's sportsmanship was first rate, but it was a tough way to lose a bet.

Joe DeBona – in his first Bendix Trophy Race – was a very close second to Mantz, loosing by just 1.3 minutes elapsed time. Third place went to another rookie race pilot, Ed Lunken. He made absolutely no plans before the race and didn't even have a refueling team spotted along the way. Lunken simply took off from Van Nuys and headed east. Early in the race, the high blower solenoid failed and he ran the entire trip in low blower. Fortunately, his V-1650-9A Merlin was running very lean and he made the trip non-stop. As it was, his tanks ran dry during roll out while landing in Cleveland and he had to be towed somewhat ignominiously from the runway.[11] Ed Lunken certainly garnered all the luck that had deserted Jim Ruble!

Bill Eddy's clean P-51D-20 sits at Cleveland airport after the Bendix race. Wing gun ports were removed and faired over, but little else was done to the airframe other than removing unneeded weight. Credit: Warren Bodie

North American P-51 Mustangs took the top six positions conclusively demonstrating their dominance in transcontinental racing. Frank Whitton's Corsair placed seventh while Bill Lear, Jr., and Jane Page took eighth and ninth, respectively. The lone P-63 Kingcobra flown by Joe Kinkella was forced out of the race at Pueblo, Colorado with mechanical problems. By 5:30 p.m. eastern time, Dianna Cyrus in her big twin engine A-26 was over Fort Wayne, Indiana, when she ran into a heavy thunderstorm. Trying to get around the storm, she mistook the Lake Huron for Lake Erie. She followed the shoreline all the way to Saginaw Bay before noticing her mistake and realizing that her compass was wasn't working properly. In frustration, she landed at Saginaw, Michigan, hopelessly out of the race.

Nine planes finished the 1947 race. Mantz's second win duplicated Frank Fuller's two victories before the war. Could Mantz do it again in 1948, and become the only three-time winner? It was a challenge the 44 year old pilot wouldn't be able to resist. And if there was any doubt that the P-51 Mustang was king of the transcontinental racers, it was gone when the final race tally was published.

NINETEEN FORTY-EIGHT

The city of Long Beach, California, hosted the Bendix race in 1948. Long Beach Municipal Airport attracted the Bendix contest committee because they wanted to have two airplanes take off at a time. Launching the racers would take less time and hopefully, they would arrive in Cleveland for a more exciting finish. The plan seemed possible as Long Beach had a primary east-west 6000 foot runway and a parallel taxiway. The taxi strip was in the process of being widened and could serve as a second runway. In the end, airport authorities vetoed the idea and a conventional staggered interval start was used once again.

A new Bendix rule permitted foreign aircraft and pilots to compete this year. This prompted the entry of three Canadian-built DeHavilland Mark 25 Mosquitoes. These were British-designed twin engine airplanes constructed largely of wood, not unlike the old Lockheed Vegas from the early thirties. Two Rolls-Royce Merlins powered the Mosquito giving it a lot more bite than the old Lockheed.

WOODEN RACERS FROM CANADA

One of the Mosquitoes was entered by Dianna Cyrus.[12] She bought the DeHavilland in Miami earlier in the year after selling her A-26 to the Standard Pipeline Company in Tulsa, Oklahoma. Dianna christened her new airplane "Huntress II," and following the Bendix race, planned to fly this fast airplane around the world in an attempt to break Bill Odom's record.[13]

Bendix race official Larry Therkelsen chats with movie actor Robert Taylor before the start of the 1948 classic long distance race. Credit: A.U. Schmidt

Unfortunately and for whatever reason, Dianna didn't fly her Mosquito in the Bendix. Another airplane entered in the race which never arrived at the starting line was A.T. Whiteside's Lockheed F-5G-6. It was to be flown by Jack Becker of Jacksonville, Florida.

Donald M. McVicar from Montreal, Canada, bought two Mosquitos from Canadian Government surplus for $1500 each.[14] Don kept one of the DeHavillands intending to race it in the Bendix. The other he sold to 40 year old Jesse F. Stallings from Nashville, Tennessee. Stallings was an ex-

Stallings' Mosquito was named "Miss Marta" and was sponsored by Capitol Airways. The Mosquito was an elegant design, but in this case, was handicapped with low altitude Merlin 225 engines having two-speed, single-stage superchargers. Credit: Emil Strasser

Chapter X: Race Pilots

Jess Stallings and Don McVicar entered de Havilland Mk 25 Mosquitos in the 1948 race. Don lost an engine en route to Long Beach for the Bendix. Stallings, however, was able to race. Credit: Birch Matthews collection

American Airlines captain who flew as a contract pilot for the Air Transport Command during World War II. After the war, he was president of Capitol Airways, a distributor for Stinson and Beechcraft and the operator of two flying schools in Nashville. He bought the Mosquito to race in the Bendix too.

Now, the DeHavilland Mosquito is a sleek greyhound of an airplane. The problem with the Mark 25s that McVicar and Stallings planned to race centered on the Merlin engines. Their Mosquitoes were powered by Packard-built Merlin 225 engines which had two-speed, single-stage superchargers.[15] The engines wouldn't give the altitude performance that Paul Mantz and the other Mustang jockeys could realize with two-stage, two-speed superchargers in their dash 3 or dash 9 Merlins. McVicar realized this but loved the smoothly finished DeHavilland "Mossies" and still felt he could give the P-51s a run for the prize money. To complete the race non-stop, McVicar added four gas tanks for a total internal capacity of 844 gallons. He planned to run the Merlins at 2850 revolutions with a manifold boost pressure of plus 14 pounds per square inch (60 inches of mercury).

Don McVicar's dreams of pushing his Mosquito across the United States in the Bendix race never materialized. After a valiant effort to reach Long Beach, he lost the starboard engine from a broken connecting rod on his way to California, and made an emergency landing at Wichita, Kansas. It was some consolation to Don that Jesse Stallings was able to reach Long Beach and start the Bendix. Unfortunately, Stallings carried almost 200 gallons less fuel in his racer and had to throttle back over Denver because his fuel consumption rate was excessive. He used cruise power for the remainder of the race.

THREE FOR THE MONEY

Paul Mantz coveted a third Bendix victory. Air racing then, as it is now, was expensive and Mantz wanted a sponsor. He turned to Glenn McCarthy with a proposition. For $75,000 in sponsorship, Mantz would enter three Mustangs which he was sure would take the top three spots in the race. It would be great publicity for McCarthy's businesses. All three P-51s would wear his racing colors. McCarthy accepted the proposal and Mantz went to work. He had two racing Mustangs. A third was needed pronto. Part of the deal included accepting McCarthy's chief pilot, Linton Boyd "Lin" Carney as the pilot of one of the Mantz Mustangs. Paul switched planes in 1948, and Carney would fly the 1947 Bendix winning Mustang. Lin Carney learned to fly as a civilian in 1933. He joined the Army Air Corp in 1941 and rose to the rank of Lt. Colonel before taking his discharge in 1945. From the Army, he went to work for the Texas oil man as a corporate pilot.

About a month or two before the race, Paul called Ed Lunken, who at the time owned a pair of Mustangs including the one he flew to third place in the 1947 Bendix. Would Lunken sell one of his P-51s? Sure. They agreed upon a price and Mantz sent him a check for the amount. This second Mustang hadn't been flown in some time, so with Mantz's check in his pocket, Lunken fired up the Merlin. He wanted to make a check flight before turning the plane over to Mantz. Just after the wheels broke ground during takeoff, both coolant lines to the header let go as the wheels were coming up. Lunken could do nothing but let the fighter settle back onto the runway for a belly landing. Ed recalls that "it was a loud noisy slide along the remainder of the runway. Forward momentum

Paul Mantz waits at the Long Beach starting line in the 1948 race. Glenn McCarthy sponsored a team of three racers this year. Paul changed airplanes, this time flying NX1204. He adopted the McCarthy colors of P-80 gray trimmed in green. Credit: Birch Matthews collection

Paul Mantz won the 1948 Bendix for an unprecedented third time. His speed was 448 miles an hour, a tad slower than the previous year. Credit: Warren Bodie

carried the plane off the end of the runway where it eventually came to rest."[16] When Lunken scrambled out of the cockpit, he still had Paul Mantz's check in his pocket. He called Paul and broke the news to him offering to fly his own racing Mustang as the third entry in the McCarthy racing stable for 1948. Time was short, Lunken was an exceptionally good pilot and Mantz accepted.

Edmund P. "Ebby" Lunken learned to fly when he was only 16 years old. He came from a distinguished Cincinnati, Ohio, family interested in aviation for many years. Indeed, his father and grandfather donated land for what became the Lunken Airport. Ed joined the Army Air Corp during the late 1920s and during his career, flew virtually every single engine aircraft the Army possessed from the P-26 to the jet powered P-59A, to say nothing of many multi-engine planes as well. In his own words, he "flew almost anything that would fly."[17] Ed went on active duty in January, 1941, and wound up in the Panama Canal Zone for much of the war. It wasn't until returning to the United States in 1944, that Lunken first flew North American's P-51 Mustang.

After the war, Lunken at one time owned three different Mustangs, two of which were P-51K models obtained in Elkhart, Indiana. The third (NX61151) was a D model purchased in 1947, from Bill Ong in Kansas City. An old time race pilot, Ong used this P-51 for pylon racing in 1946. Lunken painted his newly acquired Mustang P-80 gray with blue trim and on a nostalgic whim, entered the Bendix in 1947, no doubt surprising himself by finishing third behind Mantz and DeBona.

Chapter X: Race Pilots

A happy Mantz flashes a broad smile celebrating his third victory in this photograph. His plane was named for one of McCarthy's hotels, the "Latin American." Credit: Al Hansen collection

Carney's racer was named the "Houstonian," one of McCarthy's hotels. Four exhaust stacks are missing on the left bank of the Merlin suggesting they were burned during the race. Markings on the two racers were basically the same differing only in slight detail. Credit: Emil Strasser

Ed Lunken flew his own P-51D as one of the Mantz stable of racers in 1948. He had a unique low profile cockpit modification, new propeller and a wet wing in addition to a general airframe clean up. The aircraft is shown here at Long Beach before the race. Credit: Birch Matthews collection

Mantz apparently didn't chill the fuel used in his racer in 1948. It is believed that the fuselage tank volume was increased for the 1948 race thereby obviating the need for greater density fuel. Credit: Birch Matthews collection

Lin Carney, McCarthy's chief pilot, flew N1202 this year. Mantz used this airplane the previous two years when he won the Bendix. Carney finished second in 1948. Credit: Emil Strasser

The competition was getting tougher with every race. When he joined the Mantz-McCarthy team, it was time to do some serious rework on the racer.

The first change to his Mustang racer was installation of a brand new dash 11 Merlin. The engine was obtained from the chief engineer at Packard who had the crated Merlin in his house. His wife had been complaining loudly about this piece of decor. All it cost Lunken was a pair of tickets to the 1948 races. Ed next obtained special thin paddle blades from Hamilton Standard and replaced the stock propeller. Special fairings were added to the engine exhaust stacks for improved streamlining. The airframe was modified by replacing the stock P-51D canopy and windscreen with a low profile configuration which was blended smoothly into the fuselage contour. The airplane was flown to Burbank, California, where Hal Wendt of Aircraft Tank Service wet the wing. Lunken's fuel capacity was now around 800 gallons.[18] The P-80 gray primary color was retained for 1948. Trim was changed to green to comply with McCarthy's racing colors. The end product was a beautifully prepared, swift looking racing Mustang christened "Buttonpuss", an affectionate nickname Lunken bestowed upon his wife. All that remained was a "run for the roses."

Ed Lunken emerges from the cockpit of his racer after finishing fourth. He flew the race at 39,000 feet hoping to catch a ride on the polar jet stream. It didn't happen and the time expended climbing to that altitude probably cost him the race. Credit: Alice Eucker collection via Phil Krause

The massive YP-47M Thunderbolt entered by Bill Odom in the previous two Bendix races was again slated for this year's contest. Jane Page was to be the pilot. A pre-race accident once again kept the airplane on the sidelines. Credit: Sid Bradd collection

DEBONA GETS SERIOUS

Joe DeBona was bitten by the air racing bug. He raced a P-51D in the 1947 Bendix race finishing in second place ever so close to Paul Mantz. Following Mantz's lead, Joe wanted a B or C model Mustang which Paul and Jackie Cochran so successfully campaigned in previous Bendix races. He acquired a P-51B which, to say the least, possessed an unusual if not surreptitious background. DeBona's surplus Mustang began its civil career as a disassembled fuselage hulk, serial number 43-6822, located in Chicago, Illinois. It was sold by the Government for the callosal sum of $27.05 as "salvage and scrap" to Leland H. and Martha L. Cameron of North Hollywood, California."[19] This had to be the lowest sale price of any Mustang in history! Cameron initially planned to enter the Mustang in the 1948 Bendix and proceeded to rebuild the airframe.[20] Components to complete the P-51 came from a variety of commercial sources as well as the War Assets Administration.

Cameron used the fuselage serial number to register the airplane with civil authorities, a practice not unheard of today. Apparently changing his mind about running the Bendix, Cameron sold the airframe to the Joe DeBona Racing Company on April 7, 1948. Joe DeBona was a well known Hollywood real estate man and president of the Beverly Hills Lions Club. He was a first rate pilot and veteran of the wartime Air Transport Command with thousands of hours ferrying Army aircraft to Europe and across the Pacific.

The Mustang was moved to Santa Monica's Clover Field for race conditioning by a superb team spearheaded by Joe Katona. Joe proceeded to have the airplane modified for long distance racing by stripping every ounce of unneeded weight from the airframe. The wing was mounted on a fixture which

Joe DeBona (left) chats with sponsor and movie actor Jimmy Stewart about en route weather before the Bendix takeoff at Long Beach. Credit: A.U. Schmidt

Chapter X: Race Pilots

Joe DeBona was back for the 1948 race with a new airplane. His P-51B-5 was roughly equivalent to the Mantz airplanes including a wet wing. The cobalt blue racer was named "Thunderbird." Credit: Chalmers Johnson via Bill Larkins and Tim Weinschenker

Thunderbird gets a pre-race engine run up at Long Beach. DeBona firewalled the racer all the way across the country only to run out of fuel almost within sight of the Cleveland airport. It was a tough way to lose. Credit: A.U. Schmidt

Joe DeBona, disappointed at not being able to finish the 1948 Bendix, was determined to have another go at the trophy in 1949. The airplane is shown here at Clover Field, Santa Monica, CA, where it was prepared for the race. Credit: A.U. Schmidt

Entries came in slowly for the 1949 race. An unusual entry came from Lee Cameron in the form of this Martin B-26C-20, sponsored by Allied Aircraft Co. of North Hollywood, CA. Credit: Dusty Carter via A. Kevin Grantham

took off from Long Beach exactly ten minutes after Ed Lunken. She flew her race at around 30,000 and squeezed past Lunken while he was still climbing. Mantz was off third and had no trouble passing Jesse Stallings in the slower DeHavilland Mosquito. He eventually caught and passed Linton Carney who was the first to depart. Joe DeBona was in the thick of the race until he neared Elyria, Ohio, when his engine quit cold. He was out of gas almost within sight of the finish line at Cleveland. The end of Joe's race was a disappointing but safe dead stick landing.

Paul Mantz won the Bendix for an unprecedented third time at an average speed of 448 miles per hour with an elapsed time of four hours and 34 minutes. His team mate, Linton Carney was right behind him taking just 1.1 minutes longer to complete the race. The hoped for one, two, three finish by the McCarthy team was broken up by Jackie Cochran who squeezed ahead of Ed Lunken to take the bronze position, relegating him to fourth place. Climbing to 39,000 feet had cost Lunken at least a third place and possible the race. Stallings brought up the rear at a comparatively slow speed of 341 miles per hour. Incredibly, less than four minutes of elapsed time separated the first four airplanes to cross the finish line after a race of over two thousand miles.

NINETEEN FORTY-NINE

National Air Race management was frustrated in their desire for paired race horse takeoffs in the previous Bendix event out of Long Beach, California. Some time after the 1948 race program, a contest committee meeting was held in Washington, D.C., in which veteran race pilot Art Chester – president of the Professional Race Pilots Association – was asked to survey potential sites for a race horse start of the 1949 Bendix. As an alternative, he was asked to consider having all Bendix starters rendezvous upon takeoff and then make an air start. After talking to some of the Bendix pilots, Chester concluded that an air start was impractical. It would be a waste of precious fuel. Art evaluated several possible sites including Rosemond Dry Lake, and the airports at Palm Springs and Long Beach. The Long Beach Chamber of Commerce was quite interested in again having the race begin in their city.[25] Long Beach could offer the many needed amenities and logistics to support the race start.

Art Chester, however, had other ideas. He believed that Rosemond Dry Lake – 2300 feet above sea level in the high desert north of Los Angeles – would do nicely for a race horse start.[26] The six mile diameter lake bed was dry, hard and smooth in September. Separation of the racers on takeoff presented no problem due to the vast open space available. Further, the racers could launch toward the east because winds were typically absent in the early morning hours. True, Rosemond was remote, about 80 miles away from the heart of Los Angeles, but then as now, Angelenos thought nothing of driving such a distance.

Mantz entered both of his Mustangs in the 1949 event. No longer sponsored by Glenn McCarthy, Mantz reverted to the red and white colors of his Paul Mantz Air Service. Credit: Dusty Carter collection via A. Kevin Grantham

Chapter X: Race Pilots

Stan Reaver (left) and Fish Salmon (right) pose before Mantz's Mustang number 60 at Rosamond Dry Lake. Credit: A.U. Schmidt

A requirement this year stated that contestants had to report their approximate position four times during the race. Civil Aeronautics Administration stations at Colorado Springs, Goodland, Kansas, Peoria, Illinois, and Fort Wayne, Indiana, were designated for enroute communications. Identifying codes in sealed envelopes would be given to each pilot at a meeting the evening before the race. This would allow race management to track progress during the race and coordinate arrivals in Cleveland.

HOW MANY ENTRIES?

In 1946, there was a great deal of enthusiasm for the Bendix race and seemingly everyone with a surplus fighter wanted to compete. Pilot interest in running the Bendix race rapidly diminished thereafter. Nineteen forty-nine was no exception. The cost of preparing a first class long distance racing plane was not cheap and if one didn't at least place seventh, there was no prize money to offset the inevitable expenses. Anyone without a wet wing Mustang couldn't realistically be competitive. Perhaps for these reasons, only one application had been received by early July. The race was less than seven weeks away.[27] The lone entrant was Joe DeBona. Fearing there

Don Bussart brought this sleek de Havilland Mosquito to the party at Rosamond. He limped into Cleveland having lost his oxygen system and one engine along the way. Credit: Harry Gann collection

wouldn't be enough planes to hold a race, Walter Orr, Director of Public Relations for the races, started to beat the bushes for contestants. The situation was becoming serious if not desperate.

By early August, only four entries had been received. Paul Mantz placed his two airplanes in competition although who would fly them was undecided. The fourth entry was Leland "Lee" Cameron in a big twin engine Martin B-26C, assigned race number 24. National Aeronautics Association representative C.S. Logsdon reserved three other racing numbers – "38, 52 and 61 – for prospective Bendix starters" as the contest committee pressed for additional competitors.[28] By mid-August, The Bendix entry list had edged up to six planes. The newcomers were Larry Hadley, given race number 38 and

A last minute entry was this Republic AT-12 flown by Vincent Peron. He called it a "Super P-35," but in reality it was an aging two-place training plane based upon the Seversky P-35s of pre-war vintage. Credit: Sid Bradd collection

Another view of Vince Peron's AT-12 sitting on Rosamond Dry Lake before the race is seen in this photograph. Peron was forced out of the race with mechanical problems. Credit: Dusty Carter via A. Kevin Grantham

Don Bussart assigned number 81.[29] Hadley never did appear for the race and little is known other than the basic fact of his entry. Bussart signed on with his DeHavilland Mosquito recently acquired from Don McVicar in Canada.

A last minute entry came on 24 August when Burbank flying instructor Vince Perron wired Ben Franklin, race general manager, that he had "just returned from out of country and would appreciate special waiver to enter my Super Republic P-35 in Bendix Race."[30] In reality, Perron's super P-35 was a two-place advance trainer designated by the Air Force as an AT-12. Perron was sponsored by actor Buddy Rogers and the plane was nicknamed "Buck Rogers." Charles Logsdon responded immediately with entry forms and assigned Perron race number 61. Meanwhile, the rumor mill around Cleveland had it that Bill Odom might take another crack at the Bendix, flying one of Paul Mantz's Mustangs. Charlie Logsdon wired Mantz seeking verification and details.[31] Whether Mantz and Odom were actually dickering over this possibility is not known; however, not until 31 August did Paul Mantz reply to the inquiry, stating positively that "Odom will not fly one of our ships."[32]

In fact, Paul had not made a final decision on who would fly the second of his two Mustangs. He notified Charlie Logsdon that Stan Reaver, a pilot working for Mantz, would race NX1204 which carried race number 46 that year. The second P-51, NX1202, would be flown either by Lockheed test pilot Herman "Fish" Salmon, Ed Lunken or Mantz himself. Paul finally committed to Fish Salmon as pilot for NX1202, but on the evening before the race was overcome with a strong desire to try for victory number four. He tried to cajole both of his pilots into letting him fly. In the end, Paul stood by his commitment and stepped aside. Salmon and Reaver would, indeed, be able to race the next day.

HAPPY BOTTOM RIDING CLUB

Rosemond Dry Lake lies in the huge Antelope Valley known as the high desert region of Southern California. Even today, the area is not heavily populated in spite of tremendous development in the cities of Palmdale and Lancaster. The

Joe DeBona sits in the cockpit of his beautiful B model Mustang. Crew member Joe Torma is to the left and Joe Katona is behind the airplane. Sponsor Jimmy Stewart is on the right. Credit: A.U. Schmidt

Chapter X: Race Pilots

The 1949 race pilots met at Pancho Barnes' Happy Bottom Riding Club. From left to right, Joe DeBona, Pancho Barnes, Don Bussart and Lee Cameron sit around a table at the "Club." Pancho is smiling, but the look on Joe's face registers surprise. What happened Joe? Credit: A.U. Schmidt

In this photograph, Larry Therkelsen passes out lane numbers and radio call letters to the pilots. Standing left to right, Fish Salmon, Stan Reaver, Joe DeBona, Lee Cameron, Paul Mantz, Vince Peron and Don Bussart. Seated are E. McIver (left) and Larry Therkelsen. Credit: A.U. Schmidt

Antelope Valley high desert is an area of harsh extremes. It is very hot and very dry in the summer and fall. Huge dust storms occur when the wind kicks up. Winter brings a smattering of snow and cold weather. Early in the year, heavy rains turn ordinarily parched ground into temporary shallow lakes. As spring arrives, the lake beds dry once more forming hard, smooth surfaces.

In 1949, there weren't any super freeways leading from Los Angeles to Rosemond Dry Lake. The nearby town of Mojave, California, was little more than a railroad stop with a few bars and cafes and not much else. Nearby Muroc Army Air Field had been developed extensively during the war and some years later would grow to become Edwards Air Force Base. But in those early years, neighbors were few and far in between. In spite of the harsh desolate landscape, blowing sand and unrelenting sun, one person chose to settle on a ranch in the Antelope Valley. This was Florence Leontine Lowe,

The racers are brought up to the starting line at Rosamond Dry Lake. The dry lake is huge and the airplanes were spread out widely for the race-horse start. Credit: A.U. Schmidt

much better known as Pancho Barnes.[33] Pancho was an accomplished pilot, horsewoman, rancher, and hostess, although some might have inferred a different epithet. She had an amazing ability for short declarative sentences laced with adjectives spicy enough to make any sailor take notice. Pancho was a character and most certainly a legend in her own time among airmen.

Pancho played a small but important role in the 1949 Bendix. She hosted the pilot's meeting at her "Happy Bottom Riding Club" on September 2nd, the day before the race. This was a local watering hole and entertainment spa on her ranch near Muroc, frequented by nearly every pilot who happened along over the years. It was here that Paul Mantz tried to convince one of his two pilots to step down and let him fly the Bendix one more time. Both Reaver and Salmon resisted claiming that Mantz had won the race three times and it was their turn to have some fun.

As Pancho Barnes hovered in the background, the pilots gathered around a wooden table at the Happy Bottom Riding Club to swap stories and pose for pictures while photographer A.U. Schmidt recorded the informal ceremonies with his big Speed Graphic. Larry Therkelsen handed out starting lane positions for the racehorse takeoff and individual radio call signs for communication checks along the route. Joe DeBona was in the number one slot dwarfed by Lee Cameron's B-26 on his right wing. Vince Perron drew number three position followed by Don Bussart's Mosquito, and Paul Mantz's two Mustangs with Fish Salmon in race 60 and Stan Reaver in race 46.

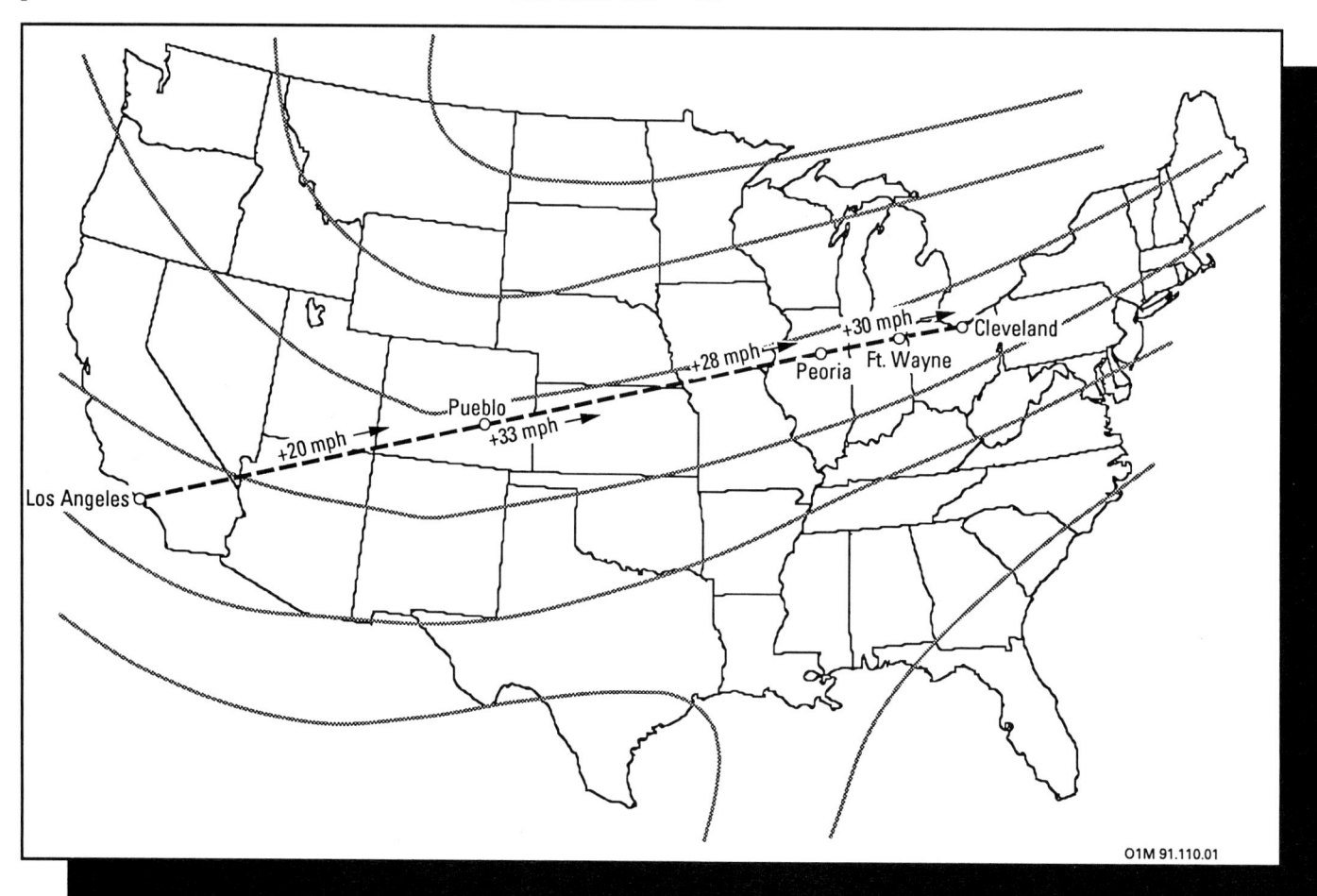

1949 Bendix Race Radio Call Signs

Pilot	Race No.	Call Sign Code
Joe Debona	90	Bendix A (Able)
Lee Cameron	24	Bendix B (Baker)
Fish Salmon	60	Bendix C (Charlie)
Stan Reaver	46	Bendix D (Dog)
Vince Perron	61	Bendix E (Easy)
Don Bussart	81	Bendix F (Fox)

This illustration shows the tail winds that pushed Joe DeBona along during the 1949 Bendix. He flew a great circle route at 27,000 feet at a blistering average speed of 470 miles per hour to win the race. Credit: John Pappas

Chapter X: Race Pilots

THE LAST RACE

The 1949 Bendix field was small, but there was serious competition arrayed along the starting line in the form of three very, very fast Mustangs. This would be the first and only racehorse start in a Bendix contest, an idea fostered by the contest committee to create more interest at the end of the race 2000 miles to the east.

Wheels were chalked on each racer as pilots and crews attended to last minute details at six o'clock, Friday morning on the day of the race. In the background was a large operations tent surrounded by a couple of dozen service vehicles and cars. This was truly a remote site located two miles off the nearest highway. The flat desert floor of Rosemond Dry Lake stretched for miles. As with any type of contest, there was a quiet air of pre-race excitement.

The three highly modified Mustangs were favored and only a miracle could change the outcome. It was a matter of which P-51 would reach Cleveland first. Joe DeBona, sponsored by Jimmy Stewart, was sure he could beat the Mantz Mustangs flown by Stan Reaver and Fish Salmon. His crew and sponsor had invested a tremendous amount of time, effort and money toward this goal. Thirty-seven year old Joe DeBona was a ruggedly good looking man with a square jaw, ready smile and a head full of unruly dark hair. He had a penchant for casual dress and loud sport shirts. Above all else, he was a fine pilot.

His wet wing racer was beautifully prepared and extremely light having an empty weight of 6223 pounds.[34] The General Petroleum Company of California produced a special run of 150 octane gasoline for DeBona.[35] The day before the race, 850 gallons of this detonation-resistant fuel, weighing 5,100 pounds, flowed into the fuel tanks of his racer. An auxiliary oil tank had been installed bringing the total oil capacity to 27 gallons adding an additional 202 pounds. Engine coolant and hydraulic oil increased the weight another 294 pounds. When DeBona climbed aboard, airframe gross weight at takeoff was a heavy 12,000 pounds. At full throttle the Merlin would burn fuel at a rate of over one thousand pounds an hour. With each passing hour, the racer would get lighter and faster. Joe DeBona was as ready as he could be for the 1949 Bendix race.

As takeoff time approached, Larry Therkelsen signaled all pilots to crank their engines. Propellers arced in the early morning sun creating a windstorm of translucent rooster tails composed fine alkaline dust which bloomed over the barren landscape behind the waiting racers. Inside each cockpit, the tasks were much the same as pilots checked magnetos and evaluated pressure and temperature gages. Minutes before the start, engine revolutions were advanced. The corresponding power output against set brakes made every airframe dance and vibrate. At 6:30 a.m., Larry Therkelsen and three assistants were spread out in front of the racers in plain view of each pilot when they simultaneously dropped their flags signaling the start of the race.

Five of the racers began to roll. Vince Perron was left behind with a stubborn engine. It was several minutes before his AT-12 began its takeoff roll. By this time, the other racers were rapidly becoming small dark flecks in the eastern sky. Perron struggled along in the race finally dropping out at Grand Junction, Colorado, with a balky engine. DeBona, Reaver and Salmon surged ahead of the others, each climbing to pre-planned flight levels.

Joe described his flight strategy saying, "I climbed to 27,000 feet and navigated a great circle course entirely by gyro compass. To confirm my on-course accuracy, I used visual checks along the way. For example, I dead-reckoned about 850 miles to Colorado Springs, and computed a course ten miles south of that city. It looked like about six to seven miles south when I passed over. Later, my course called for a heading which cut between Goshen and Fort Wayne, Indiana. When I got there, I split the two towns accurately as planned."[36]

DeBona gradually eased ahead of the other contestants. He was favored by tailwinds throughout the race.[37] Along the first one-third of the course to Pueblo, Colorado, tailwinds pushed Joe's racer at 22 miles per hours. Passing Pueblo, he radioed his position as required by the race rules saying, "this is Bendix A –Able – calling Peterson Tower. My position is seven miles south of Colorado Springs. Please transmit my position to Cleveland."[38]

From Pueblo to Peoria, Illinois, the tailwinds ran between 28 and 33 miles per hour. When DeBona reached his last checkpoint at Fort Wayne, the winds steadied at 30 miles per hour during his long down hill track to Cleveland. He had now burned off about 3,600 pounds of fuel giving him a much improved power to weight ratio.

The end of an era in transcontinental air racing is depicted in this post-Bendix race shot of Jimmy Stewart with Bendix champions Roscoe Turner and Joe DeBona. Credit: Rebman Photo Service from the Sid Bradd collection

A happy Joe DeBona emerges from the cockpit of his superb Mustang racer just after arrival at Cleveland airport. Credit: H.G. Martin photo from Robert J. Pickett collection via Kansas Aeronautical Historical Society

Joe DeBona streaked across the finish line at Cleveland, four hours and 16 minutes after Therkelsen flagged the racers away from Rosemond. He was the first to arrive and there was no doubt who had one the race. Actor Jimmy Stewart – financial sponsor for the racer – was there with his wife, Gloria, to meet Joe as the striking blue Mustang rolled to a stop. Jumping out of the cockpit, with a huge smile on his face, Joe greeted his backer saying, "hi buddy, I finally did it for you." Stewart grabbed the winning pilot's outstretched hand in both of his and shouted, "Thanks a helluva lot, Joe."[39] DeBona had done it, alright.

His elapsed time calculated to a staggering average speed of 470 miles an hour, a new Bendix record for piston engine airplanes!

It took three attempts for Joe to achieve his goal of winning the Bendix. He retired from further competition happy to win and a bit disappointed that Mantz hadn't been in the race that year. He had wanted to beat his friendly rival. On the other hand, DeBona did eclipse the two Mantz airplanes. Stan Reaver's bright red P-51 arrived eleven minutes later closely followed by Fish Salmon in the other P-51, to capture second and third places. Don Bussart's DeHavilland Mosquito was a slow fourth almost two hours behind DeBona. After leaving Rosemond, Don noticed his oil pressure dropping with a corresponding rise in oil temperature. He throttled back and kept going. His problems weren't over. At 21,000 feet above Peoria, his oxygen system failed. Don descended to a lower altitude to finish the race. The temperamental Mosquito continued to plague its pilot. As Bussart passed the finish line, the crowd noted that the propeller on his starboard engine was feathered. The engine was shut down during the last part of the race. Sadly, the promising DeHavilland Mosquito never got to show its wares against the mighty Mustangs of DeBona, Reaver and Salmon.

Chapter X: Race Pilots

Lee Cameron cruised into Cleveland way after the six o'clock deadline. He too was overcome with mechanical difficulties. Cameron set the big Martin Marauder down at North Platte, Nebraska, losing over an hour with fuel feed system problems. Once repairs were made, he took off again hoping to reach Cleveland before the deadline. He didn't. Cameron landed at 7:50 p.m., with the dubious distinction of being the last man to ever fly the Bendix.

The thirteenth and last piston engine Bendix Trophy Race faded into history with the 1949 contest, although no one realized this at the time. Two days later, Bill Odom flying Jackie Cochran's Beguine racer in the Thompson Trophy pylon race, crashed to his death, killing a mother and child in the accident. The whole concept of the air racing was called into question, including the location of the next race. Although plans were drawn for a 1950 race, North Korean army divisions swept across the 38th parallel attacking the South Koreans. American involvement followed and any thoughts of future air races vanished.

NOTES:
1 Performance estimate based upon data presented in Douglas Aircraft Corporation Report No. DS-543A, dated 1 November 1945.
2 *The Arizona Republic*, 28 August 1947, p. 12.
3 Scott A. Thompson, "Postwar Aircraft Disposal," American Aviation Historical Society JOURNAL, Vol. 37, No. 4, 1992, p. 287.
4 Correspondence to the author from A. Kevin Grantham dated 11 April 1992.
5 Don Dwiggins, *They Flew The Bendix*, J.B. Lippincott Company, Philadelphia, p. 123.
6 *Los Angeles Times*, 27 August 1947, p. 1.
7 Ibid.
8 Department of Commerce, Civil Aeronautics Administration certificate of airworthiness application, dated 29 November 1946.
9 Information contained in a chronological summary prepared by Malcolm L. Gougon based upon Civil Aeronautics Administration files from 24 June 1946 through 9 August 1951. Data supplied through the courtesy of Dick Phillips, 27 June 1992.
10 *Los Angeles Times*, 31 August 1947, p. 2.
11 Telephone interview with E.P. Lunken by the author, 28 September 1992.
12 *Aviation Week*, 23 August 1948, p. 14.
13 National Air Races 1948 Press and Radio Manual, Pilot Biographies, p. 8.
14 Don McVicar, *Mosquito Racer*, Airlife Publishing Ltd., England, 1985, p. 140.
15 Ibid., p. 141.
16 E.P. Lunken interview, op.cit.
17 Correspondence to the author from E.P. Lunken dated 30 September 1992.
18 Lunken interview, op.cit.
19 Contract of Sale of Property, Contract No. W11-120-352, dated 14 January 1948. Documentation on the history of N5528N, AAF serial number 43-6822, was gathered by Malcolm L. Gougon and provided to the author through the courtesy of Mustang enthusiast, Dick Phillips.
20 Correspondence from L.H. Cameron to the Civil Aeronautics Authority, dated 31 March 1948.
21 Airworthiness Certificate Application, 31 August 1948.
22 Long Beach Press-Telegram, 4 September 1948, p. 1.
23 William L. Donn, *Metrology*, McGraw-Hill Book Company, New York, 1965, p.245.
24 Data and correspondence from John J. Pappas to the author, dated 7 November 1992.
25 Correspondence to the National Air Race Contest Committee from D.W. Campbell, Long Beach Chamber of Commerce, dated 13 April and 23 May, 1949.
26 Correspondence from Art Chester to Ben Franklin, dated 17 February 1949.
27 Correspondence from Walter C. Orr, National Air Races director of public relations, to Charles Logsdon, National Aeronautic Association, dated 6 July 1949.
27 Correspondence from C.S. Logsdon to Larry Therkelsen, dated 12 August 1949.
29 Correspondence from C.S. Logsdon to L.E. Therkelsen, dated 17 August 1949.
30 Western Union telegram to Ben P. Franklin from Vincent J. Perron, dated 24 August 1949.
31 Western Union wire from Logsdon to Paul Mantz, dated 24 August 1949.
32 Western Union wire from Mantz to Logsdon, 31 August 1949. The wire was not received until one o'clock in the afternoon, Cleveland time.
33 Grover Ted Tate, "The Lady Who Tamed Pegasus, the Story of Pancho Barnes," A Maverick Publication, 1984, p.74.
34 The empty weight of DeBona's racer was listed on his entry form for the Bendix and provided to the author through the courtesy of Al Chute.
35 *New York Times*, 4 September 1949, p. 1.
36 *Western Flying*, November 1949, p. 25.
37 Wind conditions at 27,000 feet on the day of the race were analyzed by John Pappas of Delta Airlines and provided to the author in correspondence circa January, 1992.
38 Correspondence from Charles S. Logsdon to Larry Therkelsen, 17 August 1949, giving instructions on pilot reporting during the Bendix race.
38 *Cleveland Plain Dealer*, 4 September 1949, p. 1.

This white P-51D-25 Mustang trimmed in black belonged to Howard Olsen. He was sixth to get away from St. Petersburg only to drop out at Ocala, FL. In trying to avoid the Gulf of Mexico, Olsen ran into severe weather and was forced to land. Credit: Photoscope Corp. via Howard Olsen

Chapter XI

RENO ENCORE

There was a lapse of 15 years between the last Bendix tournament for piston engine airplanes and the resumption of transcontinental racing in 1964. The new race was called the Harold's Club Transcontinental Trophy Dash, named for the Reno hotel and casino on Virginia Street providing the impressive looking winner's trophy together with $5,000 in prize money. While the sponsor was new, the race aircraft were not. Once again, North American P-51s made up a field of eight airplanes about to bolt for Reno from the starting point at the St. Petersburg/Clearwater International Airport on the western Florida coast. The competing airplanes posed a familiar sight for an unlimited class cross-country race. All were Mustangs. The pilots who would fly them, however, were new to the sport. Most likely none had even seen an air race before. It didn't matter. It was a flying contest and they loved to fly.

THE UNINVITED PARTICIPANT

Race promoter Bill Stead and his staff scheduled the transcontinental race of the inaugural Reno air races to begin in the early morning hours of September 12, 1964, unwittingly involving the participants in the fringes and aftermath of a calamitous storm. Violent weather, that old nemesis of transcontinental racing, struck the eastern coast of Florida when the eye of Hurricane Dora moved inland across St. Augustine just after noon on September 10, a little more than 40 hours before the race was to begin. Hurricane Dora was the second hurricane to strike Florida in two weeks. Ironically, it was the first storm of full hurricane intensity to cross the northeast Florida coastline since record keeping began in 1885.[1]

The barometer dipped to 28.52 inches and gale force winds rose to 125 miles per hour just after the eye of the storm passed over St. Augustine. The center of the storm continued westward across Florida reaching southeastern Alabama the following day. Through the interior of the state, sustained winds of 100 miles an hour were reported during the night. The Jacksonville Weather Bureau airport station measured sustained wind velocities of 82 miles per hour. This was the first time in history that winds of full hurricane force were recorded at Jacksonville!

THE CONTESTANTS

The storm was accompanied by widespread and heavy rainfall, flooding and abnormally high tides along the Gulf Coast as far south as the Tampa-St. Petersburg sector. Gale force winds began affecting that area on 10 September. These conditions continued through much of the following two days. The storm hindered pilots flying in for the race. United Airlines captain Clay Lacy was

Chuck Lyford's beautiful P-51D-25 was modified for racing in the transcontinental dash as well as the pylon races. The external wing tanks were borrowed from the Navy and came from a Douglas Skyraider. Credit: Jim Larsen

Chuck taxis away for a test flight in the Bardahl Special. In the background is Bill Stead's Grumman F8F-2 Bearcat, BuAer 121751, flown by Mira Slovak in the 1964 pylon races. Credit: Jim Larsen

The Bardahl Special was all glossy white. The company logo was orange outlined in black as was the license number. Race "8" was just the opposite color combination and appeared on the vertical tail as well as on both drop tanks. Credit: Jim Larsen

Chapter XI: Reno Encore

We started talking and pretty soon he opened up his trunk, got out his tools and started helping me change the engine. His name was Dwight Thorn. He was a student going to technical school there at Boeing Field trying to earn his Aircraft and Engine license. After he helped me work on the engine that day, he came back the next morning to help again. And that was the beginning of Dwight's involvement with racing."[9]

"Dwight built up the first engine under the tutelage of Dixon "Dax" Smith – engine builder for the Bardahl race boat crew – and the two men became good friends." When Chuck decided to enter Bill Stead's air race at Reno, he obtained sponsorship from Bardahl and proceeded to clean up the P-51 airframe. Gun ports in the wings of the fighter were removed and the openings covered so that the leading edge had a smooth, uninterrupted contour. The air intake grills on the engine cowling were removed and replaced with solid aluminum sheet stock. For desert operation, the ram air intake on the Mustang could be blocked and air taken in through these side grills and filtered to keep dust and sand out of the induction system.

All airframe surface protrusions were eliminated including the attachment bolts used to secure the fuel tank access panels on the lower wing surface. The panels were reworked by countersinking each bolt hole so that flathead bolts could be used. Wing pylons were fitted to mount Douglas A-1 Skyraider 150 gallon drop tanks borrowed from the U.S. Navy. When the airframe work was finished, the racer was painted a glossy snow white. The Bardahl logo and aircraft registration number were painted in orange, outlined in black, on the sides of the fuselage. Race number eight was painted on the vertical fin as well as on each drop tank. Here, the color scheme was reversed. The number was black and the outline was orange. The final appearance of the Bardahl Special was striking and elegantly simple.

Dwight modified a new dash 9 engine for the races. In Chuck's words, "that engine wasn't stock. It was fairly well built up. It was modified about half-way to an unlimited hydroplane racing engine." A high performance Merlin generates copious amounts of waste heat, most of which goes out the exhaust stacks as hot gas. Heat that doesn't go out the stacks is transferred to the engine oil and liquid coolant. Both fluids circulate through heat exchangers or radiators located in the familiar belly scoop on a Mustang. Air flowing into the scoop and through the radiators removes heat from the oil and

This unusual view of Lyford's racing Mustang illustrates how long the drop tanks were. Chuck experienced tank vibrations during high speed descent and thus elected to let down a long way out from Reno in a more shallow approach. Credit: Jim Larsen

A disappointed Chuck Lyford is seen here just after landing at Sky Ranch. His crew confirmed that Wayne Adams won the race while Chuck was en route from Reno Municipal airport with a very sick Merlin. Credit: Jim Larsen

Another modification made to Lyford's Mustang racer was the installation of a P-51H Aeroproducts propeller which replaced a stock Hamilton Standard unit. This change was made for three reasons. The Aeroproducts propeller blades were lighter and had more blade area. Equally important, it had a self-contained hydraulic system adding a measure of safety should a dead stick landing have to be made.

One further race-specific change is worth mentioning. It was a minor alteration that would ultimately become a major factor determining the outcome of the Harold's Club transcontinental race. The dash 9 Merlin uses a two-stage, two-speed supercharger or blower. At some point between 16,000 and 18,000 feet, the high speed blower automatically engages to maintain manifold pressure. This is controlled by an aneroid switch – a pressure measuring device containing a set of electrical contacts – sensing ram air pressure delivered to the engine. As ram air pressure decreases, the aneroid switch contacts close energizing an electrical solenoid connected to a balanced hydraulic valve which, in turn, activates a clutch engaging the high speed blower drive gears.

coolant before they are pumped back to the engine. Cooling air flow through the belly scoop or duct can be modulated – governed by the thermal load to the radiators – by opening or closing the exit doors (flaps) downstream of the radiators. When the engine is pushed to high power, temperature sensing elements emersed in the two fluids transmit signals to actuators and the doors open wider. Unfortunately, this also results in more drag.

The Bardahl Special would be flown in both the forthcoming high altitude transcontinental race as well as pylon events, two very dissimilar forms of competition. At high altitudes where the outside air temperature is extremely cold, the exit doors extend only slightly if at all and the drag component is minimal even at military power.[10] For low level pylon racing, however, still higher Merlin power settings may be used producing even more waste heat causing the exit doors to remain wide open. In setting up for the 1964 Reno races, Chuck used a position indicator in the cockpit to monitor the coolant exit door position with different engine power settings and concluded that cooling augmentation was needed to eliminate the exit door drag penalty.

The problem of cooling door drag was solved by installing a water spray bar in the belly scoop of the Bardahl Mustang. A tube with an array of nozzles was mounted in front of the coolant radiator. Water was pumped under pressure from a tank built into the wing gun bay to the nozzles creating a droplet spray or mist which impinged on the radiator face. As the water droplets evaporated, additional heat was removed from the radiator surfaces.[11] The Bardahl Special was the first unlimited racing plane to employ spray bar cooling, an innovation now used on virtually every unlimited.

Dick Snyder captured fourth place in the 1964 race in this very clean P-51D-25 Mustang named "Phoebe." The range of his racer was extended with the aid of what appear to be 110 gallon drop tanks. Credit: Larry Smalley via Tim Weinschenker

The dust at the short Sky Ranch airstrip was fierce in 1964, causing more than one pilot to grumble about the conditions. Dick Snyder prepares to launch in this photograph and the dust cloud behind his plane is clearly evident. Credit: Jim Larsen

Chapter XI: Reno Encore

This close up photograph illustrates the wing tank installation on Synder's Mustang. Credit: Jim Larsen

At the high power setting – 90 inches manifold pressure at 3000 revolutions – Chuck planned to use during climb out at the start of the transcontinental race, allowing the blower to shift automatically from low to high speed would produce a very large shock to the entire supercharger drive mechanism. To avoid this potentially destructive mechanical shock, a three-position switch was mounted in the cockpit and wired into the 24 volt solenoid circuit. This allowed Chuck to inactivate or circumvent the aneroid switch and manually engage high blower under controlled conditions. Conversely, the switch could also be reset to permit automatic blower speed control.

THE 1964 RACE

Unlike Clay Lacy and Wayne Adams, Chuck Lyford arrived in Florida before hurricane Dora. Dwight Thorn also journeyed to Florida to help Chuck get off in good shape. Another Bardahl crew member, Chuck Neeley, went directly to Childress – a town in the Texas panhandle about 15 miles from the Oklahoma border – where he would refuel the aircraft during the race.

The remnants of hurricane Dora were still causing havoc. After plowing across northern Florida and then into southeast Alabama, the storm turned around and headed east into Georgia on the day of the race. Lyford was up all night before the race spending most of his time with local Weather Bureau personnel tracking the storm on their weather radar screens. He was trying to decide upon a route that would let him pass over the storm and avoid icing conditions. About three o'clock in the morning, he took time out for breakfast. It would be over ten hours before he would eat his next meal.

The race was scheduled to start at six in the morning. The first Mustang to take off was C.E. Crosby's at 6:19 a.m. with

E.D. Weiner dropped out of the Harold's Club race due to the remnants of hurricane Dora. He landed at Jacksonville, Fl. E.D. flew into Reno when the weather cleared. The aircraft he flew in the 1964 transcon, N335J, became his pylon racer subsequent to this first air race. The aircraft was bronze with white trim. Credit: Jim Larsen

Jack Shaver raced this P-51D-25 to fifth place in 1964. He too carried drop tanks to extend his range. Credit: Jim Larsen

Chapter XI: Reno Encore

Starting Sequence
1964 Harold's Club Trophy Race

Position	Pilot	Race No.	Aircraft Type
1	C.E. Crosby	3	P-51D-30
2	Dick Snyder	45	P-51D-25
3	Chuck Lyford	8	P-51D-25
4	Jack Shaver	69	P-51D-25
5	Stan Hoke	99	P-51D-25
6	Howard Olsen	1	P-51D-25
7	E.D. Weiner	14	P-51D-25
8	Wayne Adams	9	P-51D-25

the other contestants following in rapid order. Chuck released the brakes on the Bardahl Special becoming the third airplane to depart.[12] He began a long heavy climb into the dark overcast Florida sky at 200 knots (230 mph) at 90 inches of manifold pressure and 3000 revolutions using water injection.

"As I was climbing, I looked out into the Gulf of Mexico and could see this huge line of thunderstorms. Some of those clouds were as high as 35,000 feet or possibly higher. It was basically just a continuous squall line which was the edge of the hurricane. I could see one notch or break in the storm clouds. The notch I was heading for was fairly distinct. Spending the time with the weather radar people the night before really helped me. As I got closer to the storm front, I noticed that my angle of climb was not going to get me up into that notch which was probably at 22,000 or 23,000 feet."

Chuck eased the Mustang into a steeper climb. He didn't want to get into the moisture-laden clouds where he might encounter icing conditions. "I had drop tanks hanging on the plane. I had no capability of handling ice at all, let alone the drag that ice would produce. I didn't even have pitot (tube) heat. So I started increasing the climb rate. This started costing me air speed and I was getting down to about 120-130 knots (138-150 mph) which was very close to the stall speed." As his speed dropped off with the increased climb angle, ram air entering the carburetor inlet duct decreased and at about 27,000 feet the supercharger began to surge with corresponding engine power variations.

To build ram air pressure and get away from the surge condition, Chuck lowered the nose of the airplane and built up speed. "That put me into the clouds. Fortunately, at that altitude and air temperature, there wasn't any ice. It was, however, extremely turbulent and I'll never forget the ride through those clouds. It was just like riding a bucking bronco. The drop tanks were still full and I was afraid I was going to lose them. The entire airframe was shaking violently. Fortuitously, the Mustang was so heavy that it was still semi-stable. Although shock loads on the airplane were high, roll rates didn't go anywhere near 30 degrees. It was just a very violent ride!

The time Chuck spent with the weather radar specialists led him to conclude that an initial heading out over the Gulf of Mexico was the only way to circumvent the storm. He made landfall again in the vicinity of Mobile, Alabama. It was a good choice. Two of the race pilots, Howard Olsen and E.D. Weiner, elected to avoid the Gulf and fly along the Florida coastline. Weather forced both to land. Olsen came down at Ocala and E.D. dropped out at Jacksonville. Wayne Adams followed Lyford over the Gulf and threaded his way around the storm. He would trail Chuck throughout the race.

REFUELING AT CHILDRESS

The Bardahl Special landed at Childress where it was met and refueled by Chuck Neeley. Lyford kept the engine running all during the refueling operation. Pre-heated engine oil was added at the same time. Unfortunately, prop blast blew hot oil mist onto the windscreen and into the cockpit. In his haste to depart Childress, Chuck didn't have time to spend cleaning up the mess. Instead, he was handed a couple of rags and would worry about cleaning up inside the cockpit once he got to altitude.

The racer was off within minutes of refueling, climbing out of Childress with 80 inches of manifold pressure, this time without antidetonant injection. None had been added during the fast refueling stop. The blower control switch was set on manual and running in low speed while the airplane climbed. When the racer reached about 19,000 feet and manifold pressure had bled off, Chuck reduced power to 50 inches and manually shifted to high blower and once again added power. "The idea was that once I was well above the aneroid (switch) height where the blower would have shifted by itself, I would put the blower back on automatic and let it downshift in this mode during descent, which was not a violent shift. In fact, it was hardly noticeable."

With his climb complete at 28,000 feet, Chuck took time to clean up the oily mess in the cockpit. The windscreen was covered in oil virtually eliminating forward visibility. On top of that, a magneto problem developed which would persist throughout the remainder of the race. The dash 9 Merlin was equipped with a Northeast magneto as opposed to the British-made Rotax unit commonly found on the dash 7 engine. Both Chuck and Dwight Thorn preferred the Northeast magneto as it had a spark retard feature absent in the Rotax. The engine started much easier with a Northeast magneto because of this feature. At high power settings, the spark also retarded a little bit which helped control detonation. And finally, it was easier

This P-51D-25 belonged to Stan Hoke. His plane carried an extra fuselage tank aft of the pilot's seat in the cockpit as well as tanks symmetrically installed on the wing tips. Credit: Larry Smalley via Tim Weinschenker

to work on the points. The magneto had one drawback. The chamber in which the rotor is located is sealed. When the airplane is on the ground, air pressure inside the chamber is the same as outside, about 15 pounds per square inch. At 28,000 feet, ambient air pressure is between four and five pounds per square inch and pressure inside the rotor housing decays until it reaches equilibrium with the pressure at altitude. When the airplane descends to land, the chamber breathes enough to build up in pressure until it equals the outside air pressure once more.

When Chuck landed in Florida, very humid air was sucked into the magnetos. The moisture resulted in deposits. As the deposits built up, arcing occurred. Chuck went on to explain that for the "second half of the race, arcing was occurring and we lost perhaps 300 revolutions per minute. Under normal conditions of say 60 inches manifold pressure, the engine would do what we called "chunging." About every 15 seconds, this phenomenon would occur and could be felt by a shake or vibration. It was very distracting. On Climb out, this was disheartening as hell! It didn't happen as often in cruise, but the entire distance from Childress to Reno, the condition persisted. It was basically a detonation and you didn't know how much of this the engine could withstand. Needless to say, I was very uncomfortable."

RENO APPROACH

Between cleaning up the mess in the cockpit and the periodic chunging of the engine, Chuck forgot to reset the blower to automatic. He remembers rather vividly what happened next as he neared the end of the race. "Coming into Reno, I experienced a bad vibration in the external drop tanks while letting down at high speed. So instead of making a rapid high speed descent, I thought I would let down way out and not radically increase the speed of the airplane to minimize the tank vibration problem. The blower, still in high speed in the manual control setting, started to heat up. The induction temperature began to rise, which I didn't realize at the time. However, I did notice the manifold pressure start to decrease slightly. I was increasing power to keep the manifold pressure up which made the situation worse. This was actually increasing the amount of heat that the blower was generating in high gear at low altitude."

As the induction temperature increased the engine ran hotter and the ethylene glycol engine coolant temperature shot up exacerbating the problem. Solder in the aftercooler radiator core began to melt eventually becoming entrapped on the backfire screens in the air induction passageway. This created a partial blockage and a high pressure drop across the screens. Engine manifold pressure steadily decayed dropping to around 21 inches. "I got down low," Chuck recalls, "and got stuck behind some hills east of Reno and I didn't have enough power to climb over the hills. I wasn't quite sure where I was so I just kept heading west going through the low points in the terrain. The airplane was just barely flying. I finally located Reno and went straight for the municipal airport."

The Reno air races in 1964, were held at Bill Stead's Sky Ranch a few miles north of Sparks, Nevada. He had cleared a short 3000 foot dirt runway and ramp area for the racers. It was pretty crude and lacking in any amenities. The finish line for the Harold's Club Trophy Dash, author Don Berliner recorded, "was a Federal Aviation Administration (FAA) Omnirange station atop Mount Vista, ten miles east of Reno and about as far southeast of the race site."[13] Don was the chief timer for the conclusion of the "transcon" race that September 12. He and his timing crew had been notified by radio that the leading airplane appeared to be Chuck Lyford in the Bardahl Special. Don and the other race officials scanned the Reno sky for his approach.

Like most of the P-51s in that first Reno transcon race, Stan Hoke's Mustang was basically a stock airframe with added fuel capacity. The tip tanks appear to be from a Cessna 310. Credit: Jim Larsen

Chapter XI: Reno Encore

Wayne Adams flew a good race in 1964. His Mustang was not as fast as the Bardahl Special, but luck was with Wayne and he had no mechanical problems along the way. Credit: Jim Larsen

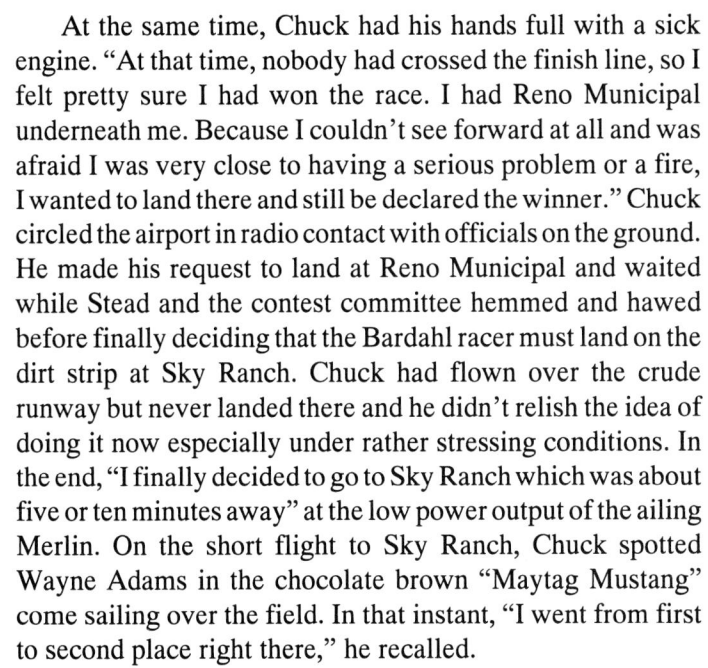

The Harold's Club Transcontinental Trophy Dash was the first cross-country race for unlimited piston engine planes since 1949. A happy Wayne Adams poses with his trophy on the wing of race 9. Interestingly, the 1949 Bendix winner, Joe DeBona, was there to greet Adams when he landed. Credit: Jim Larsen

At the same time, Chuck had his hands full with a sick engine. "At that time, nobody had crossed the finish line, so I felt pretty sure I had won the race. I had Reno Municipal underneath me. Because I couldn't see forward at all and was afraid I was very close to having a serious problem or a fire, I wanted to land there and still be declared the winner." Chuck circled the airport in radio contact with officials on the ground. He made his request to land at Reno Municipal and waited while Stead and the contest committee hemmed and hawed before finally deciding that the Bardahl racer must land on the dirt strip at Sky Ranch. Chuck had flown over the crude runway but never landed there and he didn't relish the idea of doing it now especially under rather stressing conditions. In the end, "I finally decided to go to Sky Ranch which was about five or ten minutes away" at the low power output of the ailing Merlin. On the short flight to Sky Ranch, Chuck spotted Wayne Adams in the chocolate brown "Maytag Mustang" come sailing over the field. In that instant, "I went from first to second place right there," he recalled.

For the competitive former champion boat racer, it was a frustrating conclusion to a long, physically exhausting race fraught with mechanical problems and some pretty heavy weather. Loitering over Reno Municipal and the short trip from there to Sky Ranch cost him 15 minutes more elapsed time and, as it turned out, the race. Looking back across three decades, Chuck acknowledges that he and his crew were pretty disappointed. "It was a helluva effort by my crew. We didn't quite make it though." In retrospect, Chuck Lyford's first and only transcontinental race – he would go on to be a champion pylon racer – was certainly a fine tribute to his flying skill, competitive nature and determination.

NOTES:
1 United States Weather Service synopsis of Hurricane Dora, 9-12 September 1964. Information provided by John J. Pappas, Manager, Delta Meteorology Center, Delta Airlines, Atlanta, Georgia.
2 John Tegler, *Gentlemen, You Have a Race*, Wings Publishing Company, Severna Park, Maryland, 1984, p. 34.
3 Ibid.
4 Ibid, p. 36.
5 Audio tape to the author from Chuck Lyford, 5 February 1992.
6 Robert W. Gruenhagen, *Mustang, The Story of the P-51 Fighter*, revised edition, Arco Publishing, Inc., New York, 1976, p. 186.
7 Telephone interview by the author with Jim Larsen, 6 April 1993.
8 Tegler, op.cit., p. 29.
9 Lyford audio tape, op.cit.
10 At 25,000 feet in a standard atmosphere, the temperature is -25° Fahrenheit.
11 A discussion of spray bar cooling systems used on unlimited air racers is contained in *Mustang: The Racing Thoroughbred*, by Dustin W. Carter and Birch J. Matthews, Schiffer Publishing Ltd., West Chester, Pennsylvania, 1992, pp. 42-43.
12 *Reno Evening Gazette*, 12 September 1964, p. 1.
13 Don Berliner, *Unlimited Air Racers*, Motorbooks International, Osceola, Wisconsin, 1992, p. 37.

E.D. won the 1965 Harold's Club race. The end of the race this year was at Reno Municipal airport. In this photograph, Weiner is seen just after he landed and taxied up to the race stand. The weather was rainy and overcast. Credit: Jim Larsen

Chapter XII

THE FINAL YEARS

Following the 1964 Harold's Club inaugural event, unlimited class transcontinental air racing continued on for another six years. Unlike the more glamorous high speed pylon events, transcontinental races were run at high altitudes, out of the public's view. Race fans could only see the start or finish of these long duration events and that may well be the reason they were eventually discontinued. But, to certain pilots racing in the last half of the 1960s decade, transcontinental or "transcon" races represented the supreme challenge. Isolated within their cockpits and challenged by the nuances of long distance competition, they sought to wring the last bit of speed out of their mounts. They did this by streamlining the airframe, practicing good fuel management and applying expert navigational skills. The races were often physically tough and demanding contests of endurance as well as skill. These pilots, like their marathon counterparts on the ground, were basically excellent athletes.

"E.D."

The 1964 National Championship Air Races, virtually Bill Stead's personal creation, "were a rousing success – 40,000 fans the final day according to race officials – and promoters hope to stage them again next year."[1] Intrigued with the possibilities of a set, established racing program in Reno, plans were drawn to try and increase prize money from $45,000 to $100,000 the following year. Race management was nothing if not enthusiastic. There was even talk of trying to kickoff the 1965 race with a "round-the-world jet race from nearby Stead Air Force Base."[2] This unique concept never came to pass, although it certainly would have been an interesting tournament.

    The Reno business community embraced the idea of continuing the races. The program came at a time of the year when the local tourist economy needed bolstering. The major deficiency with the first race was an environmental one. Mira Slovak, Czech refugee and winner of the championship pylon race capsulized the problem best. "The dust was so blinding that it was impossible to see the landing strip."[3] Twelve months of planning and preparation by Stead and his co-workers resulted in a much improved race program in 1965. For one thing, the landing strip was coated with dust suppressing oil. For another, the conclusion of the transcontinental race would occur at the Reno Municipal Airport, an improvement over the hastily arranged windup of the previous year. Once again, Harold's Club would sponsor this race which attracted a flock of Mustangs and one Riley "Rocket," an improved performance conversion of the twin engine Cessna 310D.

    One of the entrants was a participant in the first race, Ellis .D. "Ed" Weiner. Forty-three year old Ed Weiner – frequently known simply by his first initials – was a quiet, reserved and

E.D. Weiner built up this P-51D-25 Mustang specifically for transcontinental air racing in 1965. The modifications included a general airframe cleanup and sealing the gun and ammunition bays for fuel. The checkered paint scheme was black and white. The spinner and race number were apple green. Credit: Jim Larsen

thoughtful pilot and business man. His five feet, seven inch frame was athletically trim with only traces of grey betraying his age. Weiner's flying background included a stint in the Air Force during World War II when he ferried aircraft for the Air Transport Command all over the country. Ed longed to fly in the post-war National Air Races, but simply couldn't afford it. He never lost that ambition and when Bill Stead brought unlimited racing back in 1964, Weiner didn't hesitate. Money was no longer a problem. He was affluent now, running his own aircraft electronics business, E.D. Weiner Corporation, located in Santa Monica, California. He owned several aircraft including a brace of P-51s used for both pleasure and business trips. The Mustangs became his racing vehicles. One was set up for pylon racing and the other for cross-country competition.

Disappointed at being forced out of the 1964 Harold's Club race, Weiner set about preparing for 1965. His Mustangs were maintained at Long Beach Municipal Airport in Southern California, where they were cared for by Vern Barker at the Air Associates hangar. E.D. convinced Vern to open up his

Wayne Adams placed third in 1965. His Maytag Mustang was basically unchanged from the previous year. Note the added fuselage tank in back of the pilot's seat. Markings were slightly different this year. Credit: Jim Larsen

Chapter XII: The Final Years

Pilot Dick Kestle was a newcomer to transcontinental air racing in 1965. He flew this red and white P-51D-20 Mustang to fourth place. Credit: Larry Smalley via Tim Weinschenker

own shop. With Weiner's support, Vern Barker's Aircraft Maintenance opened for business just off Wardlow Road on the east side of the airport.

The wing of E.D.'s cross-country racer was partially wetted and a large auxiliary fuel tank fabricated and installed in the fuselage behind the pilot's seat. Ed wanted a distinctive and spectacular paint scheme on his Mustang. He believed colorful, custom paint jobs were an integral part of the sport and something that appealed to race fans. He settled on a black and white checkerboard pattern for the fuselage and vertical surfaces. Weiner was meticulous about his airplanes. He fussed over the size of the checkered pattern trying different sized squares until he was satisfied that the entire pattern had a proportional appearance, smaller at the nose and tail. The wings and horizontal tail were smoothly finished in a glossy white. The spinner and race number were painted in apple green. The cockpit appointments included the latest navigational aids together with enunciator lights to alert him in the

R. J. "Jack" Shaver was back again with his Mustang. He finished in sixth place with an average speed of 269 miles per hour. Credit: Larry Smalley via Tim Weinschenker

event any engine operating parameters were exceeding limits.

The starting point for the 1965 Harold's Club race was again the St. Petersburg region in western Florida. The race began on Labor Day, 6 September at one second after 5 a.m., eastern standard time, when Dick Kestle was flagged away in his red and white D model Mustang. Wayne Adams, the pre-race favorite and winner of the first race, launched seconds after Tom Green in the customized Cessna 310. Adams had a wet wing this year and reportedly carried nearly 700 gallons of fuel, enough for a non-stop race.[4] The sixth racer to take off was E.D. Weiner. He dropped out of the 1964 race landing at Jacksonville, encountering severe weather from hurricane Dora. E.D. lifted off this time into fair skies, guiding his Merlin-powered black and white checkerboard P-51 out over the Gulf of Mexico.

The weather at Reno, meanwhile, was cold, thick with dark overcast and punctuated with rain showers, an ominous sign for the transcontinental racers from the perspective of those waiting at the finish line. The weather was not widespread, fortunately, and really had no influence on the outcome of the race. Six and one-half hours after takeoff, a Mustang broke through the overcast at Reno and flashed across the finish line. It was 2:30 p.m. local time. There was

Weiner pushed his Merlin hard during the 1966 race. He lost an exhaust stack on the port bank, but otherwise had no trouble defeating the other two contestants. E.D. took on 400 gallons in a refueling stop at Duncan, OK, during the race. Credit: Birch Matthews

When the Harold's Club race wasn't held in 1966, E.D. Weiner put together a three-plane cross-country race from St. Petersburg to Palm Springs. Weiner won the race and is shown here just after he arrived. E.D. is in the cockpit being greeted by the air race queen. Vern Barker, his chief wrench, is standing on the wing. Credit: Birch Matthews

Chapter XII: The Final Years

Starting Sequence
1965 Harold's Club Trophy Race

Position	Pilot	Race No.	Aircraft Type
1	Dick Kestle	13	P-51D-20
2	Tom Green	6	Riley Rocket
3	Jim Fugate	83	P-51D-25
4	Wayne Adams	9	P-51D-25
5	Jack Shaver	69	P-51D-25
6	E.D. Weiner	14	P-51D-25
7	Doug Wood	7	P-51D-25
8	John Gower	11	P-51D-25
9	Clay Lacy	64	P-51D-30

no mistaking the identity of the racer. It was Ed Weiner, seven minutes ahead of second place winner, Clay Lacy and over 20 minutes in front of Wayne Adams in the Maytag Mustang. Weiner entered the pattern at Reno and landed, taxiing up to a temporary announcer's podium and grandstand erected for the race. The crowd was sparse because of the cold and rain. It didn't matter to E.D. He had beaten some first class competition and in the process, boosted the winning speed almost 30 miles per hour. With favorable weather this year, Weiner averaged 348 miles an hour to win the second Harold's Club race.

THE PICKUP RACE

There was no Harold's Club race in 1966. Disappointed by this turn of events, Ed Weiner contacted several pilots with a sporting proposition. They would run their own race this year, each pilot putting up a $1,000 stake with the winner taking the entire purse. Weiner convinced Dick Kestle of Atlanta, and Mike Carroll from the Palos Verdes Peninsula in California, to join the race. As before, the airplanes would launch from the St. Petersburg/Clearwater area. The finish, however, would occur at Palm Springs, California. The racers launched on September 4, headed for the Palm Springs airport. The skies were clear at mid-day over this exclusive enclave in Southern California's low desert. It was terribly hot and bone dry. The temperature climbed to 114 degrees Fahrenheit and that was in the shade! Weiner's well groomed racer was the first to roar across the Palm Springs airport. It was his second consecutive transcontinental victory. He pushed the Merlin hard and in the process, burned an exhaust stack on port side. The racer landed five hours and 36 minutes after leaving the humid Florida coast. Twenty minutes later, Dick Kestle arrived, finishing second. Kestle experienced an engine problem during the race loosing coolant in the process. Newcomer Mike Carroll in a freshly prepared Hawker Sea Fury was a distant third, rolling out at Palm Springs almost an hour behind Weiner's Mustang.

FLAMING FURY

Thirty-one year old Michael D. Carroll was the president of a family owned business, Signal Trucking Service, located in Signal Hill, California, near the Long Beach airport. He was

Mike Carroll was the third entry in the Florida to Palm Springs race. The photo here shows the big Sea Fury at Reno that same year. Markings were unchanged. Credit: Birch Matthews

The big Sea Fury seems to almost swallow Mike Carroll as he sits in the cockpit. The small acyrilic bubble was mounted on a frame hinged to open to one side. In an emergency, the entire frame could be jettisoned. Credit: Birch Matthews

Dick Kestle arrived at Palm Springs 20 minutes behind E.D. Weiner to take second place. It was a hot desert summer day at Palm Springs when Kestle arrived. The temperature was 114 degrees in the shade! Credit: Birch Matthews

Mike Carroll bought his Sea Fury in the summer of 1965. When the aircraft arrived at Long Beach, CA, it had a stock airframe painted red with a large gold stripe down the fuselage. The Canadian registration was CF-VAN. For a short time, it carried both a Canadian and U.S. registration as shown here. Credit: Birch Matthews

a handsome, athletic young man with a ready smile and outgoing personality.

Before Mike acquired the Sea Fury, he owned a two-place P-51 purchased from E.D. Weiner. Carroll had a grand total of 120 hours when he bought the Mustang. Before E.D. would let him fly the airplane, he gave him three hours of dual time in a North American T-6 until he was satisfied his young protege could handle the sleek fighter. Mike put about 60 hours of flying time on the Mustang and then sold it to Los Angeles attorney Peter Drucker who later entered the P-51 in the 1965 Harold's Club race with Western Airlines captain John Gower as pilot.[5]

In the summer of 1965, an unusual aircraft entered the pattern on final for runway 30 at Long Beach. It was a Hawker Sea Fury F.B. Mk.11, late of the Royal Canadian Navy and civilian ownership by Canadian pilot Robert Van der Veken. Mike bought the British-built fighter using money from the sale of his Mustang. The dark red airplane still carried Canadian registration CF-VAN when it was ferried into Long Beach. The Canadian registration was soon replaced by U.S. license, N878M, although for a short time, the big Sea Fury sported both.

Mike's new airplane joined Ed Weiner's two Mustangs at Vern Barker's Aircraft Maintenance hangar where Vern, Don Newberger and Dick Tomasulo prepared the Sea Fury for racing. Mike wrote to Hawker Siddeley Aviation Limited for advice about modifications. He was interested in drag reduction techniques. Would, for instance, clipping the wings impair performance for transcontinental racing? Hawker engineers evaluated the proposed short span racing wing and

Chapter XII: The Final Years

Lyle Shelton raced Mike's Sea Fury around the pylons during the 1966 Reno air races. The airplane was not particularly successful at this form of racing. Lyle found that it lost about 40 miles per hour during 4 G turns. Credit: Birch Matthews

Mike's racer, named the "Signal Sea Fury," sits on the ramp in front of Vern Barker's Aircraft Maintenance hangar at Long Beach airport. The airplane was extensively modified for cross-country racing. Credit: Birch Matthews

didn't "feel too concerned about the loss of lift at altitude."[6] The stock wingspan on a Sea Fury is 38 feet, 4.75 inches and Vern Barker's crew chopped the wing tips at the rib station just outboard of the center aileron hinge. New symmetrical fiberglass tips filled with balsa wood were fitted giving the racer a new span of about 32 feet.[7]

The military airframe was lightened considerably. Wing folding mechanisms were removed along with all armor plate and the arresting hook used in carrier deck landings. An accessory drive unit on the Bristol Centaurus which powered the hydraulic pump, electrical generator and compressor for the air brakes was removed. It consumed about 150 horsepower of the engine output.[8] A Douglas DC-6 electrically actuated hydraulic pump was substituted to operate the landing gear and flaps. An alternator replaced the generator and a compressed air bottle was installed to actuate the brakes. To increase range, the wings were sealed using PRC 1422, a viscous polysulfide putty made by the Product Research Company. Sections of the wing skin were removed to access the structure to be sealed. Putty was applied to form fillets at each wing structural intersection and to cover internal rivet heads. When this was done, the process was completed by painting all internal surfaces with "monkey blood," a red semi-viscous liquid more formally identified as PRC 1005.[9] The main fuselage tank and nose tank were removed and replaced by larger capacity tanks. In its military configuration, the F.B. 11 Sea Fury has an internal gasoline capacity or 240 gallons (200 Imperial gallons). With the modifications described, Mike could load 588 gallons – over 3500 pounds of fuel – into his racer, almost two and one-half times the original amount.

Fuel Capacity Race 87 Sea Fury

Tank Location	Gallons
Nose Tank	155
Fuselage Tank	213
Left Wing	110
Right Wing	110
Total	588

Data courtesy of Bill Kerchenfaut

There were two transcon races in 1967. The first ran from Palm Springs, CA, to Cleveland in connection with races held at Burke Lakefront Airport. Bob Guilford was one of four pilots entered. He flew this P-51D-30. Credit: Birch Matthews

The 1967 race to Cleveland included Weiner, Carroll, Guilford and Jim Ventura who flew this P-51D-30. Ventura was killed when this airplane crashed near Minden, NB. Credit: Birch Matthews

In the process of cleaning up the airframe, upper wing surface gun blisters were removed and these openings together with gun cooling holes and spent cartridge slots were faired over. Gaps that normally existed between the folding tips and the inboard wing panels were sealed. The Sea Fury wing was designed around an excellent laminar flow airfoil section developed by Hawker.[10] The crew working on Mike Carroll's racer spent many hours filling and smoothing the wing surface. Openings where the arresting hook had been installed were also covered and the fuselage contour smoothed. To complete the job, the large cockpit canopy was stripped away and replaced with a tiny custom-formed bubble canopy with a corresponding reduction in frontal area and wetted surface.

Sea Fury racing modifications were completed in the summer of 1966. It was almost ready to race. The airframe was primed and painted a bright yellow. The large spinner over the

E.D. has just shut down the Merlin dash 9 after landing at Stead Field. He was second in the 1967 Harold's Club race. The fuselage tank had been modified so that a portion carried oil. The fuel tank was red and the oil tank was yellow. Credit: Birch Matthews

E.D. Weiner's immaculate Bardahl II transcon racer sits in a hangar at Palm Springs before the race to Cleveland. This cross-country race marked his third straight victory in this sport. Credit: Birch Matthews

Chapter XII: The Final Years

Weiner's 1967 Bardahl II racer sits in the pits at Reno after the race. E.D. wasn't used to losing and began thinking about how to make his Mustang faster for 1968. Credit: Dusty Carter

five-blade propeller hub was snow white and this color was carried over to the leading edge of the cowling. The white faded to medium blue along the cowl. Aft of the cowl, the color changed again, first to a burnt orange and then to red depicting flames flowing aft over the forward fuselage. It was a striking, colorful paint scheme unlike any other contemporary unlimited racer. The airplane was christened the "Signal Sea Fury."

The Bristol Centaurus 18 engine was retained in the Mike's racer although it would occasionally cause problems. In the 1966 race from Florida to Palm Springs, Mike refueled at San Angelo, Texas. Instead of refueling hot, he shut the engine down. It took eight cartridges to restart the engine and Mike lost about 40 minutes in the process. That was enough to cost him the race. The brakes on the Sea Fury represented another weakness. The aircraft was designed for carrier operation where it would be arrested upon landing. Prolonged braking and a lot of taxiing around an airport were not design requirements for the big British fighter. Mike knew he had a problem. On his flight east for the start of the Florida-Palm Springs race, he landed at Atlanta and lost the brakes. Determined to continue, Mike had people at Mustangs Unlimited work on the brakes before continuing to Florida. Two men from the Mustangs Unlimited shop wing-walked the Sea Fury out to the runway for takeoff the next day. Landing at Palm Springs at the end of the race, his brakes failed again. He had to be towed from the end of the runway.[11]

TRANSCON TO CLEVELAND

E.D. Weiner put together a second transcontinental contest in 1966, to coincide with opening day ceremonies of the first air race program held at Cleveland in 18 years. This time, the races would take place at Cleveland's Burke Lakefront Airport on the shores of Lake Erie. The transcontinental race was

Vern Barker with his ever present cigar listens as Ed Weiner talks about the race. All seams on the racer were taped with Scotch Tape as a drag reduction technique. Credit: Birch Matthews

Jim Fugate finished fifth in the 1967 Harold's Club race from Rockford, IL, to Reno's Stead Field. He was penalized for a late start. Credit: Jim Larsen

Fugate's transcon racer sits in the unlimited pits in this picture. The racer was white with dark blue trim. The leading edge of the vertical fin was black and the aircraft name was the "Twinkletown Special." Credit: Dusty Carter

to begin at Palm Springs on Saturday, 2 September 1967, but poor weather in the southwest intervened and the race was delayed until Sunday.[12] Four planes were set to run. In addition to E.D. Weiner and Mike Carroll, Bob Guilford of Beverly Hills and Jim Ventura of Goleta, California, both in P-51 Mustangs, would also race.

Thirty-three year old James L. Ventura was a newcomer to unlimited air racing. His D model Mustang was basically unaltered having only two 110 gallon external drop tanks mounted underneath the wings. He flew the race on a waiver from the Federal Aviation Administration because his flight path would be over 24,000 feet in a positive control area and the aircraft was not equipped with a radar beacon transponder. Ventura was non-instrument rated and would fly under visual flight rules. He landed at McCook, Nebraska to refuel. While refueling, he was advised that weather between McCook and Omaha was poor with extremely low ceilings. In spite of this, Jim took off and headed for Cleveland. As predicted, he immediately ran into fog and light rain. Forty minutes out of McCook, Ventura became disoriented in the overcast and crashed inverted five miles east of Minden, Nebraska.[13] Sadly, the sport had claimed another victim.

Weiner's checkered racer, riding favorable tail winds, won the transcontinental dash to Cleveland. It was his third straight cross-country victory. During the summer, E.D. had the internal fuel capacity increased by wetting more of the wing than had previously been done. Total fuel capacity was now around 650 gallons. The large fuselage fuel tank installed

Tom Kuchinsky flew this P-51D-25 Mustang in 1967, and took fourth place in the transcon race. The aircraft was light blue with medium blue trim. Credit: Dusty Carter

Chapter XII: The Final Years

Mike Carroll won the 1967 Harold's Club race with his Sea Fury. It marked the first and only time an airplane other than a Mustang had won a post-war unlimited transcontinental air race. Mike is being interviewed by a reporter from Reno television channel 2, KTVN. A representative from Harold's Club holds the trophy.

in 1966, was modified, part of the capacity being converted into an auxiliary oil tank which would add perhaps five gallons to the system.

Mike Carroll brought his garish Sea Fury into Cleveland 19 minutes behind Weiner. He was getting the hang of it, improving his performance with each race.

SAILING SEA FURY

Mike Carroll and Ed Weiner returned from Cleveland with only days to get ready for the Harold's Club trophy race. The transcon race was on again after a one year absence. The race would be run on Thursday, 21 September 1967, and start from Rockford, Illinois, near the Wisconsin state line. The finish line this year was at the newly deactivated Stead Air Force Base, about 10 miles north of Reno. The move from Sky Ranch to Stead Field – named for Bill Stead's brother, Croston who was killed in a P-51 while flying for the Nevada Air Guard – was a major step forward for the Reno air races. The new site offered two paved runways, one 7600 feet and the other 8080 feet in length. There was a large tie down area, fixed base operations and numerous other facilities to accommodate race officials and large crowds. Ironically, Bill Stead was killed flying a Formula One racer during an accident at St. Petersburg, Florida, and never lived to see his creation take form at the new site.

E.D. Weiner did his own flight planning for the transcontinental races, no doubt because of his military background coupled with a genuine preference for cross-country flying and all that it entails. Mike Carroll, along with Dick Kestle and one or two other transcon pilots, utilized the flight planning services of meteorologist C.L. "Chan" Chandler at the Southeast Weather group in Atlanta. Chan laid out a pressure pattern minimum time track from Rockford to Reno for Mike and Dick Kestle for the 1967 race. Based upon upper air data and forecasts, Chan indicated the headings and altitudes Mike should fly to maximize tailwinds or at least minimize headwinds. Typically, this would not be a great circle route between the start and finish of the race due to variations in weather conditions across the United States.

Weather for this year's transcon race was exceptionally good along the entire route. The temperature at Stead Field was in the high eighties. Frank Tallman had just completed his aerobatic routine in an old Boeing F-4B and was driving back to the race announcer's stand when the first unlimited appeared. He recalled . . . "there was a subdued murmur of excitement from the crowd – the announcement had been made that the first of the unlimiteds was inbound on the Harold's Club cross-country dash. From the east a speck grew into Mike Carroll's enormous Sea Fury."[14]

Mike had flown the profile given to him by C.L. Chandler. The Sea Fury true air speed drops off rapidly above 25,000 feet. It can't compete with the dash 9 Merlin-powered Mustangs at higher altitudes. Following his flight plan, Mike took off from Rockford behind E.D. and climbed to about 6,000 feet, below the strong headwinds at higher altitudes that day. He eventually climbed to 24,000 feet for the last portion of the race following the pressure pattern track Chan had laid out for him.[15] It worked and Mike led perennial winner E.D. Weiner across the finish line by ten minutes. He encountered no real problems during the race noting only that "there were some rough winds and turbulence over the Rockies that shook me up. Other than that, everything was fine. She (the Sea Fury) really sailed."[16] Mike was one tired, happy pilot that day. All of the work that he, Vern Barker, Don Newberger and Dick Tomasulo had lavished on the Sea Fury finally paid off!

Starting Sequence
1967 Harold's Club Trophy Race

Position	Pilot	Race No.	Aircraft Type
1	E.D. Weiner	14	P-51D-25
2	Mike Carroll	87	Sea Fury
3	Dick Kestle	13	P-51D-20
4	Tom Kuchinsky	18	P-51D-25
5	Mick Rupp	17	P-51D-25
6	Jim Fugate	83	P-51D-25

The rest of the transcon racers trailed into Reno except for Mick Rupp who was down with mechanical problems. As E.D. Weiner made his low level pass over Stead, he looked down and saw the big yellow Sea Fury sitting at rest in front of the grandstands. Ed was certainly the pre-race favorite because of his previous wins.

It must have been a bit of a shock to realize that Mike had bested him this time. Commenting on Mike's victory, C.L. Chandler recalled that "it may have been a surprise to most everyone, but not to me."[17] He had pieced together a good flight plan for the fast Fury and he knew it. Third place went to Dick Kestle from Columbus, Georgia, following another Chandler minimum time track flight plan.

There was one oddity about this race. Jim Fugate from Lake Oswego, Oregon, was certainly determined to fly the Harold's Club race. On his way to Rockford the day before the race, Jim landed at Albuquerque with oil feed system problems. Repairs were made, but he didn't depart Albuquerque until three in the morning, arriving in Rockford an hour after the other pilots had departed. By this time, all of the contest officials at Rockford were gone. Undaunted, Jim refueled his P-51 and took off anyway. Five hours and 36 minutes later, his Mustang reached Stead and landed. His time was good enough for fourth place, however, the contest committee in Reno penalized him because he had not arrived in time for the official start. He was given the same takeoff time as Mick Rupp, the last to depart Rockford, which resulted in a calculated elapsed time of seven hours. Ironically, this only cost Fugate $100, the prize differential between fourth and fifth place.

Mike Carroll wanted a pylon racer and a shot at the world's speed record for piston engine airplanes. He chose this airplane, a Bell P-39Q-10 Airacobra. In 1946, this same airplane won the Thompson Trophy Race. Credit: Bell Aircraft via Birch Matthews collection

DEADLY COBRA

Mike Carroll's Sea Fury was set up primarily for transcontinental racing. Although Lyle Shelton flew the big airplane in pylon events at Reno in 1966, it didn't do exceptionally well. In later years, racing Sea Furies were successfully campaigned with the awesome Pratt & Whitney R-4360 engine providing more power up front. It should be pointed out that none raced with clipped wings. When Lyle raced the airplane, he found control to be light and very responsive with good performance in straight and level flight. The downside of Mike's clipped wing Fury occurred during pylon turns where speed bled off rapidly. "The aircraft was dissipating about 40 miles per hour during a hard four "g" turn of 180 degrees."[18] Rather than compromise what was now a champion transcon racer, Mike elected to obtain a second airplane and prepare this one for pylon racing and a shot at the world's piston engine speed record.

The airplane Mike Carroll chose for a pylon racer won the 1946 Thompson Trophy Race with Tex Johnston up.[19] This was a superbly prepared Bell P-39Q Airacobra known as "Cobra II." The same airplane took third in the 1947 Thompson. A year later, Allison Division test pilot Chuck Brown established a closed-course qualification record spinning the diminutive Bell Airacobra around the 300 mile Thompson course at 418 miles an hour. There was no doubt this P-39 could fly fast. After leading the 1948 Thompson, vapor lock forced Brown from the race in the next to last lap. The airplane wasn't raced in 1949. A backup pilot flew the plane back to Indianapolis after the 1948 race, belly landing the P-39 into a field when he encountered an engine problem.[20]

Mike bought the airframe in 1967, from Ed Maloney, Director of the Planes of Fame Museum in California. Ed had located the airplane in 1960, and trucked the remains from

Chapter XII: The Final Years

Within a few months, the P-39 fuselage had been inspected, cleaned and modifications started. The left-hand cockpit door was sealed by the time this photograph was taken. Credit: Birch Matthews

Don Newberger works on the reduction gear box in this picture. The V-1710-85 engine was run for the first time on 20 July 1968. Note the absence of a canopy member on the overhead acyrlic panel. This was removed during the modification process. Credit: Birch Matthews

Darryl Greenamyer, Mike Carroll and Ed Weiner pose for this shot in Vern Barker's hangar. The tank in the forward gun bay on Mike's P-39 was part of a boil off system used to cool the engine oil. Credit: Birch Matthews

Right: Mike bought the veteran race plane and trucked it to Vern Barker's hangar at Long Beach. The airframe looked like this when it arrived at Vern's hangar. Credit: Birch Matthews

Indianapolis to his museum. There it sat on static display until 1965, when the airframe was disassembled and trucked to Long Beach airport. Adam Robbins of Hawthorne, California, led an effort to rebuild the old racer into a contemporary unlimited. His prospectus invited investors to sponsor the Cobra project in return for advertising and promotional programs centered on the revival of unlimited air racing. This enterprise never got off the ground, so to speak, and Maloney took the airplane back to his museum. Two years later, Mike asked Don Newberger to take a look at the airframe and see if

The Bell P-39Q-10 looked like this as it was readied for the first flight. Note the sealed left door. The front shock was pumped up to raise the nose because of the large diameter four-blade propeller. Credit: Birch Matthews

Mike sits in the cockpit with Don Newberger on the wing waiting for tower approval for takeoff. The port just below the windshield exhausts steam from the boiler used to cool the oil. The shaft extending from the spinner is the pitot tube. Credit: Birch Matthews

Chapter XII: The Final Years

After losing the 1967 transcon race, E.D. determined to improve race 14 with some aerodynamic changes. The most obvious was a low profile windscreen and canopy shown here. Credit: Birch Matthews

The empennage on Weiner's Mustang was also modified. The span on the horizontal surfaces was clipped. The dorsal fin was removed and replaced with a small fillet. The dorsal was reinstalled when E.D. found stability was impaired. Credit: Birch Matthews

it was restorable. Don gave the project a thumbs up and Mike bought the veteran racer.

For the next year, Don, Mike and Dick Tomasulo rebuilt and extensively modified the old Cobra II for pylon racing and an attempt at the piston engine speed record. Mike wanted to preserve the racing history of the P-39 while simultaneously putting his own imprint on the airplane. In its reconstituted form the racer would be called "Cobra III" and painted white with gold trim. The trim geometry and race number (84) would remain the same as it had been in 1946, only the colors would change.

By August, 1968, the racer was assembled and one of Dave Zeuschel's rebuilt Allison engines installed. The pace during July and early August was fast as Mike's crew worked to ready the airplane for Reno. Major changes had been made. The wings were clipped and concave aluminum tips added. The shortened span meant that aileron length was also reduced with a corresponding decrease in area. To partially offset this

The sliding canopy was built on a stock Mustang canopy frame. The aft portion was formed using fiberglass. Credit: Birch Matthews

This is another view of the new canopy. The fiberglass aft section was trimmed to fit and blend with the fuselage contour. Credit: Birch Matthews

E.D. poses for a photograph while sitting in his pylon racer, N335J. The dorsal fin on this airplane was also removed. Flight tests convinced him to replace the fin on both racers. Credit: Hal Loomis

Right: This is the fuselage tank used by Weiner on his transcon racer. The right front portion of the tank was segmented to form an oil tank. Credit: Birch Matthews

area reduction, the aileron chord was increased by one inch. The left-hand cockpit door – the Airacobra had automobile style doors – was removed and replaced by new aluminum skin. A water spray bar system was mounted in front of the engine coolant radiator and a novel boil-off system employed to cool the engine oil. The latter was installed in the gun bay in front of the cockpit. Great care was given in finishing the wings so that all surface discontinuities were eliminated. Hundreds of manhours were expended before the airframe was finally painted in grey primer.

The racer was finally ready for high-speed taxi tests on Thursday evening, 8 August. Mike radioed the Long Beach tower and requested the use of runway 12. He was turned down. There was a conflict with a Douglas Aircraft test program then taking place. The aircraft was put back in the hangar for the night. They would try again on Friday. The Cobra was tugged out of Vern's hangar early Friday morning. Mike got in the cockpit, fired the Allison and taxied out to the long 10,000 foot runway at Long Beach airport.

The airport was quiet that morning with virtually no air traffic. With tower permission, Mike rolled onto runway 12 and gunned the engine. The Cobra reacted, accelerating down

Chapter XII: The Final Years

There were a variety of aircraft entered in the 1968 transcon race. One unusual entry was the Experimental Aircraft Association's North American P-64 flown by Carl Koeling. Electrical problems forced the airplane out of the race. Credit: Leo Kohn

Bob Guilford's light blue and white P-51D-30 placed sixth in 1968. It carried race number three applied with washable paint. Credit: Leo Kohn

Burns Byram took third in his P-51D-25. The airplane was painted black and white and was basically a stock airframe. Credit: Leo Kohn

Another stock Mustang was piloted by Dr. Mark Foutch. The airplane is shown here at Milwaukee before the race. Credit: Leo Kohn

Tom Kuchinsky was back again in the 1968 race with his stock Mustang. This year he finished fifth at a slow 245 miles per hour. The airplane was named "Miss Gen Guard," and was using a borrowed rudder. Credit: Birch Matthews

the runway gaining speed until Mike chopped the throttle. At the far end of the runway, Mike did a 180 turn and repeated the run, this time lifting off the ground for a few seconds before pulling back the power. The test was over. Long Beach air traffic controllers needed the runway for incoming traffic.

By 11:00 a.m., Saturday morning, the airplane was ready for its first flight. Mike climbed into the cockpit, ran some engine checks and then waited for tower permission to launch. E.D. Weiner took off in his pylon racer to fly chase during the initial flight. Waiting for Mike to takeoff, Weiner orbited Long Beach airport. At approximately 11:15, Mike was given permission to taxi into position and hold on runway 12. Minutes later, he advanced the throttle and the racer began to roll. After a run of about four thousand feet, the airplane lifted off, accelerating rapidly in a low level, straight out departure headed for Seal Beach, California, and the coast line. Mike was to pass over the coast before attempting any maneuver. E.D. saw the Cobra and added power trying to catch up. Mike was flying at about 2000 feet when he eased into a right turn and almost immediately lost control of the airplane.[21] Sensing disaster, Mike released the right hand door and bailed out. He was struck by the tail of the airplane as it careened out of control. Disabled, Mike never activated his parachute and was killed. The airplane impacted in an open field within the U.S. Navy Weapons Station in Seal Beach, California. The Cobra was destroyed. Cause of the accident was never determined. There was reason to believe, however, that the aircraft center of gravity may not have been within limits and this caused the Cobra to go out of control. Regardless of the cause, the racing community lost one of its most enthusiastic supporters.

FINAL RUN

After Ed Weiner lost the 1967 Harold's Club race to Mike Carroll, he decided to refine his transcon Mustang for greater speed. Vern Barker's crew was overloaded with work on Mike's Airacobra so Weiner had the modifications made in

The first Grumman to race in any unlimited class transcontinental race was Bob Kucera's F8F-2 Bearcat. He finished in fourth place using a centerline auxiliary tank to increase his range. Credit: Leo Kohn

Walt Ohlrich flew into Long Beach airport to have Vern Barker hang these auxiliary drop tanks on his F8F-2 Bearcat. Electrical problems forced Walt to land in Las Vegas on his way east to Milwaukee for the 1968 race. Credit: Harry Gann

another hangar next door. Three airframe changes were made. The first was a low profile canopy. A curved, single piece acrylic wind screen was fashioned and adapted to the fuselage. A portion of the sliding canopy frame was used as the basis for a new fiberglass structure completing the cockpit profile. The horizontal tail span was reduced by removing the tips and capping the structure just outboard of the hinge. The final change was not retained for long. The traditional D model Mustang dorsal fin was removed and replaced with a small fillet. This mod was made to both Ed's transcon and pylon racers. After testing the pylon racer without a dorsal, Weiner was unhappy with directional stability and the dorsal was quickly replaced on both airplanes. E.D. retained his trademark checkerboard paint scheme for 1968, changing only the color combination to yellow and black. The finished racer was aesthetically quite pleasing.

The 1968 Harold's Club Transcontinental Trophy Dash from Milwaukee's Mitchell Field to Reno was dedicated to the memory of Mike Carroll. A large number of aircraft were entered. One of the pilots looking forward to the race was Navy Commander Walter Ohlrich with his Grumman F8F-2 Bearcat. Walt brought the "cat" into Long Beach before the race and had Vern Barker's crew mount external wing tanks on the racer. On his flight back to Milwaukee, he was forced out at Las Vegas with electrical problems. One Bearcat did make it to the race. It was owned and flown by 43 year old Robert H. Kucera, a photogrammetric engineer from Shaker Heights, Ohio. Kucera mounted an external fuel tank on the fuselage centerline to increase fuel capacity for the 1667 mile race. In addition to Kucera's Bearcat, there was the usual gaggle of P-51D Mustangs gathered for the race and one uncommon and rare North American P-64 entry from the

Jim Fugate modified his Mustang for the 1968 race by extending the wingspan from 37 feet to 40 feet, six inches. Jim did not start the Harold's Club race, but did arrive in Reno and participated in the pylon races. Credit: Birch Matthews

Each wing tip was extended one foot, nine inches on Fugate's airplane. The additional span, fabricated from fiberglass, incorporated fuel cells to increase the range of the racer. Credit: Birch Matthews

Chapter XII: The Final Years

Experimental Aircraft Association, flown by Carl Koeling.

This fourth Harold's Club transcontinental dash was run on Sunday, 15 September, the weekend before the main program. Although a large number of racers were tentatively to compete, the field was reduced to eight planes when the race started. At the other end of the country, race management sponsored a special two hour air show at Stead that Sunday, beginning at one o'clock. It was open to the public without charge. Beside the air show, spectators would witness the finish of the Harold's Club trophy race.

Weiner's reconfigured Mustang, sponsored by Bardahl, won the race handily beating second place finisher Dick Kestle by one and a half hours elapsed time. His speed was a comparatively slow 361 miles per hour. E.D. encountered headwinds that ranged as high as 140 miles per hour, considerably diminishing his average speed.[22] The others straggled into Reno over the next four hours. Kestle, normally a competitive cross-country flyer, refueled at Casper, Wyoming. His engine coolant was overheating and he lost 50 minutes wrestling with that problem. A real rat race developed between Dr. Burns Byram flying a Mustang and Bob Kucera. Kucera was forced to make a dead stick landing at Burleigh, Idaho, when he lost oil pressure. But for this unfortunate inconvenience, he would have beaten Byram and taken third place. As it was, Byram finished a scant 39 seconds in front of Kucera's Bearcat. The venerable P-64 flown by Carl Koeling was forced back to Milwaukee with electrical difficulties and was out of the race. Mark Foutch, in another Mustang, dropped out at Laramie, Wyoming, with unspecified difficulties. Tom Kuchinsky and Bob Guilford were the last to arrive, taking fifth and sixth positions, respectively.

The 1968 transcontinental race was in the record books. E.D. Weiner became the first pilot to win the Harold's Club Trophy two times. It was also his fourth cross-country win, a record unmatched by any other pilot in the history of transcontinental racing.

NOTES:

1 Charles R. Moore, United Press International, published in the *Reno Evening Gazette*, 22 September 1964.
2 Ibid.
3 Ibid.
4 Don Berliner, "Reno Stakes Claim to National Air Race Title," *Air Progress*, January 1966, p. 8.
5 Don Downie, "The Fury of Mike Carroll," Air Progress, September 1967, p. 21.
6 Correspondence from David Lockspeiser, Hawker Siddeley, to Michael Carroll, dated 16 June 1966.
7 Bill Johnson, "Sea Fury, Low and Fast," Air Enthusiast, March-June, 1985, p. 59.
8 Martin Haynes, "TLC for the Big Birds," Private Pilot, Vol. 3, No. 11, August 1968, p. 39.
9 Details of the wet wing process were kindly provided by Bill Kerchenfaut during a telephone interview with the author on 30 March 1993.
10 Hawker high speed section H/1414/37.5 at the root and H/1410/37.5 at the tip.
11 Henry Artof and Tom Piedimonte, *Air Progress*, December 1966, p. 6.
12 *Cleveland Plain Dealer*, 3 September 1967, p. 1.
13 Richard G. Snyder and Audie W. Davis, Jr., "Medical Factors in Unlimited Class Air Racing Accidents," *Aerospace Medicine*, Vol. 43, No. 5, May 1972, p. 517.
14 Frank Tallman, "Racing Gets Hot," *Flying*, January 1968. p. 48.
15 Correspondence to the author from C.L. Chandler, 17 February 1986.
16 *Reno Evening Gazette*, 22 September 1967, p. 13.
17 Chandler correspondence, op.cit.
18 Johnson, op.cit., p. 60.
19 Birch J. Matthews, "Cobra," American Aviation Historical Society JOURNAL, Vol. 8, No. 3, 1963, p.195.
20 Correspondence from Don Nolan to the author circa August, 1963. See also, American Aviation Historical Society JOURNAL, Vol. 8, No. 4, 1963, p. 293.
21 "Factual Aircraft Accident Report - General Aviation," Civil Aeronautics Board, CAB Accident Identification No. LAX69-F-370, dated 18 October 1968.
22 Tom Piedimonte, "1968 National Championship Air Races," *Sport Flying*, Vol. 2, No. 2, February 1969, p. 16.

Weiner flew into Orange County for publicity shots with Paul Mantz's old Bendix racer. These two aircraft each won more transcontinental races than any other aircraft in history. Credit: Dusty Carter

Chapter XIII

END GAME

Transcontinental racing with unlimited class airplanes was rapidly approaching the end game, space age terminology related to the final maneuver phase before a missile reaches its destination. In a real sense, cross-country air racing was approaching that stage in 1969. Interest and sponsorship were in decline. With the loss of Mike Carroll, there was only one truly competitive airplane for this sport and it belonged to Ed Weiner and as fate would have it, he would not be able to race. The number of pilots truly enthusiastic about cross-country racing was quite small. The end was in sight, although perhaps few realized this at the time.

E.D. Weiner intended to fly in the 1969 Harold's Club race hoping to win for an unprecedented third time. He always stayed at the old Mapes Hotel in Reno and reservations for this year were in place. September was fast approaching and the races were just weeks away. Both of Ed Weiner's aircraft were ready. He had acquired sponsorship for his transcon racer from STP, makers of a well known oil treatment additive. As a consequence, the checkerboard paint scheme was discarded and the Mustang was painted a brilliant red and adorned with the sponsor's logo on the vertical fin. Race number 14 was carefully applied in black against a white oval background on the fuselage sides. Other than flying new colors this year, the aircraft was essentially unchanged.

Weiner was an accomplished pilot with over 8,000 hours of military and civilian flying time. He was meticulous about his aircraft and cautious when it came to modifications. Airframe changes were made in incremental steps, each evaluated in flight before another was completed. With an eye toward eventual sale of one or both Mustangs, Ed made no modifications that could not be easily undone. This, for instance, governed his approach to a low drag, low profile cockpit canopy installed the previous year. A portion of the original bubble canopy sliding frame was retained so that no change to the fuselage was necessary. The aft portion of the new canopy was fashioned from fiberglass to effect a long blended line fairing the canopy into the fuselage contour. Reverting to a standard P-51D cockpit enclosure was an easy change to make, only requiring reinstallation of the original wind screen and remounting the bubble canopy.

The repainted transcon racer rolled out of Vern Barker's hangar in August. The all red paint job was reminiscent of Paul Mantz's C model Mustang and three-time Bendix Race winner. Knowing this, E.D. flew his champion airplane to Orange County Airport in Santa Ana, California, where Frank Tallman obligingly rolled out the old Mantz racer for publicity photos.

Forty-six year old Ellis Weiner was seriously ill, but no one knew. Perhaps he couldn't accept the fact himself. In May, 1967, he had undergone a routine medical examination to renew his pilot's first class medical certificate. The examining physician found evidence of an old myocardial infarction – a heart attack – and denied the first class certificate.[1] Ed had heart disease. In April, 1969, he applied for and was granted a second class medical certificate searching out a different physician for this less rigorous examination. Several days before the transcon race,

E.D. Weiner acquired the sponsorship of STP for the 1969 racing season. The airplane was stripped and repainted all red. His racer is seen here at Orange County a few days after being refinished. The race number was black against a white background. Credit: Birch Matthews

E.D. flew his transcon racer to Reno intending to fly on to Milwaukee for the Harold's Club race. Instead, he checked into a Palm Springs hospital. By this time, STP markings had been applied. Credit: Dusty Carter

E.D. flew each of his racers to Stead Field, apparently intending to depart for Milwaukee from there instead of Long Beach. Returning to Southern California, he quietly checked into a Palm Springs hospital for a short time.

THE LAST RACE

E.D. never showed up to fly his bright red STP Special to Milwaukee for the start of the transcon race on Sunday, 14 September. Ten racers did get away and veteran Dick Kestle finally garnered a victory in his fifth try at this tough sport, beating Jack Sliker across the finish line by less than one minute.

Ed Weiner arrive in Reno early in the week after the Harold's Club race had been run. Climbing into his pylon Mustang racer, he proceeded to qualify at 356 miles per hour, fifth in a field of 13 unlimiteds that year. The first heat race for the big bore unlimiteds was on Friday and Ed Weiner drew this event. He got into his Mustang somewhat early and put on his oxygen mask. When it was time to taxi out for takeoff, E.D. had trouble getting the powerful Merlin started. It finally caught and he taxied out for takeoff. E.D. was the third off the runway following Darryl Greenamyer in his super fast Bearcat and Mike Loening in another P-51. Climbing rapidly, he joined with pace plane pilot, Bob Hoover as the flight assembled for an air start. The crowd watched fascinated as the racers roared down the chute onto the Reno course. It's one of

Chapter XIII: End Game

the most exciting points in unlimited racing.

Weiner declared a May Day in the second lap and pulled up and out of the race. Race control had difficulty communicating with Ed as they attempted to determine the nature of his problem. Circling the field, he finally established an approach for runway 26 and brought the Mustang safely to earth rolling out to the end before turning left onto the taxiway. Weiner braked the airplane to a stop after leaving the runway and sat there for several minutes with the engine still running. Finally, he taxied slowly toward the pit area swinging the racer toward the pit line before shutting down. His crew helped Ed out of the plane and whisked him away to a hospital. E.D. Weiner was very sick, apparently the victim of a second heart attack, this time while flying in a race. He died ten days later. The air racing fraternity lost a driving force in this most exacting of motor sports.

Starting Sequence 1970 Harold's Club Trophy Race

Position	Pilot	Race No.	Aircraft Type
1	Gunther Balz	7	F8F-1
2	Jack Huismann		P-51D-30
3	Jack Sliker	17	P-51D-30
4	Dick Kestle	13	P-51D-20
5	Ron Reynolds	44	F8F-2
6	Burns Byram	71	P-51D-25
7	Howie Keefe	11	P-51D-30

LAST OF THE HAROLD'S CLUB RACES

Nineteen seventy would see the final transcontinental contest associated with the Reno Air Races. This year, it was scheduled for Sunday, 13 September. Nine pilots were slated to race, but only seven would actually start. William S. "Sherm" Cooper was one of the entries. He bought the Hawker Sea Fury from Mike Carroll's estate, renamed the airplane "Miss Merced," and promptly entered the transcon. Bad luck followed Sherm to Reno where he stopped to refuel enroute to Milwaukee. Rolling out after touchdown, Cooper touched the brakes and promptly lost one causing the big yellow racer to ground looped. Undaunted, Sherm came back days later to run the Reno pylon events with the big Fury winning first place in the unlimited consolation race.

Without Ed Weiner in the hunt this year, the pre-race favorite was Dick Kestle from Columbus, Georgia. Kestle was a stocky 41 year old pilot with over 2000 hours, 900 of which were in P-51s. He owned a pizza franchise company in Columbus as well as a bottling operation. When Dick first began to race in 1965, his red and white Mustang was prepped by Bailey Johnson of Mustangs Unlimited based in Atlanta. In 1967, he took the Mustang back to Trans-Florida Aviation where it was reconditioned and a new tall vertical fin installed, reminiscent of a P-51H. A wet wing was added along the way and a Cavalier style paint scheme reapplied, only this time it was medium grey and white with black trim. The finished color scheme together with a highly polished spinner was very attractive if somewhat sedate.

Another ex-military pilot entered in the 1970 race was Howard Keefe, who became one of the best known pilots among the fans at Reno. Outgoing, a patriot and always willing to talk with race fans, he was easily recognized everywhere he appeared with his red, white and blue P-51 Mustang, "Miss America." The vibrant color scheme Howie applied to his racer was borrowed from the Air Force Thunderbirds jet demonstration team.

Dick Kestle won both the 1969 and 1970 Reno cross-country races. This picture was taken in 1967, but the aircraft was basically unchanged in subsequent years. Credit: Dusty Carter

John Sliker was second in the 1969 race and third in 1970. Sliker had interchangeable wing tips. For the transcon race, the aircraft sported Cessna 310 tip tanks. Credit: Birch Matthews

Howie Keefe flew one of the most recognizable planes ever to race. His red, white and blue "Miss America," was quite popular with race fans. He placed sixth in the 1969 race and gained fourth in 1970. Credit: Birch Matthews

Howie Keefe departed Los Angeles on 2 September on a circuitous route to Milwaukee for the start of this year's race. A violent storm forced him down in western Nebraska. His next port was Chicago followed by a short leg to Cleveland for three days of air shows and racing at Burke Lakefront Airport. From there he flew to New York for business, eventually reaching Milwaukee two days before the race. Howie describes what happened before and during the race. "Pete Hoyt (who accompanied Howie) and I were hoping to have a nice leisurely time getting ready for the race this year, but all that was shattered when a boost pump in the right main tank let loose. Once again, we were reminded that this was not a current model aircraft. There was no time to get one from Florida, but as always seems to happen, a guy in Milwaukee had one![2]

"The morning weather report (on the day of the race) gave us the news that we had feared. There was one solid storm area from Milwaukee to Salt Lake City along the route we had planned. This was an unusual type of bad weather caused by an exceptionally low, high speed jet stream that snaked its way across the upper third of the United States. It sucked into it everything in a 300 mile wide path just as a roaring water torrent would do. Regretfully, we had to abandon all idea of landing at Saratoga, Wyoming, because they have no instrument facilities there – just giant mountains all around.

"We chose Denver as the next best stop and planned a route to go far south over Grand Junction, Colorado, and then on up into Reno trying to get away from the headwinds which were forecast at 120 miles per hour right on our nose! I made a bad judgement which cost us one of the first three places – we missed third place by only 31 seconds over a six hour, 32 minute flight. On an instrument flight, I elected to climb to 26,000 feet hoping to get above the bad weather and then start thinking (about the route and conditions). The P-51 thrives at altitude. It cruises at 430 miles an hour at 30,000 feet." The problem, Howie recalls, was that high blower speed was not operational because he planned to compete in the pylon races after finishing the transcon.[3] Ordinarily, cruising at 26,000 feet in low blower would have been all right for this race. "My error," Howie admitted, "was that I should have calculated the devastating effect of a 120 mile an hour headwind at 26,000 feet versus a 70 mile per hour headwind at 12,000 feet." He was flying strictly on instruments and was preoccupied with keeping the Mustang straight and level flying in poor weather. While Howie was totally engrossed with controlling the racer, Pete Hoyt sat in the back seat feeding him headings and radio navigation frequencies.

Approaching Denver, Howie descended through the overcast breaking out at about 13,000 feet. It was then he realized his mistake. Preoccupied with flying, he finally realized that "had I dropped to 12,000 feet, we would have gone 12 miles an hour faster. We had been up for three hours and 15 minutes at that point. Doing nothing but staring at instruments for that long makes you see them when you close your eyes. The pit stop at Denver was great under the circumstances, but took ten minutes this year as opposed to six minutes last year." Howie refueled hot. "Wayne Houge and his gang at Jeffco Airport in the suburb of Broomfield are all heart, tackling that plane with the prop spinning and exhausts snorting.

Chapter XIII: End Game

Richard Thomas flew the first Corsair in an unlimited cross-country event since the 1947 Bendix race. The F4U-4 is seen here as it appeared in 1968. Thomas finished after the 4 o'clock deadline in 1969. Credit: Birch Matthews

"Out of Denver, we climbed to only 14,000 feet to reduce our headwinds to about 50 miles per hour and relied on radar to guide us to Reno." Air traffic control "gave us radar stears all the way, but they too misread the wind and we found ourselves 80 miles north (of our intended course) about 150 miles out of Reno. With all this going on we were glad to get a fourth place and really glad to get there with the need for only one stop. We figured that in a no-wind condition, we flew the equivalent of about 2,200 miles," as opposed to a 1,667 great circle distance.

All of the contestants faced the same extremely poor weather and the speeds and elapsed times were correspondingly poor. Dick Kestle landed at Stead five hours, 19 minutes after departing Milwaukee. He won the race with a slow average speed of 284 miles per hour. Howie Keefe recounted that Dick was so low on gas, he didn't fly over the finish line, but landed directly and rolled across. There were only eight gallons of fuel remaining in Kestle's wet wing Mustang, enough for maybe eight more minutes of flying time. Kestle really cut it close. Chan Chandler once again provided Kestle

Judy Wagner put her Beech E-33C Bonanza into the 1969 cross-country race for the fun of it. The flight from Milwaukee to Reno took her eight hours with an average speed of 207 mile per hour. Credit: Leo Kohn

Sherm Cooper bought Mike Carroll's Sea Fury and entered it in the 1969 Harold's Club race. A minor accident at Reno kept him out of the race. Credit: Birch Matthews

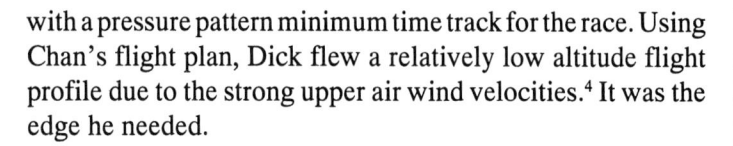

The fastest airplane of the 1969 entrants was Darryl Greenamyer's P-51D-30 owned by Dave Zeuschel. Mechanical problems kept him from starting. The following day, he flew to Reno in less time than Dick Kestle who won the race on the previous day. Credit: Leo Kohn

with a pressure pattern minimum time track for the race. Using Chan's flight plan, Dick flew a relatively low altitude flight profile due to the strong upper air wind velocities.[4] It was the edge he needed.

ADDENDA

There were two other unlimited class cross-country races which were not associated with the annual Reno program. One was run in context with the February, 1969, races held at Executive Airport, Fort Lauderdale, Florida. Six Mustangs including one rare P-51H, departed Municipal Airport, Frederick, Maryland, and headed south. As periodically happened during long distance racing, bad weather played a roll. Paul Finefrock in his D model Mustang was forced out of the race at Charleston, North Carolina, because of poor weather conditions. The other five racers made it, however, the speeds were relatively slow for this 929 mile race. Ed Bowlin won the event with a time of two hours and 59 minutes. Dick Kestle was close behind trailing by only ten minutes.

Bill Hogan flew this rare P-51H-5 to third place in the 1969 cross-country race from Frederick, MD, to Fort Lauderdale. Credit: Roger Besecker collection

Chapter XIII: End Game

The very last cross-country race took place in May, 1971. This was part of a two day affair called the P-51 Mustang Tournament staged just north of St. Louis at the Civic Memorial Airport, East Alton, Illinois. Although these contests centered around the Mustang, other fighter types were represented as well. It was an interesting air show concept. Unlimited class racers competed in a measured mile speed trial, a 30 second time-to-climb contest and a short 309 mile cross-country dash from Milwaukee to East Alton. There were ten pilots in the latter contest. Clay Lacy won the dash with a time of 52.4 minutes. Richard Foote was the last to finish this race and his arrival marked the end of an era.

The epoch of unrestricted all-out speed flights from point-to-point across the United States stretched over more than 65 years, from the sometimes faltering non-stop derbies of the late 1920s to that final flight by Richard Foote into East Alton. These races took their toll of pilots and planes over the years, mostly due to the violent weather masses which occur across our nation. The pioneers in transcontinental racing endured with scant information of what the heavens had in store. The art and science of weather forecasting gradually became more sophisticated beginning with often infrequent upper air measurements dependent upon kites and balloons. When wireless communication was reduced to practice, upper air weather measurements advanced significantly. Data could be gathered much more rapidly. More important, these data were used to construct more astute forecasts which were quickly disseminated for pilot use. The field of wireless transmission eventually developed into an entirely new field of revolutionary devices involving improved communications, weather radar and refined navigation aids.

Flight planning techniques also improved toward the end of transcon racing in the form of pressure pattern flight profiles allowing the race pilot to take full advantage of the most current upper air measurements. In spite of the modern advancements in forecasting, electronics and flight planning techniques, flying long cross-country races still took a great amount of skill, athletic ability and perhaps above all else, a generous measure of individual courage. It was, after all, a lonely journey.

NOTES:

[1] Richard G. Snyder and Audie W. Davis, Jr., "Medical Factors in Unlimited Class Air Racing Accidents," *Aerospace Medicine*, Vol. 43, No. 5, May 1972, p. 515.

[2] Howard Keefe's experiences in the 1970 transcontinental race are contained in an unpublished manuscript provided to the author by Maurice O'Brien circa November 1992.

[3] Reno pylon races are run at a physical altitude of about 5,000 feet. (Density altitude varies with the atmospheric conditions.) Racing Merlins are run in low blower which allows higher engine speeds without the corresponding power loss incurred by running in high blower. The power loss in high blower is quite significant, amounting to over 600 horsepower at 100 inches of manifold pressure. A discussion of Merlin supercharging is found in *Mustang, The Racing Thoroughbred*, by Dustin Carter and Birch Matthews, Schiffer Publishing Limited, West Chester, Pennsylvania, Appendix A, pp. 194-195.

[4] Correspondence to the author from C.L. Chandler, 17 February 1986.

Appendix A

MAJOR TRANSCONTINENTAL AIR RACES: 1928 - 1970

EARLY TRANSCONTINENTAL AIR RACES

1928 Non-Stop New York to Los Angeles Derby - 2470 Miles

Pilot	Pos.	Race No.	License Number	Aircraft	Serial Number	Time	Speed mph	Remarks
Clifford E. McMillan		101	NC4827	Stinson Detroiter SM-1	C/N M-224			Forced out, Wilkes-Barre, PA
John P. Morris		33	X7430	Lockheed Vega	C/N 19			Crashed near Decatur, IN.
Nick B. Mamer		25	NX6874	Buhl Air Sedan CA-3C	C/N 30			Forced out, Rawlins, WY
Emile Burgin		206?	NX5315	Bellanca J	C/N 106			"Veedol," Forced out, Willard, NM
Oliver C. LeBoutillier			NX3789	Bellanca J	C/N 101			"North Star"
Randolph Page				Stinson Jr.				Forced out, Allentown, PA
George W. Haldeman				Bellanca				Out at Albuquerque, NM
Jack Iseman		140	NX237	Bellanca WB-2				"Columbia," Forced out at Amarillo, TX
Arthur C. Goebel	(1)	44	X4769	Lockheed Vega 5	C/N 7			"Yankee Doodle," forced down at Prescott, AZ, due to weather. Continued on to L.A. but was disqualified for in route stop.
Owen I. Haugland		14	5835	Cessna BW-5	C/N 117			Scratched before race start.
Cesare Sabelli			NX4864	Bellanca K	C/N 107			"Roma," Late entry, not accepted.

1929 Non-Stop Los Angeles to Cleveland Derby - 2042 Miles

Pilot	Pos.	Race No.	License Number	Aircraft	Serial Number	Time	Speed mph	Remarks
Henry J. Brown	1	148	NR3057	Lockheed Air Express 3	C/N 75	13:15:07	154.091	"Black Hornet"
Leland Shoenhair	2	36	NR308H	Lockheed Vega 5A	C/N 79	13:51:10	147.407	
Roscoe Turner	(3)	192	NR8954	Lockheed Vega 5	C/N 24	15:27:00	132.168	Landed after deadline, disqualified
John P. Wood			C895E	Lockheed Vega 5	C/N 67			Crashed during a storm north of Needles, CA.
Frank Hawks			7955	Lockheed Air Express 3	C/N 5			Did not start.
Robert Cantwell			NC7429	Lockheed Vega 5	C/N 18			Did not start.
Oliver C. Le Boutillier				Bellanca				Did not start.

1930 Non-Stop Los Angeles to Chicago Derby - 1760 Miles

Pilot	Pos.	Race No.	License Number	Aircraft	Serial Number	Time	Speed mph	Remarks
Wiley Post	1	11	NR105W	Lockheed Vega 5B	C/N 122	09:09:04	192.326	
Arthur C. Goebel	2	62	NR7954	Lockheed Vega 5	C/N 24	09:39:13	182.315	
Lee Shoenhair	3	36	NR308H	Lockheed Vega 5A	C/N 79	09:53:57	177.793	
Roscoe Turner	4	25	NR3057	Lockheed Air Express 3	C/N 75	09:58:41	176.387	

1931 Bendix Trophy Race, Los Angeles to Cleveland - 2046 Miles

Pilot	Pos.	Race No.	License Number	Aircraft	Serial Number	Time	Speed mph	Remarks
James H. Doolittle	1	400	NR12048	Laird Super Solution		09:10:21	223.058	Laird Model LC DW 500
Harold S. Johnson	2	64	NR12220	Lockheed Orion 9	C/N 177	10:14:22	199.816	
Beeler Blevins	3	112	NR988Y	Lockheed Orion	C/N 174	10:49:33	188.992	
Ira Eaker	4	50	NR119W	Lockheed Altair	C/N 153	10:59:45	186.070	
Arthur C. Goebel	5	129	NR7954	Lockheed Vega 5	C/N 24	11:55:48	171.500	
James G. Hall	6	125	NR15W	Lockheed Altair	C/N 145	12:51:16	159.167	
Louis T. Reichers		11	NR998Y	Lockheed Altair	C/N 176			Forced landing, Beatrice, NB, out of fuel.

Appendixes

Pilot			Race No.	License Number	Aircraft				Remarks
Walter Hunter			16	NR614K	Travel Air Model R				Crashed on takeoff, Terre Haute, IN. Aircraftt burned, pilot not seriously hurt.

1932 Bendix Trophy Race, Burbank to Cleveland - 2042 Miles

Pilot	Pos.	Race No.	License Number	Aircraft	Serial Number	Time	Speed mph	Remarks
James H. Haizlip	1	92	NR536V	Wedell-Williams	C/N 104	08:19:45	245.162	
James R. Wedell	2	44	NR278V	Wedell-Williams	C/N 103	08:47:31	232.258	
Roscoe Turner	3	121	NR61Y	Wedell-Williams		09:02:25	225.878	
Lee Gehlbach	4	7	NR2101	Gee Bee R-2		09:41:39	210.642	
Claire K. Vance		61	NR12700	Vance Flying Wing				Returned to Burbank with fuel leak.
Frank Hawks		13	NR12265	Northrop Gamma 2A	C/N 1			Did not start.
Frank Lynch			NR13205	Hall Cicada				Did not start due to persistent engine problems.
Robert Hall		6	NR2111	Hall Bulldog				Did not get permission to compete in time
James H. Doolittle		400	NR12048	Laird Super Solution				Modified from 1931 configuration. Aircraft crashed prior to Bendix Race.

1933 Bendix Trophy Race, New York to Los Angeles - 2470 Miles

Pilot	Pos.	Race No.	License Number	Aircraft	Serial Number	Time	Speed mph	Remarks
Roscoe Turner	1	2	NR61Y	Wedell-Williams		11:30:00	214.780	
James R. Wedell	2	44	NR278V	Wedell-Williams	C/N 103	11:58:18	209.230	Correct speed is 206.320 mph.
Russel Boardman		11	NR2100	Gee Bee R-1				Fatal crash, Indianapolis, IN.
Russel Thaw		7	NR2101	Gee Bee R-2				Ground looped, Indianapolis, IN.
Arthur K. Knapp		77	NR10538	Laird Solution				Did not start. Racer modified with new wing.
Lee Gehlbach		92	NR536V	Wedell Williams	C/N 104			Forced landing, New Bethal, IN.
Amelia Earhart		88	NR965Y	Lockheed Vega	C/N 171			Dropped out at Wichita, KS.
Ruth Nichols		112	NR988Y	Lockheed Orion	C/N 174			Dropped out, Wichita, KS.
Claire K. Vance			NR12700	Vance Flying Wing				Did not start.
Alex. de Seversky			X1206	Seversky SEV-3	C/N 1			Did not start.

1934 Bendix Trophy Race, Burbank to Cleveland - 2042 Miles

Pilot	Pos.	Race No.	License Number	Aircraft	Serial Number	Time	Speed mph	Remarks
Douglas Davis	1	44	NR278V	Wedell Williams	C/N 103	09:26:41	216.237	
John Worthen	2	45	NR62Y	Wedell Williams		10:03:00	203.213	
Lee Gehlbach		77	NX14307	Gee Bee QED				Finished after 6:00 pm deadline, disqualified.
Roscoe Turner		57	NR61Y	Wedell Williams				Set coast-to-coast record one day after Bendix Race was held.
Harold Neumann		40	NR273Y	Howard DGA-6				Aircraft damaged on trip to West Coast. Did not race.
Murray Dilley			NR12700	Vance Flying Wing				Did not start.
Roy Minor		7	NR2101	Gee Bee R-1/R-2				Damaged in pre-race accident, did not race.
James Granger		9	R14215	Rider R-3				Did not start.
Lee Miles		92	NR536V	Wedell Williams	C/N 104			Did not start.
Jacquelin Cochran			NX13761	Northrop Gamma 2G	C/N 11			Did not start.

1935 Bendix Trophy Race, Burbank to Cleveland - 2042 Miles

Pilot	Pos.	Race No.	License Number	Aircraft	Serial Number	Time	Speed mph	Remarks
Ben O. Howard	1	40	NR273Y	Howard DGA-6		08:33:16.3	238.704	
Roscoe Turner	2	57	NR61Y	Wedell Williams		08:33:39.8	238.522	
Russel Thaw	3	35	NR2111	Northrop Gamma 2D-2	C/N 12	10:06:45.0	201.928	
Roy O. Hunt	4	72	NR232Y	Lockheed Orion 9D-1	C/N 204	11:41:03.1	174.766	
Amelia Earhart	5	88	NR965Y	Lockheed Vega	C/N 171	13:47:06.35	149.578	Correct speed is 148.131 mph.
Royal Leonard		90	R14307	Gee Bee QED				Forced down at Wichita, broken oil line.
Cecil Allen		7	NR2101	Gee Bee R-1/R-2				Crashed fatally on Bendix Race takeoff.
Earl Ortman		9	NR14215	Rider R-3				Forced out at Kansas City, loose cowling.

254 WET WINGS & DROP TANKS

Pilot	Race No.	License Number	Aircraft	Serial Number	Remarks
Jacquelin Cochran	55	NX13761	Northrop Gamma 2G	C/N 11	Dropped out of race at Kingman, AZ.
William Ong	92	NR536V	Wedell Williams	C/N 104	Damaged in accident before the race.
Howard Hughes		NR258Y	Hughes Racer		Did not start.
Seward W. Pulitzer	27	NX14220	Northrop Delta 1D	C/N 73	Did not start.
Maurice Rossi			Renault Racer		Did not arrive from France.
Vance Breese		X12899	Breese-Dallas Transport		Did not arrive.

1936 Bendix Trophy Race, New York to Los Angeles - 2466 Miles

Pilot	Pos.	Race No.	License Number	Aircraft	Serial Number	Time	Speed mph	Remarks
Louise Thaden	1	62	NR15835	Beechcraft C-17R	C/N 77	14:55:01	165.346	
Laura Ingalls	2	53	NR14222	Lockheed Orion 9D	C/N 211	15:39:38	157.466	
William Gulick	3	83	NR14255	Vultee V1A	C/N 20	15:45:25	156.429	Sponsored by Crusade Oil Co.
George Pomeroy	4	82	NC1000	Douglas DC-2	C/N 1324	16:16:51	151.467	
Amelia Earhart	5	20	NR16020	Lockheed Electra 10E	C/N 1055	16:34:53	148.720	
Joe Jacobson		73	NR12265	Northrop Gamma 2A	C/N 1			Aircraft exploded in mid-air, pilot bailed out.
Ben O. Howard		40	NR273Y	Howard DGA-6				Did not finish, crash-landed in New Mexico.
Lee Miles		77	R14307	Gee Bee QED				Did not finish.
Roscoe Turner		29	R263Y	Turner-Laird LTR-14				Construction not completed in time.
Roscoe Turner/ Frank Clark		57	NR61Y	Wedell Williams				Clark to fly # 57. LTR-14 not finished and Turner flew #57, pre-race crash in New Mexico.
Steve Wittman		101	NR13688	Wittman "Bonzo"				Reported entry, did not race.
George W. Haldeman		29	NR190M	Bellanca 28-70	C/N 902			Irish Swoop." Did not start.
Jacqueline Cochran			X12899	Breese-Dallas Transport				Planned entry by J. Cochran. P&W Twin Wasp to be installed for race.

1937 Bendix Trophy Race, Burbank to Cleveland - 2042 Miles

Pilot	Pos.	Race No.	License Number	Aircraft	Serial Number	Time	Speed mph	Remarks
Frank Fuller	1	23	R70Y	Seversky SEV-S2	C/N 43	07:54:26.31	258.242	
Earl Ortman	2	4	R14215	Marcoux-Bromberg R-3		09:49:21.73	224.833	Correct speed is 207.784 mph.
Jacqueline Cochran	3	13	R18562	Beechcraft D-17W	C/N 164	10:29:08.70	194.740	
Frank Sinclair	4	63	R18Y	Seversky SEV-1XP	C/N 2	11:02:33.08	184.920	
Milo Burcham	5	20	R18130	Lockheed 12A	C/N 1226	11:03:58.28	184.526	
Eiler Sundorph	6	17	R2599	Sundorph Special		12:17:08.26	166.210	
Roscoe Turner		29	R263Y	Turner-Laird LTR-14				Fire damaged racer prior to Bendix Race.
Robert Perlick		64	NX12583	Beechcraft A-17F	C/N 5			Collapsed landing gear during takeoff.
Joeseph C. Mackey		25	NR61Y	Wedell Williams				Did not finish.
Arthur J. Davis		92	NR536V	Wedell Willilams	C/N 104			Ground accident. Did not start.
Alex. de Seversky			R1250	Seversky AP-2	C/N 40			Damaged during belly landing before race at Floyd Bennett Field, N.Y.
Alex Pampana		37	NX2432	Bellanca 28-92				Did not reach West Coast due to weather.
Reg Robbins Dick Merrill/ Jack Lambie				Wedell Williams				

1938 Bendix Trophy Race, Burbank to Cleveland - 2042 Miles

Pilot	Pos.	Race No.	License Number	Aircraft	Serial Number	Time	Speed mph	Remarks
Jacqueline Cochran	1	13	NX1384	Seversky AP-7	C/N 145	08:10:31.4	249.774	
Frank Fuller	2	77	R70Y	Seversky SEV-S2	C/N 43	08:33:29.2	238.604	
Paul Mantz	3	9	NR12222	Lockheed Orion 9C	C/N 180	09:36:25.4	206.579	Correct speed is 212.552 mph.
Max Constant	4	31	R18562	Beechcraft D-17W	C/N 164	10:14:39.6	199.330	
Ross Hadley	5	44	NC18776	Beechcraft D-17S	C/N 199	11:13:46.4	181.842	Forced down at Woodriver, IL
John Hinchey	6	72	NX17615	Spartan Executive	C/N 7W-14	11:30:27.2	177.449	
George Armistead		61	R14307	Gee Bee QED				Did not finish.
Lee Gehlbach		92	NR536V	Wedell Williams	C/N 104			Did not finish.
Frank Cordova		99	NX2433	Bellanca 28-92				Did not finish.
Bob Perlick		85	NX12583	Beechcraft A-17F	C/N 5			Did not finish.
Bernarr MacFadden			NR13761	Northrop Gamma 2G	C/N 11			Did not start.

Appendixes

1939 Bendix Trophy Race, Burbank to Cleveland - 2042 Miles

Pilot	Pos.	Race No.	License Number	Aircraft	Serial Number	Time	Speed mph	Remarks
Frank Fuller	1	77	NX70Y	Seversky SEV-S2		07:14:19.02	282.100	
Arthur Bussy	2	39	NX2433	Bellanca 28-92		08:21:08.00	244.486	
Paul Mantz	3	23	NR12222	Lockheed Orion 9C	C/N 180	08:41:38.38	234.875	
Max Constant	4	31	NX18562	Beechcraft D-17W	C/N 164	08:49:33.01	231.570	
Arlene Davis	5	51	NX17605	Spartan Executive 7W	C/N 7W-10	10:22:25.66	196.842	
William Maycock	6	66	NC20768	Beechcraft D-17S	C/N 306	10:54:32.16	187.186	
Jacqueline Cochran		13	NX1384	Seversky AP-7	C/N 145			Did not start.

1946-1949 BENDIX TROPHY RACES

1946 Bendix Trophy Race, Van Nuys to Cleveland - 2048 Miles

Pilot	Pos.	Race No.	License Number	Aircraft	Serial Number	Time	Speed mph	Remarks
A. Paul Mantz	1	46	NX1202	P-51C-10	44-10947	04:42:14	435.501	
Jacqueline Cochran	2	13	NX28388	P-51B-15	43-24760	04:52:00	420.925	
Thomas J. Mayson	3	60	NX1204	P-51C-10	42-103831	05:01:06	408.220	Entered by Paul Mantz.
William E. Eddy	4	31	NX66851	P-51D-20	44-63539	05:29:18	373.252	
James L. Harp, Jr.	5	95	NX79123	F-5G-6	42-28235	05:31:48	370.447	
Donald E. Husted	6	45	NX37482	A-26C-55	44-35956	05:34:06	367.889	Entered by Caribbean Air Transport.
Charles Tucker	7	30	NX63231	P-63C-5	44-4126	05:34:47	367.149	
Harvey M. Hughes	8	70	NX70087	F-5G-6	44-53173	05:44:51	356.428	Entered by Hughes & G.R. Marsh.
Walter R. Bullock	9	50	NX70005	F-5G-6	44-27026	05:45:21	355.908	Entered by DePonti Aviation, Inc.
Harold S. Johnson	10	63	NX21765	F-5G-6	44-53045	05:57:57	343.380	
John C. Carroll	11	22	NX33697	F-5G-6	44-53218	06:03:47	337.880	
H. Marshall	12	99	NX66108	F-5G-6	44-53134	06:05:53	335.938	Entered by H. Marshall & R. Brown.
Rex Mays	13	55	NX57492	F-5G-6	44-53015	06:15:17	327.526	
William P. Lear, Jr.	14	71	NX66613	F-5G-6	44-53026	06:15:46	327.105	
Thomas Call	15	90	NX63382	FG-1D	88086	06:17:29	325.612	Entered by Dave Wyler.
William Fairbrother	16	58	NX69800	P-38L-5	44-53059	06:17:54	325.255	Entered by Anderson Air Activities
Andrew Grant	17	82	NX33698	F-5G-6	43-50281	07:49:44	261.665	Entered by Serviss Aviation, Inc.
Spiro "Sammy" Dilles		47	NX67115	P-63C-5	44-4178			Forced out, Windslow, AZ. Entered by Dilles & R. Foltz.
John E. Schields		36	NX66692	P-38L-5	44-26545			Arrived after time deadline, disqualified.
H. Calloway		48	NX26927	P-38L-5	44-26927			Forced out, Toledo, OH. Entered by H.L. Pemberton.
Herman Salmon		74	NX56687	F-5G-6	44-53138			Started but returned to Van Nuys with mechanical problems. Entered by D. Mercer.
J. Yandell		11	NX66678	F-5G-6	44-53159			Forced out of race, Kansas City, MO
J. Redwine		26	NX	F-5G				Did not start.
Paul J. Franklin		67	NX33699	P-51D-10	44-14377			Did not start. Raced by J. DeBona in 1947.
Nadene B. Ramsey			NX34993	F-5G-6				Entered by Wynn Motors. Aircraft not ready to start. Disqualified.
Earl H. Ortman		43	NX65419	F-5G-6	44-27207			Withdrew before start of race.
James Philpott		49		P-47				Did not start.
W. Clayson				FG-1D				Did not start.
J. Alexander		16	NX62805	P-38M-6	44-53082			Did not start.
William Odom		42	NX4477N	YP-47M	42-27385			Did not start.
Robert A. Swanson		80	NX66111	P-51K-10	44-12140			Possible entrant. Did not start.

1947 Bendix Trophy Race, Van Nuys to Cleveland - 2048 Miles

Pilot	Pos.	Race No.	License Number	Aircraft	Serial Number	Time	Speed mph	Remarks
A. Paul Mantz	1	46	NX1202	P-51C-10	44-10947	04:26:57	460.423	
Joe C. DeBona	2	90	NX33699	P-51D-10	44-14377	04:28:15	458.203	
Edmund P. Lunken	3	33	NX61151	P-51D-20	44-63592	05:00:45	408.723	
Bruce Gimbel	4	13	NX28388	P-51B-15	43-24760	05:04:11	404.080	
William E. Eddy	5	31	NX66851	P-51D-20	44-63539	05:26:25	376.549	
Thomas J. Mayson	6	60	NX1204	P-51C-10	42-103831	05:26:49	376.084	
Frank P. Whitton	7	99	NX63382	FG-1D	88086	06:24:04	320.025	
William P. Lear, Jr.	8	25	NX56687	F-5G-6	44-53217	06:59:57	292.680	

Pilot	Pos.	Race No.	License Number	Aircraft	Serial Number	Time	Speed mph	Remarks
Jane Page Hlavacek	9	63	NX21765	F-5G-6	44-53045	08:15:60	247.812	
James O. Ruble		88	NX5101N	P-38F-15	43-2181			Pilot bailed out over Arizona, plane crashed.
Dianna C. Cyrus		91	NX67807	A-26B	44-34766			Did not finish, landed in Michigan
Joeseph M. Kinkella		92	NX62822	P-63C-5	44-4393			Mechanical problems, forced out at Pueblo, CO.
William P. Odom		42	NX4477N	YP-47M	42-27385			Did not start.

1948 Bendix Trophy Race, Long Beach to Cleveland, 2044 Miles

Pilot	Pos.	Race No.	License Number	Aircraft	Serial Number	Time	Speed mph	Remarks
A. Paul Mantz	1	46	NX1204	P-51C-10	42-103831	04:33:49	447.980	
Linton B. Carney	2	60	NX1202	P-51C-10	44-10947	04:34:57	446.112	
Jacqueline Cochran	3	13	NX28388	P-51B-15	43-24760	04:35:07	445.847	
Edmund P. Lunken	4	33	N61151	P-51D-20	44-63592	04:37:46	441.594	
Jesse F. Stallings	5	81	N66313	DH Mk 25 Mosquito	KB984	05:59:35	341.120	
Joe C. DeBona		90	N5528N	P-51B-5	43-6822			Forced down near Cleveland out of fuel.
Jane Page Hlavacek		42	NX4477N	YP-47M	42-27385			Did not start.
Donald M. McVicar		41	CF-FZG	DH Mk 25 Mosquito	KB377			Broken engine, did not start.
Dianna C. Cyrus				DH Mk 25 Mosquito				Did not arrive.
Jack Becker		50	N70005	F-5G-6	44-27026			Did not arrive.

1949 Bendix Trophy Race, Rosemond, California to Cleveland - 2008 Miles

Pilot	Pos.	Race No.	License Number	Aircraft	Serial Number	Time	Speed mph	Remarks
Joe C. DeBona	1	90	N5528N	P-51B-5	43-6822	04:16:17	470.136	
Stanley H. Reaver	2	46	N1204	P-51C-10	42-103831	04:27:38	450.221	
Herman R. Salmon	3	60	N1202	P-51C-10	44-10947	04:28:14	449.214	
Donald Bussart	4	81	N37878	DH Mk 25 Mosquito	KB377	05:50:31	343.757	
Leland H. Cameron		24	N5546N	B-26C-20	41-35071			Arrived after deadline, disqualified.
Vincent Perron		61	N55811	Republic AT-12	41-17515			Out at Grand Junction, CO. (c/n 483-22)
Larry Hadley		38						Did not race. Details unknown.

MODERN TRANSCONTINENTAL AIR RACES

1964 Harold's Club Transcontinental Trophy Dash, St. Petersburg to Reno - 2254 Miles

Pilot	Pos.	Race No.	License Number	Aircraft	Serial Number	Time	Speed mph	Remarks
Wayne Adams	1	9	N332	P-51D-25	45-11471	7:04:07	318.880	
Charles A. Lyford	2	8	N2869D	P-51D-25	44-84390	7:19:32	307.780	
C.E. Crosby	3	3	N35N	P-51D-30	44-74602	8:08:27	276.920	
Richard Snyder	4	45	N651D	P-51D-25	44-73857	8:32:00	264.240	
Jack Shaver	5	69	N351D	P-51D-25	44-73483	9:12:06	245.000	Blew out tires at Oklahoma City, OK.
Stan Hoke	6	99	N551D	P-51D-25	45-11489	9:25:32	239.180	
Ellis D. Weiner		14	N335J	P-51D-25	44-74506			Landed at Jacksonville, FL due to bad weather.
Howard Olsen		1	N5073K	P-51D-25	44-73656			Landed at Ocala, FL due to bad weather.
Clay Lacy		64	N182XF	P-51D-30	44-74423			Did not arrive for start due to storm.

1965 Harold's Club Transcontinental Trophy Dash, St. Petersburg to Reno - 2254 Miles

Pilot	Pos.	Race No.	License Number	Aircraft	Serial Number	Time	Speed mph	Remarks
Ellis D. Weiner	1	14	N335	P-51D-25	44-72902	6:28:38	347.989	
Clay Lacy	2	64	N182XF	P-51D-30	44-74423	6:36:07	341.415	
Wayne Adams	3	9	N332	P-51D-25	45-11471	6:49:02	330.633	
Richard D. Kestle	4	13	N6303T	P-51D-20	44-63481	7:48:02	288.954	
John Gower	5	11	N12064	P-51D-25	44-73683	8:04:32	279.114	
Jack Shaver	6	69	N351D	P-51D-25	44-73483	8:22:29	269.143	Again blew tires at Oklahoma City.
Doug Wood	7	7	N469P	P-51D-25	44-73240	8:47:36	256.331	Refueled at Hobbs, NM.

Thomas Green		6	N191R	Riley Rocket	C/N 35229			Cessna 310D conversion. Forced out with engine problems.
James R. Fugate		83	N5077K	P-51D-25	44-73856			Forced out with engine problems.

1966 Transcontinental Race, St. Petersburg to Palm Springs, CA - 2038 Miles

Pilot	Pos.	Race No.	License Number	Aircraft	Serial Number	Time	Speed mph	Remarks
Ellis D. Weiner	1	14	N335	P-51D-25	44-72902	5:36	363.9	
Richard D. Kestle	2	13	N6303T	P-51D-20	44-63481	5:56	343.5	
Michael D. Carroll	3	87	N878M	Sea Fury F.B. Mk. 11	606878	6:16	305.7	Correct speed is 325.2 mph.

1967 Palm Springs CA to Cleveland - 2020 Miles

Pilot	Pos.	Race No.	License Number	Aircraft	Serial Number	Time	Speed mph	Remarks
Ellis D. Weiner	1	14	N335	P-51D-25	44-72902	4:55	411	All speeds approximate in this race.
Michael D. Carroll	2	87	N878M	Sea Fury F.B. Mk. 11	606878	5:14	386	
Robert Guilford	3	11	N511D	P-51D-30	44-74950	9:00	224	Three refueling stops.
James L. Ventura		25	N2871D	P-51D-30	45-11367			Crashed fatally near Minden, NB.
Clay Lacy		64	N182XF	P-51D-30	44-74423			Did not start.
Robert Garrison				F4U				Did not start.
John Gower		11	N12064	P-51D-25	44-73683			Did not start.

1967 Harold's Club Transcontinental Trophy Dash, Rockford IL to Reno - 1620 Miles

Pilot	Pos.	Race No.	License Number	Aircraft	Serial Number	Time	Speed mph	Remarks
Michael D. Carroll	1	87	N878M	Sea Fury F.B. Mk. 11	606878	3:50:55	417.346	
Ellis D. Weiner	2	14	N335	P-51D-25	44-72902	4:01:20	399.332	
Richard D. Kestle	3	13	N6303T	P-51D-20	44-63481	5:16:15	304.736	
Thomas Kuchinsky	4	18	N6165U	P-51D-25	44-84634	5:50:00	275.349	
James R. Fugate	5	83	N5077K	P-51D-25	44-73856	5:36:00	286.821	Penalized for late start and arrival.
H.F. "Mick" Rupp		17	N5151R	P-51D-25	44-73163			Forced out shortly after takeoff.
John W. Church		11	N148F	F8F-2	121787			Did not race.

1968 Harold's Club Transcontinental Trophy Dash, Milwaukee to Reno - 1667 Miles

Pilot	Pos.	Race No.	License Number	Aircraft	Serial Number	Time	Speed mph	Remarks
Ellis D. Weiner	1	14	N335	P-51D-25	44-72902	4:37:03	361.141	Correct speed is 361.083 mph.
Richard D. Kestle	2	13	N6303T	P-51D-20	44-63481	5:59:15	278.458	
Burns M. Byram	3	7	N169MD	P-51D-25	44-73140	6:17:58	264.669	
Robert H. Kucera	4	99	N212KA	F8F-2	121528	6:18:37	264.214	
Thomas Kuchinsky	5	18	N6165U	P-51D-25	44-84634	6:47:01	245.789	
Robert Guilford	6	3	N511D	P-51D-30	44-74950	8:48:33	189.265	
Mark Foutch		16	N2870D	P-51D-20	44-63350			Forced out with engine problems, Laramie, WY.
Carl Koeling		1	N840	P-64	41-19086			One hour out, returned to Milwaukee with electrical problem.
Walter Ohlrich		10	N7827C	F8F-2	121752			Did not start.
John Sandberg				P-51D				Did not start.
John Silberman				P-51D				Did not start.
Wendel Trogdon			N6325T	P-51D-25	44-73973			Did not start.
Peter Brucia				F6F ?				Did not start.
James R. Fugate		77	N5077K	P-51D-25	44-73856			Did not start.
Michael D. Carroll		87	N878M	Sea Fury F.B. Mk. 11	606878			Crashed fatally before the race.
Gunther W. Balz		9	N9G	F8F-1	90454			Did not start.

1969 Florida Cross-Country Race, Frederick, MD to Ft. Lauderdale - 929 Miles

Pilot	Pos.	Race No.	License Number	Aircraft	Serial Number	Time	Speed mph	Remarks
Ed Bowlin	1	51	N5151R	P-51D-25	44-73163	2:59:15	310.96	
Richard D. Kestle	2	13	N6303T	P-51D-20	44-63481	3:09:35	294.01	
William Hogan	3	3	N313H	P-51H-5	44-64415	3:21:55	276.05	
John M. Sliker	4	17	N5428	P-51D-30	44-74466	3:38:50	254.71	
Wallace Garrick	5	4	N103TL	P-51D-25	44-73422	4:28:00	207.99	
Paul Finefrock		6	N119H	P-51D-25	44-73275			Forced out by weather at Charleston, NC.

1969 Harold's Club Transcontinental Trophy Dash, Milwaukee to Reno - 1667 Miles

Pilot	Pos.	Race No.	License Number	Aircraft	Serial Number	Time	Speed mph	Remarks
Richard D. Kestle	1	13	N6303T	P-51D-20	44-63481	5:19:26	313.120	
John M. Sliker	2	17	N10607	P-51D-30	44-74466	5:20:22	312.210	
Thomas Kuchinsky	3	18	N6518D	P-51D-25	44-84634	5:48:35	286.930	
Burns M. Byram	4	71	N169MD	P-51D-25	44-73140	5:53:06	283.260	
Charles Doyle	5	0	N711UP	P-51D-25	44-73856	5:57:47	279.880	
Howard Keefe	6	11	N991R	P-51D-30	44-74536	6:03:16	275.340	
Gunther W. Balz	7	7	N9G	F8F-1	90454	6:16:47	265.460	
Walter Ohlrich	8	10	N7827C	F8F-2	121752	6:32:15	254.990	
Richard Thomas		22	N6667	F4U-4	97259	7:39:06	217.860	Finished after 4 pm deadline.
Judy Wagner		21	N775JW	Bonanza E-33C		8:02:46	207.180	Finished after 4 pm deadline.
Darryl Greenamyer		1	N332	P-51D-30	45-11471			Mechanical problems. Did not start.
Ellis D. Weiner		14	N335	P-51D-25	44-72902			Entered but did not arrive for start.
William S. Cooper		87	N878M	Sea Fury F.B. Mk. 11	606878			Did not start.
Merril				MM1				Did not start.
Robert Guilford			N511D	P-51D-30	44-74950			Did not start.

1970 Harold's Club Transcontinental Trophy Dash, Milwaukee to Reno - 1667 Miles

Pilot	Pos.	Race No.	License Number	Aircraft	Serial Number	Time	Speed mph	Remarks
Richard D. Kestle	1	13	N6303T	P-51D-20	44-63481	5:52:36	283.664	
Gunther W. Balz	2	7	N9G	F8F-1	90454	6:05:46	273.453	
John M. Sliker	3	17	N10607	P-51D-30	44-74466	6:32:11	254.983	
Howard Keefe	4	11	N991R	P-51D-30	44-74536	6:32:42	254.698	
Burns M. Byram	5	71	N169MD	P-51D-25	44-73140	6:46:31	246.042	
Jack Huismann			N5471V	P-51D-30	45-11381			Forced out at North Platte, NB with electrical problem.
Ron Reynolds		44	N5005	F8F-2	121731			Forced out with engine problem at Sioux City.
William S. Cooper		87	N878M	Sea Fury F.B. Mk. 11	606878			Did not start.
Paul Finefrock			N167F	P-51D-25	44-73877			Did not start.

1971 Alton P-51 Tournament, Milwaukee to East Alton, IL - 309 Miles

Pilot	Pos.	Race No.	License Number	Aircraft	Serial Number	Time	Speed mph	Remarks
Clay Lacy	1	64	N64CL	P-51D-30	44-74423	0:52.40	353.8	
Sherm Cooper	2	87	N878M	Sea Fury F.B. Mk. 11	606878	0:52.44	353.5	
Gunther Balz	3	7	N9G	F8F-1	90454	0:55.00	337.1	
Leroy Penhall	4	81	N6519D	P-51D-25	44-73857	0:56.26	329.5	
Howard Keefe	5	11	N991R	P-51D-30	44-74536	0:56.26	329.0	
William Hogan	6	3	N3131	P-51H-5	44-64415	0:58:43	317.3	
Burns M. Byram	7	71	N169MD	P-51D-25	44-73140	0:59.28	312.8	
Paul Finefrock	8		N119H	P-51D-25	44-73877	0:59.58	311.2	
Wallace Oakes	9		N5423V	P-51D-30	45-11586	1.01.43	301.8	
Richard Foote	10		N8676E	P-51D-25	44-73028	1:07.32	275.4	

Appendix B

GORDON D. CARTWRIGHT: METEOROLOGIST

The following biographical information on Gordon D. Cartwright was extracted from the World Meteorological Organization Bulletin, Vol. 41, No. 2, April 1992.

Gordon Cartwright entered the United States Weather Bureau in 1929, and did not retire until 1983, some 54 years later. Gordon didn't in any real sense retire. For the past ten years he has been under contract to the United States Government providing reports to the Departments of Commerce and State from his post in Geneva, Switzerland. The biographical information presented in the following narrative relates to Gordon's early career in the Weather Bureau where he was very actively involved with aviation weather forecasting operations. Following is a brief summation of his experiences in the Weather Bureau from 1929 to 1939.

"I was born on 14 August 1909, the middle of seven children, five boys and two girls. We lived in the west of the state of Pennsylvania at the industrial town of New Castle, named after the English city of Newcastle-upon-Tyne. At that time, New Castle had the world's largest tin plate center and that was where my father worked.

"I graduated from high school in June 1926. Always on the lookout for a better job, I saw in the local post office one day about open examinations for appointment as airway beacon maintenance assistant or as junior meteorological observer. I applied for both. Luckily for me, the Weather Bureau application forms came through first. I passed the examination and soon after had a letter instructing me to report to the Weather Bureau's Pittsburgh office on 1 June 1929. That was an exciting day! Pittsburgh was all of 50 mile away, and with its extensive steel works would surely offer much more than my home town.

"In those days there were about 100 (weather) stations, and no upper-air observations except at a few research centers. The total Weather Bureau staff was of the order of 1000 and its annual budget a little over three million dollars. We received weather observation messages in Morse code through the Western Union Telegraph network. They were in word form because a digit cost the same to transmit as a full word. Each office had its radio operator to take down these messages. Incidently, the Western Union's telegraph lines all converged on its center at Chicago, where girls on roller skates carried messages received to the appropriate operators for onward transmission.

"It was not considered necessary for all Weather Bureau stations to get all the observations. At Pittsburgh I believe we plotted about 60 stations spread over the USA, and this chart was the basis for making our daily weather forecast.

"I had been assigned to Pittsburgh for the propose of aviation, but since there was no proper airport I had to make my observations at the city office. When the civil airport was built I was transferred out there. We did three hourly observations, but the daily synoptic chart was based on observations at 8 a.m. There were few scheduled passenger flights in those days, but the airmail service between Pittsburgh and Cleveland was important. After three years at Pittsburgh I was transferred to the forecast office at Cleveland airport.

"At Cleveland I was introduced to the ways by which measurements in the upper air were currently being made. This was by pilot balloon observations and a daily flight by a light aircraft on contract to the Weather Bureau. Weather permitting, this airplane took off no later than 6:30 a.m. and carried a small aerograph recording pressure, temperature and humidity up to a height of 16,000 feet. There were then only six or eight stations in the whole of the United States that did these aircraft soundings, but by the end of the 1930s the number had risen to about 30.

"Cleveland was one of the major aviation forecast centers in the eastern U.S., which made it a particularly interesting assignment for me. Observations were received via various circuits in the form of teletype tapes. It was a big improvement when page printers were installed. Another technological development of that time was the transmission of weather maps by teletype, because of course there was no facsimile in those days. For the purpose of transmission a basic map suitable for the teletype machines was designed and printed and supplies sent to all stations. The duty forecaster at the main forecast center depicted the current synoptic situation (isobars and fronts) on one of these charts and fed it into the communications printer from which the data were copied to a teletype tape for transmission. All the receiving stations placed one of the blank maps in their printer and stood by for the bell to ring signaling the beginning of the transmission. Three or four minutes later they would have their copy of the weather map.

"The Cleveland aviation forecast area was sandwiched between that of Kansas City to the west and Newark to the east, and the analyses of the three centers did not always coincide. It was decided to exchange analyses prior to dissemination, but eventually a center analysis unit was created at Washington, D.C.

"My function was the observation of the upper air soundings by aircraft (APOBS or aircraft observations). The Army Air Corps agreed to cooperate in extending the network of these valuable observations, and in 1936, it was decided that in view of my experience I should be transferred to Barksdale Field at Shreveport, Louisiana, where APOBS were to be started.

"The morning meteorological reconnaissance ascent was flown by a different (Army) pilot each day, and one of my jobs was to brief them on what was needed. Some were quite good at maintaining a steady rate of climb, others not so good. One pilot failed to watch his altimeter properly and reached the ceiling of his aircraft - 22,000 feet. He managed to land safely in a field and had succeeded in making the highest sounding reached during my stay at Barksdale! After a year at Barksdale I was transferred to the aviation forecast center at Dallas, Texas. I was considered to have had a pretty good apprenticeship in my previous assignments. Now, I was expected to learn the art of forecasting on the job, picking the brains of my more experienced colleagues and reading all the available literature. In fact it was a fairly gradual transition from the observing to the forecasting side. There simply were not enough data to draw regular upper air charts, and one had to rely a lot on experience.

"Texas is noted for its severe storms which can last for many hours. That was one challenge. Another was posed by the strong summer airflow bringing in moist air from the Gulf of Mexico. On clear nights an extensive area of low cloud could form very rapidly over the air route from Brownsville to Dallas and predicting it was one of our trickiest tasks. Apparently the problem has still not been solved because the University of Texas now has a special research project on it.

"It was in 1939, that I was transferred once again although not because of the war. I was sent to the new airport - La Guardia - that had just been built on the shore of the East River to serve New York City. There was now a regular transatlantic air service by flying boat that used the marine terminal, and I was very pleased when after a few months at La Guardia I was put on to forecasting for these flights. The need for observations from the ocean became critical, especially with all the additional military traffic, and the North Atlantic weather ship network came into being just before the war in Europe began.

"The Pan American Boeing 314 flying boats usually would take off early in the morning to fly to Lisbon via Bermuda and Lagens in the Azores or to Foynes, Ireland via Botwood, Newfoundland and Lagens. The passengers would be called in their New York hotels and asked to be at the marine terminal by 4:30 or 5 a.m. Their baggage would be lined up ready for loading, but all this was done before the weather forecast was available, so that sometimes the captain had to cancel the flight if conditions were not acceptable. Quite frequently, the state of the sea made it unfit for takeoff or landing at Lagens, and wave forecasts were critical. There were cases of aircraft being held up in the Azores for as long as two weeks, the airline having to pay the hotel bills of both passengers and crew."

Appendix C

PACKARD-BUILT MERLIN ENGINES

MODEL	AIRCRAFT TYPE	REMARKS
MERLIN 28	LANCASTER III/X	MERLIN XX R.M. 3 S.M.
MERLIN 29	CANADIAN HURRICANE	EQUIVALENT TO MERLIN XX
MERLIN 31	CANADIAN MOSQUITO	EQUIVALENT TO MERLIN 21
MERLIN 33	CANADIAN MOSQUITO	EQUIVALENT TO MERLIN 23
MERLIN 38	LANCASTER III/X	EQUIVALENT TO MERLIN 22
MERLIN T38	LANCASTER III/X	MODIFIED PACKARD MERLIN 38
MERLIN 68	LINCOLN II	SIMILAR TO V-1650-7
MERLIN 69	CANADIAN MOSQUITO	EQUIVALENT TO MERLIN 67
MERLIN 225	MOSQUITO	PACKARD-BUILT MERLIN 25
MERLIN 266	SPITFIRE 16LF	PACKARD-BUILT MERLIN 66
MERLIN 300	LINCOLN (PROJECT ONLY)	PACKARD-BUILT MERLIN 100
MERLIN 301	LINCOLN (PROJECT ONLY)	PACKARD-BUILT MERLIN 101
V-1650-1	P-40F WARHAWK	SIMILAR TO MERLIN 28
V-1650-3	P-51B/C MUSTANG	
V-1650-5	XP-63B KINGCOBRA	NO PRODUCTION. PROPOSED AIRCRAFT ONLY
V-1650-7	P-51D/K MUSTANG	SIMILAR TO MERLIN 68
V-1650-9	P-51H MUSTANG	WATER-METHANOL INJECTION, SIMMONDS POWER CONTROL
V-1650-9A	P-51M MUSTANG	SIMMONDS POWER CONTROL
V-1650-11	P-51L MUSTANG	WATER-METHANOL INJECTION, SIMMONDS POWER CONTROL
V-1650-13	NO PRODUCTION	SIMMONDS POWER CONTROL, NO PRODUCTION
V-1650-15	NO PRODUCTION	SIMMONDS POWER CONTROL, NO PRODUCTION
V-1650-17	NO PRODUCTION	SIMMONDS POWER CONTROL, NO PRODUCTION
V-1650-19	NO PRODUCTION	VARIABLE SUPERCHARGER GEAR RATIO, NO PRODUCTION
V-1650-21	XP-82 TWIN MUSTANG	LEFT-HAND PROPELLER ROTATION
V-1650-23	P-82B/C/D TWIN MUSTANG	
V-1650-25	P-82B/C/D TWIN MUSTANG	LEFT-HAND PROPELLER ROTATION

SOURCES:
1.) Rolls-Royce Limited, "Mark Number Chart for Rolls-Royce Piston Engines," February 1953.
2.) Gruenhagen, Robert W., *Mustang, The Story of the P-51 Fighter*, Arco Publishing, New York, 1969.

Appendix D

ALLISON V-1710 ENGINE MODELS

MILITARY MODEL	ALLISON MODEL	AIRCRAFT TYPE	REMARKS
V-1710-1	C-1	NONE	1ST ARMY ENGINE, 750 HP (1933)
V-1710-2	A1	NONE	1ST NAVY ENGINE, 650 HP (1932)
V-1710-2	A2	NONE	NAVY ENGINE REBUILD, 750 HP
V-1710-3	C4	A-11A	INSTALLATION MOCKUP FOR A-11A MODIFICATION, ATTEMPTED TYPE TEST
V-1710-4	B	NONE	REVERSIBLE NAVY ENGINE, DIRIGIBLE PUSHER
V-1710-5	C?	NONE	MODIFIED V-1710-3 WITH FUEL INJECTION
V-1710-6	E1	XFL-1	BELL/NAVY AIRABONITA, 1150 HP
V-1710-7	C4	A-11A	FIRST FLIGHT ENGINE, 300 HOURS
V-1710-9	D	XFM-1	"C" TYPE ENGINE, 5 FT EXTENSION SHAFT
V-1710	C7		INTENDED FOR XP-37, XP-38, NO PROP, FEATHERING CAPABILITY
V-1710-11	C8R	XP-37/XP-38	C7 WITH PROP. FEATHERING
V-1710-13	D1	YFM-1	PUSHER CONFIGURATION, SIMILAR TO -11
V-1710-15	C9L	XP-38	LEFT-HAND ROTATION, PAIRED WITH -11
V-1710-17	E2	XP-39	FIRST "E" SERIES ENGINE, REMOTE PROP, REDUCTION GEAR BOX AND EXTENSION SHAFT
V-1710-19	C13	XP-40	FIRST "ALTITUDE RATED" ENGINE, -11 WITH, HIGHER S/C GEAR RATIO
V-1710-21	C10	YP-37	SIMILAR TO -11
V-1710-23	D2	YFM-1A	SIMILAR TO -13, BUT WITH BACKFIRE SCREENS
V-1710-25	F1	NONE	TEST ONLY, NEW SERIES WITH EXTERNAL SPUR TYPE PROP. REDUCTION GEARS
V-1710-27	F2R	XP-38/YP-38 P-38D/P-38E	1ST PRODUCTION "F" ENGINE
V-1710-29	F2L	XP-38/YP-38 P-38D/P-38E	LEFT-HAND ROTATION, SIMILAR TO -27
V-1710-31	E2A	YP-39A	NOT FLOWN, SIMILAR TO -17, WOULD HAVE USED TURBOSUPERCHARGER
V-1710-33	C15	P-40/P-40B P-40C/P-40G H-81A LOCKHEED P-322 LIGHTNING I	FIRST MAJOR PRODUCTION MODEL, SIMILAR TO -19
V-1710-35	E4	P-39C/P-400 P-39D/P-39D-1 P-39F	"ALTITUDE RATED" VERSION OF -17, HIGHER S/C GEAR RATIO
V-1710-37	E5	XP-39B/YP-39	INTERIM MODEL OF -17, "ALTITUDE RATED," 16 BUILT FOR YP-39
V-1710-39	F3R	P-40D/P-40E XP-46/XP-46A XP-51/P-51 NA-73	SIMILAR TO -27, BUT WITH MORE EFFICIENT SUPERCHARGER ROTATING GUIDE VANES
V-1710-41	D2A	YFM-1B	"ALTITUDE RATED" FOR USE WITHOUT TURBOSUPERCHARGER, OTHERWISE SIMILAR TO -23
V-1710-43	F8	XP-40K	SIMILAR TO -39, BUT WITH IMPROVED CRANKSHAFT, NEW VALVE TIMING AND LUBRICATION
V-1710-45	F7R	NONE	FIRST "F" WITH AUXILIARY SUPERCHARGER STAGE
V-1710-47	E9	XP-39E/XP-63 XP-63A/P-76	FIRST "E" WITH AUXILIARY SUPERCHARGER STAGE
V-1710-49	F5R	P-38F/XF-5D	SIMILAR TO -27, BUT WITH INCREASED SUPERCHARGER GEAR RATIO AND IMPROVED IMPELLER GUIDE VANES
	XF-5E		
	P-322-II		

Appendixes

MILITARY MODEL	ALLISON MODEL	AIRCRAFT TYPE	REMARKS
V-1710-51	F10R	P-38F/P-38G P-38H/F-5A F-5B/XF-5D	SIMILAR TO -49, NEW CARBURETOR
V-1710-53	F5L	P-38F/XF-5D XF-5E/P-322-II	LEFT-HAND ROTATION -49
V-1710-55	F10L	P-38F/P-38G P-38H/F-5A F-5B/XF-5D	LEFT-HAND ROTATION -51
V-1710-57	F11R	NONE	SIMILAR TO -55, BUT WITH 2-SPEED BIRMANN-TYPE 10.25" DIAMETER SUPERCHARGER IMPELLER
V-1710-59	E12	P-39J	SIMILAR TO -35, BUT WITH HIGHER SUPERCHARGER GEAR RATIO AND AUTOMATIC MANIFOLD PRESSURE REGULATOR
V-1710-61	F14	NONE	SIMILAR TO -39, BUT WITH HIGHER SUPERCHARGER GEAR RATIO AND AUTOMATIC MANIFOLD PRESSURE REGULATOR
V-1710-63	E6	P-39D-2/P-39K P-39L	SIMILAR TO -35, BUT WITH HIGHER SUPERCHARGER AND PROPELLER GEAR RATIOS, LARGER OIL PUMP
V-1710-65	E16	NONE	SIMILAR TO -47, DIFFERENT AUXILIARY SUPERCHARGER GEAR RATIO
V-1710-67	E8	P-39M	SIMILAR TO -63, DIFFERENT ACCESSORY DRIVES
V-1710-69	F18R	NONE	SIMILAR TO -51, CYLINDER PORT FUEL INJECTION, SEA LEVEL RATED
V-1710-71	F19R	NONE	SIMILAR TO -69, DIRECT CYLINDER FUEL INJECTION, DIFFERENT SUPERCHARGER GEARS
V-1710-73	F4R	XP-40K/P-40K	SIMILAR TO -39, INCREASED RATINGS AND AUTOMATIC BOOST CONTROL
V-1710-75	F15R	P-38K/XP-60A XP-60B	SIMILAR TO -51, DIFFERENT PROP. REDUCTION GEAR RATIO, WATER INJECTION, INCREASED RATINGS, MODIFIED FOR HYDRAMATIC PROP
V-1710-77	F15L	P-38K	SIMILAR TO -75, LEFT-HAND ROTATION
V-1710-79	F4L	NONE	EXPERIMENTAL ENGINE, NOT FLOWN, SIMILAR TO -73
V-1710-81	F20R	P-40M/P-40N P-40R/P-51A MUSTANG II F-6B	SIMILAR TO -73, DIFFERENT SUPERCHARGER GEAR RATIO AND AUTOMATIC BOOST CONTROL
V-1710-83	E18	P-39L/P-39M P-39N/P-39Q	SIMILAR TO -63 EXCEPT FOR SUPERCHARGER GEAR RATIO AND AUTOMATIC BOOST CONTROL
V-1710-85	E19	P-39M/P-39N P-39Q	SIMILAR TO -83, DIFFERENT PROP. REDUCTION GEAR RATIO
V-1710-87	F21R	A-36/A-36A	SIMILAR TO -51
V-1710-89	F17R	P-38H/P-38J F-5B/F-5C F-5F VEGA XB-38	SIMILAR TO -75, DIFFERENT PROP. REDUCTION GEAR RATIO, IMPROVED CONTROLS
V-1710-91	F17L	P-38H/P-38J F-5B/F-5C F-5F	SIMILAR TO -89, LEFT HAND ROTATION
V-1710-93	E11	XP-63A/P-63A RP-63A/P-63C XA-42/XB-42	SIMILAR TO -47, DIFFERENT AUXILIARY SUPERCHARGER CONFIGURATION
V-1710-95	F23R	XP-55	SIMILAR TO -81, PUSHER INSTALLATION, PROPELLER JETTISONING DEVICE
V-1710-97	G1R	NONE	FIRST OF NEW ENGINE SERIES, NEW CRANKSHAFT, IMPROVED ROCKER CASTINGS AND 10.25" S/C IMPELLER
V-1710-99	F26R	P-40N-20 P-40N-35	SIMILAR TO -81, AUTOMATIC BOOST CONTROL
V-1710-101	F27R	NONE	2-STAGE SUPERCHARGER, MAY HAVE BEEN CLOSE-COUPLED, I.E., WITHOUT AUXILIARY STAGE

MILITARY MODEL	ALLISON MODEL	AIRCRAFT TYPE	REMARKS
V-1710-103	E23	NONE	TWO E TYPE POWER SECTIONS WITH AUXILIARY SUPERCHARGERS CONNECTED TO V-3420 COUNTER-ROTATING REDUCTION GEAR BOX
V-1710-105	F29R	NONE	SIMILAR TO -75, NEW CRANKSHAFT, CONTROLS AND RATINGS
V-1710-107	F29L	NONE	SIMILAR TO -105, LEFT-HAND ROTATION
V-1710-109	E22	P-63D/P-63E	SIMILAR TO -93, NEW CRANKSHAFT, DIFFERENT SUPERCHARGER GEAR RATIO AND CONTROLS
V-1710-111	F30R	P-38L/P-38M F-5E,F-5F F-5G	SIMILAR TO -105, DIFFERENT PROPELLER REDUCTION GEAR RATIO AND RATINGS
V-1710-113	F30L	P-38L/P-38M F-5E/F-5F F-5G	SIMILAR TO -111, LEFT-HAND ROTATION
V-1710-115	F31R	P-40N-40	SIMILAR TO -99, NEW CRANKSHAFT, STRONGER ACCESSORY HOUSING, NEW ACCESSORY GEARS
V-1710-117	E21	P-63C/RP-63C	SIMILAR TO -93, NEW CRANKSHAFT, STRONGER ACCESSORY HOUSING, NEW ACCESSORY GEARS AND AUXILIARY SUPERCHARGER, WATER INJECTION
V-1710-119	F32R	XP-51J	SIMILAR TO -101, LOWER COMPRESSION RATIO, AFTERCOOLER, WATER INJECTION AND SPEED DENSITY FUEL PUMP, ENGINE FOR XP-81A WHICH WAS CANCELED
V-1710-121	F28R	XP-40Q	SIMILAR TO -101, DIFFERENT CARBURETOR AND NEW CRANKSHAFT
V-1710-123	F28L	NONE	LEFT-HAND ROTATION VERSION OF -121
V-1710-125	E24	XB-42/XB-42A	TWO E-24 POWER SECTIONS, 24 FOOT EXTENSION SHAFTS CONNECTED TO COUNTER ROTATING V-3420 GEAR BOX AND PUSHER PROPELLERS
V-1710-127	E27	XP-63H NOT FLOWN	SIMILAR TO -109, AFTERCOOLER, GE CT-1 TURBO-COMPOUND POWER TURBINE CONNECTED TO CRANKSHAFT VIA AUXILIARY SUPERCHARGER DRIVE, ENGINE TESTED, AIRCRAFT MOCKUP, PROJECT CANCELED
V-1710-129	E?	XB-42	SIMILAR TO -125
V-1710-131	G3	XC-114/YC-116	SIMILAR TO -97, REDUCED COMPRESSION RATIO
V-1710-133	E30	P-63F	SIMILAR TO -109, LOWER COMPRESSION RATIO
V-1710-135	G4	RP-63G	NEW CRANKSHAFT AND "E" TYPE REMOTE REDUCTION GEAR HOUSING
V-1710-137	E23C	XB-42A	PAIRED INSTALLATION, REDUCTION GEARS FROM -103
V-1710-139	F33R	FOR P-82 NOT FLOWN	SIMILAR TO -133, "F" TYPE REDUCTION GEARS
V-1710-141	F33L	FOR P-82 NOT FLOWN	LEFT-HAND ROTATION VERSION OF -139
V-1710-143	G6R	F-82E/F-82F F-82G	SIMILAR TO -101, LOWER COMPRESSION RATIO, NEW SUPERCHARGER GEAR RATIO, WATER INJECTION
V-1710-145	G6L	F-82E/F-82F F-82G	LEFT-HAND ROTATION VERSION OF -143
V-1710-147	G9R	P-82	NO PRODUCTION, SIMILAR TO -143, CYLINDER PORT FUEL INJECTION, REDESIGNED SUPER CHARGER DRIVE
V-1710-149	G9L	P-82	NO PRODUCTION, LEFT-HAND ROTATION VERSION OF -147

SOURCES:
1.) "Army Aircraft Characteristics," Air Materiel Command, Wright Field, Report No. TSEST-A2, Revised December, 1947.
2.) Various Bell Aircraft Specifications for P-39, P-400, P-63, and XFM aircraft.
3.) Correspondence from Dan Whitney dated 18 Dec. 1992 and 17 Jan. 1993.

Bibliography

In a sport as fluid as air racing, and one in which there is little necessity for structured documentation, the researcher is faced with compiling a narrative by examining a multitude of real and potential sources. The reader will find a number of bibliography references which at first glance seemingly have nothing to do with air racing or perhaps with aviation in general. One example is David L. Lewis' biography of Henry Ford. This impressive work details Ford's initial acceptance of a program to build the Rolls-Royce Merlin in the United States and his later angry refusal, much to the consternation of William Knudsen and indeed, of President Franklin D. Roosevelt. Another book by Augusta Fink, *Time in the Terraced Land*, truly has nothing to do with aviation; however, it sets the historical background to the eventual location of Mines Field, later the Los Angeles International Airport.

This bibliography is divided into five parts; books, periodicals, reports and documents; newspaper articles and oral history. Wherever possible, facts were checked with more than one source. Although newspaper articles are contemporary sources of information, they are not always accurate. Technical reports and documents are the most precise sources one can find. Unfortunately, there are not many available on the topic of air racing aside from ancillary materials covering engines, aerodynamics and fuels. Nonetheless, these sources are valuable. One of the most valuable sources of historical information is found in oral history provided by the people who were there. Again, one must approach these remembrances with some caution. Memories fade with the passing years.

BOOKS

Allard Noel E., *Speed, The Biography of Charles W. Holman*, Noel E. Allard, Chaska, Minnesota.

Allen, Richard Sanders, *The Northrop Story, 1929-1939*, Orion Books, New York, 1990.

Allen, Richard Sanders, *Revolution in the Sky*, The Stephen Greene Press, Brattleboro, Vermont, 1967.

Anon., *Aviation Weather*, U.S. Government Printing Office, Washington, D.C., Revised, 1975.

Anon., *The Pratt & Whitney Aircraft Story*, Pratt & Whitney Aircraft Division, United Aircraft Corporation, 1950.

Aymar, Brandt, *Men in the Air*, Crown Publishers, Inc., New York, 1990.

Byttebier, Hugo T., *The Curtiss D-12 Aero Engine*, Smithsonian Institution Press, Washington D.C., 1972.

Baker, W.J., *A History of the Marconi Company*, St. Martin's Press, New York, 1971.

Berry, Peter, *Beechcraft Staggerwing*, Tab Books, Blue Ridge Summit, PA, 1990.

Carter, Dustin W. and Birch J. Matthews, *Mustang: The Racing Thoroughbred*, Schiffer Publishing Ltd., West Chester, Pennsylvania, 1992.

Cochran, Jacqueline, *Stars at Noon*, Little Brown & Company, Boston, 1954.

Collier, Peter and David Horowitz, *The Fords*, Summit Books, New York, 1987.

Domonoske, Arthur B. and Volney C. Finch, *Aircraft Engines,* John Wiley & Sons, Inc., New York, 1936.

Donn, William L., *Meteorology*, McGraw-Hill Book Company, New York, 1965.

Dwiggins, Don, *The Air Devils*, J.B. Lippincott Company, New York, 1966.

Dwiggins, Don, *They Flew the Bendix Race*, J.B. Lippincott Company, New York, 1965.

Dyke, A.L., *Dyke's Aircraft Engine Instructor*, The Goodheart-Willcox Company, Inc., Chicago, 1928.

Emme, Eugene M., *Aeronautics and Astronautics*, National Aeronautics and Space Administration, U.S. Government Printing Office, Washington, D.C., 1961.

Eyman, Scott, *Mary Pickford, America's Sweetheart*, Donald I. Fine, Inc., New York, 1990.

Fink, Augusta, *Time and the Terraced Land*, Howell-North Books, Berkeley, California, 1966.

Fraas, Arthur P., *Aircraft Power Plants*, McGraw-Hill Book Company, Inc., New York, 1943.

Gordon, Louis and Alan Gordon, *American Chronicle: Six Decades in American Life, 1920-1980*, Atheneum, New York, 1987.

Gruenhagen, Robert, *Mustang*, Arco Publishing Co., New York, Revised 1976.

Gunston, Bill, *World Encyclopaedia of Aero Engines*, 2nd Edition, Patrick Stephens Ltd., Northamptonshire, England, 1989.

Hardie, George, Jr., Editor, *E.M. "Matty" Laird's Super Solution*, EAA Aviation Foundation, Inc., 1981.

Haffke, Henry A., *Gee Bee – The Real Story of the Granville Brothers and Their Marvelous Airplanes*, VIP Publishers Inc., Colorado Springs, 1989.

Herndon, Booton, *Mary Pickford and Douglas Fairbanks*, W.W. Norton & Company, Inc., New York, 1977.

Heron, S.D., *Development of Aviation Fuels*, Graduate School of Business Administration, Harvard University, Boston, 1950.

Hull, Robert, *A Season of Eagles*, Bob Hull Books, Bay Village, Ohio, 1984.

Hughes, Patrick, *A Century of Weather Service, 1870-1970*, Gordon and Breach, Science Publishers, Inc., New York, 1970.

Jordanoff, Assen, *Power and Flight*, Harper & Brothers, New York, 1944.

Kimes, Beverly Rae, Editor, *Packard, A History of the Motor Car and the Name*, Princeton Publishing, Inc., Princeton, N.J., 1978.

Larsen, Jim, *Air Racers*, American Air Museum, Inc., Kirkland, Washington, 1971.

Lewis, David L., *The Public Image of Henry Ford*, Wayne State University Press, Detroit, 1976.

Maloney, Edward T., *Sever The Sky, Evolution of Seversky Aircraft*, World War II Publications, Corona Del Mar, California, 1979.

Mandrake, Charles G., *National Air Races – 1932*, Speed Publishing, Ashtabula, Ohio, 1976.

McMahon, Morgan E., *A Flick of the Switch, 1930-1950*, Vintage Radio, Palos Verdes Peninsula, California, 1975.

McMahon, Morgan E., *Vintage Radio, 1887-1929*, Vintage Radio, Palos Verdes Peninsula, California, 1972.

McVicar, Don, *Mosquito Racer*, Airlife Publishing, Ltd., Shrewsbury, England, 1985.

Mead, Cary Hoge, *Wings Over the World, The Life of George Jackson Mead*, The Swannet Press, Wauwatosa, Wisconsin, 1971.

Miller, A. Austin and M. Parry, *Everyday Meteorology*, Philosophical Library, 1959.

Mikesh, Robert C., *Excalibur III*, Smithsonian Institution Press, Washington, D.C., 1978.

Mohler, Stanley R. and Bobby H. Johnson, *Wiley Post, His Winnie Mae, and the World's First Pressure Suit*, Smithsonian Institution Press, Washington, D.C., 1971.

Mooney, Michael MacDonald, *Evelyn Nesbit and Stanford White*, William Morrow and Company, Inc., New York, 1976.

Moss, Sanford A., *Superchargers for Aviation*, New York Aeronautics Council, Inc., 1942.

O'Neil, Paul, *Barnstormers & Speed Kings*, Time-Life Books, Alexandria, VA, 1981.

Post, Wiley and Harold Gatty, "Around the World in Eight Days," Orion Books, New York, 1989.

Rashke, Richard, *Stormy Genius, The Life of Aviation's Maverick, Bill Lear*, Houghton Mifflin Company, Boston, 1985.

Reynolds, Quentin, *The Amazing Mr. Doolittle*, Appleton-Century-Crofts, Inc., New York, 1953.

Rich, Doris L., *Amelia Earhart, A Biography*, Smithsonian Institution, Washington, D.C., 1989.

Roseberry, C.R., *The Challenging Skies*, Doubleday & Company, Inc., Garden City, New York, 1966.

Schlaifer, Robert, *Development of Aircraft Engines*, Graduate School of Business Administration, Harvard University, Boston, 1950.

Schmid, S.H. and Truman C. Weaver, *The Golden Age of Air Racing*, EAA Aviation Foundation, Inc., Times Printing Co., Random Lake, WI, Revised 1991.

Setwright, L.T.J., *The Power to Fly*, George Allen & Unwin Ltd., London, 1971.

Sloan, Alfred P., Jr., *My Years With General Motors*, Doubleday & Company, Inc., Garden City, New York, 1964.

Sloat, Warren, *1929 – America Before the Crash*, MacMillan Publishing Co., Inc. New York, 1979.

Smith, Herschel, *A History of Aircraft Piston Engines*, Sunflower University Press, Manhattan, Kansas, 1981.

Solberg, Carl, *Conquest of the Skies*, Little, Brown and Company, Boston, 1979.

Sonnenburg, Paul and William A. Schoneberger, *Allison – Power of Excellence: 1915 -1990*, Coastline Publishers, Malibu, California, 1990.

Taylor, George F., *Elementary Meteorology*, Prentice-Hall, Inc., New York, 1954.

Tate, Grover Ted, *The Lady Who Tamed Pegasus, the Story of Pancho Barnes*, A Maverick Publication, 1984.

Tegler, John, *Gentlemen, You Have A Race*, Wings Publishing Company, Severna Park, Maryland, 1984.

Thomas, Lowell, and Edward Jablonski, *Doolittle, A Biography*, Doubleday & Company, Inc., Garden City, New York. 1976.

U.S. Bureau of the Census, *Historical Statistics of the United States, Colonial Times to 1957*, Washington D.C., 1960.

Wedlake, G.E.C., *SOS – The Story of Radio Communication*, Crane, Russak & Company, Inc., New York, 1973.

Whitnah, D.R., *A History of the United States Weather Bureau*, University of Illinois Press, Urbana, 1965.

Whitnah, Donald R., *Safer Skyways, Federal Control of Aviation, 1926-1966*, Iowa State University Press, Ames, Iowa, 1966.

PERIODICALS

Allen, Richard Sanders, "Barrel-Nosed Cigars," American Aviation Historical Society JOURNAL, Vol. 9, No. 1, 1964, pp. 28-39.

Anon., "Speed Planes of 1931," *Aviation*, November, 1931.

Anon., "Bristol Centaurus," *FLIGHT*, 5 July 1945, pp. 13-17.

Anon., "The Bristol Centaurus," *THE AEROPLANE*, 6 July 1945, pp. 11-17.

Berliner, Don, "Cloak-and-Dagger," *American Aircraft Modeler*, August 1972, pp. 40-68 passim.

Berry, Peter, "The Spartan Executive," American Aviation Historical Society JOURNAL, Vol. 25, No. 2, 1980, pp. 145-152.

Brown, Philip, C., "The Fabulous Gee Bees," American Aviation Historical Society JOURNAL, Vol. 24, No. 3, 1979, pp. 187-201.

Deering, Roscoe, "Bellanca," (Part I), *Sport Flying*, July 1968, pp. 46-66 passim.

Deering, Roscoe, "Bellanca," (Part II), *Sport Flying*, August 1968, pp. 42-64 passim.

Downie, Don, "The Fury of Mike Carroll," *Air Progress*, September 1967, pp. 20-73 passim.

Emmert, Thomas M. and William T. Larkins, "Electra Junior, Lockheed's Model 12," American Aviation Historical Society JOURNAL, Vol. 19, No. 4, 1974, pp. 307-319.

Emmert, Thomas M. and William T. Larkins, "Lockheed's Model 10 Electra," American Aviation Historical Society JOURNAL, Vol. 23, No. 2, 1978, pp. 141-153.

Friedman, Paul D., "Birth of An Airport," American Aviation Historical Society JOURNAL, Vol. 23, No. 4, 1978, pp. 285-295.

Haynes, Martin, "TLC for the Big Birds," *Private Pilot*, Vol. 3, No. 11, August 1968, pp. 37-40.

Hazen, Ronald M., "Allison Division, General Motors Corporation," *Aeronautical Engineering Review*, November 1942, p. 81.

Hazen, Ronald M., "The Allison Aircraft Engine Development," Society of Automotive Engineers JOURNAL, (Transactions), Vol. 49, No. 5, November 1941, pp. 488-500.

Hirsch, Bob, "Wedell-Williams Air Service Corporation and Air Racing," American Aviation Historical Society JOURNAL, Volumes 32, 33 and 34, 1987-1989.

Johns, Russell C. "Observations at the National Air Races and Exposition," *Aero Digest*, October 1929.

Bill Johnson, "Sea Fury, Low and Fast," *Air Enthusiast*, March-June 1985, pp. 52-78.

Johnson, Chalmers A., "Thirty Years of Lockheed Vegas," American Aviation Historical Society JOURNAL, Vol. 2, No. 1, 1957, pp. 1-35.

Larkins, William T., "Bellanca Production List," American Aviation Historical Society JOURNAL, Vol. 3, No. 3, 1958, pp. 179-185.

Lear, Bill Jr., "Bill Lear, Jr., and His P-38," *Sport Flying*, Vol. 6, No. 4, August 1972.

Lippincott, Harvey, "The Navy Gets An Engine," American Aviation Historical Society JOURNAL, Vol. 6, No. 4, 1961, pp. 247-258.

Matthews, Birch J., "Often a Bridesmaid," American Aviation Historical Society JOURNAL, Vol. 7, No. 2, 1962, pp. 83-96.

Matthews, Birch J., "Cobra," American Aviation Historical Society JOURNAL, Vol. 8, No. 3, 1963, pp. 185-198.

Overton, John, "Those Hush-Hush Bellancas," *Air Progress*, September 1966, pp. 24-82 passim.

Phillips, Ed, "Mystery Ship," American Aviation Historical Society JOURNAL, Vol. 27, No. 4, 1982, pp. 286-295.

Plehinger, Russell, "Endurance Flying: The Pilots and Planes," American Aviation Historical Society JOURNAL, Vol. 9, No. 4, 1964, pp. 280-287.

Schirmer, Robert F., "AAC & AAF Civil Primary Flying Schools, 1939-1945," Part VIII, Santa Maria Primary, American Aviation Historical Society JOURNAL, Vol. 37, No. 4, 1992, pp. 300-309.

Schuyler, Norm, "The Jet Stream and General Aviation Pilots," *Airways*, Vol. 3, No. 5, May 1969, pp. 57-59.

Snyder, Richard G. and Audie W. Davis, Jr., "Medical Factors in Unlimited Class Air Racing Accidents," *Aerospace Medicine*, Vol. 43, No. 5, May 1972, pp. 512-519.

Thompson, Scott A., "Postwar Aircraft Disposal," American Aviation Historical Society JOURNAL, Vol. 37, No. 4, 1992, pp. 274-287.

Underwood, John, "A Racer for Ireland, Bombers for Spain," *Air Classics*, October 1975, pp. 16-67 passim.

REPORTS AND DOCUMENTS

Anon., "Fifty Years of Aeronautical Research," National Aeronautics and Space Administration, Washington, D.C., Report No. EP-45 1965.

Anon., "Memorandum on Density-Altitude," Air Weather Service Technical Report, AWS TR 105-101 (Rev. 2), United States Air Force, September 1957.

Anon., "National Implementation Plan for the Modernization and Associated Restructuring of the National Weather Service," Fiscal Year 1992 Annual Update, Department of Commerce, National Oceanic and Atmospheric Administration, Washington, D.C., June 1992.

Anon., "Pratt & Whitney Aircraft Engine Model Designations and Characteristics," Pratt & Whitney document PWA-SD 14, 1 January 1945, revised 1 September 1955. Document furnished to author through the courtesy of Dan Whitney.

Anon., Rolls-Royce Limited, "Mark Number Chart for Rolls-Royce Piston Engines," Derby, England, February 1953.

Anon., "Service Instructions, V-1710 Aircraft Engines," Report No. An 02-5AD-2, USAF, 5 May 1945.

Chandler, C.L., "Flying Jet Winds," a privately published booklet by the author, Babylon, Long Island, New York, November 1958.

Grice, Gary K., "National Weather Service Snapshots, Portraits of a Rich Heritage," A National Weather Service Publication, 1991.

Horkey, E.J. and J.G. Beerer, "Performance Calculations for Model P-51D Airplane," North American Aviation, Inc., Report No. NA-46-130, dated 6 February 1946.

Lieurance, N.A., "The Development of Aeronautical Meteorology," Aeronautical Meteorology, Technical Note No. 95, 1969.

Maize, Kennedy P., "Weather Forecasting," Vol. 1, No. 5, Congressional Quarterly Inc., 1979.

Mantz, Paul, personal scrap book volumes on file at the San Diego Aerospace Museum Library. These five volumes were made available for inspection through the courtesy of Ray Wagner and George Welsh of the museum staff, 7 August 1987.

O'Brien, Kaye and Gary K. Grice, Editors, "Women in the Weather Bureau During World War II," A National Weather Service Publication, 1991.

Stoddard, V.M., "Model Specification for Single Engine Offensive Fighter Airplane," Model No. P-63C-5-BE, Report No. 33-947-007, 15 November 1944.

Voglewede, T.J. and E.C.B. Danforth, "Flight Tests of the High-Speed Performance of a P-51B Airplane," National Advisory Committee for Aeronautics, Memorandum Report No. L4L18, 18 December 1944.

NEWSPAPERS

Arizona Republic, various editions, 1946-1949.

Cleveland News, various editions, 1946-1949.

Cleveland Plain Dealer, various editions, 1946-1949.

Cleveland Press, various editions, 1946-1949.

Los Angeles Times, various editions, 1946-1949.

New York Times, various editions, 1928-1949.

Reno Evening Gazette, various editions, 1964-1970.

Tulsa Tribune, various editions, 1946.

ORAL HISTORY

Jack Daniels: Telephone interview with the author on 11 March 1993, concerning the parasitic drag coefficients on the P-51C and P-51D airplanes.

George Gehrkens: Telephone interview with author on 11 March 1993, about wetting the wing on a P-51 Mustang.

Howard Keefe: Transcription of Howie Keefe's recollections of his experiences in the 1970 Harold's Club Trophy Dash race. This transcription was provided through the courtesy of Maurice O'Brien, a member of Howie's crew for several years.

Bill Kerchenfaut: Telephone interview with author on 30 March 1993, about Mike Carroll's Hawker Sea Fury.

Harvey H. Lippincott: Audio recording of a talk presented to the Society of Air Race Historians, 4-5 May 1990. Harvey is a retired Pratt & Whitney engineer and company archivist.

Harvey H. Lippincott: Telephone interview, 19 February 1993.

Charles Lyford: Telephone interview with author on 1 December 1992, regarding his 1964 transcontinental Harold's Club Trophy Race.

Charles Lyford: Audio recording of his experiences in the 1964 Harold's Club Trophy Race, February 5, 1993.

Howell Miller: Telephone interview with author on 1 December 1992, concerning Russel Boardman.

John Nollan: Telephone interview with author on 11 March 1992, concerning his work preparing cruise control charts for the 1946 Bendix for both Paul Mantz and Jackie Cochran.

Charles Tucker: Telephone interview with author on 23 April 1992, and 12 March 1993, regarding his 1946 Bendix Trophy Race flight.

Index

Adams, Wayne, 214, 219, 221, 223, 228, 229
Air Commerce Act, 16
Airplane observations (APOBS), 16, 19
Allison, John, 178
Allison Division, 38-43
Allison, Sarah Cornelius, 41
Allison, James A., 38-42
Allison Experimental Co., 39
Allison, V-1710-117, 180
Allison racing engines, 43-44
Allison Engineering Co., 39, 42
Andrus, C.G., 19
American Cirrus Engines, Inc., 124
Analytical Methods, Inc., 143
Art Chester, 204
Ashley, Sylvia, 83
Ashton, C.J., 18
Atlantic Ferrying Organization, 138
Aviation Maintenance Corp., 183, 189

Barker, Vern, 226, 230, 231, 235, 241, 242, 245
Barns, Pancho, 208
Bayles, Lowell, 123, 124-126
Becker, Jack, 196
Beechcraft D-17W airplane, 96
Beechcraft A-17F airplane, 96
Beechcraft C-17R, 133
Beery, Wallace, 96
Bell P-63 characteristics, 153-155
Bell, Larry, 155
Bell Aircraft Corp., 43 155, 156, 179
Bell XFM-1 fighter, 43
Bell P-39Q "Cobra II" racer, 236, 239
Bellanca Trimotor airplane, 135
Bellanca "Columbia," 52, 53, 55
Bellanca "Northstar", 52
Bellanca "Veedol," 54
Bendix Aviation Corporation, 72, 151
Bendix, Vincent, 72, 85, 87, 131, 151
Benjamin, Delmar, 145
Benjamin, Earl, 147
Benjamin, Robert, 147, 148
Bennett, Andrew, 47
Bent, A.E., 18
Berliner, Don, 222
Berry, Major John, 63
Bijur Starting & Lighting Co., 72
Bingham, Senator Hiram, 71
Black, T. Campbell, 81
Bleriot, Louis, 72
Blevins, Beeler, 74
Boardman Aviation Corp., 128
Boardman, Russell N., 128, 130-131
Boeing 247 airplane, 132
Boeing 247-D prototype airplane, 90
Boeing, Bill Jr., 215

Borton, Jim, 91
Bowlin, Ed, 250
Breese, Vance, 87, 88, 134, 135
Bricker, William, 189
Bristol Centaurus 18 engine, 44
Bromberg, Jack L., 89, 91, 92
Bromley, Harry, 65
Brown, Herman, 190
Brown, George, 190
Brown, Henry J., 63, 64
Brown, Philip C., 125
Brown, Chuck, 236
Brown, Larry, 59
Burcham, Milo, 96
Burgin, Emile, 54, 57
Bushey, Ralph, 91
Bussart, Don, 206, 208, 210
Byram, Burns, 243

California Air Race Association, 48
Call, Thomas F., 190, 193
Cameron, Leland H., 200, 205, 208, 211
Cameron, Martha L., 200
Canadian Pacific Airways, 137
Cantwell, Robert, 63, 64
Capone, Alphonse, 60
Carney, Linton Boyd "Lin," 197, 202, 204
Carroll, Mike, 14, 25, 44, 229-230, 232, 233, 234-235, 239-241, 242, 245, 247
Carroll Hawker Sea Fury racer, 230-233
Carroll's P-39 "Cobra III" racer, 236-241, 239
Cartwright, Gordon D., 19
Cassidy, George, 84
Ceilometer, 19
Chandler, C.L. "Chan," 235, 236, 249, 250
Chenault, General, 178
Cirrus Derby, 124
Civil Aeronautics Administration, 205
Clark, Edith Boydston, 79, 90
Clarke, Lt. H.B., 51
Cleveland Speed Foundation, 73
Clinometer, 19
Cochran, Jacqueline, 33-34, 35, 79, 84, 96, 134, 135, 156-158, 184-186, 189, 193, 200, 202, 203-204, 211
Cochran P-51 racer characteristics, 156-158
Coffman starter, 44
Cole, R.A., 190
Collyer, Capt. Charles B.D., 50
Compton, California air race, 81
Consolidated A-11A conversion, 43
Constant, Max, 135
Continental Motors Corp., 215
Cooper, William S. "Sherm," 247
Cord Cup Race, 79
Cordova, Frank, 135
Crawford, Fred, 151

268

Index

Crosby, C.E., 214, 219
Curtiss D-12 engine, 33, 34
Curtiss Pusher, 66
Curtiss Conqueror engine, 33, 41, 85
Curtiss XP-37, 43
Cyrus, Dianna, 189, 196

Daniels, Jack, 186
Davis, Douglas, 62, 84-85, 87, 123
Davis, Harry L., 87
Day, Capt. Stephen D., 50, 51, 53, 57
De Forest, Lee, 17
DeBona, Joe, 26, 189, 192, 193, 195, 198, 200-202, 204, 205, 208, 209-210
DeBona P-51 racer "Thunderbird," 202
Defense Plant Corp., 152
DeHavilland Mark 25 Mosquito, 196
Denslow, Fred, 83
Destefani, Bill, 143
Detroyat, Michael, 92
Dilley, Murray, 84, 87
Dole Race, 55
Doolittle, James, 25, 29, 72-77, 83, 117, 123, 129, 145
Douglas A-26 "Reynolds Bombshell," 190
Douglas A-26 airplane, 187
Douglas DC-2 airplane, 87, 132, 146
Douglas DC-3 airplane, 132, 137
Drucker, Peter, 230
Dwiggins, Don, 157

E.D. Weiner Corp., 226
E.M. Laird, Inc., 73
Earhart, Amelia, 51, 71, 133
Eclipse Machine Co., 72
Eclipse-Pioneer Division, 72
Eddy, William, 177, 186-187, 189, 194
Ellenstein, Meyer, 137, 138
Ethylene glycol, 33, 39-41
Experimental Aircraft Association, 243

Fairbanks, Douglas, 83
Fairchild PT-19 airplane, 182
Federal Aviation Administration, 234
Ferguson, Malcolm, 151
Finefrock, Paul, 250
Fischer, Carl, 41
Fisher Investment Trust, 43
Fokker F10 airplane, 48
Folkerts, Clayton, 59
Foote, Richard, 251
Ford, Edsel, 36
Ford Motor Company, 35, 36
Ford, Henry, 35-36
Foutch, Mark, 243
Franklin, Paul J., 177, 192
Franklin, Ben T., 151, 206
Freeman, Daniel, 47
Freeman, Ron, 202
Fugate, Jim, 236

Fuller, Frank Jr., 25, 133, 134, 135, 196

Gale, Charles, 120
Gatty, Harold, 67, 68
Gee Bee Q.E.D. airplane, 84, 85, 90
Gee Bee E airplane, 128
Gee Bee R-1/R-2 airplane, 84
Gee Bee Y airplane, 128
Gee Bee R-2 analytical model, 143-145
Gee Bee R-1 airplane, 84, 128-129
Gee Bee R-2, 84
Gee Bee R-2 airplane, 128-131, 139-140
Gee Bee Z airplane, 124-126
Gee Bee Y airplane, 128
Gehlbach, Lee, 29, 84, 85, 123, 129-130
General Petroleum Co. of California, 209
General Airmotive Corp., 91
Gibson, Inez, 135
Gilman, Norman H., 39, 41, 43
Gilmore, Earl, 89
Gilmore, Arthur Fremont, 89
Gilmore Oil Company, 88, 89, 91, 92, 118
Gimbel, Bruce, 189, 193
Giuseppe M. Bellanca, 52
Glenn Curtiss (airplane), 18
Goebel, Arthur C., 52, 55-57, 63, 64, 68
Goodlin, Charles "Slick," 155
Goodyear Aircraft Corp., 156
Gower, John, 230
Granger, James E., 79, 81, 84, 87-88, 89
Granger, James E., Inc., 79
Granger, Glema, 81
Granville Brothers, 29, 59, 123, 124, 128
Granville, Zantford "Grannie," 123, 143, 145
Green, Tom, 228
Greenamyer, Darryl, 246
Greve, Louis W., 71, 87, 136
Guilford, Bob, 234, 243

Hadley, Larry, 205, 206
Haizlip, James, 73, 85, 117-123, 133
Haldeman, George, 52, 55, 71, 72
Hall, Ben, 215
Hall, Florence C., 66, 96
Hancock, Capt. G. Allen, 89
Hancock Foundation College, 89, 178
Happy Bottom Riding Club, 208
Harp, Jim, 187
Harrison, Henry T., 19
Haslett, Major Elmer, 138
Hawks, Frank, 63, 64, 73, 76
Heaton, William, 129
Henderson, Phil, 136
Henderson, Clifford W., 48, 59, 63, 66, 71, 72, 73, 82, 83, 88, 136, 151, 183
Hercules engine, 44
Herrick, C.A., 53
Hertz, Heinrich R., 17
Hill, Ivis V., 191

Hirsch, Bob, 117
Hispano-Suiza aircraft engine, 26
Hitchman, W.H., 83
Hlavacek, Jane Page, 189, 194, 196
Hoke, Stan, 214
Holman, Charles "Speed," 73
Hoover, Bob, 246
Hopkins, W.R., 61
Hornet engine, 28, 29
Houge, Wayne, 248
Houston, George H., 26
Howard DGA-6 "Mr. Mulligan", airplane, 29-33, 84, 139-140
Howard, Benny, 29-31, 59, 84, 132
Hoyt, Pete, 248
Hughes, Howard, 134, 135
Hughes Racer, 134, 135
Hunter, Walter, 73
Hurricane Dora, 213-214, 219, 228
Husted, Don, 187

Indianapolis Speedway Team Co., 38
Ingalls, Laura, 133
Iseman, Lt. Cmdr. Jack, 55, 57

Jet Stream, 202-203
Joe DeBona Racing Co., 200
Johnson, Bailey, 247
Johnson, Harold, 182
Johnson, Cort, 159
Johnston, Alvin "Tex," 155, 236
Jones, C.S. "Casey," 71

Katona, Joe, 200
Keefe, Howie, 247-249
Keefe P-51 racer "Miss America," 247
Kelly, J. Nelson, 123
Kenworthy, Robert, 137
Kestle, Dick, 14, 228, 229, 236, 243, 246, 247, 249, 250
Kimball, Dr. James, 19
King, Bob, 158, 159
Kingsford-Smith, Major, 128
Kinkella, Joseph M., 189, 196
Klemin, Professor Alexander, 143
Knudsen, William S., 35-36
Koeling, Carl, 243
Kucera, Robert H., 242, 243
Kuchinsky, Tom, 14, 243
Kusenda, Mike, 84

La Guardia, Fiorello, 138
Lacy, Clay, 213-214, 219, 229, 251
Laird, E.M. "Matty," 73, 74, 95
Laird "Solution," 73-74
Laird "Super Solution," 73-74
Laird Super Solution, 29, 73-77
Lange, K.O., 18
Larsen, Jim, 215
Lawrance J-1 engine, 26

Lawrance, Charles L., 26
Lear, William Powell, Jr., 182
Lear, Bill Jr., 187, 190, 194, 196
LeBoutillier, Oliver, C., 51, 52, 54, 63, 64
Lednicer, Dr. David, 143-146
Leonard, Royal, 85
Levine, Charles A., 52, 55
Liberty engine, 39
Lindbergh, Ann Morrow, 61
Lindbergh, Charles A., 19, 28, 47, 48, 50, 61
Lockheed P-38/F-5G characteristics, 153-155
Lockheed Vega "Winnie Mae," 66, 68, 96, 139-140
Lockheed Aircraft Corp., 156
Lockheed P-38/F-5G racer characteristics, 181-183
Lockheed Vega "Miss Silvertown,", 64
Lockheed Vega,"True Story Magazine", 52
Lockheed Vega "Yankee Doodle," 52, 55, 56
Lockheed 12 airplane, 96
Loening, Mike, 246
Logsdon, Charles S., 205
Loutt, Bobby, 65
Lowe, Florence Leontine (see Pancho Barnes)
Lunken, Edmund, 189, 192, 195, 197-199, 202-203, 204, 206
Lunken P-51 racer "Buttonpuss," 199
Lyford, Chuck, 38, 214-223
Lyford P-51 "Bardahl Spl.," 215-219
Lyon, Capt. Harry W., 128

MacCracken, William P., Jr., 61
Mackey, Joe, 96
MacPherson, Robertson, 79
Macready, Lt. John A., 73
MacRobertson Race, 33, 79, 81, 84, 85, 87
Maloney, Ed, 236, 237
Mamer, Nick, 54
Mantz, Paul, 245
Mantz P-51 racer characteristics, 158-160
Mantz, Paul, 26, 38, 135, 157, 158-160, 183-184, 189, 190, 191, 194-195, 196, 197-198, 200, 204, 206, 208, 209, 210
Marconi, Guglielmo, 17
Marcoux, Hal, 89, 91
Marcoux-Bromberg racer, 139-140
Marcoux-Bromberg racer (see also Rider R-3), 91-94, 96
Marvin, Charles F., 14
Maxwell, James C., 17
Mayson, Tommy, 177, 189, 192, 194
McCarthy, Glenn, 190, 194, 195, 197
McCarthy Oil & Gas Corp., 191, 199
McCurdy, J.A.D., 18
McMillan, Clifford, 53
McReynolds, Charles F., 134, 135
McVicar, Donald M., 196-197, 206
Mead, George J., 28
Merlin 225 racing engine, 197
Merlin V-1650-9A racing engine, 195
Miller, Ward, 65
Miller, Howell "Pete," 143
Mines Field, 48

Index

Mines, William W., 48
Minimum time track, 14
Minor, Roy, 84
Moffett, Admiral William A., 26
Morris, Jack P., 52
Morris, John, 55
Morse, Samuel F.B., 18
Mortenson, Dr. Elmer, 87
Mosher, O.N., 138
Muncy, Bill, 214
Mussett, Lucille, 41, 42
Mussett, George W., 41
Mustangs Unlimited, 233

National Defense Advisory Commission, 35
National Air & Space Museum, 135
National Aeronautics Association, 205
National Rifle Association, 77
Neeley, Chuck, 219, 221
Neumann, Harold, 84
New England Air Museum, 145, 148
Newberger, Don, 230, 235, 237, 239
Nikrent, Joe, 83
Nollan, John, 157, 158
North American AT-6, 215
North American P-51 characteristics, 153-155
North American Aviation, 155, 156
North American T-28, 215
Northeast magneto, 221
Northrop, John, 33
Northrop Gamma 2G racer, 33, 34, 85, 139-140
Northrop A-17A, 92, 147
Noyes, Blanch, 133
Nutt, Arthur, 34

Odlum, Floyd B., 85, 156
Odom, Bill, 189, 190, 194, 196, 206, 211
Ohlrich, Walter, 242
Olsen, Howard, 214, 221
Ong, William, 88, 89, 198
Ortman, Earl H., 89-93, 96, 114, 133, 137, 147, 148, 156, 182

P-51 Strega, 143
Pacific School of Aviation, 79
Packard Motor Car Company, 36-37, 202, 215
Packard-Merlin, 36
Page printer teletype, 19
Page, Randolph, 54, 55
Pangborn, Clyde, 79
Pappas, John J., 203
Penrose, Paul, 156
Perlick, Bob, 96, 135
Perron, Vince, 206, 208, 209
Perseus engine, 44
Pickford, Mary, 82-83, 87
Pilot balloons, 15
Piper J2 Cub airplane, 178, 182
Planes of Fame Museum, 236

Polando, John L., 128, 130
Post, Will Francis, 66
Post, Mae Quinlan, 66
Post, H. Wiley, 66-68, 96
Powell, Dick, 183
Pratt & Whitney Wasp S1D1 engine, 90, 92
Pratt & Whitney, 25-28
Pratt & Whitney Twin Wasp Jr. S2A5-G, 92, 146
Pratt & Whitney Wasp S4D1-G engine, 90
Pratt & Whitney Wasp Jr., S/N X-27, 81
Pritchard, Robert J., 48
Professional Race Pilots Association, 204

Radio Corporation of America, 17
Radiosonde, 16, 18
Ramsey, Nadine, 181
Rancho Redondo, 47
Randall, I.S., 138
Reaver, Stan, 206, 208 209
Reconstruction Finance Corp., 152, 179
Reed, Wilson, Jr., 19
Renault racer, 88
Rentschler, Frederick B., 26, 28
Republic YP-47M racer, 190, 194
Rickenbacker, Eddy, 42-43
Rider R-3 airplane, 79-91
Rider R-1 airplane, 79
Rider B-1 airplane, 79
Rider, Keith, 29, 59, 79-81, 87-88, 146
Rider R-2 airplane, 79
Rider-Clark Aeroplane Corp., 91
Robbins, Adam, 237
Roberts, F.J., 92
Roggers, Buddy, 206
Roosevelt, President Franklin D., 35, 36
Rossi, Maurice, 88
Rotax magneto, 221-222
Ruble, James C., 190, 194, 195
Ruble's P-38 racer "Flying Shamrock," 190-192, 194
Rupp, Mick, 236
Ryder, Earle A., 28

Salmon, Herman "Fish," 206, 208, 209, 210
Sawyer, Grant, 215
Schields, John, 187
Schmidt, A.U., 208
Schneider Trophy Race, 132
Schory, Carl, 51
Scott, C.W.A., 81
Seversky Aircraft Co., 95
Seversky P-35 pursuit, 95, 132, 133, 147
Seversky racers, 95-96
Seversky, Alexander P., 95, 133
Shaver, Jack, 214
Shaw, Wilbur, 135
Shell Speed Dashes, 130
Shelton, Lyle, 236
Shoenhair, Lee, 63, 64
Shogran, Ivar, 81

Sinclair, Frank, 95, 133
Sleeve valves, 44
Sliker, Jack, 246
Sloan, Alfred P., Jr., 43
Slovak, Mira, 225
Smith, Dixon "Dax," 217
Smith, Art, 66
Smith, E.B., 65
Snyder, Dick, 214
Spray bar cooling system, 218
Stallings, Jesse F., 196-197, 204
Standard Pipeline Co., 196
Stanley, Robert M., 179
Stead, Bill, 213, 215, 217, 222, 225, 226
Steele, Dudley M., 48, 50, 51, 56
Stewart, Jimmy, 209, 210
Stewart, Gloria, 210
Stillman, Mrs. James A., 52, 54
Stromberg Carburetor Division 72
Sundorph, E.C. "Sonny," 96
Sundorph Special airplane, 96
Surplus Property Act, 152

Taylor, Robert, 202
Tegler, John, 214
Telefunken Company (Germany), 17
Texas Railway Equipment Corp., 190, 191
Thaden, Louise, 79, 133
Thaw, Evelyn Nesbit, 130
Thaw, Russell K., 130-131
Thaw, Col. William K., II, 52, 55-56
Thaw, Harry K., 130
Therkelson, Larry, 84, 96, 183, 194, 202, 208, 209
Thorn, Dwight, 38, 217, 219, 221
Timm Aircraft Corp., 134
Tomasulo, Dick, 230, 235, 239
Townsend, George, 54
Trans-Florida Aviation, 247
Travel Air "Mystery Ship," 73
Tucker, Harry J., 52, 55, 56-57
Tucker P-63 racer characteristics, 178-181
Tucker, Charles, 156, 178-181, 187
Turner, Roscoe, 29, 33, 64, 65, 79, 83, 87, 96, 118

U.S. Army, 39, 41
U.S. Navy, 17, 39
U.S. Navy Allison engines, 43
U.S. Army Allison engine development, 43

Van der Veken, Robert, 230
Vance, Claire, 84
Vance "Flying Wing" airplane, 84

Ventura, Jim, 234
Vern Barker Aircraft, 227
VSAERO analytical model, 143-144
Vultee BT-13 airplane, 182, 190

Waco UPF airplane, 178
Wait, Louis, 156
War Assets Administration, 152, 177, 183, 200
Warner, Edward P., 71
WASP (Women Air Force Service Pilot), 189
Weather kites, 14, 16
Weather Bureau, 13-16, 18, 19, 22
Weatherhead, Albert J., 151
Weaver, Truman, 84
Wedell Williams #92 airplane, 84, 88, 139-140
Wedell Williams Corp., 88
Wedell Williams Air Service, 118
Wedell Model 44 racers, 117, 134
Wedell, Jimmy, 29, 59, 79, 117-118, 123, 133
Weiner P-51 racer, 242, 245
Weiner, E.D., 214, 221, 225-229, 230, 233-234, 235, 236, 241, 243, 245-247
Wetzel, Harry H., 48
White, Stanford, 130
Whiteside, A.T., 196
Whitton, Frank P., 190, 196
Wilkins, Sir Hugh, 52
Willgoos, Andrew Van Dean, 28
Williams, Harry Palmerson, 117, 118
Williams, Al, 71
Wing twist, 144, 145
Wireless Telegraph Company of America, 17
Wireless (radio), 17
Wittman, Steve, 33
Wittman Bonzo racer, 33
Wood, Major John P., 21, 22, 63, 64-65
Woolams, Jack, 155
Worthen, John, 84, 85
Wright J-5 Whirlwind engine, 28
Wright Aeronautical, 25, 26-27
Wright J-3 engine, 28
Wright-Martin Company, 26
Wygle, Brian, 214
Wyler, Dave, 193

Yost, John, 96
Young, Dr. T.C., 48,

Zeuschel, Dave, 239
Zimmerman, Eugene F., 75, 76, 77
Zink, William C., 135